JOURNAL FOR THE STUDY OF THE NEW TESTAMENT SUPPLEMENT SERIES
158

Executive Editor
Stanley E. Porter

Sheffield Academic Press

'Mysticism' in the Gospel of John

An Inquiry into its Background

Jey J. Kanagaraj

Journal for the Study of the New Testament
Supplement Series 158

To Pamela,
the never-failing life-companion

Copyright © 1998 Sheffield Academic Press

Published by
Sheffield Academic Press Ltd
Mansion House
19 Kingfield Road
Sheffield S11 9AS
England

Typeset by Sheffield Academic Press
and
Printed on acid-free paper in Great Britain
by Bookcraft Ltd
Midsomer Norton, Bath

British Library Cataloguing in Publication Data

A catalogue record for this book is available
from the British Library

ISBN 1-85075-865-4

CONTENTS

FOREWORD

Since the early centuries of the Christian era John's Gospel has been regarded as a 'mystical' Gospel. Apart from anything else, it was a way of characterizing the clear differences between John's Gospel and the other three. But the concept was lost to sight in the long debates of the nineteenth century about the historical value of the Gospel, and became something of an embarrassment as the evaluation of 'mysticism' in Protestant circles became less positive. In the twentieth century the attempt to illuminate John's Gospel, particularly the theme of mutual indwelling, against the background of gnostic or hermetic spirituality only succeeded in rendering the concept of Johannine 'mysticism' more confused, if not a subject of still deeper suspicion.

All this time it was the classic mediaeval understanding of mysticism that prevailed—that of mystical union with the divine (hence the focus on the Johannine theme of mutual indwelling). Almost entirely ne-glected was the fact that there was a form of Jewish mysticism already attested in the more immediate context of John's Gospel. During the last 50 years the nature and extent of this Jewish mysticism became clearer, as attested not least in the Dead Sea Scrolls. Surprisingly, however, very little attempt was made to read the Gospel against this background or to reopen the question of Johannine mysticism.

It is to Dr Kanagaraj's credit that he identified this large gap in late-twentieth-century Johannine research. He has demonstrated the preva-lence of a form of Merkabah mysticism within the Judaism of John's time, and has clearly shown how much of John's language and motifs, of ascent–descent, of seeing and sending, as well as of indwelling, is indeed illuminated when set over against the language and imagery of contemporary Jewish Merkabah mysticism. Thanks to Dr Kanagaraj we can now speak once again of Johannine mysticism, but in a much more historically valid sense and in a way that informs our continuing appreciation and use of the Gospel. I commend his book with considerable enthusiasm.

James D.G. Dunn
Lightfoot Professor of Divinity,
University of Durham

PREFACE

The Gospel of John first excited my deep interest during teaching and interaction with students of the Union Biblical Seminary, Pune, India. I found, in particular, the fascinating theme 'Johannine mysticism' had been given little previous attention. Until recent times, Johannine study has taken seriously the background of the Gospel, literary and source criticism, the problem of authorship, parallelism with the Synoptics, the christological titles and the like, but '"mysticism" in the Fourth Gospel' has been regarded as secondary or even a doubtful theme. The primary reason for this attitude in Johannine research may be attributed to the equivocal expression 'mysticism'.

There is no consensus among English dictionaries in rendering the meaning of 'mysticism' or 'mystical'. For example, Klein's etymological dictionary treats the word 'mysticism' as the combination of the adjective 'mystic' and the suffix '-ism' and explains 'mystic' as from the Latin *mysticus* and the Greek μυστικός, meaning 'pertaining to secret rites' or more probably 'pertaining to an initiated'.[1] The word is also understood allegorically, especially in connection with the interpretation of Scripture.[2] The French equivalent *mystique* seems to mean, among many other meanings, 'special skill in the management of some kind of enterprise'.[3] Webster's dictionary displays four different meanings for 'mysticism'.[4] The uncertainty of this enigmatic word is recognized in the scholarly circles as well. To cite a few, W.R. Inge gives a list of 26 definitions for the word 'mysticism' or 'mystical theology'

1.   E. Klein, *A Comprehensive Etymological Dictionary of the English Language* (Amsterdam: Elsevier, repr. 1971), p. 485.

2.   See *The Compact Edition of the Oxford English Dictionary* (1971), I, col. 817.

3.   See A.J. Bliss, *A Dictionary of Foreign Words and Phrases* (London: Routledge & Kegan Paul, repr. 1972), p. 254.

4.   P.B. Gove (ed.), *Webster's Third New International Dictionary of the English Language* (London: G. Bell & Sons, 1961), p. 1497.

and indeed the list can become longer if he takes up the views of all theologians, including Roman Catholics;[5] A. Schweitzer, in his study on Pauline mysticism, rightly poses in the very beginning the crucial question, 'When we say that Paul is a mystic, what do we mean by mysticism?' and then attempts to explain 'mysticism' under two categories: primitive and developed;[6] in our time, L.W. Countryman, by realizing the variety of senses in which the word 'mystical' is used, says, 'I take it to describe an experience of things or persons outside myself as direct and unmediated as my experience of myself is.'[7] D.J. Halperin, who uses the word 'mysticism' in his work *The Merkabah in Rabbinic Literature*, plainly states at the outset, 'Given the limited scope of this study, I do not think it necessary to undertake the extremely difficult task of formulating a general definition. I merely indicate how I use the word in the course of this book.'[8] Although right understanding of 'mysticism' is the core of a study on 'mysticism', surprisingly enough, the inner meaning of the term is usually assumed by scholars rather than logically derived.

Our study also evokes the question, 'What is mysticism?' But we need to put the question in a different form: What was meant as 'mysticism' in the late first century CE when the Gospel of John was supposedly written? What are the elements treated as 'mystical' at the time of John? In answering these questions, I have taken two factors seriously: first and foremost, the socio-religio-historical context in which John's Gospel was composed. Dunn's remark, cited below, gave me a fresh inspiration in this direction:

> Consequently *the task of setting John in its historical context must be given a place of priority* in any enquiry into the gospel and the Fourth Gospel. Unfortunately it is a task which has often been ignored, or which

5.   W.R. Inge, *Christian Mysticism: The Bampton Lectures 1899* (London: Methuen, 1899), pp. 335-48.

6.   A. Schweitzer, *The Mysticism of Paul the Apostle* (London: A. & C. Black, ET 1931), p. 1. By primitive mysticism, Schweitzer means the entry into communion with a divine being by means of a magical act in such a way that the participant shares the deity's supernatural mode of existence; and by developed form of mysticism, he means the believer's attainment of union with the divinity and thereby becoming a partaker in the immortality for which he yearns.

7.   L.W. Countryman, *The Mystical Way in the Fourth Gospel* (Philadelphia: Fortress Press, 1987), p. 1.

8.   D.J. Halperin, *The Merkabah in Rabbinic Literature* (New Haven: American Oriental Society, 1980), p. 1 n.1.

has been pursued without sufficient care. In both cases, because the historical context has not been clarified, John has been *mis*understood, the Fourth Gospel has not been heard in its own terms, John has not been allowed to be John.[9]

Second, is the question of the author of the Fourth Gospel and his religious background. C.A. Evans is right when he states:

In my judgment scholars who uncritically make and accept assertions that the authorship of the Fourth Gospel is unknown and irrelevant undermine the exegetical task. Exegesis based on this kind of thinking lacks a historical orientation and is in danger of becoming docetic, in that it only appears to be genuine historical-literary exegesis.[10]

He argues that as per the internal evidence, the author was a Palestinian Jew, familiar with Judaea and Jerusalem, who wrote in a Diaspora context in a way that is best understood against the background of the late-first-century synagogue.

Being convinced with these observations, I have ventured to define 'mysticism' by paying attention to the late-first-century socio-religious context of Palestinian Judaism. This attempt necessitates an examination of the relevant Palestinian Jewish texts, including the major works of the Jewish apocalyptic literature that belong to the first century or even earlier. An analysis of these texts gives evidence that 'mystical' practice based on Ezekiel's throne-vision existed before the first century and that John's Gospel contains the same 'mystical' thought reinterpreted with the aim of making the message relevant to the people of John's time. The observation that either Hellenistic mysticism or Hellenistic-Jewish mysticism does not show complete parallelism with John's Gospel strengthens our thesis that John can be better understood mainly against the background of Jewish mysticism. This, however, is not to ignore the question often raised: do the examined writings deal with real, psychic experiences such as the ascetic practices and an ascent to heaven? Or are they merely concerned with literary conventions, having exegesis in focus? The apocalyptic visionary language and the dramatic style of narration make it hard to accept that the

9. J.D.G. Dunn, 'Let John Be John: A Gospel for its Time', in P. Stuhlmacher (ed.), *Das Evangelium und die Evangelien: Vorträge vom Tübinger Symposium 1982* (WUNT, 28; Tübingen: J.C.B. Mohr [Paul Siebeck], 1983), p. 311 (emphasis his).

10. C.A. Evans, *Word and Glory: On the Exegetical and Theological Background of John's Prologue* (JSNTSup, 89; Sheffield: JSOT Press, 1993), p. 193.

authors of the Jewish mystical texts did not mean the actual experiences of the mystics. Dreams, epiphanies and visionary experiences were not uncommon in Judaism, Hellenism and Christianity, particularly of the first century CE.[11]

The original form of this work was submitted in March 1995 as a doctoral dissertation at the University of Durham and there are several individuals and organizations without whose support this would not have been published in book form. I am most grateful to Professor James D.G. Dunn, my supervisor and *mystagogue*, who took personal interest in guiding my insights and recommending my work for publication. His warm heart and gentleness enabled me to cope with my studies throughout several ups and downs in my time as a student in Durham. I greatly appreciate his depth of understanding and willingness to help me in all possible ways. I thank him for his careful reading of all my research papers and for drawing my attention to some recent publications of relevance which otherwise would have gone unnoticed by me. It is appropriate for him who has put several years of labour to understand the origins of Christianity by setting it in its historical context to write a foreword to a volume such as this and I salute him for having done this with great pleasure.

I am indebted to Professor Philip S. Alexander and Revd Dr Stephen Barton, my external and internal examiners respectively, for their encouragement and valuable suggestions to revise my thesis for publication. But for their recommendation to make this work known to the students of the New Testament and of Jewish studies, I would probably not have thought of publishing this at an early stage. My special thanks are due to Dr C.T.R. Hayward for kindly reading some of the key chapters of this work; his comments enabled me to present my thoughts with much care and improved clarity. I am happy to record my appreciation to Professor C.K. Barrett, who was kind enough to read more than half of my work and to give me an opportunity to have a friendly discussion with him on the subject. I also thank Professor D.A. Carson for stimulating my thinking during my dialogue with him more than once at Tyndale House, Cambridge. I am deeply grateful to the Editorial Board of Sheffield Academic Press, to Professor Stanley Porter in particular, for their kindness in accepting my work for publi-

11.   On this see J.D.G. Dunn, *Jesus and the Spirit: A Study of the Religious and Charismatic Experience of Jesus and the First Christians as Reflected in the New Testament* (Philadelphia: Westminster Press, 1975), pp. 303-307.

cation. I am glad to record my appreciation to Revd Dr John Stott and Revd Dr Bruce Nicholls who took great interest and effort to arrange finance for me to go and work at Sheffield in order to revise my thesis to an acceptable level for publication. A special word of thanks is due to Professor D.J.A. Clines, the Head of the Biblical Studies Department at Sheffield University, for generously allowing me to use the facilities available in the department and to Mrs Gillian Fogg for all the office help given to me during my stay at Sheffield.

I acknowledge with gratitude the financial support and warm fellowship given by the organizations such as Crosslinks, Interserve, Langham Trust, TEAR Fund, Tyndale House, World Evangelical Fellowship of India, and World Vision International. I deeply appreciate their generosity in rendering pastoral care in a remarkable way to me and my family in all circumstances. I am indebted to the vicar, Revd Michael Wilcock, and to the members of St Nicholas Church, Durham, for their pastoral heart and unstinted hospitality shown to us throughout our stay in Durham.

I gratefully acknowledge the love and support rendered by my parents, Mr and Mrs Joseph Durairaj, all my years, particularly during the period of my research, by relieving me of major family responsibilities so that I could better concentrate on my studies. Since my father departed to heavenly glory while I was approaching the end of my study programme, my affectionate regards and thanks are offered to him posthumously.

My heartiest thanks are due to our lovely boys, Hanson and Theoson, who bore with several inconveniences and restraints particularly during my work at home by understanding in an extraordinary way the cause of their dad.

Finally it is my privilege and pleasure to record my deep appreciation and warmest thanks to my wife, Pamela, for undertaking all family responsibilities with love and forbearance during the whole period of my theological study both in India and in the UK. As a small token of my love and gratitude, this work is affectionately dedicated to her.

Jey Kanagaraj
Pune
July 1997

ABBREVIATIONS

AB	Anchor Bible
AJSL	*The American Journal of Semitic Languages and Literatures*
AnBib	Analecta Biblica
ANRW	H. Temporini and W. Haase (eds.), *Aufstieg und Niedergang der römischen Welt: Geschichte und Kultur Roms im Spiegel der neueren Forschung* (Berlin: W. de Gruyter, 1972–)
ArBib	The Aramaic Bible
ATR	*Anglican Theological Review*
ATANT	Abhandlungen zur Theologie des Alten und Neuen Testaments
BDB	F. Brown, S.R. Driver and C.A. Briggs, *A Hebrew and English Lexicon of the Old Testament* (Oxford: Clarendon Press, 1907)
BEvT	Beiträge zur evangelischen Theologie
Bib	*Biblica*
BeO	*Bibbia e oriente*
BT	*The Bible Translator*
BJRL	*Bulletin of the John Rylands Library*
BJS	Brown Judaic Studies
BKAT	Biblischer Kommentar Altes Testament
BSTS	Bible Speaks Today Series
BZ	*Biblische Zeitschrift*
ConBOT	Coniectanea biblica, Old Testament
CBQ	*Catholic Biblical Quarterly*
CH	*Church History*
ChristCent	*Christian Century*
DownRev	*Downside Review*
EncJud	*Encyclopaedia Judaica*
ER	*Encyclopaedia of Religion*
ERE	J. Hastings (ed.), *Encyclopaedia of Religion and Ethics* (Edinburgh: T. & T. Clark, 1917)
ETL	*Ephemerides theologicae lovanienses*
ExpTim	*Expository Times*
FBBS	Facet Books, Biblical Series
GTJ	*Grace Theological Journal*
HBT	*Horizons in Biblical Theology*
HE	Eusebius's *Historia Ecclesiastica*

HNT	Handbuch zum Neuen Testament
HNTC	Harper's NT Commentaries
HR	*Hekhalot Rabbati*
HSS	Harvard Semitic Studies
HTR	*Harvard Theological Review*
HZ	*Hekhalot Zutarti*
IBS	*Irish Biblical Studies*
ICC	International Critical Commentary
IEJ	*Israel Exploration Journal*
IJT	*Indian Journal of Theology*
Int	*Interpretation*
IOS	*Israel Oriental Studies*
JAOS	*Journal of the American Oriental Studies*
JBL	*Journal of Biblical Literature*
JewEnc	*The Jewish Encyclopedia*
JETS	*Journal of Evangelical Theological Society*
JJS	*Journal of Jewish Studies*
JSJ	*Journal for the Study of Judaism*
JSNTSup	*Journal for the Study of the New Testament*, Supplement Series
JSOTSup	*Journal for the Study of the Old Testament*, Supplement Series
JSQ	*Jewish Studies Quarterly*
JSS	*Journal of Semitic Studies*
JTS	*Journal of Theological Studies*
JU	Judentum und Umwelt
Judaica	*Judaica: Beiträge zum Verständnis des jüdischen Schicksals in Vergangenheit und Gegenwart*
LCL	Loeb Classical Library
NTAbh	Neutestamentliche Abhandlungen
NCBC	New Century Bible Commentary
Neot	*Neotestamentica*
NIDNTT	C. Brown (ed.), *The New International Dictionary of New Testament Theology* (3 vols.; Exeter: Paternoster Press, 1975)
NOT	*Notes on Translation*
NovT	*Novum Testamentum*
NovTSup	*Novum Testamentum*, Supplements
NTS	*New Testament Studies*
NumSup	*Numen: International Review for the History of Religions*, Supplements
OG	Old Greek
OTP	J.H. Charlesworth (ed.), *The Old Testament Pseudepigrapha* (2 vols.; New York: Doubleday, 1983–85).
OTS	*Oudtestamentische Studiën*
SBS	Stuttgarter Bibelstudien

SBLDS	Society for Biblical Literature Dissertation Series
SBT	Studies in Biblical Theology
SE	*Studia Evangelica*
SJ	Studia Judaica
SJLA	Studies in Judaism in Late Antiquity
SJT	*Scottish Journal of Theology*
SNTSMS	Society for New Testament Studies Monograph Series
Synopse	P. Schäfer (ed.), *Synopse zur Hekhalot-Literatur* (TSAJ, 2; Tübingen: J.C.B. Mohr [Paul Siebeck], 1991)
TDNT	G. Kittel and G. Friedrich (eds.), *Theological Dictionary of the New Testament* (trans. G.W. Bromiley; 10 vols.; Grand Rapids: Eerdmans, 1964–)
TDOT	G.J. Botterweck and H. Ringgren (eds.), *Theological Dictionary of the Old Testament*
TheolEduc	*Theological Educator*
TLZ	*Theologische Literaturzeitung*
TSAJ	Texte und Studien zum Antiken Judentum
TU	Texte und Untersuchungen zur Geschichte der altchristlichen Literatur
TynBul	*Tyndale Bulletin*
ThWAT	G.J. Botterweck und H. Ringgren (eds.), *Theologisches Wörterbuch zum Alten Testament* (Stuttgart: W. Kohlhammer, 1970–)
VC	*Vigiliae Christianae*
VT	*Vetus Testamentum*
VTSup	*Vetus Testamentum*, Supplement
WBC	Word Biblical Commentary
WMANT	Wissenschaftliche Monographien zum Alten und Neuen Testament
WUNT	Wissenschaftliche Untersuchungen zum Neuen Testament
ZNW	*Zeitschrift für die neutestamentliche Wissenschaft*

Chapter 1

INTRODUCTION: IS JOHN A 'MYSTICAL' DOCUMENT?

The view that the Gospel of John contains 'mysticism' or 'mystical' ideas was prevalent in patristic circles in the early centuries of Christianity. For example, as early as the second century CE, Clement of Alexandria labelled John a 'spiritual Gospel'[1] and the gnostic commentators, from Heracleon to Steiner, found in John support for their 'mystical' experience of attaining knowledge by individual enlightenment. Origen accepted John as a 'mystical' document, because it teaches that knowledge of God, which, for Origen, means divinization (θεοποίησις), is possible through contemplation, or a 'transforming vision' of the Word (and through him of God).[2] After him, Augustine, under the influence of Neoplatonism, gave 'mystical' interpretation to John, arguing that its author had ascended to reach the presence of God and to contemplate the godhead of the Word.[3] He also gave 'mystical' value to the 153 fishes of Jn 21.11 by stating that 17 (1 + 2 + 3 +...17 = 153) is formed by adding 10, which stands for the Law, and 7, which denotes the Spirit.[4]

1. See *HE* 6.14. E.C. Hoskyns, *The Fourth Gospel* (ed. F.N. Davey; London: Faber & Faber, 2nd rev. edn, repr. 1961), p. 17, suggests that the word 'spiritual' may imply 'some peculiar religious intuition or emotion or experience which the 'spiritual' man...may only too easily identify with the life that is not relative but eternal'.

2. Cf. A. Louth, *The Origins of the Christian Mystical Tradition: From Plato to Denys* (Oxford: Clarendon Press, 1981), pp. 60-66, 73-74; C.W. Macleod, 'Allegory and Mysticism in Origen and Gregory of Nyssa', *JTS* 22 (1971), pp. 362-79 (368-69).

3. St Augustine, *Homilies on the Gospel According to St John and his First Epistle* (2 vols.; trans. H. Browne; Oxford: John Henry Parker, 1848–49), I, pp. 5-6. Augustine's mystical theology is concerned with the soul's ascent to God out of her inward longing to return to him—see Louth, *Christian Mystical Tradition*, pp. 141-58.

4. See J.H. Bernard, *A Critical and Exegetical Commentary on the Gospel*

Nevertheless, Johannine scholars in the modern period have shown much reserve on the subject of 'mysticism' in John. While Dodd and Barrett take neutral position in this area of study,[5] scholars such as B.F. Westcott, A. Plummer, E.C. Hoskyns, J.H. Bernard, R.H. Lightfoot, R.E. Brown, F.F. Bruce, G.R. Beasley-Murray and T.L. Brodie, in their commentaries, and L. Newbigin and B. Milne, in their expositions, are almost reluctant to discuss this subject. J. Ashton's two recent studies on John's theology give no place for 'mysticism'.[6] Although Bultmann perceived in 1955 the influence of 'mystical' language on the Johannine concepts such as mutual knowing, mutual abiding and oneness among the disciples, he discouraged in his commentary on John any form of mystical interpretation.[7] This contrast between the ancient views of John and their modern counterparts is puzzling. Has 'mysticism' no part in the background and thought of John's Gospel? In other words, is the Gospel of John a 'mystical' document? The question is at least worth posing afresh, in case modern commentators are missing something of importance for our understanding of John.

The Problem of Definition

Any study on 'mysticism' has to face the primary question: what is meant by 'mysticism' or 'mystical'? Few words, if any, have such ambiguous connotations as the word 'mysticism' or 'mystical'. The reason is not only that each writer has assumed different meaning(s) for this enigmatic term, but also that, as far as Christianity is concerned, this term does not appear either in the Old Testament or in the New Testament at all.[8] Previous studies have shown that it is difficult to

According to St John (2 vols.; ICC; Edinburgh: T. & T. Clark, repr. 1948–49), I, p. lxxxvii.

5.   For their positions, see below, pp. 25-26, 31-32.

6.   See J. Ashton, *Understanding the Fourth Gospel* (Oxford: Clarendon Press, 1991); *idem*, *Studying John: Approaches to the Fourth Gospel* (Oxford: Clarendon Press, 1994).

7.   R. Bultmann, *Theology of the New Testament* (2 vols.; London: SCM Press, ET 1955), II, p. 84; *idem*, *The Gospel of John: A Commentary* (Philadelphia: Westminster Press, ET 1971), esp. p. 16 n. 6, pp. 69, 382, 536, 541, 605-606, 613-14. However, he supposes that the ἐν ἡμῖν of Jn 1.14 refers to the indwelling of the Logos in the soul of the Gnostic or of the mystic (see: *John: A Commentary*, pp. 66-67 n. 6).

8.   J.T. Pring, *The Oxford Dictionary of Modern Greek: Greek–English and English–Greek* (Oxford: Clarendon Press, 1982), p. 207 of English–Greek section

reach a commonly accepted definition for the term 'mysticism',[9] particularly in the present context of religious pluralism. For, as Scholem rightly maintains, 'There is no mysticism as such, there is only the mysticism of a particular religious system, Christian, Islamic, Jewish mysticism and so on.'[10] Therefore I will not take the risk of giving any definition for the word 'mysticism' until the word is connected with the religious system that may provide a relevant background for understanding John.[11] Since scholars, both in the past and present, have sought to extract 'mystical' elements from John without settling initially this basic issue, early studies on Johannine mysticism have failed to do justice to John's message. Are we justified, then, if we claim John as a 'mystical' Gospel in the sense that it contains 'mystical' features in any acceptable sense? Do the early claims for Johannine mysticism retain validity? Was there an 'ism' so that we can call 'mysticism' as early as the first century CE? Is there anything more to be explored in this field of study?

Past Research on Johannine Mysticism

Although the issue is many-sided and the exponents of John do not talk much about the 'mystical' dimension of the message of John's Gospel, there are several scholars who have argued for 'mystical' features in John. We can classify the proponents under three categories and examine their views to see whether any of these provides a key to understanding the context and thought of John:

1. Those who have argued for what we can call the 'traditional view of mysticism' in John. These scholars can be divided into two groups: (a) those who hold the *unio mystica* theory; and (b) those who hold the *communio mystica* theory. Whereas the former argues for the presence of 'mysticism' in John in the sense of deification (i.e. the mystic's

---

gives μυστικισμός as the Greek equivalent to the term 'mysticism'. Its cognate terms occur in Wis. 8.4 (μύστις); 12.5 (ET v. 6—μυστής); and in *3 Macc.* 3.10 (μυστικῶς). The Symmachus version of Isa. 3.3 has μυστική. However, in their own contexts they give different meanings and therefore they do not help us much to arrive at a specific meaning for the term μυστικισμός.

9.   See above, pp. 11-12.

10.   G.G. Scholem, *Major Trends in Jewish Mysticism* (London: Thames & Hudson, 3rd rev. edn, 1955), p. 6.

11.   Until then I prefer to use the word 'mysticism' or 'mystical' within quotation marks.

union with God in the course of which he himself becomes god), the latter stresses 'mysticism' in John in the sense of closest relationship (i.e. the mystic communes with God in such a way that his identity and responsibility are preserved).

2. Those who find in John an influence of or a parallel to Hellenistic mysticism.

3. Those who view John against the background of Jewish mysticism.

The Traditional Understanding of Johannine Mysticism

I am identifying here only a few modern scholars who give a 'mystical' interpretation to John's Gospel basically in the sense of 'union with God'. I have not added any critical comments against each scholar's views in order to avoid repetition, but an analysis of the traditional view as a whole is undertaken in the latter part of this section.

The Unio Mystica Theory. W.R. Inge, in his Bampton lectures 1899, described 'Religious mysticism' as 'the attempt to realize the presence of the living God in the soul and in nature'.[12] A mystic's ultimate aim, according to him, is *scala perfectionis* (i.e. the gradual transformation into the likeness of God), which takes three stages, namely the purgation life, the illuminative life and the unitive life, and it is in the final stage that the mystic beholds God and is joined to Him.[13] In this sense Inge argues that the Fourth Gospel is 'the charter of Christian mysticism'.[14] For him Johannine mysticism is 'that *centripetal* tendency in thought and feeling which always strives to see unity in difference, the one in the many' (cf. Jesus' prayer for oneness in Jn 17.22-23); he understands this unity as 'mutual inhabitation' or the 'ethical harmony' of human souls with God.[15] According to Inge, the 'Word-become-flesh', through whom God was revealed as the Father, is the central fact in the mystical theology of John and this revelation was further illuminated by the Holy Spirit.[16] He highlights two main features in Johannine mysticism: the union that exists between Christ and

12. Inge, *Christian Mysticism*, p. 39.
13. Inge, *Christian Mysticism*, pp. 9-13.
14. Inge, *Christian Mysticism*, p. 44.
15. W.F. Howard, *The Fourth Gospel in Recent Criticism and Interpretation* (London: Epworth Press, 4th rev. edn, repr. 1961), p. 198 (emphasis his).
16. Inge, *Christian Mysticism*, pp. 47-49.

the Church collectively, although union with individual souls is not thereby ruled out, and between one another as members of Christ.[17]

Commending the Fourth Gospel, B.F. von Hügel wrote in 1911: 'The book's method and form are pervadingly allegorical; its instinct and aim are profoundly mystical.'[18] Thus he seems to treat the deeper meaning(s) of any Johannine word as 'mystical'; this is also known from his statement that there is everywhere in the Gospel the mystic's deep love of double, even triple meanings.[19] According to von Hügel, Johannine mysticism implies 'an emotional intuitive apprehension' of Jesus and of God (1 Jn 4.10, 19; Jn 4.14; 6.35, 44)[20] and by its nature it is both sacramental and ecclesiastical in the sense that the Church, as 'one fold', is united to the 'one Shepherd' (Jn 10.16) by means of the two great sacraments: baptism (Jn 3.5) and eucharist (Jn 6.53-58).[21]

Evelyn Underhill, in her comprehensive study on 'mysticism', recognizes the Fourth Gospel as a 'mystical' writing with a poetic and devotional nature rather than a historical one.[22] She defines 'mysticism' as an inward experience and passionate communion with reality and perceives John as a mystic who had intuitive communion with the spiritual order and who retranslated his visions in his Gospel by means of such images as the vine, paraclete, etc.[23] The 'plot' of the Fourth Gospel, as Underhill observes, is the union with the Logos of all those who have inherited the life offered by him by virtue of his entry into time from

17.   Inge, *Christian Mysticism*, p. 51; Inge also expressed the same idea in his Paddock lectures in 1906—see W.R. Inge, *Personal Idealism and Mysticism* (London: Longmans Green, 1907).

18.   B.F. von Hügel, 'John, Gospel of St', *Encyclopaedia Britannica* (Cambridge: Cambridge University Press, 11th edn, 1911), XV, p. 455.

19.   Von Hügel, 'John, Gospel of St', p. 454. For instance, the word 'again' in Jn 3.3 (wrongly cited by him as 3.2), for him, means literally 'to be physically born again', morally 'to become as a little child', mystically 'from heaven, God' or 'to be spiritually renewed'. So too he understands the Johannine word κρίσις in the popular sense as 'condemnation', denoting a future act, but in the mystical sense as 'discrimination', denoting a present fact.

20.   See Howard, *The Fourth Gospel* (1961), pp. 200-201.

21.   W.F. Howard, *The Fourth Gospel in Recent Criticism and Interpretation* (London: Epworth Press, 1931), p. 202.

22.   E. Underhill, *The Mystic Way* (London: J.M. Dent, repr. 1914), p. 217.

23.   Underhill, *The Mystic Way*, pp. 226, 254-55; she (p. 231) concedes with Resch, who argues that John was written in an ecstasy, which caused the author to confuse his visions and memories.

eternity and of his triumphant return after his fight with 'darkness'.[24] Thus for her the mystic way in John starts with the Logos Christology even in the first chapter and runs through the whole Gospel, comprising his death, resurrection, ascension and parousia.[25]

M. Charan Singh, in his incomplete commentary on John, maintains that John's Gospel promotes the idea that God is within every one of us and that we have to search for him within ourselves under the guidance of Christ who himself realized God within his lifetime.[26] On the under-standing that the teachings of Jesus coincide with the teachings of all saints in all other religions, Singh finds in John the Hindu mystical notion that the human form is given to us to enable us to get out of this prison, the wheel of 84, and go up and merge back into the Lord.[27]

J.A. Sanford, in his recently published commentary on John entitled *Mystical Christianity*, argues for 'mysticism' in John in an 'interior, psychological, and esoteric sense'.[28] He maintains that John, as a Gospel that has been influenced by mainly Hellenistic and Platonic thought, contains the 'esoteric or psychological' meaning within the literal meaning.[29] However, it is not clear how 'esoteric' can be identified with 'psychological' and why he calls esoteric 'mystical'. Adopting uncritically the terminologies and concepts used by C.G. Jung and F. Kunkel, Sanford argues that 'mystical unity' is 'the integration of the personality that is the result of the process of individuation'.[30] That is, for him, the Word of God is indwelling within the human soul as an *imago dei*, and the knowledge of God that comes from within us is a direct knowledge inspired in us by that indwelling *logos*.[31] Similarly, Sanford describes the Johannine light in the psychological, and hence mystical, sense as a source of 'enlightened consciousness', for it comes from a deeper reality and lights the ego to give forth light, analogous to

24.   Underhill, *The Mystic Way*, p. 226.

25.   Underhill, *The Mystic Way*, pp. 241-57.

26.   M. Charan Singh, *St John the Great Mystic* (Punjab: Radha Soami Satsang Beas, 3rd edn, 1974), p. 2.

27.   Charan Singh, *The Great Mystic*, p. 157.

28.   J.A. Sanford, *Mystical Christianity: A Psychological Commentary on the Gospel of John* (New York: Crossroad, 1993), p. 1.

29.   Sanford, *Mystical Christianity*, pp. 4-5.

30.   Sanford, *Mystical Christianity*, p. 303; by 'individuation' he means the discovery of one's inner identity.

31.   Sanford, *Mystical Christianity*, pp. 23-24.

a candle that gives forth light when it is lit by a flame.[32] He treats the vine imagery of John 15 as denoting 'pure mysticism, concerned with the mystery of the transformation of the soul through union with God', which he calls 'deification'.[33] He agrees with Streeter for whom John's stories and discourses might have been seen and heard by him in a mystic trance.[34]

The Communio Mystica Theory. C.K. Barrett, in both editions of his commentary on John,[35] accepts the definition of the word 'mysticism' given by *Chambers' Dictionary* and R. Otto and in that light describes John's emphases on the mediation of Christ to attain communion with God, on the intellectual content of Christian truth, and on its ethical expression, as the non-mystical features of John.[36] Barrett, who denies that Johannine mysticism speaks of the union of the mystic with God so that he himself becomes divine—that is, deified—identifies mystical elements particularly in John's portrait of the abiding of the Father and the Son with the believer (Jn 14.23), of the Spirit with and in him (Jn 14.17) and of the abiding of the believer in Christ (Jn 15.1-6).[37] He argues that the Johannine Christ himself is 'the one true mystic', for he had so close a communion with God that he was sharing oneness (Jn 10.30) and equality with him (Jn 5.18) and that no worded prayer was necessary for him (Jn 11.42).[38] Thus, for Barrett, Johannine mysticism, probably by borrowing from contemporary mystical thought, describes Christ as the one who had communion with God, whereas the 'mystical' life of Christians is derivative and rests upon the essential relation of Jesus with the Father (Jn 17.23).[39]

In similar tone, R. Schnackenburg argues that John produces a

32. Sanford, *Mystical Christianity*, pp. 100-101, 180-81.
33. Sanford, *Mystical Christianity*, pp. 279, 299, 302-305; cf. also p. 294.
34. Sanford, *Mystical Christianity*, p. 9; cf. Underhill, who also takes a similar position (pp. 23-24 above).
35. C.K. Barrett, *The Gospel According to St John* (London: SPCK, 1955), pp. 71-74; *idem*, *The Gospel According to St John* (Philadelphia: Westminster Press, 2nd edn, 1978), pp. 85-87. The latter work will hereafter be referred to as *John*.
36. Barrett, *John*, pp. 85-86.
37. Barrett, *John*, pp. 86-87.
38. Barrett, *John*, p. 87.
39. Barrett, *John*, p. 87.

Christian answer to the 'mystical' desires and language of his time.[40]
According to him, the so-called Johannine mysticism is concerned with
the believer's 'being in' and 'abiding in' Christ and through him in
God. The fellowship with God is made possible in the earthly Jesus (Jn
14.7-11), but is given in its full reality only through the glorified Christ.
Since the 'Johannine mysticism' of union with Christ and God is
intrinsically linked with the self-revelation of the earthly Jesus as well
as to the glorification of the Christ, it is not a timeless mysticism
detached from history.[41] Moreover, Schnackenburg does not think of
'union' in terms of complete transformation into the deity and therefore
argues that the Johannine 'mysticism' of fellowship with Christ is
inseparable from ethical qualities such as love and obedience (Jn 15.4-
10; 13.14-15, 34).[42]

J. McPolin's article, 'Johannine Mysticism', published in 1978, is
entirely devoted to the study of having communion with God through
Christ.[43] McPolin argues that although 'mysticism' generally means 'a
special experience of those chosen to enter into a privileged
communication with God', for John it denotes 'communion with God',
the essential principle of Christian life.[44] Communion with God does
not mean, as it does in Hellenistic mysticism, that humankind and the
world is 'in God', but it denotes personal relationships. McPolin
observes that in John's theology of communion there is no trace of an
ecstatic possession by divine inspiration, as in Hellenistic mysticism,
nor of a separation between morality and 'mysticism', as one finds in
the neo-platonic 'contemplative mysticism', but that there is a communication of will and action through which those united with God can
pray and do the works of God (Jn 15.13, 16-17; 17.20-23).[45] Like
Schnackenburg, McPolin also maintains that the communion with God
that is centred on Christ is not a 'timeless mysticism', detached from
space and time, but something that is possible in the earthly life of
Jesus (Jn 14.7-11); the core of Johannine mysticism for him is that

40.   R. Schnackenburg, *The Gospel According to St John* (3 vols.; New York:
Crossroad, ET 1968), I, pp. 161-62.
41.   Schnackenburg, *St John*, I, p. 161.
42.   Schnackenburg, *St John*, I, p. 162. For similar understanding of Johannine
mysticism see M.P. John, 'Johannine Mysticism', *IJT* 5 (1956), pp. 15-21.
43.   J. McPolin, 'Johannine Mysticism', *Way* 1 (1978), pp. 25-35.
44.   McPolin, 'Johannine Mysticism', pp. 25-26.
45.   McPolin, 'Johannine Mysticism', pp. 26-28.

communion with God that integrates humans into community within God, bringing a radical change in their lives.[46] He also shows that communion is the action and gift of Three Persons: God the Father, Jesus the Son and the Holy Spirit, who together abide in the believer.[47]

Reflecting the thoughts of McPolin, B. Maggioni argues in his article, 'La Mistica di Giovanni Evangelista' (1984), that John's mysticism can be envisaged in the use of Johannine vocabularies, 'to know', 'to see', 'to remain', etc., which reflect the idea of 'an intimacy with God' or of 'entering into communion with God'.[48] Like others who hold the *communio mystica* view, Maggioni too maintains that one can meet God neither in a direct and personal vision nor through ascetic techniques or contemplation, but in the historical Christ alone.[49] He drives home this point by referring to the Johannine themes such as incarnation, eternal life, knowing, faith, love and the Holy Spirit, but concludes that John's mysticism is synthesized into two commands: faith in Jesus and practice of love.[50] In contrast to his discussion in the article, Maggioni concludes that the way to search for God is through faith in the *apostolic witness* and through fraternal love. Like McPolin, he too argues that Johannine mysticism is markedly 'Trinity based'.[51]

The idea of 'mystical union' in the sense of 'the complete opening of two realities into one another' has been detected in John by L.W. Countryman in a naïve manner. In his book, *The Mystical Way in the Fourth Gospel*,[52] Countryman views the word 'mystical' in two categories: 'mystical enlightenment', by which he means an experience of the order of the cosmos and of one's place in it, and 'mystical union', by which he means an experience of full knowledge of another specific being. He believes that John treats 'mystical enlightenment' as a

46.   McPolin, 'Johannine Mysticism', p. 28.
47.   McPolin, 'Johannine Mysticism', pp. 34-35.
48.   B. Maggioni, 'La Mistica di Giovanni Evangelista', in E. Ancilli and M. Paparozzi (eds.), *La Mistica: Fenemenologia e Riflessione Teologia* (2 vols.; Rome: Citta Nuova, 1984), I, pp. 223-24, 248-49. I am indebted to Mrs Alison Snow of Durham for kindly providing me with the English translation of this Italian article.
49.   Maggioni, 'La Mistica', pp. 229, 248.
50.   Maggioni, 'La Mistica', p. 248; for similar treatment of the subject see W.J. Fulco, *Maranatha: Reflections on the Mystical Theology of John the Evangelist* (New York: Paulist Press, 1973).
51.   Maggioni, 'La Mistica', p. 249.
52.   Countryman, *The Mystical Way*, p. 1; cf. above p. 12 n. 7.

prelude to 'mystical union'.[53] John, as Countryman conceives, portrays the very life of the believer (i.e. his conversion, participation in the Eucharist, enlightenment to see the reality in Jesus, and his new life) as emerging from the primaeval union of God and the Logos and as progressing towards a mystical goal: union with Father and Son and with one another, which is also known as 'the mystical path'.[54] By treating Jn 1.1-34 as the prologue of John, in contrast to the well-established theory that Jn 1.1-18 constitutes the prologue, he argues that John's mysticism is tied to a historical character, Jesus, who has 'crossed over' to the Father from this cosmos through his death and resurrection so that he might bring his followers into union with himself and God (cf. Jn 17.20-23).[55]

An Analysis of the Traditional View. The mystical interpretation of John in terms of union or communion with God has been rewarding, particularly in bringing John's message to the people of modern times in terms of what they understand today as 'mysticism'.[56] However, we can hardly overlook the basic issues involved in the traditional view of Johannine mysticism:

1. The interpretation of John's Gospel in terms of 'mystical' union or communion only proves that the theology of union had been known in the first century CE, but there is no convincing evidence that this was recognized as 'mysticism' at that time particularly in Palestine. This has been overlooked by those who hold the traditional view, because they have failed to study John in its religio-historical context. Schnackenburg is right in proposing that John gives a Christian answer to the 'mystical' longings of his time, but unfortunately he did not demonstrate fully the then 'mystical' tendency of the people. Similarly,

53.   Countryman, *The Mystical Way*, p. 1.
54.   Countryman, *The Mystical Way*, pp. 1-2, 11, 14, 90, 106-107, 109, 128.
55.   Countryman, *The Mystical Way*, pp. 87-91.
56.   Another typical example in this regard is the work of an Indian bishop, A.J. Appasamy, 'The Mysticism of Hindu Bhakti Literature, Considered Especially with Reference to the Mysticism of the Fourth Gospel' (DPhil Thesis, University of Oxford, 1922), who associated John's mysticism with the Hindu ideas of *bhakti* (loving devotion to God), *moksa* (release or salvation), *antaryamin* (indweller), and *avatara* (god assuming human form). He found these ideas as the best available Indian instrument for the proclamation of the Christian message. See R.H.S. Boyd, *An Introduction to Indian Christian Theology* (Delhi: ISPCK, repr. 1989), pp. 110-43.

Maggioni's opinion that Johannine mysticism is markedly 'Trinity based' (so also McPolin) assumes that John was already aware of the doctrine of Trinity and thus misses the first-century context and meaning of Johannine passages.[57] Thus an inquiry into what elements, if any, were actually known as 'mystical', particularly in the first century, has been largely ignored and this we undertake in our work.

2. The adherents of the traditional view have attempted to give a definition to such an abstract word as 'mysticism' or 'mystical' and in this attempt they have largely been dominated by their own presuppositions. Deriving a definition for the word 'mysticism' from modern dictionaries and scholars (e.g. Barrett and McPolin) or by assumption (e.g. Countryman and Sanford), is not helpful in examining a first-century text such as John. Underhill and Sanford have understood John's Gospel as no more than the reproduction of John's mystical visions or 'active imagination' (Sanford by borrowing Jung's phrase) and hence have undermined the historical value and the rich theology embedded in the Gospel. However, M.P. John and Maggioni deny that Johannine mysticism is concerned with visions, auditions and ecstatic experiences.[58]

3. Most of the proponents of *unio mystica* and of *communio mystica* have removed several verses and passages from their contexts and joined them together to argue for 'mysticism' in John. Johannine expressions and themes are interpreted at the *prima facie* level without giving enough attention not only to the valuable work done previously on them, but particularly to exegesis and scholarly analysis. It is not clear, for example, how von Hügel derives the mystical idea of 'an emotional intuitive apprehension' of Jesus and of God by referring to Jn 4.14; 6.35, 44 and 1 Jn 4.10, 19. Charan Singh's comment on Jn 1.51 that by means of the indwelling sound current, the Holy Ghost (= the Logos), Christ could go back to the Father and come back to this earth as he wishes[59] has no support in the text. Maggioni's emphasis on one's meeting with Jesus as well as on the meeting of the 'brothers' in the world as essential to having concrete experience of God shows that one can attain 'mystical' experience by performing deeds of love. Such an interpretation is based more on the subjective and naïve attitude than on an objective analysis of the Johannine themes.

57.   Cf. Dunn, 'Let John Be John', pp. 311-12.
58.   M.P. John, 'Johannine Mysticism', p. 21; Maggioni, 'La Mistica', p. 229.
59.   Charan Singh, *The Great Mystic*, p. 14.

4. The traditional view has not grappled with the issues: why did John prefer to use 'mystical' language in his Gospel? What role does it play in fulfilling the author's christological and soteriological purpose (cf. Jn 20.31)? How is the theme of Johannine mysticism related to the other important themes in John? For instance, Countryman's study on Jn 20.30-31 is focused mainly on the idea of 'believing', ignoring the question 'believing in whom?'[60] and therefore the important titles, Messiah and Son of God, as well as John's name theology are left unexamined, leaving the study incomplete.

Due to these problems the traditional understanding of Johannine mysticism has not taken firm root in biblical studies. The idea of 'deification', which differentiates the *unio mystica* view from the *communio mystica* view, remains to be taken up in our study on John to examine whether John contains this 'mystical' element in it. Our next task is to set the views of those who argue for the background of Hellenistic mysticism for John.

John in the Light of Hellenistic Mysticism
The works of three scholars, A. Schweitzer, C.H. Dodd and D.L. Mealand, emerge as key to an understanding of John against the background of Hellenistic mysticism.

By 'mysticism' Schweitzer means 'the entry into the super-earthly and eternal' either by means of a 'mystery', a magical act (primitive mysticism) or through an act of thinking (intellectual mysticism).[61] He argues that Paul speaks of Christ-mysticism by means of which one comes into relation to God.[62] That is, the mystical experience of being-in-God is achieved by being-in-Christ in Paul. In John, however, as Schweitzer perceives, both God-mysticism and Christ-mysticism interpenetrate, for the Johannine Logos-Christ speaks both of a being-in-him and a being-in-God and represents the being-in-God as mediated by the being-in-Christ.[63] In this sense John represents the Hellenistic mystical doctrine of redemption through the being-in-Christ, that is, through union with the Logos-Christ.[64] The Logos-Christ preaches a

---

60. Countryman, *The Mystical Way*, pp. 127-32.
61. Schweitzer, *The Mysticism of Paul*, pp. 1-2; see also above, p. 12 n. 6.
62. Schweitzer, *The Mysticism of Paul*, p. 3.
63. Schweitzer, *The Mysticism of Paul*, p. 5.
64. Schweitzer, *The Mysticism of Paul*, pp. 349-53. Schweitzer seems to imply by 'Hellenistic mysticism' the 'Hellenistic union-with-Christ mysticism'

faith in Jesus Christ that includes faith in the sacraments (Baptism and Eucharist) which are derived from him.[65] According to Hellenistic mysticism, the Spirit unites with the baptismal water and the elements of the Eucharist in a way capable of being appropriated by the believer, whereas in John the Logos-Christ on earth was carrying the Logos-Spirit and after his death the Spirit flows in the sacraments as the power of communicating eternal life to humans.[66]

Schweitzer does not demonstrate whether the ideas of deification and immortality embedded in Hellenistic mysticism occur in John. He also has failed to analyse the passages such as Jn 3.5 and 6.56 by setting them in their contexts before suggesting that for John the sacraments are the vehicles of the Spirit to communicate eternal life to humans. The major weakness in Schweitzer's study is his presupposition that the idea of union with God or of being-in-God belongs to Hellenistic mysticism alone. Our study below shows that the theology of union is as old as some of the oldest parts of the Old Testament and that it occurs in the New Testament also.[67]

C.H. Dodd, in his extensive study on the hermetic literature, has drawn several points of contact, both verbal and conceptual, between the *Hermetica* and the Fourth Gospel.[68] Like Schweitzer, he too attempts to show how the expression ἐν θεῷ, used in Hellenistic mysticism, provides a basis for interpreting the Johannine doctrine of mutual indwelling.[69] Dodd affirms that the religious experience of union with God with a background of pantheistic thought can properly be called mystical.[70] How he arrives at this definition is unclear. When he describes the Johannine concept that through love we become one by mutual indwelling with the Father and the Son and with one another in him, he raises the question: can the type of religion represented by the Fourth Gospel be properly called 'mysticism'?[71] By citing Bauer, Dodd argues that the Fourth Evangelist is not a mystic in the sense of

(p. 348), i.e. the hellenized form of Christian faith as held by Paul and Ignatius.

65. Schweitzer, *The Mysticism of Paul*, p. 352.

66. Schweitzer, *The Mysticism of Paul*, pp. 352-69.

67. See below, pp. 271-72.

68. C.H. Dodd, *The Interpretation of the Fourth Gospel* (Cambridge: Cambridge University Press, repr. 1958), pp. 10-53; see particularly the lists of parallels on pp. 34-35, 50-51.

69. Dodd, *Interpretation*, pp. 187-200.

70. Dodd, *Interpretation*, p. 190.

71. Dodd, *Interpretation*, p. 197.

the one who has ecstatic experience or of the one who is absorbed in the divine. He goes on to say that the Johannine ideas of mutual indwelling and of bearing fruit meet in the notion of divine ἀγάπη, the ἀγάπη which is expressed in acts of brotherly love to the extent of laying down one's life, and above all in the act of love performed in history, the crucifixion of Jesus.[72] Dodd's final remark here, 'Whether this should be called "mysticism" I do not know',[73] is puzzling. For, after supposing a definition for Hellenistic mysticism, why should he show such reluctance to speak plainly of Johannine mysticism? Some of Dodd's findings are taken up in the next chapter. However, here it should be mentioned that his work, though valuable, reflects insufficient exegesis, particularly of the ideas of ἐν θεῷ, ἀγάπη, and mutual indwelling. Bühner comments that Dodd's interpretation of the sending-statements in terms of the pre-existent Son of God, who entered the earth as a prophet, conclusively lacks exegetical support.[74] This comment applies to his 'mystical' interpretation of John as well.

D.L. Mealand, in his study of Johannine 'mutual indwelling', shows that Hellenistic mysticism is one of the cultural aspects that provide background to the Johannine idea of 'mystical union'.[75] Using Dodd's citations from the *Hermetica* which state that God is in the world and the world in God (*CH* 8.5; 2.6, 18), and that God is in mind and mind in God (*CH* 11.2, 4, 15), Mealand argues that Hellenistic mysticism does speak of the mutual indwelling of God and human, but he is not certain whether this has influenced Johannine Christianity.[76] Following Dodd, he maintains that, unlike some Hellenistic formulae, the Johannine theme of mutual indwelling does not take the form of absorption but of communion, and that it is in the dynamic of *agapê* that the mutuality consists.[77] He also observes that the intermediate role of

72.   Dodd, *Interpretation*, pp. 198-200.

73.   Dodd, *Interpretation*, p. 200. See also below p. 67 n. 12.

74.   Jan-A. Bühner, *Der Gesandte und sein Weg im 4. Evangelium: Die kultur- und religionsgeschichtlichen Grundlagen der johanneischen Sendungschristologie sowie ihre traditionsgeschichtliche Entwicklung* (WUNT 2.2; Tübingen: J.C.B. Mohr [Paul Siebeck], 1977), p. 70.

75.   D.L. Mealand, 'The Language of Mystical Union in Johannine Writings', *DownRev* 95 (1977), pp. 19-34 (23-25, 34).

76.   Mealand, 'Mystical Union', pp. 24-25.

77.   Mealand, 'Mystical Union', p. 31.

Christ in 'mystical union' with God and its ethical implications are alien to Hellenism.[78]

It is notable that, though Mealand refers to Hellenistic mysticism as the background for understanding John's doctrine of 'mystical union', eventually he concludes that this doctrine has roots in the Hebrew Scriptures and associations with the piety of Hellenistic Judaism and of Hellenism, even while it reflects the Christian tradition.[79] Thus one can see a shift in scholarly concentration from Hellenistic mysticism to other forms of religious background for John. As Mealand himself puts it:

> In recent years, the Jewish background to the Fourth Gospel has been strongly emphasized. Historical and archaeological detail, the arguments employed in the controversy chapters, and affinities with the modified dualism of the Qumran texts have all been adduced in this cause.[80]

However, Mealand refers only to a few *Hodayoth* passages of Qumran and without any discussion he concludes, 'They do not speak of a mutual indwelling'.[81] The 'mystical' doctrine as found in Jewish literature, then, remains largely unexplored. However, there have been some attempts in the scholarly circles to argue for the Jewish mystical background to John's Gospel. A brief analysis of their views will advance our investigation further.

Those Who Interpret John in the Light of Jewish Mysticism
In 1929 H. Odeberg argued that both John's Gospel and early Jewish mysticism show close correspondence not only with rabbinic Judaism but also with Mandaeism.[82] Commenting on the notion of salvation and judgment found in Jn 5.24-29, he holds that the religious atmosphere of John can be called 'the Johannine (Christian) salvation-mysticism' and that parallels between John and several features of salvation-mysticism that existed in Palestinian Judaism in the first and second centuries CE can be demonstrated.[83] He finds 'mystical' teaching in John in at least

78. Mealand, 'Mystical Union', p. 25.
79. Mealand, 'Mystical Union', p. 34.
80. Mealand, 'Mystical Union', p. 23.
81. Mealand, 'Mystical Union', p. 25.
82. H. Odeberg, *The Fourth Gospel: Interpreted in its Relation to Contemporaneous Religious Currents in Palestine and the Hellenistic-Oriental World* (Uppsala: Almqvist & Wiksell, 1929; repr. Chicago: Argonaut Publishers, 1968), pp. 5-6.
83. Odeberg, *Fourth Gospel*, pp. 215-16.

two ways: (1) in an inclusive sense as seen in the term ὁ υἱός τοῦ ἀνθρώπου; and (2) in the sense of Merkabah mysticism.[84]

1.   According to Odeberg, the title 'Son of Man' in Johannine passages bears an inclusive connotation, referring to his intimate relationship with the Father on one hand, because the Father works through the Son, and with the believers on the other hand, because the Son's work is related to the believers (cf. Jn 5.17-21). He maintains that Jn 3.13 conveys the 'essentiality of the Son of Man' in the sense that there is no ascent into heaven apart from the Son of Man. Because the Son of Man bears the image of God, only those who are united together in the Son of Man can be born from above and ascend to heaven to perceive the kingdom of God and gain heavenly knowledge (cf. Jn 14.2-4, 6, 23).[85] In a sense, Odeberg seems to fall within the 'traditional view of mysticism', leaving room for three important questions. First, it is unclear whether he implies 'deification' when he argues for the idea of union with the Son and in him with the Father. Secondly, is this understanding of 'mystical union' the primary concern of John in the Son of Man passages such as Jn 1.51 and Jn 3.13? This needs to be judged by an exegetical study of these Son of Man passages, which Odeberg fails to undertake. Thirdly, what date does he ascribe to 'early Jewish mysticism', to 'Rabbinical Judaism' and also to the Fourth Gospel? He presumes that rabbinic Judaism existed along with other religious traditions in the first centuries of our era.[86] Even though the beginnings of rabbinic Judaism are usually dated to the period following 70, the same period as that of John, it is doubtful whether it had been fully recognized as 'Rabbinic Judaism' in the sense in which Odeberg sees it.

2.   Odeberg mentions both apocalyptic and Merkabah mystical traditions as important for understanding Jn 3.13. The essential feature of these traditions, according to him, was: 'the vision of the heavens... the Divine Abode, and the knowledge concerning Divine secrets of Past, Present and Future derived therefrom'.[87] He is aware of two forms of Merkabah mysticism: one is esoteric, or Merkabah experiences proper, which he designates 'salvation mysticism', and another is the

84.   For the meaning of 'Merkabah mysticism' see below, pp. 48-50.
85.   Odeberg, *Fourth Gospel*, pp. 95-98. Odeberg (pp. 98-100) argues that for John even the patriarchs and the prophets ascended to heaven only in union and communion with the Son of Man (Jn 8.56-58).
86.   Odeberg, *Fourth Gospel*, p. 5.
87.   Odeberg, *Fourth Gospel*, pp. 94-95.

popular or coarsened theories about Merkabah mysticism which emphasize ecstasy, magic and abstruse revelations. Odeberg argues that Jn 3.13 is directed against the coarse form of Merkabah mysticism. However, the question remains: when did this coarsened form of mysticism become popular? If the evidence points to a period after John's Gospel, as Abelson shows,[88] then we can hardly accept it as the background for John. On the other hand, it may be argued that Jn 3.13 itself is an evidence for the older form of 'mysticism', but this needs to be investigated. Probably Bühner is right in saying that Odeberg has provided a 'basic framework' to interpret John on the background of Palestinian mysticism.[89] Further, Odeberg has not dealt with the question of the relationship between apocalyptic and Merkabah mysticism as to whether they are identical or separate.

By using the rabbinic principle of *shaliah* (i.e. 'the one who is sent is as he who sends him') T. Preiss brings out the juridical aspect of Johannine mysticism. He argues that, at the time when John wrote his Gospel and Epistles (70–100 CE), the Church was engaged in apologetics against the Synagogue and therefore that John, unlike Paul, presents the doctrine of justification in terms of a cosmic conflict between God and the Prince of this World, having the Son of Man as judge and witness and, after resurrection, having the Spirit as the witness *par excellence*.[90] In this context Preiss indicates that Johannine mysticism is concerned with life in the Spirit, who, by his indwelling, performs the juridical function of judging the world.[91] Inasmuch as Jesus is the Son of Man sent as a witness from heaven, that is, as an ambassador sealed by God (Jn 3.33; 6.27), he is according to rabbinical law 'as he who sends him'. Preiss calls this a sort of 'juridical mysticism', for through the Spirit both Father and Son come and take up their abode in the hearts of the believers (Jn 14.18, 23) and through the witness of the witnessing Spirit the Father's testimony is present with his own (1 Jn 5.10).[92] The essence of juridical mysticism is that God the Father, by the death of

---

88.   J. Abelson, *Jewish Mysticism* (London: G. Bell and Sons, 1913), esp. pp. 48-49, mentions that the coarsened form of Merkabah mysticism belongs to the mid-second century CE.

89.   Bühner, *Der Gesandte*, p. 55.

90.   T. Preiss, *Life in Christ* (London: SCM Press, 1954), pp. 11-31, esp. 11-14, 24-28.

91.   Preiss, *Life in Christ*, p. 24.

92.   Preiss, *Life in Christ*, p. 25.

his Son, exercises justice, not by condemning man (not *justitia passiva*) but by forgiving (*justitia activa*) their sins, by bestowing the Holy Spirit (Jn 20.22), and by enabling the believers to love one another (1 Jn 3.7-10) and to have divine life both now and in future (1 Jn 3.1-2). This kind of mysticism, as Preiss observes, has also the inclusive significance of the idea of the Son of Man. That is, this Son of Man by his death will draw all men unto him making them his brothers (Jn 20.17) so that they might be in him (1 Jn 2.5), in the Son and in the Father (1 Jn 2.12).[93] Although Preiss is right in indicating a situation of conflict with the Synagogue in the late first century, he fails to identify what, if any, was actually called 'mysticism' at that time. He uses the Jewish law of 'sending' to argue for Johannine mysticism, but the underlying thought carries what we call 'the traditional view' of mysticism. Therefore the criticisms that we have posed against this view are applicable also to Preiss's juridical mysticism. Was the idea of justification of sinners by the Son of Man known as 'mysticism' in John's time? How is the rabbinic sending-principle, which belongs to the late second century, related to the 'mystical' practices of John's time? These issues that emerge from Preiss's study need careful analysis.

Another scholar who interprets John in the light of Jewish mystical tradition is N.A. Dahl. He rightly perceives that the real issue in John's time, when there was severance between Jews and Christians, was the authority of Jesus and therefore that John presents a historical continuity between Old Testament witness and the witness borne by the Johannine Church.[94] He argues that Jn 1.51 can be interpreted in the light of the *Haggadah* in which Gen. 28.12 is combined with other visionary texts such as Daniel 7 and Ezekiel 1[95] and that Moses and Abraham had heavenly visions in which they saw the 'hidden' Christ.[96] Similarly, referring to Jn 12.41, where the vision of Isaiah 6 is interpreted as a vision of Christ, Dahl argues that within Jewish 'Merkabah mysticism' Isaiah's vision, mentioned in Jn 12.41, must have been thought to imply a visionary ascent to heaven.[97] He suggests that the Merkabah

93.   Preiss, *Life in Christ*, p. 26.
94.   N.A. Dahl, 'The Johannine Church and History', in W. Klassen and G.F. Snyder (eds.), *Current Issues in New Testament Interpretation: Essays in Honour of O.A. Piper* (New York: Harper & Row, 1962), pp. 124-42 (128-30).
95.   Dahl, 'Johannine Church', p. 136.
96.   Dahl, 'Johannine Church', pp. 132-36.
97.   Dahl, 'Johannine Church', p. 131.

mystical tradition can also be envisaged in *Ascension of Isaiah*, according to which Isaiah saw not simply the glory of the pre-existent *Logos asarkos*, but the glory of Christ incarnate and crucified and that precisely this is meant in Jn 12.41.[98] Like Odeberg, Dahl sees a 'polemical note' in Jn 1.18; 3.13; 6.46 directed against Merkabah mysticism, which made the Old Testament patriarchs and prophets heroes of 'mystical' visions of the heavenly world.[99] Thus Dahl interprets some passages of John against a Merkabah mystical background. However, he assumes, without showing any evidence, that Merkabah mysticism had been known at the time when John was written. So also, Dahl's study does not clarify whether *Ascension of Isaiah* belongs to the same time as John. If Merkabah mysticism had been known or practised in the late first century, then Dahl's view of the Merkabah mystical background for John strengthens Odeberg's thesis. Though Dahl himself has not pursued the study of Merkabah mysticism, he has been followed by other scholars to whom we refer below.

P. Borgen argues that the Jewish background of John, particularly the idea of the vision of God (Jn 6.46), belongs to Merkabah mysticism, which cherished the belief in Israel as the nation that sees God. That is, the theophanic ideas and the spiritualizing tendency found in Jn 6.31-58 suggest for him the early stages of Merkabah mysticism as the background of John.[100] He adopts Preiss's term 'juridical mysticism' to say that for John the life of the Father is transferred to the agent (שליח), his Son as ὁ πεμφθείς (Jn 5.26; 6.57), so that everyone who sees the Son will see God the Father (Jn 1.18; 6.40, 46; 12.45; 14.9).[101] According to Borgen, in Jn 6.31-58 the concepts of Torah, wisdom and agency are woven together and among these the halakhic principle of agency (i.e. 'an agent is like the one who sent him') has solved the problem of the denial of the vision of God, because the mediating function of the agent has made it possible.[102] The concept of agency also explains that through his Son God takes possession of those who belong to him by

98. Dahl, 'Johannine Church', pp. 131-32.
99. Dahl, 'Johannine Church', pp. 141-42.
100. P. Borgen, *Bread from Heaven: An Exegetical Study of the Concept of Manna in the Gospel of John and the Writings of Philo* (NovTSup, 10; Leiden: E.J. Brill, 1965), pp. 2, 147, 177.
101. Borgen, *Bread from Heaven*, pp. 162-63; cf. *idem*, 'God's Agent in the Fourth Gospel', in J. Neusner (ed.), *Religions in Antiquity: Essays in Memory of E.R. Goodenough* (NumSup, 14; Leiden: E.J. Brill, 1968), pp. 137-48.
102. Borgen, *Bread from Heaven*, pp. 162-63.

transferring them to the Son and that those who belong to God accept the claim of the Son by believing in him.[103] Borgen gives importance to the exegesis of the Johannine passages, though not sufficiently. He neither clarifies the meaning of Merkabah mysticism nor gives enough attention to it. He introduces this as the Jewish background of John, but later he makes only a casual reference to it in connection with the vision of God. He traces the Merkabah mystical tradition in Philo (*Conf.* 145–47) and in a Nag Hammadi text,[104] but does not investigate as to what extent this tradition was alive among first-century Jews in Palestine. The key question is: are we justified if we interpret John in the light of later texts such as *b. Qam.* 70a, *Mek.* 12.3-4 and *Qid.* 43a, which contain the law of agency? The halakhic principle emphasizes that an agent is like the sender only in terms of representation or of rank, but there is no reference to 'seeing' the sender in his agent. If so, how does it explain the vision of God? A detailed exegetical study alone will provide the right understanding of John as to whether the vision of God in Jesus is possible because he is the Son of God or he is the שליח or both.

The 'mystical' background of John is brought out by W.A. Meeks by using Moses-tradition. He demonstrates that in the early centuries of the Christian era there was among some Jews a mystical preoccupation with heavenly mysteries and that Moses was regarded by them as one of the greatest prototypes of the mystic ascent to heaven.[105] Some Jews from at least the second century BCE believed that when Moses went up to God on Mt Sinai to receive the Torah and the heavenly secrets, he was crowned there as king of Israel and became the mediator of all kinds of heavenly secrets.[106] He proves his case by using the non-rabbinic Jewish sources such as Philo, Josephus's writings, *Pseudo-Philo*, *Ezekiel the Tragedian* and the Qumran texts, which antedate John, as well as by using the rabbinic *Haggadah*, Samaritan Sources and Mandaean Sources, which are probably later than John.[107] Meeks, however,

---

103. Borgen, *Bread from Heaven*, p. 163.

104. Borgen, 'God's Agent', pp. 144-48.

105. W.A. Meeks, *The Prophet-King: Moses Traditions and the Johannine Christology* (NovTSup, 14; Leiden: E.J. Brill, 1967), pp. 205, 215.

106. Meeks, *Prophet-King*, pp. 206, 215; cf. *idem*, 'Moses as God and King', in J. Neusner (ed.), *Religions in Antiquity: Essays in Memory of E.R. Goodenough* (NumSup, 14; Leiden: E.J. Brill, 1968), pp. 354-71.

107. Meeks, *Prophet-King*, pp. 100-285.

maintains that in the first century there were overlapping traditions and mutual influence between the Samaritan and Jewish *Haggadah*. He detects in John a Moses-centred Jewish piety as 'Prophet-King'. John, for instance, describes the mediatory function of Jesus in delivering to his disciples the 'words' and 'commandment' that God gave him (Jn 1.17) similar to Moses' mediatory role in giving the Law. Jesus reveals God's Name (Jn 17.6, 11-12) just as the Name YHWH was revealed to Moses (Exod. 3.13-14; 6.2-3).[108] He also states that just as Moses became God's שליח after his ascent and was sent to earth as prophet and king to reveal divine secrets, Jesus was sent by the Father as God's prophetic agent to reveal God's name, to testify and judge the world (Jn 17.6, 8, 11, 14; 3.11-21, 31-36).[109] However, the question remains: is Jesus described as prophet-king in John in the same way as Moses was described in the 'mystical' traditions of the first century? Both Ashton and de Jonge argue that the Johannine Jesus is prophet and king only because he is the Son sent by the Father.[110] What, then, is the nature of Jesus' kingship, according to John? Should the functions of performing the Father's will, testifying and judging the world necessarily be attributed only to a prophetic figure? What is the significance of the sending-formula used by John? Had John any form of 'mystical' tradition in mind when he presented Jesus as prophet and king? Only if we allow John's Gospel to speak for itself will we be able to clarify these issues and determine whether it contains 'mystical' thought in it.

Following Odeberg and Dahl, Meeks argues that the expressions 'to ascend into heaven' (Jn 3.13), 'seeing' (Jn 3.3) and 'entering (the king-dom of God)' (Jn 3.5) are used polemically against the mystical prac-tice of the Johannine opponents centred on Moses' ascent.[111] We noticed earlier that Odeberg, Dahl and Borgen have argued that Merkabah mysticism is the tradition that emphasizes an ascent to heaven and a vision of God. If so, is there a connection between Merkabah mysticism and Moses-centred mystical piety? Meeks himself draws parallels between Merkabah mysticism and Moses' ascent and says,

> The medieval 'revelations' show that Moses, like Enoch, Ezra, Baruch, Rabbi Akiba, Rabbi Joshua ben Levi, and others, was in some circles

108. Meeks, *Prophet-King*, pp. 286-91.
109. Meeks, *Prophet-King*, pp. 301-307.
110. See Ashton, *Understanding*, p. 100 n. 76.
111. Meeks, *Prophet-King*, pp. 297-301.

regarded as the pathfinder to the heavenly mysteries so ardently desired
by mystical circles of Judaism.[112]

Does this imply that Moses-centred mysticism was one branch of
Merkabah mysticism? Are the Johannine passages such as Jn 3.3, 5 and
13 a polemic against only Moses' heavenly ascent? These questions
can properly be answered by undertaking a study of the 'mystical' trend
of the first century CE.

Odeberg's inclusive understanding of the Son of Man concept,
Borgen's halakhic principle of agency, Meeks's study of the mystical
ascent of Moses are jointly treated by Jan-A. Bühner in his study, *Der
Gesandte und sein Weg im 4. Evangelium*. Bühner is convinced that the
Johannine tradition can be fitted into the religio-historical development
of the Jewish environment.[113] According to him, the 'mystical' understanding of Christ's function in John originated from the Johannine
community, which had seen Christ in its 'mystical' worship as a heavenly figure, as the hierophant, who mediates the mystical vision of God
(*die mystische Gottesschau*) and the vision thus received is described in
John by means of sending-Christology.[114] However, it is unclear why
Bühner does not name the mystical tradition with which the Johannine
community had been associated. Can it be Merkabah mysticism, which
is believed by scholars such as Odeberg, Dahl and Borgen to be a religious background for John? In fact, Bühner criticizes Goodenough for
not taking Palestinian mysticism into view,[115] but he himself does not
clarify what Palestinian mysticism is.

Bühner suggests that John's sending-Christology is based, at the
level of cultural history, on the three stages of a messenger's path (i.e.
he is sent out, he implements his commission, and returns to the sender), and that at the level of the history of religions the descent of a
heavenly angel to function as a prophetic שליח, as held in the Jewish
apocalyptic-esoteric tradition, is a possible background for the Johannine Son of Man Christology, which is also equal to the 'sending of the
Son' Christology.[116] He goes on to say that by portraying the ascent–
descent of the Son of Man, John gives an apocalyptic-prophetic picture
of Jesus, who could reveal God because of his visionary experience of

112. Meeks, *Prophet-King*, p. 209.
113. Bühner, *Der Gesandte*, pp. 62-69, 72, 374.
114. Bühner, *Der Gesandte*, p. 49.
115. Bühner, *Der Gesandte*, p. 48 n. 1.
116. Bühner, *Der Gesandte*, pp. 270-421, 430-32.

heavenly things and of his consecration in heavenly δόξα.[117] Thus the idea of the prophet-angel that had been associated with the Jewish esoteric traditions gives basis to the Johannine Christology of 'the path of the emissary'. It is not clear whether Bühner means Merkabah mystical tradition when he speaks of the 'apocalyptic-esoteric' tradition of Judaism. Does Merkabah mysticism form a part of the Jewish apocalyptic-esoteric tradition? Did it have a role in shaping John's sending-Christology? Can Merkabah mysticism provide a meaningful background to the descent–ascent of the Son of Man? These need to be examined in this study.

The method of initially setting John in its historical context has been further advanced by J.D.G. Dunn in recent years.[118] Realizing the need to understand John's message as it was intended for its original readers, Dunn attempts to decide the milieu of the Gospel and maintains that John reflects a dialogue with broader strands of apocalyptic and mystical Judaism, with Jabnean rabbis, and possibly with other Christians.[119] John's references to 'the Jews' as the opponents of Jesus and to ἀπο-συνάγωγος in Jn 9.22, 12.42 and 16.2 indicate the christological situation that existed after 70, during which both the apocalyptic and Merkabah mystical strands of Judaism survived.[120] Dunn points out that in late-first-century Judaism, or even earlier, there was an interest in experiencing for oneself a mystical ascent to or revelation of the throne of God by meditating on the Chariot vision of Ezekiel 1 as well as on Isaiah 6, Dan. 7.9-10 and Genesis 1 (cf. *1 En.* 14; Sir. 49.8; 4QS1 40.24).[121] In the second edition of his *Christology in the Making*, Dunn observes that in the period between the Jewish revolts (70–132 CE) the main issue among most of the Jews was monotheism, which they felt was being threatened by the Merkabah mystical interest (i.e. interest in glorious angels, divine throne, the man-like figure of Dan. 7 and the like) found among both Jews and Jewish Christians and by the developing Christian devotion to Jesus as divine.[122] This explains why John

117. Bühner, *Der Gesandte*, pp. 425-26.

118. Dunn, 'Let John Be John', pp. 309-39.

119. Dunn, 'Let John Be John', p. 333.

120. Dunn, 'Let John Be John', pp. 317-23.

121. Dunn, 'Let John Be John', pp. 323-25.

122. J.D.G. Dunn, *Christology in the Making: An Inquiry into the Origins of the Doctrine of the Incarnation* (London: SCM Press, 2nd edn, 1989), pp. xxviii-xxxi.

presents Jesus as no more than God's self-revelation. Dunn comments that for John the real mystical goal, that is, 'to see God', is realized and perceived in Jesus (Jn 1.51; 6.29-58) and that Jn 3.3, 5, 13, with a polemic note, states that true knowledge of heaven comes only from Christ who is from above and who bears witness to what he (alone) has seen there.[123]

Dunn has rightly developed the works of Preiss and Dahl, who had only referred to the late-first-century historical context. He also rightly emphasizes the Merkabah mystical interest that was current at the time of John. However, his references to the 'mystical' strands in John, as in the case of the works of others who argued for Merkabah mystical background, are only outlined without detailed exegesis. It has not been cogently proved that Merkabah mysticism was being practised in the late first century, although some Johannine references point in that direction. Moreover, Dunn has not disproved the parallels between John and the non-Jewish mystical traditions which also emphasized mostly on heavenly ascents, seeing God, etc., and which also had possibly been known in the first century CE.[124] Therefore an extensive study of the subject to trace the mystical elements that could have probably known in the late first century and of the mode of their influence, if any, on John is called for.

The New Trend in Johannine Research

We have seen earlier that the traditional view of 'mysticism' can scarcely be accepted as the 'mystical' thought of John mainly because of its failure to undertake an exegetical analysis of the passages concerned in the light of its first-century religio-historical context.

Although Dodd, who was one of the proponents of the presence of the Hellenistic mystical elements in John, has drawn parallels between the *Hermetica* and John, he concludes that similarities between these

---

123. Dunn, 'Let John Be John', pp. 326-27.

124. Cf. L.W. Hurtado, *One God, One Lord: Early Christian Devotion and Ancient Jewish Monotheism* (London: SCM Press, 1988), p. 6, for the criticism that Dunn, in his *Christology in the Making*, has ignored the pagan religious traditions of Graeco-Roman world about divine beings appearing on earth as humans. Dunn does not respond to this criticism in his 'Foreword to Second Edition' (see *Christology*, pp. xi-xxxix), but concentrates more on the primary issue faced by the Jews and Christian Jews in the late first century.

two documents suggest a common background of religious thought (e.g. Philo) rather than any substantial borrowing from one to the other.[125] We have also observed that Mealand, in his final analysis, suggests Hellenistic piety as only one of several religious systems that influenced John's concept of 'mystical' union.[126] These studies in fact discourage us from arguing confidently for the use of Hellenistic mysticism by the Fourth Evangelist. My own study in this regard has confirmed this to me all the more. It should also be borne in mind that Dodd's *The Interpretation of the Fourth Gospel* was completed in 1953 before Qumran texts were published and therefore his work remains inadequate in terms of resources now available to us to inquire into Johannine mysticism.

Our survey indicates that it is the Jewish background that provides the best key for understanding John in its historical context. Recent studies make it more clear that the matrix of John is Palestinian Judaism and that its author was a Palestinian Jew.[127] By citing the archaeological and topographical evidence as well as the Qumran documents which speak of the contrast of light and darkness, truth, etc., Albright argued in 1956 that both narratives and *logia* of John come from the oral tradition in Palestine before 70 CE and that they were transmitted orally in the Diaspora for one or two decades before being put into writing.[128] That the place of writing is most probably Asia Minor points to the possibility that John was one of the Palestinian Jewish Christians who took refuge among the Christians in Diaspora during the persecution of Christians both by Jews and pagans in 66–70 CE.[129]

125. Dodd, *Interpretation*, pp. 12-13, 53.

126. See above, pp. 32-33.

127. See W.H. Brownlee, 'Whence the Gospel According to John?', in J.H. Charlesworth (ed.), *John and the Dead Sea Scrolls* (New York: Crossroad, 1991), pp. 166-94; M. Hengel, *The Johannine Question* (London: SCM Press; Philadelphia: Trinity Press International, 1989), pp. 109-35; Evans, *Word and Glory*, pp. 146-86, 191-99.

128. W.F. Albright, 'Recent Discoveries in Palestine and the Gospel of John', in W.D. Davies and D. Daube (eds.), *The Background of the New Testament and its Eschatology: Studies in Honour of C.H. Dodd* (Cambridge: Cambridge University Press, 1956), pp. 153-71.

129. Cf. Albright, 'Recent Discoveries', p. 156. Hengel, *Johannine Question*, p. 123, thinks that most probably John the Elder, the author of the Fourth Gospel, moved to Asia Minor and founded the school there. Wengst points to Syria, the province of Agrippa II in the late first century, as the capital of the Johannine

The thesis that John was written in the phase of conflict between Jewish Christians and the synagogue has been vigorously defended by Brown, Martyn and Dunn.[130] Recently Evans has persuasively proved the Palestinian Jewish origin of the Fourth Gospel and of its author. He refers not only to the Qumran parallels and to the expulsion of Christians from the Synagogue, but also to some rabbinic terms and methods, targumic traditions, and to John's christological apologetic that is rooted in the Old Testament as evidence that John belongs to the milieu of first-century Palestinian Judaism, particularly of the synagogues.[131] Though we cannot maintain the first century as the date for targumic and midrashic traditions without difficulty,[132] John's use of the Old Testament, the first-century context of the conflict with the Synagogue, and the discovery of the Qumran scrolls, which have given valuable insights into the Jewish Apocrypha and Pseudepigrapha, clearly indicate that John should be interpreted primarily against a Palestinian Jewish background. Thus, Evans categorically states that research of the last three decades has underlined K. Schubert's statement that Qumran research has proven 'the Jewish origin of the Gospel of John conclusively'.[133] This recent trend in Johannine research makes it necessary to undertake a fresh and detailed study of the whether and what of Palestinian mysticism of the first century CE.

community on the assumption that Judaism was incapable of influencing the Christians in Ephesus in such a radical manner that is implied in John's Gospel (K. Wengst, *Bedrängte Gemeinde und verherrlichter Christus: Der historische Ort des Johannesevangeliums als Schlüssel zu seiner Interpretation* [Biblisch-Theologische Studien, 5; Neukirchen–Vluyn: Neukirchener Verlag, 1981], pp. 77-93, esp. 78). However, he fully ignores the political power held by the Jews in Asia and the conflict that existed between the Christians of Asia Minor and the Jews there (cf. Rev. 2.9; 3.9) in the first few centuries after Christ. See also Hengel's careful refutation of Wengst's hypothesis in Hengel, *Johannine Question*, pp. 115-17, 161 n. 5, 217 n. 88. See also below, pp. 58-61.

130. See R.E. Brown, *The Gospel According to John*. I. *I–XII* (AB, 29; New York: Doubleday, 1966), pp. lxxiii–lxxv; *idem, The Community of the Beloved Disciple* (New York: Paulist Press, 1979), pp. 166-67; J.L. Martyn, *History and Theology in the Fourth Gospel* (Nashville: Abingdon Press, 2nd edn, 1979), pp. 37-62; Dunn, 'Let John Be John', pp. 318-25.

131. Evans, *Word and Glory*, pp. 146-86.

132. However, see Evans, *Word and Glory*, pp. 18-28, for the four criteria that should be considered in evaluating the relevance of concepts found in a document that postdates New Testament writings.

133. Evans, *Word and Glory*, pp. 148-49 n. 5.

Scope, Purpose and the Terms of This Inquiry

Scholars who have argued for a Jewish mystical background to John suggest that John polemizes against the Merkabah mystical practice prevalent at that time. As we have noticed, Odeberg at first mentioned this in 1929 and it was reiterated by Dahl and Borgen. Dunn brought this to our notice again in 1983, although most of the Johannine scholars today do not show any knowledge of the mystical aspiration of the people in John's day. Evans, for instance, insists that an apologetic is intended in John, particularly in Jn 12.38–19.37, to answer the objections to Christian faith raised by the Synagogue,[134] but he does not show awareness of any form of 'mystical' practice that was current at that time. This raises the question of whether a mystical praxis, called 'Merkabah mysticism', had been known in the late first century at all. Other related questions are: if yes, then who practised it? What are the sources of evidence for such a praxis? Are we justified in using the term 'Merkabah mysticism' with '-ism' in it to refer to the first-century-CE religious context? For P.S. Alexander categorically states that any solid evidence for the existence of Merkabah mysticism as a distinctive system comes from not earlier than the third century CE,[135] whereas Scholem treats Merkabah mysticism as the development stretching from the first century BCE to the tenth century CE.[136] We should also observe that even though leading scholars of Merkabah mysticism constantly indicate that Palestine is the cradle of the Merkabah mystical movement and that Merkabah literature itself has Palestinian roots,[137] sufficient attention has not been given thus far to the Jewish mystical literature, Apocrypha and Pseudepigrapha, Qumran scrolls, and also to a study of John's Gospel against the background of this wide range of materials. These observations lead us to set the following twofold purpose in this work:

1. To examine whether or not Merkabah mysticism was in practice in

---

134. Evans, *Word and Glory*, pp. 176-77.

135. P.S. Alexander, 'Comparing Merkavah Mysticism and Gnosticism: An Essay in Method', *JJS* 35 (1984), pp. 1-18 (8, 12).

136. Scholem, *Major Trends*, pp. 40-79. See also below, pp. 50-53, on Merkabah mysticism.

137. See, for example, Scholem, *Major Trends*, pp. 41-43; I. Gruenwald, *Apocalyptic and Merkavah Mysticism* (Leiden: E.J. Brill, 1980); P.S. Alexander, '3 (Hebrew Apocalypse of) Enoch', *OTP*, I, pp. 223-315 (232).

the late first century; if it was, what are the dominant elements in it
which may help us to arrive at some definition of Jewish mysticism?

2. To inquire whether it forms a meaningful background for understanding John's message.

This end can be achieved in three progressive stages: by tracing the
first-century 'mystical' attitude in general and Merkabah mystical features in particular; by undertaking an exegetical study of Johannine
passages, arranging them in themes; and by comparing our findings
with the current mystical traditions. This will enable us not only to
understand the interaction between the Jewish Christians and the Jews
of John's time, but particularly to appreciate John's message in that
context.

Although John is basically a Jewish document, we can hardly overlook many other systems of thought that existed both in and outside
Palestine in the first and second centuries.[138] M. Smith demonstrates
that 'Palestine in the first century was profoundly Hellenized and that
the Hellenization extended even to the basic structure of much Rabbinic thought'.[139] If so, it is worth investigating Hellenistic mysticism[140]
in order to see whether John was in any way influenced by or at least
would be better understood by such thought. No doubt, we need to
study the platonic idea of a transcendent God and stoic pantheism,
should we get a broader picture of Hellenistic mysticism. However, it is
the *Hermetica* which give the fullest expression of the 'mystical'
tendency of Greek religions and philosophy, for the thought expressed
in the *Hermetica* is a 'syncretism of Platonic and Stoic philosophy with
the religious tradition of the Near East'.[141] If the materials used in the
Hermetica belong to the first century CE or earlier, then the *Hermetica*
offer the nearest comparable thought to John. Moreover, Dodd has set a

138. See E.E. Ellis, *The World of St John* (London: Lutterworth; New York:
Abingdon Press, 1965), p. 17; Barrett, *John*, p. 22.

139. M. Smith, 'Palestinian Judaism in the First Century', in Moshe Davis
(ed.), *Israel: Its Role in Civilization* (New York: Harper & Brothers, repr. 1956),
pp. 67-81 (71). Similarly M. Hengel, *The 'Hellenization' of Judaea in the First
Century after Christ* (London: SCM Press; Philadelphia: Trinity Press International,
1989).

140. I am aware of the ambiguity involved in the term 'Hellenistic', particularly in a first-century historical context, as Hengel (*Hellenization*, pp. 1-6, 53-54)
indicates. By this term I mean 'a syncretism of Greek philosophical and religious
thoughts'.

141. See Brown, *John*, I, p. lviii.

precedent by treating the *Hermetica* as a basic source for the study of Hellenistic mysticism, that too by giving more attention to the parallels between John and the *Hermetica*. Therefore I use the *Hermetica* for an analysis of Hellenistic mysticism in the early section of Part I (Chapter 2), allowing the possibility that the tradition behind it goes back even earlier than the first century.

Another system that is important for understanding the writings of first-century Christians is the Hellenistic Jewish thought known from Philo (c. 20 BCE–50 CE), a contemporary of Jesus, Paul and John. Since Philo's aim was to make Judaism intellectually respectable in the eyes of the Gentile world, he interpreted the Jewish Scripture in the light of the contemporary philosophy and theology of the Hellenistic age.[142] His writings, then, reflect the exegetical and philosophical mind of the first-century Hellenistic Jews and is therefore important for our purpose of studying John. Although it cannot be decisively argued that Alexandria is the place of the composition of John's Gospel, the correspondence between Alexandria and Palestine, both religiously and culturally, is inevitable. Hengel points out the close connection that existed between Jerusalem and Alexandria even from the third century BCE in terms of culture and education.[143] Jeremias, by citing Eusebius, indicates that Philo himself made a pilgrimage to Jerusalem.[144] This would have given Philo ample opportunity to interact with the Palestinian Jews and his writings thus had been known at least to the elite group in Palestine.[145]

Both Colson and Whitaker comment that Philo is a link not only between Judaism and Hellenism, but also between Judaism and Christianity in two different ways: besides the common allegorical treatment of the Old Testament, there is a close affinity between Philo's Logos

142. See R. McL. Wilson, 'Philo and the Fourth Gospel', *ExpTim* 65 (1953–54), pp. 47-49 (48); Dunn, *Christology*, p. 221, observes that Philo's thought is 'a unique synthesis of Platonic and Stoic world-views with Jewish monotheism'.

143. M. Hengel, *Judaism and Hellenism* (Minneapolis: Fortress Press, 2nd edn, 1991), pp. 65-78.

144. J. Jeremias, *Jerusalem in the Time of Jesus: An Investigation into Economic and Social Conditions during the New Testament Period* (Philadelphia: Fortress Press, repr. 1975), p. 69.

145. R. Marcus (trans.), *Philo: Questions and Answers on Genesis* (LCL, 1; Cambridge, MA: Harvard University Press, repr. 1993), p. xiv, observes that it has been found that in certain points Philo's legal exegesis agrees with the Palestinian exegesis of the pre-Roman period rather than that of his Palestinian contemporaries.

and the Johannine Logos on the one hand, and between Philo's conceptions of conscience, Spirit, faith, sonship, immortality, etc., and those of Paul on the other.[146] However, scholars have paid much attention so far to the conceptual parallels between Philo's Logos and the Johannine Logos.[147] Although the 'mystical' theology of Philo has been discussed by E.R. Goodenough and in our time by A. Louth,[148] no significant work has been done to compare Philo's mysticism with Johannine thought. However, Dodd has outlined the 'mystical' awareness of Philo in comparison with John[149] and therefore his work can be used as a starting point. Hagner's comparative study of the vision of God in Philo and in John throws light on one 'mystical' aspect: seeing God.[150] Therefore a study focusing on Philo's mysticism is called for. Was Philo a mystic? Do his writings contain 'mystical' teachings? If so, in what sense? Do they show similarity in any sense with Johannine motifs? An attempt is made to answer these questions in the latter section of Part I (Chapter 3). I compare his teachings with John's theology, wherever necessary, in Part III and this will throw light on why Philo's mystical thought is inadequate to serve as an interpretative background to John's Gospel.

In Part II I analyse some of the Jewish and Christian writings to see whether the third-century Merkabah mysticism was already being practised in the late first century.[151] What do we mean by Merkabah mysticism? What are the salient features of this practice?

146. F.H. Colson, G.H. Whitaker *et al.* (trans.), *Philo* (LCL; Cambridge, MA: Harvard University Press, repr. 1991), I, pp. xx-xxi. However, they infer that the connection between Philo and Christian thought is based on their common heritage and atmosphere without direct contact and conscious borrowing.

147. For example, A.W. Argyle, 'Philo and the Fourth Gospel', *ExpTim* 63 (1951–52), pp. 385-86; Wilson, 'Philo and the Fourth Gospel', pp. 47-49; S. Sandmel, *Philo of Alexandria: An Introduction* (Oxford: Oxford University Press, 1979), pp. 148-50; Dunn, *Christology*, pp. 220-30; C.A. Evans, *Noncanonical Writings and New Testament Interpretation* (Peabody, MA: Hendrickson, 1992), pp. 83-84.

148. See E.R. Goodenough, *By Light, Light: The Mystical Gospel of Hellenistic Judaism* (New Haven: Yale University Press, 1935); Louth, *Christian Mystical Tradition*, pp. 18-35.

149. Dodd, *Interpretation*, pp. 54-73, 191-200.

150. D.A. Hagner, 'The Vision of God in Philo and John: A Comparative Study', *JETS* 14 (1971), pp. 81-93.

151. The mystical elements detected in the first-century literature, or even earlier, should only be understood as denoting the earliest form of Merkabah mysticism or the pre-Merkabah mysticism rather than a full-fledged mystical system.

According to Alexander, Merkabah mysticism is concerned with an ecstatic experience through which the mystic aims to achieve a personal and intimate communion with God.[152] Although this experience is common to all 'mystical' systems, in Merkabah mysticism such an experience is centred around the 'mystical explication' of Ezekiel 1.[153] As Segal puts it,

> The vision of the throne-chariot of God in Ezekiel I, with its attendant description of Glory (*Kavod*), God's Glory or form, for the human figure, is a central image of Jewish mysticism, which is closely related to the apocalyptic tradition.[154]

Thus it is called Merkabah or throne-chariot mysticism. It was believed by some Jewish rabbis that certain 'mystical' expositions of, or even discussion on, Ezekiel 1 would cause God to appear.[155] The content of such expositions, which inculcated a theosophical interest, was known as *Ma'aseh Merkabah* (i.e. 'the Work of the Divine Chariot').[156] In the course of time, however, not only Ezekiel 1, but also Ezekiel 8–10; Isaiah 6; and Daniel 7 contributed to the development of the Merkabah mystical tradition in different aspects. Even from the early tannaitic era the exposition of *Ma'aseh Merkabah*, together with the cosmological

---

152. P.S. Alexander (ed. and trans.), *Textual Sources for the Study of Judaism* (Manchester: Manchester University Press, 1984), p. 26.

153. See I. Gruenwald, *Merkavah Mysticism*, p. vii. Although the word 'Merkabah' does not occur in Ezek. 1, it was used to mean 'chariot-throne' as early as 1 Chron. 28.18.

154. A.F. Segal, *Paul the Convert: The Apostolate and Apostasy of Saul the Pharisee* (New Haven: Yale University Press, 1990), p. 39. He also points out that the name 'Merkabah mysticism' was designated for these mystical traditions as early as the mishnaic period (c. 220 CE). Scholem, *Major Trends*, pp. 43-44, concedes that the earliest Jewish mysticism is 'throne mysticism'. According to Fossum, Jewish mysticism in the first centuries was centred on the man-like figure upon the throne (see J. Fossum, 'Jewish-Christian Christology and Jewish Mysticism', *VC* 37 [1983], pp. 260-87 [260]).

155. See A. Biram, 'Ma'aseh Bereshit; Ma'aseh Merkabah', *JewEnc*, VIII, p. 236.

156. The term 'ma'aseh' literally means 'work' (Biram, 'Ma'aseh Bereshit; Ma'aseh Merkabah', p. 235), but it can also mean 'practice', 'occupation', 'pursuit', 'undertaking', 'construction', etc. (see C.R.A. Morray-Jones, 'Merkabah Mysticism and Talmudic Tradition: A Study of the Traditions Concerning Hammerkabah and Ma'aseh Merkabah in Tannaitic and Amoraic Sources' [PhD Thesis, Cambridge University, 1988], pp. 4-5).

speculation, called *Ma'aseh Bereshit* (i.e. the Work of Creation), was considered as 'esoteric' or as containing 'hidden truths', 'secrets' in the sense that 'they are meant only for the initiated, not for the vulgar, who might misunderstand them'.[157] The esoteric nature of these 'mystical' doctrines is implied in the talmudic restriction, which states, '*Ma'aseh Bereshit* must not be explained before two, nor *Ma'aseh Merkabah* before one, unless he be wise and understands it by himself' (*m. Hag.* 2.1).[158]

It is important to note that both *Ma'aseh Bereshit* and *Ma'aseh Merkabah* alike point to God and the world in different dimensions. While the former, dealing with such questions as: what was created first, whether heaven or earth? What was the material that was used in creating the world? What did exist before creation? ultimately leads to the truth that it is God who is the 'Nothing' (*Nichts*) or the 'Original Substance' (*Urstoff*), from which everything was created,[159] the latter focuses on God as the One who, being seated on the throne of Glory, exercises lordship over the world. Thus the early Jewish mysticism was known not only as 'throne-mysticism',[160] but also as the 'mysticism of the ruler of the cosmos (*Kosmokratorenmystik*)'.[161] Another mystical aspect of *Ma'aseh Bereshit* is its claim that even before the creation of the world, the Torah and the Throne of Glory were created (*Gen. R.* 1.4). Thus both these disciplines complement each other by displaying the same theosophical and cosmological interest and our study shows that such an interest was existent even earlier than the first century CE.

Merkabah mysticism is fully treated in the so-called *Hekhalot* literature, a collection of the Jewish mystical writings, composed mainly in 200–700 CE.[162] Although this literature is later than John, the

---

157. Alexander, *Judaism*, p. 27.

158. Cf. *m. Meg.* 4.10, which prohibits the use of Ezek. 1 as a prophetic reading in the synagogue.

159. See H-F. Weiss, *Untersuchungen zur Kosmologie des hellenistischen und palästinischen Judentums* (TU, 97; Berlin: Akademie-Verlag, 1966), pp. 78-79. Cf. Alexander, *Judaism*, p. 27, who states that *Ma'aseh Bereshit* strives to get behind the world of appearance to a world of unity and ultimate reality.

160. See above, pp. 48-49.

161. See P. Schäfer, *Der verborgene und offenbare Gott* (Tübingen: J.C.B. Mohr [Paul Siebeck], 1991), p. 144.

162. See Gruenwald, *Merkavah Mysticism*, p. vii. The *Hekhalot* means 'the heavenly "halls" or "palaces" through which the mystic passes in order to reach the divine throne' (see P. Schäfer, 'The Aim and Purpose of Early Jewish Mysticism',

oldest text, *Hekhalot Zutarti*, is dated by J. Greenfield to the second or third century CE[163] and the whole of *Hekhalot* literature claims the authority of R. Ishmael and R. Akiba, the late-first-century/early-second-century rabbis. Therefore the *Hekhalot* tradition possibly goes back to the late first or early second century. Moreover, commenting on the angelology found in the *Hekhalot* literature, Elior says that, at a time when the earthly temple had been destroyed and God was thought of as having removed himself from apprehension, the priests, who were the authors of *Hekhalot* literature, transferred the essence of the earthly worship to the realm of angelic beings.[164] This situation indeed places the mystical tradition found in *Hekhalot* texts in the historical context following 70.[165] This raises the possibility that the Merkabah mystical tradition can be traced back in the late first century when John was composed. Therefore, after displaying in Chapter 4 the 'mystical'

in *idem*, *Hekhalot-Studien* [Tübingen: J.C.B. Mohr (Paul Siebeck), 1988], pp. 277-95 [279]). Schäfer ('Tradition and Redaction in Hekhalot Literature', in *idem*, *Hekhalot-Studien*, pp. 8-16) lists nine *Hekhalot* texts, excluding *Re'uyyot Yehezkel*, which, he thinks, being a Midrash, does not fit easily into the same picture as the other *Hekhalot* texts.

163. See Gruenwald, *Merkavah Mysticism*, p. 142.

164. R. Elior, 'Mysticism, Magic, and Angelology: The Perception of Angels in Hekhalot Literature', *JSQ* 1 (1993–94), pp. 3-53 (24-27). In similar vein, see J. Maier, *Vom Kultus zur Gnosis: Studien zur Vor- und Fruhgeschichte der 'judischen Gnosis': Bundeslade, Gottesthron und Merkabah* (Salzburg: Otto Müller Verlag, 1964), esp. pp. 129-46. However, P.S. Alexander suggests to me that interest in the heavenly temple predates the destruction of the earthly temple. My own study on Qumran texts undertaken below attests this.

165. Cf. *HR* 15.1 (*Synopse* §198) which states that the secret of the Merkabah vision was revealed by R. Nehunyah b. Ha-Qanah when he saw that Rome had taken counsel to destroy the mighty ones of Israel. Thus Merkabah mysticism is linked with the destruction of Jerusalem in 70. The historical link of the *Hekhalot* texts with the Roman and Sasanian empires of their time (c. the late third century CE) has been detected by Alexander in their use of the terms *familia shel ma'alah* ('the family above') and *pargod* ('curtain') respectively—see P.S. Alexander, 'The Family of Caesar and the Family of God: The Image of the Emperor in the Heikhalot Literature', in L.C.A. Alexander (ed.), *Images of Empire* (Sheffield: JSOT Press, 1991), pp. 276-97. In his article, 'Comparing Merkavah Mysticism and Gnosticism', pp. 12-17, Alexander argues that both Gnosticism and Merkabah mysticism are parallel reactions to the socio-historical conditions of that time. Although Alexander refers to a third-century context, what is clear is that the Merkabah mystical tradition did not develop outside the socio-historical situation of its time.

elements found in the *Hekhalot* literature, an inquiry into some of the Jewish documents that belong to pre- and post-Christian periods is undertaken in the subsequent chapters to see whether the *Hekhalot* mystical components can be traced in them. If traced, then they give us a clue that Merkabah mysticism had been practised even from the pre-Christian period.[166]

The Qumran documents give some evidence for the practice of Merkabah mysticism in the Qumran community. On the two fragments of the Sabbath Shirot, 4QSl 39 1.1.16-26 (= 4Q403 1.1.16-26) and 4QSl 40.24.2-9 (= 4Q405 20.2.7-14), published by Strugnell,[167] Scholem commented that these fragments undoubtedly show that there is a connection between the oldest Hebrew Merkabah texts preserved in Qumran and the subsequent development of Merkabah mysticism as preserved in the *Hekhalot* texts.[168] Now G. Vermes has published in English some more fragments of this Qumran text (4Q400; 4Q402; 4Q403; 4Q405; 11Q5–6).[169] The full material, consisting of eight MSS from Cave 4 (4Q400–407), small fragments from Cave 11 (11QShirShabb 3–4, 5–6, 8–7, etc.) and Masada ShirShabb, the composition of which is dated c. 75 BCE–50 CE, has been edited, with English translation and commentary, by Carol Newsom.[170] A study of the

166. Cf. Evans, *Word and Glory*, pp. 18-19, who shows that the first criterion in evaluating the relevance of concepts found in a document later than any New Testament writing is to look for the components of the later tradition in documents that are contemporaneous with or prior to the New Testament.

167. J. Strugnell, *The Angelic Liturgy at Qumran: 4Q Serek Shirot 'Olat Ha-shabat* (VTSup, 7; Leiden: E.J. Brill, 1959), pp. 318-45.

168. Scholem in the second edition of his *Jewish Gnosticism, Merkabah Mysticism, and Talmudic Tradition* (New York: Jewish Theological Seminary of America, 1965), as cited by L.H. Schiffman, 'Merkavah Speculation at Qumran: The 4Q Serekh Shirot 'Olat ha-Shabbat', in J. Reinharz and D. Swetschinski (eds.), *Mystics, Philosophers, and Politicians: Essays in Jewish Intellectual History in Honor of A. Altmann* (Durham, NC: Duke University Press, 1982), pp. 15-47 (16). Strugnell himself commented that the type of angelic liturgy found in these fragments is associated with the early form of Merkabah vision (see Scholem, *Jewish Gnosticism* [1960]), p. 29.

169. G. Vermes, *The Dead Sea Scrolls in English* (Sheffield: Sheffield Academic Press, 4th edn, 1995), pp. 254-63.

170. C. Newsom, *Songs of the Sabbath Sacrifice: A Critical Edition* (HSS, 27; Atlanta: Scholars Press, 1985). More recently 4Q400–4Q405 and 11QShirShabb (11Q17) have been published in English by F.G. Martínez in his *The Dead Sea*

relevant portions of these documents, which I undertake in Chapter 5, seems to endorse Schiffman's remark that Merkabah mysticism had its origin at Qumran, from where it somehow was absorbed by the pharisaic and tannaitic tradition,[171] although Merkabah tradition had already been familiar in some circles in ben Sira's time. The Aramaic *Testament of Levi*, discovered in Qumran (4Q213 TLevi[a]), uses, though in broken form, the Merkabah vision of Levi that appears in *Testament of Levi* 2–5 (second century BCE).[172] This confirms our observation that the tradition concerning an ascent to the third heaven to see God on the throne was current in the second century BCE and that the community in Qumran, as also other Qumran documents show, had great interest in such visionary experiences.

A. Louth writes, 'Can there, indeed, be such a thing as Christian mystical theology? There are many—particularly Protestants—who say not; yet the phenomenon seems persistent, however impossible.'[173] Although Louth does not mean Merkabah mysticism, a Christian mystical practice in terms of Merkabah mysticism is sufficiently attested by Paul's experience described in 2 Corinthians 12 and by *Ascension of Isaiah*, a Jewish work that shows a definite Christian influence in its narration of the vision of Isaiah (6–11).[174] Bowker suggests that the question of whether Paul had been trained in Merkabah contemplation can be answered only if points of connection with other descriptions of Merkabah visions can be found.[175] A comparison of Paul's experience with the elements of *Hekhalot* mysticism, which is undertaken in Chapter 6, reveals that Merkabah mysticism was familiar in Christian circles as early as 40 CE.

Rowland argues that apocalyptic must be recognized as a valuable source for the reconstruction of the origins of Jewish mysticism and

Scrolls Translated: The Qumran Texts in English (Leiden: E.J. Brill; Grand Rapids: Eerdmans, 2nd edn, ET 1996), pp. 419-31.

171. Schiffman, 'Merkavah Speculation', p. 46.

172. See H.W. Hollander and M. de Jonge, *The Testaments of the Twelve Patriarchs* (Leiden: E.J. Brill, 1985), p. 19. F.G. Martínez, *The Dead Sea Scrolls Translated: The Qumran Texts in English* (Leiden: E.J. Brill, ET 1994), pp. 266-68.

173. Louth, *Christian Mystical Tradition*, p. xiv.

174. J.M.T. Barton, 'The Ascension of Isaiah', in H.F.D. Sparks (ed.), *The Apocryphal Old Testament* (Oxford: Clarendon Press, 1984), pp. 775-812 (779), argues for Christian authorship of *Asc. Isa.* 6–11.

175. J.W. Bowker, '"Merkabah" Visions and the Visions of Paul', *JSS* 16 (1971), pp. 157-73 (159).

particularly for ascertaining the earliest meditation on Ezekiel.[176] Thus Gruenwald rightly analyses seven major apocalypses and demonstrates the Merkabah mystical features in them.[177] However, his focus is not mainly on the apocalypses that belong to the first century, although he does treat first-century documents such as *1 Enoch* 71, *2 Enoch*, *Apocalypse of Abraham*, *Ascension of Isaiah*; and Revelation. The major weakness in Gruenwald's analysis is his failure to discuss the 'son of man' (or 'man') who appears in the Merkabah visions of *1 Enoch* 71 and Revelation 1. This failure has led him to ignore such important works as Daniel 7, *4 Ezra* and *Testament of Abraham*. In order to give a wider picture of the Merkabah mysticism that is embedded in the apocalypses that belong to the first century CE, I examine six apocalyptic books in Chapter 7. Since Segal's 'Two Powers in Heaven' apostasy is centred on the man-like figure of Merkabah visions, a brief treatment of that apostasy is appended in this chapter.

The Jewish texts that I have examined are not exhaustive. The pseudepigraphal books such as *Testament of Levi* and *3 Baruch* should also be considered as evidence for the familiarity of and interest in Merkabah-like visions in the inter-testamental era.

In Chapter 8 I examine whether Yohanan ben Zakkai (c. 1–80 CE), a member of the pharisaic community in Jerusalem before 70 and the founder of school at Yavneh after 70,[178] and his pupils practised Merkabah mysticism. Since Yohanan was a contemporary of John and also was the champion of the restored religious life of Judaism at that time, an analysis of the mystical practice of Yohanan, if we can so speak, will provide strong evidence of the existence of the type of mysticism known in John's time.[179] By pointing out the common features between

176. C. Rowland, 'The Visions of God in Apocalyptic Literature', *JSJ* 10 (1979), pp. 137-54 (148, 154); Alexander, 'Gnosticism', pp. 10-11, 17, argues that Merkabah mysticism, albeit with different emphases, can be an inner-Jewish development of pre-70 apocalyptic.

177. Gruenwald, *Merkavah Mysticism*, pp. 29-72.

178. See J. Neusner, *A Life of Yohanan ben Zakkai: Ca. 1–80 C.E.* (Leiden: E.J. Brill, 2nd rev. edn, 1970), p. xii.

179. Morray-Jones's argument that Yohanan was not the authoritative source of Merkabah mystical tradition, as he did not have access to the esoteric and mystical tradition, is not compelling (see C.R.A. Morray-Jones, 'Paradise Revisited [2 Cor. 12.1-12]: The Jewish Mystical Background of Paul's Apostolate. Part 1: The Jewish Sources', *HTR* 86 [1993], pp. 177-217 [188 n. 32]); *idem*, 'Talmudic Tradition', pp. 282-307. Against his view, see below, pp. 155-58.

these two Jewish leaders (i.e. emphasis on individual obedience and ethics in daily life), Barrett notes that a thoroughgoing comparison between John and Yohanan would prove rewarding.[180] However, a study of Yohanan has been largely overlooked in Johannine studies. If John reflects awareness of and reaction to a mystical practice such as the one attested for Yohanan and his school, then it is most likely that he is addressing not only the Jews who were influenced by the mystical thought of his day, but also those who were actually practising it, calling them to faith in Jesus Christ. In my study of John I am more convinced that the term ἵνα πιστεύ(σ)ητε of Jn 19.35 and 20.31 can no longer be maintained as a major criterion for deciding the audience of the Gospel. For John uses ἵνα πιστεύητε (present subjunctive) in Jn 6.29, though aorist subjunctive in Jn 6.30 and 11.42, to refer to the unbelieving crowd; ἵνα πιστεύῃ (present subjunctive is well attested— cf. Jn 17.22, 23, 24) in Jn 17.21 to refer to the world; ἵνα πιστεύσητε (aorist subjunctive) in Jn 11.15, 13.19 and 14.29 to refer to the disciples; ἐὰν πιστεύσῃς (aorist subjunctive) in Jn 11.40 to refer to Martha; and ἵνα πιστεύσω (aorist subjunctive) in Jn 9.36 in reference to the healed blind man who already had a certain amount of faith in Jesus (cf. Jn 9.17, 33).[181] The corollary is that early Tannaim, though non-Christians, cannot be excluded from the audience to whom John intended his Gospel.

I do not argue, however, that John is spending all his time and energy simply addressing such a small group of Judaism. Small though the group is, one cannot ignore the fact that it was the core group at Yavneh whose decisions and customs influenced the *halakah*, the editing of Mishnah and the major part of the tractate *Eduyyot* and thus which was making tremendous impact on the religious life of the Jewish mass. Therefore there is little wonder that John aimed to reach with his Gospel the Jewish nation through this elite and dynamic group, without at the same time ignoring other people in the Graeco-Roman world, calling them to faith in Jesus as the Messiah, the Son of God.[182]

180. See C.K. Barrett, *The Gospel of John and Judaism* (London: SPCK, 1975), pp. 45, 85 n. 20.

181. D.A. Carson, *The Gospel According to John* (Leicester: IVP; Grand Rapids: Eerdmans, 1991), p. 661, shows awareness of these points when he says that John elsewhere in his Gospel can use *either* tense to refer to *both* coming to faith and continuing in faith (italics his), but he does not illustrate.

182. It should be noted that the mishnaic term *hakam* who is eligible to

We have seen above that the basic texts for the Merkabah mystical experience are Ezekiel 1, 8–10; Isaiah 6; and Daniel 7. If so, an analysis of these passages will shed light on important elements of Merkabah mysticism. Precisely such an analysis is undertaken in Chapter 9. John's use of the same passages and themes (e.g. Jn 1.51a; 12.40-41) reflects his awareness that such Merkabah mysticism as was being practised in his time was undoubtedly rooted in the Scripture. Therefore one can argue that if John is read against the background of Merkabah mysticism, it can be seen that the author confronts the Jews of his day by using their own Scripture and practice.

Even though Merkabah mysticism can be briefly defined as 'seeing God in his kingly glory', there are other components that are connected with such a vision. Chapter 10 lists, in the light of analysis of first-century Jewish and Christian texts, at least 14 interrelated aspects of Merkabah mysticism. By treating them collectively as a definition for 'mysticism', the stage is set for discussion in Part III to find out what light, if any, our findings with regard to Merkabah mysticism in the late first century CE throw on John's Gospel. Does it provide a clue to the background of John's thought? Is he in any way engaged in dialogue with the Merkabah mystics of his time? In order to answer these questions I undertake a study of the Johannine themes, ascent to heaven, seeing God, glory, kingship of Jesus, sending, indwelling, light, and the Logos. This will shed light on whether John can rightly be described as 'mystical Gospel'.

Alexander argues that 'Jewish esotericism' can usefully replace 'Jewish mysticism'. According to him, Jewish mysticism is concerned with 'secrets' and 'hidden things' in two ways: first, it strives to get behind the world of appearance and diversity to a world of unity and ultimate reality; and secondly, it is esoteric, for the teachings of secrets are meant only for the initiated rather than for the vulgar who might misunderstand them.[183] If John can be read in the light of Merkabah

---

expound *ha-merkabah*, i.e. Ezek. 1 (*m. Ḥag.* 2.1) does not denote originally a scholar in a rabbinic sense, but rather a 'mantic sage' (e.g. Daniel who was an exile in Babylon), who possesses esoteric knowledge and visionary-mystical experience—see Morray-Jones, 'Paradise Revisited. Part 1', p. 188. Therefore mystical experiences in the first century were not confined, at least in principle, to the rabbinic group alone, although they were effectively practised in conventicles—cf. Alexander, '3 (Hebrew Apocalypse of) Enoch', pp. 238-39.

183.   Alexander, *Judaism*, p. 27.

mysticism of the first century CE, does it show an esoteric tendency in the sense noted by Alexander? J. Dan rightly warns us that not everything that is esoteric is also mystical,[184] but 'mysticism' has always been concerned with 'secrets'; for the root word from which μυστικισμός ('mysticism') is derived is μέμυσται, the third person singular perfect passive of μύειν, which means 'to shut or close the mouth or eyes'. Thus C. Richardson suggests that μέμυσται means 'that which is shut up, hidden or concealed'.[185] μύειν, which is the contracted form of μύσιειν, itself is derived from μῦ-, meaning 'a muttering sound made with lips' or even 'a groan'[186] and this may imply either the muttering sound of the μυστής which comes out of his yearning for the transcendent reality or the muttering sound caused by the mystic's inability to reveal his experience in words. At any rate, as 'mysticism' seems to be concerned with secrets that are, however, revealed to the initiates, at least to the extent that they can be grasped, any 'mystical' experience can be treated as 'esoteric'. Therefore detecting the esoteric nature of John, which is undertaken in Chapter 18, will prove not only that the Fourth Evangelist is addressing particularly the Merkabah mystics of his time, but also that he and his associates themselves had been in some way connected with mystical practice.

Three observations, which are directly relevant to our exegetical task, should particularly be made at this point. They are the probable date, author and place of writing of the Gospel of John.

The general consensus of the scholars is that the most probable date of the composition of John is c. 100. The earliest papyri that contain Johannine passages, P[52], P[90] (= POxy 3253) and P[66] are dated to the second century CE.[187] There are traces of John's influence on such apocryphal Gospels as the Gospel of Peter, the Gospel of Thomas, and the Gospel contained in the Egerton Papyrus, which belong to the end

184. J. Dan, 'The Revelation of the Secret of the World: The Beginning of Jewish Mysticism in Late Antiquity' (Brown University Program in Judaic Studies Occasional Paper No. 2; Rhode Island: Brown University, 1992), p. 12. I am grateful to Professor Dan for sending me the printed form of this paper.

185. Charles Richardson, *A New Dictionary of the English Language: Volume the Second* (London: William Pickering, 1844), p. 1329. Cf. μεμύνημαι in Phil. 4.12, which, in its present grammatical construction, means 'I have been instructed in the secret of' (cf. G. Bornkamm, 'μυστήριον, μυέω', *TDNT*, IV, p. 828).

186. See Klein, *Etymological Dictionary*, p. 485.

187. See Hengel, *Johannine Question*, pp. 6-7, p. 144 n. 27.

of the first half of the second century.[188] Therefore Barrett is probably right in suggesting a date earlier than 140 CE as the *terminus ante quem*, since John must have been in existence some little time before the date of the papyrus.[189] If we allow a time of 30 years for the Gospel to have been circulated in Palestine, Asia Minor and other Christian centres before it came to be published in Egypt, a date c. 110 CE is the most probable *terminus ad quem* for the writing of the Gospel.[190] The reference to the destruction of the Temple at an early stage of the Gospel (Jn 2.19) suggests a date later than 70 CE and the reference to ἀποσυνάγωγος (Jn 9.22; 12.42; 16.2), though it may not allude to the *birkath ha-minim* as early as the first century CE,[191] suggests a date c. 85 CE as the *terminus post quem* for the composition of John.[192] I presume that John was written c. 85–110 CE and that the period between the two Jewish revolts (66–132 CE) may provide the best historical context for understanding John.[193]

The question of the authorship of the Fourth Gospel, which is vital to the exegetical study, still remains unsolved despite the scholarly undertaking of this issue by M. Hengel in his *The Johannine Question*. Both P[66] (second century) and P[72] (probably third century) contain the inscription *Euangelion kata Iônnên*.[194] For the question, 'Which John, among several Johns, is the author of the Fourth Gospel?', Hengel, on the basis of the internal and external evidence, suggests that he, as the name itself shows, was a Palestinian Jew who was one of the disciples

188. Hengel, *Johannine Question*, p. 11.

189. Barrett, *John*, pp. 110, 128. Barrett treats 140 CE as the extreme limit for the *publication* of John.

190. Cf. Hengel, *Johannine Question*, p. 3, who observes that P[52] makes it improbable that John was written after 110. For him the *terminus ad quem* is the time of the rule of Trajan (98–117 CE).

191. See P.W. van der Horst, 'The Birkat ha-minim in Recent Research', *ExpTim* 105 (1993–94), pp. 363-68. Hengel, *Johannine Question*, pp. 114-15, seems to confuse the agreement reached among the Jewish authorities to put Christians out of Synagogue, which John portrays, with the conflict, violence and persecution faced by the Church in the hands of the Jews even from the early first century.

192. See Barrett, *John*, p. 127; J.D.G. Dunn, *The Partings of the Ways: Between Christianity and Judaism and their Significance for the Character of Christianity* (London: SCM Press; Philadelphia: Trinity Press International, 1991), pp. 221-22.

193. Cf. Dunn, 'Let John Be John', pp. 318-25.

194. Hengel, *Johannine Question*, p. 6.

(or rather the 'beloved disciple') of the Lord, who founded a school that existed between c. 60–70 CE and c. 100–110 CE in Asia Minor, and who, in his extremely old age, was known in the school as 'the elder' and 'teacher'.[195] He goes on to say that the final redactor(s) of the Gospel, after the death of John the Elder, the author of the Fourth Gospel, around 100 CE, merged him with John the son of Zebedee in order to bring the Gospel as near to Jesus as possible.[196] Even Hengel's proposal does not exclude difficulties. If, as Hengel argues, the 'beloved disciple', who was lying close to the breast of Jesus, was not one of the twelve, but was another disciple of Jesus with the name John, then it runs counter to the synoptic tradition, which the Fourth Evangelist had known and which mentions the twelve as the only companions of Jesus in celebrating the Passover (Mt. 26.20-24; Mk 14.17-21; Lk. 22.14, 21-23); it seems that throughout John the group of twelve, who are addressed as οἱ ἴδιοι and οἱ ἄνθρωποι οὓς ἔδωκάς μοι, is assumed. If John the Elder himself was an eyewitness of Jesus' ministry, then what necessitated the redactors to fuse John the Elder and John the son of Zebedee?[197] At the same time, the theory that John the son of Zebedee, the 'beloved disciple' of the Lord, wrote the Fourth Gospel also poses a serious problem, for it does not explain the Palestinian Jewish character of the author, which has been proved beyond doubt,[198] and his priestly background.[199]

That the author was from a priestly family has special relevance to the subject of Merkabah mysticism, whose remarkable interest in priests and the heavenly temple is well attested in the Jewish texts. It

195. Hengel, *Johannine Question*, esp. pp. 80, 109-10.

196. Hengel, *Johannine Question*, esp. pp. 80-81, 124-35.

197. Since neither John the son of Zebedee nor John the Elder is addressed as 'apostle' both in John's Gospel and in the writings of Polycrates and Papias, one cannot argue that the fusion took place to give apostolic authority to the Fourth Gospel. In fact Papias equally identifies all the disciples of the Lord, including John the son of Zebedee, as οἱ πρεσβύτεροι—see Hengel, *Johannine Question*, p. 155 n. 100 for the Greek version of Papias's writing, as preserved by Eusebius, *HE* 3.39.3, 4.

198. See above, pp. 43-44.

199. Cf. Jn 18.15-16, which speaks of the other disciple as ὁ γνωστὸς τοῦ ἀρχιερέως. Polycrates wrote in c. 190 '...*John, who reclined on the Lord's breast, bore the (priestly) front shield, was priest* (ὃ ἐγενήθη ἱερεὺς τὸ πέταλον πεφορεκὼς), *witness to the faith and teacher; he entered into rest in Ephesus*' (cited by Hengel, *Johannine Question*, pp. 7, 144 n. 29 [italics Hengel's]).

was Ezekiel, the priest, who had a Merkabah vision by the river Chebar (Ezek. 1.3) and Isaiah had the throne-vision in the temple (Isa. 6.1). The Qumran community saw itself as a priestly community and practised Merkabah mysticism by realizing its oneness in worship with the priestly angels in the heavenly temple.[200] According to Elior, the *Hekhalot* literature describes that the priestly worship and service in the earthly temple, and the high-priest's entry into the holy of holies all correspond to the songs and adoration of the angels in the celestial sanctuary, and their ritual attendance before the Throne of Glory.[201] P.A. Alexander rightly points out to me that there is strong priestly interest in the Merkabah/*Hekhalot* texts. Does John reflect priestly concerns in any way? Unlike the Synoptists, John pictures Jesus, in the so-called 'high-priestly prayer' (Jn 17), as the one in whom God in his glory can be perceived (Jn 17.22, 24; cf. 1.14, 18; 12.41) and who, when the hour came, entered into the presence of the Father in order to give at the end-time a vision of his glory to his own (Jn 17.24; cf. Heb. 9.24-28, where the entry of Christ, the high priest, into the Holy of Holies is connected with his re-appearance to his own at the end-time). It is John who pictures Jesus as the one who will come back and take his followers with him to enter into the Father's house (Jn 14.2-3);[202] and thus, by having a communion with the heavenly high-priest, the disciples themselves become priests who will see God's glory in the celestial worship and dwell with him. One can also see in John the temple and its worship being transferred to the person, Jesus Christ, in whom alone a true worship of God is possible (see Jn 2.19-21; 4.20-26). The prophetic utterance of Caiaphas, the high-priest, which is recorded only in John (Jn 11.49-52), seems to contain an allusion to the duty of the high-priest to enter the holy of holies, and offer the atonement for *that* year (cf. ἀρχιερεὺς ὢν τοῦ ἐνιαυτοῦ ἐκείνου in 11.49) and thus to the atoning sacrifice of Christ himself.[203] Thus John connects the death of Christ at the time of Passover with the high-priestly office and prophecy. This again indicates that John, as a priest,

---

200. See below, pp. 95-98.

201. See Elior, 'Mysticism, Magic, and Angelology', pp. 22-27, 43-53.

202. For the temple theme in Jn 14.1-3, see J. McCaffrey, *The House with Many Rooms: The Temple Theme of Jn. 14:2-3* (AnBib, 114; Rome: Pontificio Istituto Biblico, 1988).

203. See Hengel, *Johannine Question*, p. 215 n. 64; Schnackenburg, *St John*, II, pp. 348-49.

presents Jesus as the high-priest as well as the sacrifice in which the glory of God was revealed to the people.[204] Therefore, when I mention 'John' as the author of the Fourth Gospel, I primarily mean a Palestinian Jew who migrated to one of the churches in the Diaspora, probably to Asia Minor, before 70.

The possibility that the writer of the Fourth Gospel was John the Elder, who was a disciple of the Lord and who headed a school in Asia Minor until he died in Ephesus at the time of Trajan, brings us to the consideration that the Gospel originated from Asia Minor. Now there is a strong case to argue that the terminologies used in Colossians and in Revelation show that Merkabah mysticism, which is rooted in Palestine, was also known and practised in Asia Minor.[205] Recent studies prove that Paul and Matthew show traces of influence of Merkabah mysticism in their writings. J.M. Scott has shown that 2 Cor. 2.14, which alludes to Ps. 67.19 LXX, describes Paul's Merkabah experience, as 2 Corinthians 12 does.[206] This yields another evidence that Paul had most probably practised Merkabah mysticism. In his study on the Gospel of Matthew, C. Rowland observes that there are sufficient indications in the Gospel of Matthew to warrant a closer consideration of its indebtedness to the Jewish apocalyptic and mystical tradition (by which he implies the throne-theophany) and that what can be said of Matthew can be said, *mutatis mutandis*, for other parts of the New Testament.[207] Can the same not be said of John also?

The probable date, author and place of the writing of John, then, does not exclude the possibility that Merkabah mystical practice was alive among the Jews in the late first century CE both in and outside Palestine and that John is interacting with such a religious fervour. It is our task

204. See J.P. Heil, 'Jesus as the Unique High Priest in the Gospel of John', *CBQ* 57 (1995), pp. 729-45, who argues that as the Johannine Jesus sacrifices himself rather than an animal, for John he is the one and only true high-priest in contrast to a plurality of Jewish high-priests.

205. See C. Rowland, 'The Influence of the First Chapter of Ezekiel on Jewish and Early Christian Literature' (PhD Thesis, Cambridge University, 1974), pp. 239-48; J.D.G. Dunn, 'The Colossian Philosophy: A Confident Jewish Apologia', *Bib* 76 (1995), pp. 153-81 (176-79).

206. J.M. Scott, 'The Triumph of God in 2 Cor 2:14: Additional Evidence of Merkabah Mysticism in Paul', *NTS* 42 (1996), pp. 260-81. See also below, pp. 104-109.

207. C.C. Rowland, 'Apocalyptic, the Poor, and the Gospel of Matthew', *JTS* NS 45 (1994), pp. 504-18.

in this volume to inquire into this. I have taken the liberty to use the word 'John' sometimes to denote the Fourth Gospel and other times its implied author and the context will tell the readers the sense in which it is used. Needless to say, of course, that since Part III is entirely a Johannine study, in all references to Johannine passages the usual 'Jn' does not appear.

Part I

HELLENISTIC AND HELLENISTIC-JEWISH MYSTICISM

Chapter 2

HELLENISTIC MYSTICISM

The question, 'What are the main features of Hellenistic mysticism?'
can best be answered in the light of Dodd's systematic study of the
hermetic literature. Since his comparison of John with the *Hermetica*
has been the most thoroughgoing attempt to find an interpretative
background for John in Hellenistic mysticism, his work is valuable for
our purpose.[1] If it is true that the materials on which the *Hermetica* are
based may go back to the first century CE, then they closely reflect the
Hellenistic religious thought that existed at the time of John. In this
chapter, therefore, I will focus on the 'mystical' features in the *Hermetica*, as noted by Dodd. This, in turn, will enable me to examine in Part
III whether or not Hellenistic mysticism can give a possible background for understanding John.

'Mysticism' in the Hermetica

The 'Mystical' Vision
Dodd points out that in the *Hermetica* the knowledge of God is
described clearly in terms of mystic vision,[2] which means 'beholding
the beauty of the Good (τὸ ἀγαθόν) and thereby becoming a god
(ἀποθεωθῆναι)' (*CH* 10.5-6). However, the author of the *Hermetica*
adds that in this life humans are too weak to have that sight and that
'beholding the Good' can never allow a person to live on earth. A
vision is possible in one's mind but not to one's physical eyes, and that
by 'drawing his soul up out of the body' and transforming him into
pure οὐσία, that is, by changing him into a god.[3] In other words, the

---

1.   See above, pp. 31-32.
2.   Dodd, *Interpretation*, pp. 16-17.
3.   W. Scott (ed.), *Hermetica* (2 vols.; Oxford: Clarendon Press, 1924, 1925),
II, p. 241.

Hermetica nullify any possibility of seeing God here on earth and even to behold him in the other world one needs to train the soul in this life by rigorous means (cf. *Stob.* 6.18-19) in order to liberate it from the world of sense and to subject it to the νοῦς or ψυχή (cf. *Stob.* 6.19; *CH* 13.11a). The vision of God, however, is described with the notion that ultimately the seeker could only say, 'I see that I am the All' (*CH* 13.13a).[4]

The knowledge of God in the *Hermetica* is based on the knowledge of the whole body of the universe, including the seven astronomical powers such as the five planet-stars, the sun, the moon and the 36 *decans* (*Stob.* 6), for God contains within himself the *kosmos* and all things are contained in him (*CH* 11.20a). As Dodd puts it, 'The metaphysical speculations which bulk so largely in the *Hermetica* are propaedeutic to the vision of God'.[5] Hermes instructs Tat that the one who has not failed to acquire knowledge of these things is able to see God with his own eyes and be blessed (αὐτόπτης γενόμενος θεάσασθαι, καὶ θεασάμενος μακάριος γενέσθαι) (*Stob.* 6.18), but quickly adds that it is impossible for one who is yet in the body to attain this happiness (*Stob.* 6.18). That is, one can know God by what some mystics call the 'cosmic consciousness', that is, 'an experience of liberation from the limits of individuality and identification with the All'.[6] It is an act of making oneself equal to God in order to apprehend God. This is possible by imagining oneself to be everywhere at once, in earth, in the sea, in heaven, and as dead or as not yet born. Only by grasping all these at once in one's thought can any human apprehend God (*CH* 11.20; cf. 13.11). The underlying principle here is that 'like is known by like (τὸ ὅμοιον τῶν ὁμοίων νοητόν)' (*CH* 11.20b)', that is, in order to see God one should thus rise above all time and become eternal. The knowledge of God is the only way of salvation and it is required if one is to have the right understanding of life.[7]

The hermetic doctrine of the knowledge of God also contains an experience of 'entering into God' (θεωθῆναι) by an ascent, that is,

---

4.   W. Scott (ed.), *Hermetica*, II, p. 391.
5.   Dodd, *Interpretation*, p. 17.
6.   Dodd, *Interpretation*, p. 16.
7.   Dodd, *Interpretation*, pp. 14-15, points out that the 'knowledge' that the Hermetists proclaim is a 'saving knowledge' which is concerned with the nature of God and the eternal world, the origin and constitution of the visible world, the nature and destiny of humankind, and the like.

being deified. However, only at the dissolution of the body does a person mount upward to the Father and enter into God and this is the final good for those who have received γνῶσις: to be made God (*CH* 1.24-26a). In order to enable people to ascend to God, God sent down to earth a great basin (κρατῆρα μέγαν), after filling it with mind (νοῦς), with a mission of proclaiming to people to dip themselves in mind, to recognize for what purpose they have been made and to believe that they will ascend to him who sent the basin down; those who heeded the proclamation and dipped themselves in mind participated in γνῶσις and became perfect because they received mind; they are immortal (ἀθάνατοι) and could see the Good, for in their own mind they have comprehended all—things on earth, things in heaven and even what lies beyond heaven (*CH* 4.4-6; cf. 1.28). According to the *Hermetica*, then, the final aim of Hellenistic mysticism is deification—the mystic's experience of becoming so closely united with God that he himself becomes god.

The idea of 'mystical' vision is described in the *Hermetica* also in terms of 'seeing' τὸ φῶς. The *Poimandres* speaks of the mystic's gazing at the light in Poimandres who appeared to him, but it is the seeing not so much with one's physical eyes as in one's mind (cf. θεωρεῶ ἐν τῷ νοΐμου τὸ φῶς in *CH* 1.7 and εἶδες ἐν τῷ νῷ τὸ ἀρχέτυπον εἶδος in *CH* 1.8a). Moreover, φῶς in the *Poimandres* is not the revelation of ὁ θεός nor of ὁ λόγος, but of ὁ νοῦς, who is the Father of all (*CH* 1.6-7, 12). The *Poimandres* refers to life and light (*CH* 1.9, 12, 21, 26b) recalling the Johannine identification of the life (of the Logos) as light (Jn 1.4; 8.12b). For the Hermetist, it is the νοῦς that is known as ζωή καὶ φῶς, ζωή being the union of father (νοῦς) and son (λόγος) (*CH* 1.6). Both ζωή and φῶς are bisexual who gave birth to ἕτερος νοῦς, the δημιουργός (*CH* 1.9) and to man (ἄνθρωπος) (*CH* 1.12). In response to Hermes' request to Poimandres, 'Tell me how I shall enter into life' (*CH* 1.24), *CH* 1.26b describes the final destination of the visionary as an entry (χωρῶ) into ζωή and φῶς. Dodd calls this 'light mysticism', which was later adapted both in Ephesians and in the Fourth Gospel.[8] The emphasis on ζωή in association with seeing the light may indicate, as Goodenough suggests, the passionate desires of the Greeks for the ideal quality of life, which is the background for the origin of Hellenistic mysticism.[9]

8.   Dodd, *Interpretation*, p. 210.
9.   See Goodenough, *By Light, Light*, pp. 3-4.

Union with God

Dodd, in his attempt to show how the phrase ἐν θεῷ, used in Hellenistic mysticism, provides a basis for interpreting the Johannine doctrine of mutual indwelling, observes that in the *Hermetica* ἐν θεῷ occurs mainly in a pantheistic sense (cf. *CH* 8.5; 9.9) and occasionally in the psychological sense that all things are 'in God' just as thoughts are in the mind (cf. *CH* 11.18-20).[10] He holds that ἐν θεῷ has 'mystical' significance in the sense that, when a person is born 'in God', he is actually united with the universe and thus with God through the divine Logos, the cosmic principle (*CH* 13.6-7). Union with God is the most essential aspect in human life, because in the general thought of the *Hermetica* and of Hellenistic mysticism the separate personality of the individual, without being ἐν θεῷ, is an insecure and vanishing concept.[11] The Hermetist portrays union with God as the birth of the deity (ἡ γένεσις τῆς θεότητος) within the visionary, when the latter stops the working of his bodily senses, which contain 'the irrational torments of matter', for these senses imprison humans in the body and cause them to suffer (*CH* 13.7). These senses will depart from anyone if only God's mercy will come upon them and then the reason (λόγος) is built up in them; and in order to receive mercy one should keep 'solemn silence' (εὐφήμησον). Precisely this experience is, for the Hermetist, rebirth (παλιγγενεσία) (*CH* 13.7, 8a). Dodd argues that, by using the expressions provided by the contemporary religions, John gives a Christian sense to 'union with God' in that the only kind of personal union that one can attain is ἀγάπη.[12]

Conclusions

Hellenistic mysticism, as described in the *Hermetica*, is concerned with the knowledge of God and having union with him so that one can become god. Though philosophically the knowledge of God is attainable by 'beholding the beauty of τὸ ἀγαθόν', practically it seems impossible because of the bodily senses with which humans live on

10.   Dodd, *Interpretation*, pp. 188-89.
11.   Dodd, *Interpretation*, p. 189.
12.   Dodd, *Interpretation*, p. 199. He affirms (p. 200) that if 'mysticism' means 'entering into the relation of ἀγάπη', which made the 'mutual dwelling' possible, then one can accept the idea of 'mysticism' in John.

earth. Even to behold him in the other world, one needs to train the soul in this life by subjecting it to the νοῦς or ψυχή.

This form of Hellenistic mysticism, as our survey shows, is born out of pantheism and therefore it treats cosmic vision as an essential means to obtaining a vision of God. That is, one can rationally apprehend God by surpassing everything, by comprehending within oneself all sensory perceptions of created things, by imagining oneself to be everywhere at once, by apprehending all things at once, and thus by making oneself like God. However, this 'mystic' vision can hardly be obtained unless one liberates himself from the limits of individuality and identifies with the All. Thus, the knowledge of God in the *Hermetica* is saving knowledge and clearly the goal of Hellenistic mysticism is 'absorption into divine' or 'deification'. The 'mystic' vision in terms of entering into God is also possible by an ascent to the Father as well as by seeing the light in one's mind. However, how can one ascend to God? An ascent is possible only at the dissolution of the body and for those who participate in knowledge by dipping themselves in the mind that was sent by God down to earth.

The idea of 'mystical union' in the sense of 'deification' is repeated in the *Hermetica* by using the ἐν θεῷ concept, which affirms that when a person is born 'in God', he or she is united with the universe and thus with God through the cosmic principle, the divine Logos. For the author of the *Hermetica*, union with God implies the birth of the deity in the mystic, which is called 'rebirth'. But here too the condition is that one must get rid of bodily senses before the Logos (i.e. reason) can be built up within oneself.

Does John develop the idea of 'union with God' by borrowing words and ideas drawn from Hellenistic mysticism? Does he give Christian colour to the Hermetic ἐν θεῷ concept by using the ἀγάπη concept, as Dodd maintains? John also refers to 'knowing God and Jesus Christ' as the means of salvation/eternal life, though he never uses the noun γνῶσις (e.g. Jn 1.10, 26; 4.42; 10.14, 15, 38; 17.3; 21.4, 12). Does this indicate that John was influenced by the Hellenistic mystical concepts? We can answer these questions only by undertaking an exegetical study of the Johannine passages concerned and this is taken up in Part III.

Chapter 3

HELLENISTIC-JEWISH MYSTICISM AS IN PHILO

Philo of Alexandria is the only Hellenistic Jew contemporary with the origins of Christianity who is well known to us from his own writings.[1] Apart from his writings there is little evidence for the existence of other writings that could reflect the exegetical and philosophical mind of the first-century Hellenistic Jews.[2] Therefore Philo's thoughts are valuable resources for studying the New Testament in general, and John in particular, against a Hellenistic-Jewish background. However, the question is: do Philo's writings show a 'mystical' character in any form? To pose the question in Sandmel's words: 'can we use the word "mystic" respecting Philo?'[3] His own answer is that Philo was a 'mystic' in no other sense than a 'philosophical mystic', for the goal implied in Philo's writing is for a person to be united with God.[4] Goodenough means the same when he suggests that the mystic background of Philo and his group is the Greek mystery religions which developed the symbols of 'mystic ascent' out of their longing to find the whole God in place of fragments and to have union with him.[5] Dunn argues that Philo was more mystic than philosopher, whose highest aim was to soar beyond the world of sense, beyond the world of ideas to see God, τὸ ὄν, as such.[6] In what sense does Philo develop the idea of seeing God and

1. See C.K. Barrett, *The New Testament Background: Selected Documents* (London: SPCK, rev. edn, repr. 1993), p. 252.
2. See above, pp. 47-48.
3. Sandmel, *Philo of Alexandria*, p. 124.
4. Sandmel, *Philo of Alexandria*, p. 124.
5. Goodenough, *By Light, Light*, pp. 15, 20.
6. Dunn, *Christology*, p. 227. Cf. D. Winston, 'Philo and the Contemplative Life', in A. Green (ed.), *Jewish Spirituality. I. From the Bible through the Middle Ages* (London: Routledge & Kegan Paul, 1986), pp. 198-231 (226), for whom Philo was a 'mystical theorist', if not a practising mystic; Louth, *Christian Mystical Tradition*, pp. 18-35.

of having union with him? A brief analysis of the concerned passages in Philo will enable us to understand an important 'mystical' trend prevalent in the Hellenistic-Jewish circles at the time of John.

The Revelation of God in Philo

The content of 'mysticism' developed by the Jews of the Diaspora, even two centuries before Philo, is that God reveals himself in his light-stream, the Logos or Sophia, and that one can find ὁ θεός through this lower type of divinity, which was called θεός without the article and which is the radiation or emanation of God himself. For God, being light, can only be discerned by the light-rays that he shot forth (φωτὶ φῶς).[7] Precisely this was amplified by Philo and hence we can categorize his 'mystical' thought in two principal themes: a vision of God and union with him.

Light as God's Self-Manifestation

Philo holds that the seekers for truth are those who envisage God through God, light through light (οἱ τὸν θεὸν θεῷ φαντασιωθέντες, φωτὶ φῶς—*Praem. Poen.* 46). He uses the symbol of the ark of the covenant to describe the essence of God that is unknowable and his manifestation through the Logos and his two powers—creative power (θεός) and royal power (κύριος) (*Quaest. in Exod.* 68; cf. *Vit. Mos.* 2.95-100), for the light streaming from God is too brilliant for humans to endure (*Deus Imm.* 77–81; *Leg. Gai.* 4–7). Goodenough calls this 'the descending Light-Stream of God', which necessitates the mystic ascent in successive stages to see τὸ ὄν.[8] Philo, by using Ps. 27.1, describes God not only as Light but also as the archetype of every other light (ἀρχέτυπον φῶς) and even prior to and high above every archetype (*Somn.* 1.75). Dodd rightly observes that one of the fundamental ideas associated with Philo's light-symbolism is that of the self-revealing character of light.[9] However, for Philo this light is perceptible to mind and to the eye of understanding (τὸ τῆς διανοίας ὄμμα) alone (*Op. Mund.* 71).

---

7.   Goodenough, *By Light, Light*, pp. 7-8.
8.   See Goodenough, *By Light, Light*, pp. 23-33, esp. 27-28.
9.   Dodd, *Interpretation*, pp. 55-56.

The Logos as God's Self-Manifestation

For Philo God is high above every archetype and the Logos contains all his fullness of Light (*Somn.* 1.75). A communion with (κατὰ μετου-σίαν) the divine Word (θεῖος λόγος) gives light to the soul in which even other things desire to become sharers (φωτός κοινωνῆσαι ψυχικοῦ) (*Leg. All.* 3.171). In *Somn.* 1.117-18 he gives more emphasis to the illumination of the soul (τήν ψυχὴν ἀφώτιστον) by the divine Word.

Philo's 'mystic' vision is focused more on the Logos, the place (ὁ τόπος) where stands God (*Conf. Ling.* 96). However, he also says that one can see God in his very essence only from afar by having his place in the divine Word (*Somn.* 1.66). In Goodenough's description of the 'pleroma' of the light-stream, the Logos, being the lower manifestation, holds the second place next to God.[10] In *Quaest. in Gen.* 2.62 the Logos is described as the 'second God'. The Logos, which exists nearest to the Existent, manifests him in a higher degree than even the δυνάμεις do. In *Cher.* 27–28 which describes the Logos (Reason) as being in between the two chiefest δυνάμεις, goodness and sovereignty, 'the picture is one of God as revealed in the Logos and the two higher powers...'[11] Philo says that God, the Existent (τὸ ὄν), and his very nature cannot be seen by anyone (*Mut. Nom.* 7–10), but that if one cannot see God, he can see his image, the most holy word (*Conf. Ling.* 97), for the Logos is 'he that sees God', that is, Israel (*Conf. Ling.* 146). 'Seeing God', for Philo, is seeing not his real nature, for that is impossible, but that he is (*Praem. Poen.* 44). Although in *Quaest. in Exod.* 2.39-40 Philo refers to a vision of God, he understands it in the sense of the 'divinization' of a holy soul. However, having Jewish upbringing, he does keep the distinction between God and human.[12] Hagner, by citing *Leg. All.* 3.102 and *Quaest. in Gen.* 4.4, argues that the direct apprehension of the Existent is possible.[13] However, these passages prove neither the direct apprehension of God nor the ecstatic experience caused by that vision. The idea in *Leg. All.* 3.100-102 is that Moses' mind gained knowledge of God neither from God himself nor from the created things, but from the first cause (τὸ αἴτιον); and *Quaest. in Gen.* 4.4 indicates only that Abraham could see the oneness

10. Goodenough, *By Light, Light*, pp. 23-25.
11. Goodenough, *By Light, Light*, p. 30.
12. See Dodd, *Interpretation*, pp. 60, 62.
13. Hagner, 'The Vision of God', pp. 89-90.

of God in the likeness of a triad. In the light of *Abr.* 132 it is clear that Abraham's mind had been prepared by his union with Sarah to see the one God in the form of three men who appeared to him, particularly in the middle one, the Logos.[14] Philo also freely uses the term θεός for λόγος in a context of God's self-manifestation (*Somn.* 1.229-30). In brief, as Dunn puts it:

> The Logos for Philo is 'God' not as a being independent of 'the God' but as 'the God' in his knowability—the Logos standing for that limited apprehension of the one God which is all that the rational man, even the mystic may attain to.[15]

'Mystical' Ascent in Philo

The 'mystical' doctrine in Philo is inevitably linked with the divine vision one gets by an ascent to God. The symbol of the ark used by Philo implies that, as the human mind cannot bear the stream as it comes directly from τὸ ὄν, it needs 'mystical' ascent which progresses from stage to stage, that is, an attempt to go up to τὸ ὄν from the sensible world (κόσμος αἰσθητός) through his two powers, creative and royal, then, in the Logos, and finally to God in his essence.[16] Stating that the Logos belongs to the intelligible world (κόσμος νοητός) (*Op. Mund.* 4, 16; *Mos. Vit.* 2.127), Philo shows that the Logos never descends from the intelligible world into the sensible world, but that one should move into the intelligible world to encounter the Logos.[17]

Louth uses the term the 'mystic way' to explain Philo's teaching on the search of the soul for God for himself alone rather than for benefits.[18] According to him, the 'mystic way', as held by Philo, is pursued by seeking the Word and thus a direct communion with God, particularly by meditation on the Scriptures (cf. *Quaest. in Gen.* 4.140). However, observes Louth, this is still only a stage; the soul that seeks God as he is in himself will seek to ascend beyond God's manifestation of himself through the Logos to God in himself (cf. *Somn.* 1.66).[19] The final apprehension of the soul's quest can only be to see that God is

---

14.   See further below, pp. 74-75.
15.   Dunn, *Christology*, p. 241.
16.   Cf. Goodenough, *By Light, Light*, pp. 27-28.
17.   See Sandmel, *Philo of Alexandria*, p. 95. Cf. below, p. 297.
18.   Louth, *Christian Mystical Tradition*, p. 29.
19.   Louth, *Christian Mystical Tradition*, p. 31.

incapable of being seen (ἰδεῖν ὅτι ἐστὶν ἀόρατος—*Poster. C.* 15).[20]
Therefore this quest is unending and is itself a source of joy.[21]

In Philo's description of 'mystical ascent', Moses occupies a prominent place. In *Quaest. in Exod.* 2.40 Philo says that Moses, by ascending the mount, goes beyond the heaven into God, where he is so united
with the deity that he himself becomes light and obtains the better part,
namely God, than the part obtained by Aaron (*Quaest. in Exod.* 2.44).
Goodenough comments that clearly it was through these experiences
that Moses came to be the hierophant who holds the secrets of God and
whose spirit guides people on the royal road (cf. *Poster. C.* 101–102).[22]

The idea of 'mystical ascent' in Philo presupposes the human soul's
severance from the world of mortality. In *Cher.* 31, for example,
Abraham is described as the one who took 'fire and knife' (Gen. 22.6)
as a symbol of his desire to sever and consume the mortal element
away from himself in order to fly upward to God (ἵνα...πρὸς θεὸν
ἀναπτῇ). In Philo's picture of the story of the 'Call of Abraham' (*Migr.
Abr.* 1–6), Abraham is the type of the soul that turns from the things of
the sense to the invisible world to know τὸ ὄν. As Dodd conceives, the
way κάτωθεν ἄνω to know God *that* he is, is preceded in Philo by the
way of ascetic practice, by which the soul is freed from the bonds of
matter.[23]

'Mystical' Union with God

Philo's Theme of Indwelling
D.L. Mealand presents Philo's 'indwelling motif' as one of the back-
grounds for the Johannine theme of 'mutual indwelling'.[24] He traces the
idea of 'cosmic inclusion' in *Somn.* 1.63 which describes God as a
place by reason of his containing things and being contained by nothing
whatsoever and he is a place for all to flee into. Philo, by using Num.
14.9, speaks of the divine Logos as dwelling (ἐνοικεῖ) and walking

20. See also W. Michaelis, 'ὁράω, κ.τ.λ', *TDNT*, V, pp. 336-38; H.A.
Wolfson, *Philo: Foundations of Religious Philosophy in Judaism, Christianity, and
Islam* (2 vols.; Cambridge, MA: Harvard University Press, 1948), II, pp. 91-93.
21. Louth, *Christian Mystical Tradition*, p. 33. The soul's yearning to see God
as he is in himself is described by Louth as Philo's 'mysticism of love' (p. 32).
However, this yearning is a common phenomenon in any mystical thought.
22. Goodenough, *By Light, Light*, p. 215.
23. Dodd, *Interpretation*, p. 61.
24. Mealand, 'Mystical Union', pp. 19-34.

(ἐμπεριπατεῖ) among those for whom the soul's life is an object of honour (*Poster. C.* 122). On this basis, Schnackenburg comments that Philo's Logos is the mediator or teacher of (mystic) union with God, because he governs the world and the souls of the just in which he dwells and moves in a city, bringing them bliss and regaling them as God's cup-bearer.[25] In similar vein, Philo uses in *Somn.* 2.248 the expression 'I will walk in you (ἐν ὑμῖν)' of Lev. 26.12 LXX referring to 'the soul of the Sage (σοφός)' in which God is said to walk. He emphasizes that God walks noiselessly only 'in the understandings (διανοίαις) of those who have been purified to the utmost' and that in the understandings of those who have not yet fully washed but who are still undergoing cleansing, the angels, divine words (λόγοι θεῖοι), walk making them clean (*Somn.* 1.148). By citing these passages, Mealand argues that Philo has extracted from the LXX the idea that God dwells within human souls, an idea that occurs also in Hellenistic mysticism, and that he not only spiritualizes the biblical texts, but also individualizes them.[26] Philo's idea of an indwelling-concept does not seem to reflect stoic pantheism; though he agrees that God contains all things, he does not say that God is himself contained.[27] There is no clear indication in Philo in this context that he has in mind the Hellenistic idea of 'absorption into divine'. He identifies complete purification of mind as the most essential for God's indwelling the wise men. Also, he speaks only of the divine 'indwelling', but not of 'mutual indwelling'. That is, there is no teaching in Philo that the human souls walk or dwell in God or in the divine Logos as the result.[28]

'Mystical' Union with God by Union with Sophia

The idea of 'mystical union' with God is illustrated in Philo by what Goodenough calls 'the Female Principle' of Greek mystery religions, in which the 'mysticism of sex' played a key role. That is, a supreme deity, having sexual relations with a 'Female Principle of nature', begets the world and now human beings can have 'mystical' union with

25.   Schnackenburg, *St John*, I, p. 487.
26.   Mealand, 'Mystical Union', p. 28.
27.   Mealand, 'Mystical Union', p. 28.
28.   Philo's notion of 'cosmic inclusiveness' cannot be treated as the humans' dwelling in God, for it simply shows that God cannot be contained by anything (cf. *Somn.* 1.64).

the supreme deity by a 'sexual mystic union' with that 'Principle'.[29] As a typology for this kind of 'mystical' practice, Philo develops the idea that in the stream of Sophia/Logos, who is the effluence of God's power and nature, humans may hope to find God.[30] Wisdom in Philo is often allegorically represented by the wives of the patriarchs. The experience of the latter with their wives illustrates the 'mystic marriage' of human souls with Sophia, the 'divine force and life'[31] (cf. *Abr.* 100–102; *Poster. C.* 75–79; *Cher.* 43–48). In other words, for Philo 'mystical union' with God is to be achieved not by merging one's identity with God, but by union with Sophia, who, as the mother of the universe, flows out in a river the 'generic virtue' (cf. *Leg. All.* 1.43, 64-65; 2.49; *Det. Pot. Ins.* 54). One of the names given to Sophia by Philo is 'vision of God' (ὅρασιν θεοῦ—*Leg. All.* 1.43), for the one who is given Virtue (ἀρετή) or Sophia is prepared for a vision of God as next stage (cf. *Abr.* 103, 106-23).[32] Thus Philo's 'mystical union' with God by being united with Sophia or Virtue results in a vision of God himself. However, even this vision does not seem to be a vision of God as he is in himself, but of him as revealed in the Logos who holds the central place among the three who appeared to Abraham (*Abr.* 121–22, 132; cf. *Cher.* 27–28). Nevertheless, Philo considers the purification of mind (διανοία) as essential to see the Existent in the three (*Abr.* 122), and in *Abr.* 104–105 he describes the need for God to discipline human soul with painful tortures before Virtue comes into it.[33]

Conclusions

We have seen that Philo's 'mystical' teaching highlights two important aspects of the yearning of the human soul: to see God, the Existent, and to have union with him.

Like Hellenistic mysticism, Philo's mysticism also is based on the principle: φωτὶ φῶς. Though God can be seen as Light through his

---

29. See Goodenough, *By Light, Light*, pp. 14-22. A.J.M. Wedderburn, *Baptism and Resurrection: Studies in Pauline Theology against its Graeco-Roman Background* (Tübingen: J.C.B. Mohr [Paul Siebeck], 1987), pp. 90-163, argues that the mystery religions were widespread in the Graeco-Roman world in the first century, having indirect influence on early Christianity.

30. Goodenough, *By Light, Light*, pp. 22-23.

31. Goodenough, *By Light, Light*, p. 23; cf. also pp. 139-79.

32. Cf. Goodenough, *By Light, Light*, pp. 139-40.

33. Cf. Goodenough, *By Light, Light*, p. 140.

δυνάμεις, he is revealed in a higher degree through the Logos. For Philo's Logos contains all the fullness of Light and, as Israel, it is always seeing God, being nearest to him. According to him, it is almost impossible to 'see' the real nature of God, that is, God as he is in himself, but it is possible to see *that he is* by seeing the Logos. Even this vision is perceptible only to human mind or to the 'eye of under-standing' rather than to one's physical eyes.

Since God, τὸ ὄν, exists above all his powers, the mystic's mind should ascend from the world of sense (κόσμος αἰσθητός) to the intelli-gible world (κόσμος νοητός) through his powers in order to see God. The soul seeks to have direct communion with God by seeking the Word, particularly through meditation on the Scriptures. It yearns to go beyond the Logos up to God, but only to know that he is incapable of being seen. Philo describes Moses as hierophant, who was deified dur-ing his ascent to Mt Sinai and became light to guide the mystics on the royal road. However, the prerequisite for 'mystical ascent', according to Philo, is that the soul should be freed from the bonds of matter through ascetic practice.

Philo's doctrine of 'mystical union' is two-sided: the indwelling of God with the wise and the seeker's communion with him. Although we have evidence in Philo for God dwelling in the wise man, we do not have evidence for the concept of 'mutual indwelling'. God dwells in human minds also by means of the Logos, but the prior condition is that they must show utmost purification.

Philo describes the experience of 'mystical union' with God in the pattern of the 'Female Principle' of Greek mystery religions. For him union with God is possible by way of union with Sophia, the effluence of God's power and nature. This is allegorically described by the experiences of the patriarchs with their wives. Union with Sophia may lead to a vision of God, but only to the extent that he can be seen in the Logos. The 'mystical union' of the human soul is an impossible exer-cise until it is disciplined by painful tortures and the mind is highly purified. Although Philo speaks of what Goodenough calls 'the mystic marriage' of man with Sophia, he does not maintain the view of deifica-tion in his 'mystical' thought except in the case of Moses.

The parallels between Philo's 'mystical' thought and some of the Johannine themes are striking. The idea that God reveals himself through φῶς and λόγος appears both in Philo and in John. Similarly, the 'mystical' aspect of the indwelling of God in humans occurs in both their writings. Philo's idea of 'mystical' union with God through union with Sophia/Logos has parallel in John's teaching of 'abiding in' and 'knowing'. Both Philo and John show familiarity in different ways with the tradition of human ascent to God. If so, is John using Philo's 'mystical' ideas in his Gospel? Or can John be meaningfully read against the background of Philo's mysticism? Do the similarities show mutual dependence or a common religious thought from which both the writers drew materials? Is John probably addressing the Hellenistic Jews of his time? I will suggest solutions to these issues in the study of John in Part III.

Part II

PALESTINIAN MYSTICISM IN THE FIRST CENTURY CE

Chapter 4

MYSTICAL FEATURES IN THE *HEKHALOT* LITERATURE

We have surveyed in Part I the 'mystical' attitude probably prevalent in Hellenistic circles and in Hellenistic-Jewish circles in the late first century CE when John was written. We have noticed that this 'mystical' tendency contains two major aspects: seeing God and having union with him. Now it is appropriate for us to examine the primary aspects of Jewish mysticism. As mentioned above, we have now more evidence to argue confidently that John can mainly be interpreted against a Palestinian Jewish background. Since no detailed study of John against a Jewish mystical background has been undertaken so far, the main focus of this book is to investigate whether there was a 'mystical' practice in first-century Palestine and whether John can be better understood in the light of such a practice. Because of this we treat Palestinian mysticism more elaborately than we have treated Hellenistic or Hellenistic-Jewish mysticism. Scholars who have viewed John against his Jewish background have set the Gospel in a historical situation in which Merkabah mysticism was being widely practised by some Jews and Christians alike at the time of John. Therefore Part II is entirely devoted to a study of major elements of Merkabah mysticism as described in the later *Hekhalot* literature and in other Jewish and Christian documents which are commonly accepted as belonging to the first century CE. Can we maintain, then, that, although the *terminus post quem* of the *Hekhalot* literature is 200 CE, the 'mystical' tradition expressed in it may go back to the first century or even earlier?[1] What

---

1.   See Scholem, *Major Trends*, p. 45, who argues that the revelations about the Merkabah, vouchsafed to the Tannaim R. Ishmael and R. Akiba and transmitted by them, are related to the old traditions about the Merkabah that belong to the first to fourth centuries (see also Scholem, *Jewish Gnosticism* [1960], pp. 6-8). Schäfer, 'Aim and Purpose', p. 279, seems to accept Scholem's view that the oldest texts go back to the second century.

are the major components of Merkabah mysticism that is described in the *Hekhalot* literature?

Gruenwald mentions three subjects as chiefly dealt with in the *Hekhalot* literature: heavenly ascensions, the revelation of cosmological and other secrets, and the special secret method of studying and memorizing the Torah.[2] Elior treats three aspects in the *Hekhalot* literature as important: mysticism, angelology and magic, which are revealed to those who descend to the Merkabah and ascend upward.[3] On closer analysis, the following 'mystical' elements seem to emerge from the *Hekhalot* literature.

The Merkabah Mystical Elements: A Review

1. The goal of the Merkabah mystical practice is 'to enter before the Throne of Glory' (*HR* 22.2; *Synopse* §§236, 248) and 'to gaze on the King, on his Throne, on his majesty and his beauty' (*HR* 15.1 = *Synopse* §198). This experience is initiated by the mystic's yearning to have communion with God.[4]

2. The mystic gazes not merely on God who is on the throne, but also on many other elements connected with his throne such as the holy creatures (*Cherubim* and *Ofannim*), the *Hashmal*, the River of Fire, the fiery flames, the chambers of the palace (*heikhal*) of the seventh heaven,[5] the fiery clouds, and Surya, the Prince of the Divine Presence (*HR* 15.1 = *Synopse* §198). If anyone wishes to descend to the Merkabah, he should invoke Suryah 112 times by using the name '*Totrasi* YHWH' (*HR* 16.4 = *Synopse* §204; cf. also §300).

3. The throne-vision could be achieved only by the 'one who is worthy' (*HR* 15.1). In other words, in order to gain this glorious vision, the mystic should prepare himself by undergoing some spiritual exercises through fasting and keeping every positive and negative commandment (*HR* 15.1, 2; 20.4 = *Synopse* §§198-99, 228). According to *Ma'aseh Merkabah*, the Merkabah mystic should fast for 40 days and his morsel should be eaten with salt only (*Synopse* §§560-62).[6]

2.   Gruenwald, *Merkavah Mysticism*, pp. 98-99.
3.   See Elior, 'Mysticism, Magic, and Angelology', p. 14.
4.   See Alexander, *Judaism*, p. 29.
5.   *Re'uyot Yehezkel* refers to the opening of seven heavens to reveal the 'Glory of the Holy One'. Cf. *1 En.* 14.13-15; 71.5; *T. Levi* 3–5; *2 En.* 3–22. *HZ* 25 refers to the sixth palace.
6.   See Scholem, *Jewish Gnosticism* (1960), p. 108 §11; for English rendering

4. The 'mystical' practice mainly takes the form of heavenly ascent to God's throne, but the mystic is often called 'one of the *Yordei Merkabah*' ('the descenders of the Chariot').[7] Those who were 'worthy' practised ascent in trance to God's heavenly throne by reciting hymns and magical formulae, and by invoking the angels (*HR* 19–22 = *Synopse* §§219-36). However, we also have evidence that mystical visions took the form of the descent of the deity on earth (e.g. Ezek. 1; Isa. 6; the Yohanan tradition).[8] The *Hekhalot* text speaks of the descent of the Prince of the Torah in a sheet of flame to reveal secrets (*Synopse* §313).

5. The *Hekhalot* literature portrays angelology as a key aspect in Merkabah mystical practice.[9] The angels possess the 'keys' for ascent to heaven and for contemplating the Merkabah and hence the revelation of their secrets conditions descent to the Merkabah.[10] They are classified into several groups and are often associated with the 'streams of fire' (cf. *3 Enoch* and *Sefer ha-Razim*). Notable among them are the *Hayyot*, the *Cherubim* and the *Ofannim*, who, as the heavenly priests and Levites, sing and worship before the Throne of Glory (*Synopse* §§103, 161, 184-85).[11] At a time when the temple had been destroyed and God was thought of as having removed himself from apprehension, the authors of the *Hekhalot* literature transferred the essence of the earthly worship to the realm of angelic beings, who, in fact, 'represent God and promise His closeness to human beings and the action of His power by means of them' (cf. *Synopse* §123).[12]

see Gruenwald, *Merkavah Mysticism*, p. 101. Gruenwald (pp. 52, 99-102) also gives a detailed description of the ascetic practice to achieve 'mystical' visions.

7.　　The peculiar use of 'descent' instead of 'ascent' to the Merkabah is attributed by Scholem, *Jewish Gnosticism* (1960), p. 20 n.1, to the influence of the talmudic phrase יורד לפני התבה used for prayer before the ark (i.e. the throne) containing the scrolls of the Torah. So also Smith, 'Palestinian Judaism in the First Century', p. 150. But D.J. Halperin, *The Faces of the Chariot: Early Jewish Responses to Ezekiel's Vision* (Tübingen: J.C.B. Mohr [Paul Siebeck], 1988], pp. 226-27, thinks that the expression 'descent into His chariot' reflects the influence of midrashic tradition (*Exod. R.* 23.14) which calls the Israelites first 'those who went down' to the Red Sea and then 'those who came up' from it.

8.　　See below, pp. 153-54, 165, 167, 199-201.

9.　　See particularly P. Schäfer, 'Engel und Menschen in der Hekhalot-Literatur', in *idem, Hekhalot–Studien* (Tübingen: J.C.B. Mohr [Paul Siebeck], 1988), pp. 250-76; Elior, 'Mysticism, Magic, and Angelology', pp. 3-53.

10.　　Elior, 'Mysticism, Magic, and Angelology', p. 9.

11.　　Cf. Elior, 'Mysticism, Magic, and Angelology', pp. 25-27.

12.　　Elior, 'Mysticism, Magic, and Angelology', pp. 24-27, esp. 27. But the

HR 20.5–22.2 (*Synopse* §§229-36) describes how the angels, who are known as the 'Gatekeepers', 'Princes' and even the 'scribe (Gabriel)', guided R. Nehunya b. Ha-Qanah, the mystic, until he descended to the Merkabah. The angels in the seventh palace lead him into the Throne of Glory with all kinds of melody and song with music, and seat him with the heavenly creatures around the throne. While beholding the divine glory, the mystic joins in his ecstasy with the angels in the celestial Sanctus (the *Qedusha*). *HR* 20.3 and 22.2 make it clear that the mystic too recites the songs of praise along with the angelic host to him who sits on the throne.[13] Thus, the worship of the angels in the heavenly temple is an inspiration from Ezekiel's chariot-vision and is parallel not only to the worship of the priests and Levites in the earthly temple, but also to the worship of the descenders to the Merkabah.[14] The mystics were also transformed into one of the angels or an archangel (cf. *3 En.* 4).

6. The name of God attains significance in several ways in the Merkabah mystical tradition. Each of the angels who are the guardians of the seventh *Heikhal* is called 'by the name of the King of the World' (*Synopse* §240). *HZ* refers to a group of exalted forces which is called by the name of YHWH and *Sefer Hekhalot* (*3 Enoch*) mentions eight great princes called YHWH in the name of their king (*Synopse* §13).[15] However, these figures do not seem to 'share' in the divinity of God. When Metatron gave the impression to 'Aher, the visionary, that he is one of the divine powers, Metatron was struck with 60 lashes of fire at the command of God (*3 En.* 16.2-5). Therefore, Elior's statement that the mystical attitude in the *Hekhalot* traditions does not focus on a single, unique God[16] is open to question.

The angels recite the name *Totrasi*, YHWH, 112 times (*Synopse* §§306, 590), and pronounce the 'Explicit Name' just like the high-

interest in worship before the Throne of Glory along with the angels is not bound to the destruction of the temple in 70 CE (see below pp. 95-98) for the earthly worship in Qumran in union with the heavenly worship of the angelic priests).

13.   When R. Akiba descended into the Merkabah, he heard the angelic hymns and learned them as he was standing in front of the divine throne—see Gruenwald, *Merkavah Mysticism*, pp. 151-52; Scholem, *Major Trends*, p. 57; Scholem, *Jewish Gnosticism* (1960), p. 21; *Synopse* §106.

14.   See Elior, 'Mysticism, Magic, and Angelology', p. 44.

15.   Elior, 'Mysticism, Magic, and Angelology', pp. 31-35.

16.   Elior, 'Mysticism, Magic, and Angelology', p. 29.

priest used to pronounce it when he entered the holy of holies.[17] Those who descend to the Merkabah should learn and imitate the uttering of the name, along with the praises and prayers recited by the angels.[18] To get past the angels at each palace, the mystic must have a secret knowledge of the correct magical names, which will seal the powers of the hostile gatekeepers, so that they might let him in and lead him beyond each gate (*HR* 17–22). *HZ* refers to the revelation of a name to R. Akiba when he gazed upon the sight of the Merkabah (*Synopse* §337) and the use of that name will bring great success and blessing. As it is revealed only to those who descend to the Merkabah, the name has esoteric character. Schäfer rightly argues that the name of God, as implied in *HZ*, is the decisive revelation of a transcendent God to the Merkabah mystic.[19] It is noteworthy that *Ma'aseh Bereshit* reveals God in his name, אהיה (I AM/I WILL BE there), which is closely associated with God's first utterance, יהי ('Let it be there') and which Hayward identifies as the *Memra* of the Targums.[20] Since the entire universe was designed with the 'irrefutable name', according to the story of the 'Four rabbis who entered in *Pardes*', Morray-Jones thinks that this idea concerns the forbidden mysteries of *Ma'aseh Bereshit*.[21]

7. The mystic, after his descent back to earth, is called upon to reveal the content of his mystical vision of the Merkabah. *HZ* shows that soon after R. Akiba descended, he proclaimed the revealed name to his students (*Synopse* §337). Ezekiel was expected to reveal his vision to the people of Israel only to the extent that the eye can see and the ear hear (*Re'uyot Yehezkel*).[22]

8. Another important part of the *Hekhalot* literature is the mystical

---

17.   Elior, 'Mysticism, Magic, and Angelology', p. 46.

18.   Elior, 'Mysticism, Magic, and Angelology', p. 9.

19.   Schäfer, *Der verborgene und offenbare Gott*, pp. 56-57, 143-45.

20.   C.T.R. Hayward, 'The Holy Name of the God of Moses and the Prologue of St John's Gospel', *NTS* 25 (1979), pp. 16-32, esp. pp. 21-23. Finding the existence of the idea of *Memra* as 'HYH even in the first century BCE (cf. 1QapGen 22.30-31), Hayward argues that the Fourth Evangelist had known and used this meaning of *memra* in his Gospel, particularly in the prologue (pp. 24-31).

21.   C.R.A. Morray-Jones, 'Paradise Revisited (2 Cor 12: 1-12): The Jewish Mystical Background of Paul's Apostolate. Part 2: Paul's Heavenly Ascent and its Significance', *HTR* 86 (1993), pp. 256-92 (278, 280). He argues that the story of *Pardes*, which constitutes a part of Jewish mysticism, belongs to the time of R. Akiba.

22.   See Gruenwald, *Merkavah Mysticism*, p. 137.

doctrine, known as *Shi'ur Qomah*, which sprang up from the speculation on the man-like figure who sits upon the throne in Ezek. 1.26. It, in
association with the description of the lover in Song 5.10-16, describes
in extenso the measurement of the body of God.[23]

9. The above-mentioned 'mystical' elements show in themselves a
strong influence of Ezekiel 1, 8 and 10; Isaiah 6, and Daniel 7. Nevertheless, not all scholars agree that the *Hekhalot* texts describe the Merkabah mystical *experience* as such. Halperin, for example, argues that
the *Hekhalot* texts are a mere continuation of the exegetical tradition
and a succession in the homiletic speculation on Ezekiel's chariot.[24]
Schäfer denies that an ascent to the Merkabah and attaining a vision of
God on his throne are the ultimate aim of the mystic. For him, basic to
Merkabah mysticism is the heavenly journey that culminates in the
liturgy and the knowledge of the Torah by adjuration.[25] Unfortunately,
the study of these scholars concentrates more on the context in which
the *Hekhalot* tradition was developed or the means by which the
mystical goal is achieved than the content of the *Hekhalot* literature.
HR 22.2 clearly indicates that the mystic's heavenly song is not the end
of his journey, but that he is further led to be seated with the *Cherubim*,
Ofannim and the *hayyot* until he sees the majesty. *HZ* emphasizes more
the experience of 'seeing the king in his beauty' and the attached
doxology is merely the outward expression of the joy of the one who
sees the 'glorious king' (*Synopse* §§411-12). Similarly, study of the
Torah is not the culmination of the heavenly journey, but is one of the
qualifications and effective means to descend into the Merkabah (see
HR 21.4 = *Synopse* §234). Elior, who reviews Halperin's *The Faces of
the Chariot*, comments, 'He [Halperin] focuses upon certain specific
lines and fragments of verses, often removed from their proper context,
and thereby fails to perceive the overwhelming esoteric content and
spiritual experience with which these texts are imbued.'[26]

If we accept that the *Hekhalot* literature gives details of the mystical

23.   See Scholem, *Jewish Gnosticism* (1960), pp. 36-42; Gruenwald, *Merkavah
Mysticism*, pp. 213-24. However, M.S. Cohen, *The Shi'ur Qomah: Liturgy and
Theurgy in Pre-Kabbalistic Jewish Mysticism* (New York: Lanham, 1983), pp. 4-9,
31, argues that the link between the *Shi'ur Qomah* and the description of the lover
in the Song of Songs is weak.
24.   Halperin, *Faces*, pp. 7-9, 15, 30, 34.
25.   Schäfer, 'Aim and Purpose', pp. 277-95.
26.   R. Elior, 'Merkabah Mysticism: A Critical Review', *Numen* 37 (1990),
pp. 233-49 (241).

experiences of certain Jews and the date of which covers a period from the second to the seventh century CE, then the moot question is: had these important aspects of Merkabah mysticism been already known and practised in the first century CE? Alexander maintains that the Merkabah tradition has its roots far back in the Palestinian Jewish apocalyptic of the first century CE or even earlier.[27] Gruenwald mentions the Qumran literature as earlier witness for the existence of Merkabah mysticism.[28] But both Halperin and Schäfer argue against an early date for Merkabah mysticism.[29] Therefore an inquiry into some of the major Jewish as well as Christian writings that are earlier than the second century CE is called for if we are to know whether or not Merkabah mysticism had already been known and practised at the time when John was written. This I undertake in the following chapters.

27.   Alexander, *Judaism*, p. 29; cf. C.R.A. Morray-Jones, 'Transformational Mysticism in the Apocalyptic-Merkabah Tradition', *JJS* 43 (1992), pp. 1-31 (1).

28.   Gruenwald, *Merkavah Mysticism*, p. vii. Cf. Schiffman's position mentioned above, p. 53.

29.   Halperin, *Merkabah*, pp. 107-40, 179-85; and P. Schäfer, 'New Testament and Hekhalot Literature: The Journey into Heaven in Paul and in Merkabah Mysticism', *JJS* 35 (1984), pp. 19-35.

Chapter 5

EVIDENCE OF MERKABAH MYSTICISM IN PRE-CHRISTIAN WRITINGS

There is considerable evidence of the fact that Merkabah mysticism had been known and even practised in pre-Christian time. While the book of ben Sira shows that people of ben Sira's time had given importance to the chariot-vision of Ezekiel, the newly discovered texts in Qumran throw enough light on the practice of Merkabah mysticism by the Qumranites. Therefore we will take up for our study in this chapter the Wisdom of Jesus ben Sira and the Qumran literature.

The Wisdom of Jesus ben Sira

Sirach 49.8
The first reference to Merkabah speculation is found in the Wisdom of Jesus ben Sira, a Jewish document that was originally written in Hebrew in 190–175 BCE.[1] In his attempt to warn of the present threat posed by Hellenization, the author highlights the divine activity in the world through Israel's history and shows his high appreciation for the wisdom of his predecessors.[2] Prior to mentioning Job, a non-Israelite, in the 'praise of our ancestors', ben Sira refers in 49.8 to Ezekiel's vision of the Lord's chariot-throne:

> It was Ezekiel who saw the vision of glory,
> which God showed him above the chariot of the cherubim (NRSV).[3]

1. See E. Schürer, *The History of the Jewish People in the Age of Jesus Christ (175 B.C.–A.D. 135)* (Edinburgh: T. & T. Clark, rev. edn, 1986), III.1, pp. 202-203; Hengel, *Judaism*, p. 131; G.W.E. Nickelsburg, *Jewish Literature between the Bible and the Mishnah* (London: SCM Press, 1981), p. 64.
2. See R.A.F. MacKenzie, *Sirach* (OT Message, 19; Wilmington, DE: Michael Glazier, 1983), p. 166.
3. NRSV follows the Greek version of ben Sira. Skehan, whose translation is mainly based on the Hebrew Text of the Geniza MSS, which renders: 'Ezekiel

This makes it clear that Ezekiel's Merkabah vision had occupied a significant place in the mind of ben Sira and that people in Palestine were familiar with it as early as the second century BCE.

Sirach 3.21-23

Moreover, ben Sira's negative attitude towards preoccupation in matters beyond one's ability gives us evidence for the presence of esoteric teachings, particularly of Merkabah speculation, at that time.

> Neither seek what is too difficult for you, nor investigate what is beyond your power. Reflect upon what you have been commanded, for what is hidden is not your concern. Do not meddle in matters that are beyond you, for more than you can understand has been shown you (Sir. 3.21-23 NRSV).

That this passage was in discussion among the rabbis is known from its citation in *b. Ḥag.* 13a; *y. Ḥag.* 77c and *Gen. R.* 8. What precisely are the hidden things that are described here as difficult to be grasped? Perhaps they may denote the secrets of the Law, which have not yet been revealed (cf. Deut. 29.29), for ben Sira considers wisdom and the Law as practically one (Sir. 24). Thus Hengel thinks that Sir. 3.21-23 is a warning against 'false "striving for wisdom"'.[4] Di Lella thinks that in 3.21, 22b, 23a, 24 ben Sira cautions his readers about the futility of Greek speculations, which glorified the achievements of the Greeks in science, technology and philosophy.[5] Though this is possible, it does not seem probable, for Greek intellectualism was not considered esoteric at all.

In view of ben Sira's exhortation to be humble and of his reference to the Lord's glorification (3.17-20), 3.21-24 may refer to 'what is above the height of the heavens' or 'the ways above' (cf. *4 Ezra* 4.21-23). This indicates the interest that was common among the people of ben Sira's time in heavenly ascents and in knowing the secrets of the heavenly realm, giving us a clue that a kind of Merkabah mystical practice had been familiar to at least a section of the Jews. Weiss has convincingly shown that Sir. 3.21-24 may refer to *Ma'aseh Bereshit*

---

beheld the vision and described the different creatures of the chariot throne'—see P.W. Skehan and A.A. Di Lella, *The Wisdom of Ben Sira* (AB; New York: Doubleday, 1987), p. 540.

4. Hengel, *Judaism*, p. 139.
5. Skehan and Di Lella, *Ben Sira*, pp. 160-61.

and *Ma'aseh Merkabah*, which was already being shaped at the time before Christ.[6] As we will see later, at the time of Yohanan b. Zakkai both these doctrines were treated as secret doctrines which should be taught only to the wise and to the people of certain age (cf. *y. Ḥag.* 2.1; *b. Ḥag.* 13b). *B. Ḥag.* 11b states that it is permissible to inquire concerning the events of the six days of Creation, but not regarding what happened before Creation. Therefore it is not improbable that ben Sira primarily meant the early forms of *Ma'aseh Bereshit* and *Ma'aseh Merkabah* in 3.21-23.

The Qumran Literature

After the Wisdom of ben Sira, clear reference to Merkabah vision occurs in the Qumran literature. Some Qumran texts show that the community, by contemplating the throne-chariot and heavenly palaces, realized a sense of communion with the angels, who used to accompany the enthroned Glory of the Lord. The fragments of the *Shabbat Shirot* (4Q *Serek Shirot 'Olat ha-Shabbat* = 4QShirShabb, i.e. *Songs of the Sabbath Sacrifice*) are of prime importance for our analysis. The recently published MSS, 4Q286–287, also throw further light on the Merkabah mystical practice in Qumran.[7]

4QShirShabb

Strugnell observes that the *Shabbat Shirot* are more consistently concerned with the angels and the heavens than any other surviving work from Qumran.[8] It seems that the author attempts to communicate an experience of worship ascribed to God in the celestial temple, by describing its various sections such as the holy of holies, the Merkabah and its priestly angels. These songs of angelic praise, being thirteen altogether, are assigned to the first thirteen sabbaths.

4Q403.1.2.1-16. Our concern focuses on the latter part of the seventh *Sabbath Song* (4Q403.1.2.1-16), which refers to the heavenly chariots and which, according to Newsom, occupies the emphatic position in the

---

6.   Weiss, *Untersuchungen zur Kosmologie*, pp. 80-82.
7.   See R. Eisenman and M. Wise, *The Dead Sea Scrolls Uncovered* (Shaftesbury, Dorset: Element, 1992), pp. 222-30. See also above, pp. 52-53.
8.   Strugnell, 'Angelic Liturgy', p. 318.

whole body of the *Shabbat Shirot*.[9] She maintains that although the end
of 4Q403.1.1 and all the lines of 4Q403.1.2 are more fragmentary, in
the initial lines of 4Q403.1.2 a brief description of the appearance of
the Throne of Glory and its attendant spirits can be deduced.[10] The language used in the succeeding lines recalls particularly Ezekiel 1 and 8–
10, the basic biblical texts, as we have noticed, for the Merkabah mystical practice. 'The appearance of the glorious form' (מראי תבנית כבוד)
in line 3, for instance, reflects the expression, 'The appearance of the
likeness of the glory of the Lord' (הוא מראה דמות כבוד־יהוה) of Ezek.
1.28. The seventh *Sabbath Song* portrays the glory of the attendant
angels ('the chiefs of the realm of the spirits') who 'constitute the
visible appearance of the Glory' and hence in 4Q405.22.5-6 the language which describes God's glory is applied to the angels who attend
the chariot-throne.[11] Commenting on the תבנית of 4Q405.20.2-21-22.8
and the בדמות of 4Q405.20.2-21-22.10, Schiffman holds that they
exhibit a tendency to guard against anthropomorphism.[12] Even though
we are not sure of the significance of תבנית, it is likely that by this term
the author of the *Shabbat Shirot* shows more reticence in describing
God's glory than Ezekiel does.

The terms כבודו ('his glory') and שערי ('gates') of line 4 are reminiscent of Ezekiel's throne-vision (Ezek. 10.19; cf. also 8.3-4; 43.1-5).
The word *kabod*, which implies 'majesty', is used to denote the visible
manifestation of God in Exod. 16.7; 24.16-17; 40.34-35; etc.[13] In the
seventh *Sabbath Song* it is also closely associated with the divine
kingship. The concepts of 'his footstool' in line 2 and of 'the glory of
His kingdom' in line 10 attest the fact that God is glorious as king and
that he sits on the throne as a royal figure (cf. 4Q405.20.2-21-22.2 and
4, where the idea of the chariot thrones of glory is attached with that of
his royal throne). The close link between 'glory' and 'king' takes us to
the heart of the Merkabah mystical vision, for the goal of Merkabah

9.   See Newsom, *Sabbath Sacrifice*, pp. 13-17. This song is dated by Newsom
(p. 186) to c. 25–1 BCE.
10.   Newsom, *Sabbath Sacrifice*, pp. 9 and 232.
11.   As observed by Newsom, *Sabbath Sacrifice*, p. 233.
12.   Schiffman, 'Merkavah Speculation', pp. 38-40; cf. also Rowland, 'The
Visions of God', p. 143.
13.   Cf. BDB, p. 458 §2c; Gruenwald, *Merkavah Mysticism*, pp. 153-54.
Schiffman, 'Merkavah Speculation', p. 35 indicates that *Kabod* is a surrogate for
the divine name in *1 En.* 14.20; 102.3; and *T. Levi* 3.4 and that in the Scrolls it is
both an attribute of God and a reward for humans.

mystic is 'to see the King in His beauty'.[14]

The appearance of 'coals of fire' (line 6) is an important element in Ezekiel's throne-vision (Ezek. 1.13, 14) as well as in the Jewish mystical tradition we have cited above (cf. 4Q405.20.2-21-22.10 where the most holy spirits, that is, the angels, bear the appearance of fire. *1 En*. 14.19 refers to the 'streams of flaming fire' as issuing from beneath the divine throne; cf. 'rivers of fire' in *3 En*. 19.4.) The adverb סביב along with מתהלך (line 7) means 'moving round about', implying most probably the movement of the angels who attend the chariot throne (cf. 4Q405.20.2-21-22.11-12, where the angels, the spirits of the godlike beings, are described as moving with the glory of the chariot) and thus in both line 7 and line 9 the word סביב implies the presence of the Merkabah around which the 'shapes of flaming fire' move.

It is noteworthy that 4Q403.1.2.15 presents the term מרכבה in plural by saying, 'The chariots of His debir give praise together'.[15] Does this point to the Qumranites' belief in the multiplicity of heavenly chariots? Is this plural a real plural, as Newsom[16] and Schiffman[17] have taken it, or the plural of majesty, as Strugnell[18] has understood? Both Newsom and Schiffman apparently have identified the plurality of chariot thrones mainly in the light of *Ma'aseh Merkabah*, without checking whether such a concept occurs in any other Qumran texts or at least in any other place in the *Shabbat Shirot*. The cited passage, Isa. 66.15, speaks of '*his* [i.e. the Lord's] chariots', without implying multiple chariots placed in numerous debirim.[19] It is more likely that מרכבות, in this context, is the plural of sovereignty[20] and so the underlying motif in the seventh *Sabbath Song* is the angelic praise offered to God, who is

14.   See above, p. 81.

15.   Both Newsom and Martínez translate thus.

16.   Newsom, *Sabbath Sacrifice*, pp. 48-49, 237-38. However, she accepts the same phrase in 4Q405 20.2-21-22.11 as a plural of majesty, denoting a single throne (p. 117).

17.   Schiffman, 'Merkavah Speculation', pp. 42, 45.

18.   Strugnell, 'Angelic Liturgy', pp. 328-29 n. 4; he shows that the idea of plurality of heavens is not very much found in the works that belong to the first century BCE, although in certain circles this belief might have been evolving.

19.   In similar vein, line 15 refers to 'the chariots of *his* debir', implying the chariot(s) of a single debir.

20.   Cf. the singular מרכבה in 4Q405 20.2-21-22.8, where the subject of praise is the *Cherubim* and the object of praise is the image of the chariot-throne (Newsom, *Sabbath Sacrifice*, pp. 306, 314).

symbolized by מרכבות דבירו.[21] The climax of the Song occurs in line
16, which reiterates the praise offered to God, who dwells in his holy
debir, this time, by the chief priestly angels (cf. line 11). The central
idea in the latter part of the seventh *Sabbath Song*, then, is the epiphany
of God's glory on the chariot throne in the heavenly sanctuary and the
praise offered to him by the angels.[22] This we have noticed as the principal part of Merkabah mysticism described in the *Hekhalot* literature.
It is also apparent that Ezekiel 1 and 8–10 have greatly influenced the
chariot vision described in the Qumran document.

4Q405.20.2-21-22. The Merkabah mystical features can also be traced
in 4Q405.20.2-21-22, which consists of the latter part of the eleventh
and the early part of the twelfth *Sabbath Songs*.[23] The text of the
eleventh *Song* (lines 1-5) exhibits the heavenly scene in which God is
seated on his royal throne, surrounded by the *Cherubim* and *Ofannim*,
who do not sit, probably guarding the Throne of Glory (cf. *1 En.* 71.7).
Newsom argues that the author of the eleventh *Sabbath Song*, in
describing the movement of the chariot(s), has followed the model
provided especially by Ezek. 43.1-5, enriching it with details from
Ezekiel 1 and 10.[24] However, the verb הלך used in line 5 echoes the
same verb used in Ezek. 1.19-21 to denote the movements of the *hayyot*

---

21.   It is to be noted that in no other *Shabbat Shirot* are the chariots unam-
biguously described as praising God. However, *HR* 24.1 asserts that the Throne of
Glory sings every day—see Gruenwald, *Merkavah Mysticism*, p. 104 n. 26. Such a
development of tradition may be due to the ambiguity in such texts as *Shabbat
Shirot*.
22.   The ecstatic/hypnotic quality of the middle songs (6–8) is underlined by
Newsom (p. 15) because of their different style and content carrying sevenfold
sequences (e.g. seven chief princes, seven debirim, seven angelic priesthood, etc.).
She supposes that this would have produced an intense effect on the religious
emotions of the worshippers.
23.   This text is dated by Newsom, *Sabbath Sacrifice*, p. 258, to c. 50 BCE. Its
content is also found in 11QShirShabb 3–4, 5–6 as well as in 4Q405 23.1. The
fragment 11QShirShabb 5–6, however, is so broken that we are unable to know
what the subject of the praise is, whether the chariot-throne or the angelic hosts
around the temple. The same is true with 11QShirShabb f-c-k, which seem to contain such expressions as 'wondrous thrones', 'eternal thrones', 'godlike beings',
'praise', 'glory' and so on, but the passage is hard to restore with full sense (see
Newsom, *Sabbath Sacrifice*, pp. 366-67, 378-79). See also Martínez, *Dead Sea
Scrolls Translated* (1996), pp. 430-31.
24.   Newsom, *Sabbath Sacrifice*, pp. 54-55.

and of the wheels of the chariot rather than the verb באו of Ezek. 43.1-
5. Whereas in the *Sabbath Song* the movement of the chariot is within
the most holy place, in Ezek. 43.1-5, which does not bear any explicit
reference either to the אופנים or to the כרובים or to the אלוהים, the
movement of God's glory is from outside into the temple. It is more
likely, therefore, that the idea of the movement of the chariot(s) in has
closer parallel to Ezekiel 1 and 10, the basic texts for mystical experience in Judaism.

The hymns of blessing sung by the *Cherubim* and *Ofannim*, and by
all the divisions of the angels, are described in the twelfth *Sabbath
Song* with more clarity and vividness (see 4Q405.20.2-21-22.6-14).
The praising angels, by following the wheels, move in and out of the
heavenly temple (cf. 11QShirShabb 5–6; 4Q405.23.1). The act of praising God is portrayed as an act of worship on the part of the *Cherubim*,
which adore God by lifting their wings up (cf. the stretching of the
wings by the *hayyot* in Ezek. 1.11-12 and 10.16),[25] and the lifting up of
their wings causes the sound of 'divine stillness', that is, the sound of
blessing God. The expression קול דממה דקה ('a still small voice'—
cf. 1 Kgs 19.12), which is parallel to קול דממת אלוהים of line 8 and
קול דממת ברך of lines 12 and 13, has similarity in *Ma'aseh Merkabah*
33, where the angels are described as טעונים דממה דקה, who stand
silent before the Throne of Glory.[26]

The blessing of the *Cherubim* is directed to the 'likeness' (תבנית) of
the chariot throne, which is 'above the firmament', as well as to the
'splendour of the luminous firmament', which is beneath his glorious
seat. Both the chariot throne and the firmament are thought to deserve
praise and blessings because they bear the glory of God. According to
Schiffman, the phrase מושב כבודו (line 9), which denotes the divine
throne or Merkabah, is parallel to the phrases מושב יקרו and כסא הכבוד
of the Merkabah literature.[27] The expression, 'the hubs of His glory' in

---

25.   In targumic tradition the movement of the *Cherubim* and the lifting-up of
their wings were understood as a sound of blessing and adoration (*Targ. Ezek.* 1.24,
25). For the terminological parallels between the twelfth Sabbath Song and Ezek. 1
and 10, see Newsom, *Sabbath Sacrifice*, pp. 55-56.

26.   See Scholem, *Jewish Gnosticism* (1960), p. 116; *Synopse* §596; Schiffman, 'Merkavah Speculation', p. 37; Newsom, *Sabbath Sacrifice*, p. 314. Schiffman
shows that in the *HR* God is pictured as sitting in a *hekhal demamah*, a 'chamber of
silence'.

27.   Schiffman, 'Merkavah Speculation', pp. 38-39; cf. Newsom, *Sabbath
Sacrifice*, pp. 314-15.

line 10, can be properly understood only in the light of Ezek. 1.12-14 as a fiery substance (cf. Martínez's rendering 'a luminous substance') which moves among the *hayyot* and which flashes like lightning.[28] Obviously, the primary function of the angelic spirits is not just singing praises, but also to follow the movement of the wheels (lines 9, 11-13). In Ezek. 1.19-21 and 10.16, 17, however, it is the wheels which follow the *hayyot/Cherubim* closely.[29]

The appearance of the 'streams of fire' (מראי שבולי אש) in line 10b (= מראי אש in 10a) is like חשמל and this recalls Ezek. 1.4, 27. 'Fire' is seen 'beneath the glorious seat' (line 9), whence the *Cherubim* sing praises to the throne and to the firmament (cf. Ezek. 1.13, 27; 10.6, 7). The term גלגלי אש, without כבודו, occurs in *Ma'aseh Merkabah* 3[30] and the association of the angels with fire is a common motif in the *Hekhalot* texts, particularly in the *Sefer ha-Razim*.

The classification of the angels in ranks is peculiar to the twelfth *Sabbath Song*. The expressions מחכי אלוהים in line 13 and דגליהם in line 14 ('the divisions of angelic beings') reflect the idea, which occurs in the *War Scroll* also, of the formations of the eschatological troops for battle. The implication of the expression, 'There is a stillness of divine blessing in all the camps of the godlike beings' (line 13) closely resembles the idea behind the expression, 'The peace of God be in the camps of His saints' (1QM 3.6). According to Schiffman, the notion that the angels were divided into camps is a basic motif in such Merkabah texts as *3 Enoch*, *Sefer ha-Razim*, the Aramaic magic bowls, etc.[31] However, the author of the *Shabbat Shirot* has added a cultic flavour here by recognizing the marshalled troops of angels as the priestly figures, who are stationed in the battle-front wearing their war-garments of multi-coloured embroidery work (cf. 1QM 7.8-18).[32]

28. See W. Zimmerli, *Ezechiel* (BKAT, 13.1; Neukirchen–Vluyn: Neukirchener Verlag, 1969), I, pp. 121-22; M. Greenberg, *Ezekiel 1–20* (AB, 22; New York: Doubleday, 1983), p. 46; Newsom, *Sabbath Sacrifice*, p. 315.

29. Although it is not until *1 En.* 71.10 that the *Cherubim* and the *Ofannim* appear as angelic bands, one can see the origin of such a tradition in the *Shabbat Shirot*, where they are mentioned in parallel (see Strugnell, 'Angelic Liturgy', pp. 339-40).

30. Scholem, *Jewish Gnosticism* (1960), p. 103 §3; *Synopse* §546.

31. Schiffman, 'Merkavah Speculation', p. 44.

32. The *War Scroll*, which was written about the same period as the *Shabbat Shirot*, makes it clear that the Qumran community believed in an eternal struggle between the spirits of light and of darkness, in which the warrior angels participated

Our investigation shows that in 4Q405.20.2-21-22 the appearance of the glory of God is experienced, albeit not explicitly mentioned, as 'a multitude of angelic spirits who appear to surround and move with the chariot throne'. The examined concepts such as the angelic praise to God, the fiery appearance of the angels and their division in ranks, the chariot-throne motif, the appearance of the streams of fire, the small still voice of God, etc., have parallels with similar concepts expressed in the Jewish mystical literature. Since there are numerous parallels, both verbal and conceptual, between this song and the throne-vision described in Ezekiel 1, 8 and 10, one can argue that these prophetic passages, which constituted the basis for mystical interest in Judaism, provide the background to understand the twelfth *Sabbath Song* too.

Communal Mysticism. Does this mean that the *Songs of Sabbath Sacrifice* were used in Qumran as a means of mystical experience at the point of worship? After her detailed study of these songs, Newsom asserts that the purpose of the Shirot, recited at the time of sabbath whole-offering, is to describe 'the praxis of something like a communal mysticism'.[33] She goes on to say that during the course of this 13-week cycle, 'the community is...gradually led through the spiritually animate heavenly temple until the worshippers experience the holiness of the Merkabah and of the sabbath sacrifice as it is conducted by the high priests of the angels'.[34] 4Q286–287 are added testimony to the community's ecstatic visions of the chariots of God's glory with the multitudes of wheel-angels (אופניהמה).

Nevertheless, some of the key aspects of Merkabah mysticism are entirely missing in the *Shabbat Shirot*. Although God is the primary object of praise, we find more descriptions of the angels than of God. There is no reference in the *Shirot* either to a visionary or to the

---

in accordance with their ranks and stations, just like the priests did—cf. T. Gaster, *The Scriptures of the Dead Sea Sect* (London: Secker & Warburg, 1957), pp. 269, 280, who uses the word 'ranks' in 1QM 7.8 instead of the literal 'gates'. It seems that the song shows the classification of the angels in various ranks in a military pattern, although the traditional word צבאות is not used.

33. Newsom, *Sabbath Sacrifice*, p. 19. See above, p. 51, for the worship of the angels in the heavenly temple as an aspect of *Hekhalot* mysticism.

34. Newsom, *Sabbath Sacrifice*, p. 19. The newly discovered Aramaic Levi documents (4Q213 TLevi^a) confirm that the sectarians in Qumran showed much interest in the Merkabah mystical practice (see above, p. 53).

heavenly ascent/journey,[35] and, because of this, Schiffman concludes that the visions described are 'the result of intellectual endeavour in interpreting the biblical material rather than of a mystical experience'.[36] Rowland has observed that, despite a few independent ideas that the *Shabbat Shirot* contain, there is no anthropomorphic description of God's form, as we have in Ezek. 1.26, *1 Enoch* 14 and Dan. 7.9.[37] Moreover, in contrast to *Hekhalot* tradition, the *content* of the angelic hymns remains largely unknown in the *Shabbat Shirot*, although the angelic praises are frequently mentioned.

This raises the questions: are the *Shabbat Shirot* in any way related to Merkabah mystical practice? Did the Qumran community consider the time of the sabbath sacrifice as an opportunity to attain the experience of being present in the heavenly sanctuary, as Newsom maintains or at least as a means of 'intersection between the earthly and heavenly realms', as Maier has postulated?[38] Did the author of the *Shabbat Shirot* intend to place the Merkabah elements in an emphatic position? What is the significance of his presentation of Merkabah speculation in a cultic context? These questions can be answered by identifying the context in which the *Shabbat Shirot* were designed and used.

The Context of 4QShirShabb

By examining the points of contact between the *Shabbat Shirot* and 4QBerakot, Newsom has demonstrated the Qumran provenance of the *Shabbat Shirot*,[39] that is widely accepted by the Qumran scholars. A tradition that combined the heavenly and the earthly priestly notions was very much alive in the postexilic period (Zech. 3; Jub. 31.13-14; *Ap. Levi* 7; *T. Levi* 2–5, 8) and it would have been natural for such a priestly community as that in Qumran to adopt an existing tradition in their worship so that they might experience at present the eschatological joy with the priestly angels.

The members of the Qumran community believed that, as the initiates of their own 'new covenant', they had already been united on earth

---

35. See Strugnell, 'Angelic Liturgy', pp. 335-36.
36. Schiffman, 'Merkavah Speculation', p. 19.
37. Rowland, 'The Visions of God', pp. 143-44.
38. Newsom, *Sabbath Sacrifice*, p. 19; Maier, *Vom Kultus zur Gnosis*, pp. 106-12, 133.
39. Newsom, *Sabbath Sacrifice*, pp. 1-4.

with the angels of heaven (1QS 11.8; cf. 1QH 3.21-22; 11.10-13).[40] The
blessing of the priests in 1QSb 4.24-26 focuses on the shared priestly
service of the Qumranites with the angels of the presence (1QSb 4.24-
26). Hence the use of the *Shabbat Shirot*, being a part of the Sabbath
observance in Qumran, would have offered an occasion to realize the
sense of communion as well as of their shared priestly service with the
angels. One can see clearly, then, the practice of 'community mysticism' in Qumran in the sense of 'Einheit von himmlischen und
irdischem Kult' ('unity of the heavenly and earthly worship').[41] Now it
is easier to understand why the Merkabah material occupied central
position in the *Sabbath Songs*. The Merkabah speculation, which contains the idea of the angelic accompaniment of God's glory, would
have provided the author a better source to inculcate the 'mystical'
awareness during the sabbath whole-offering.[42] This proves that the
Qumranites, following Isaiah, Ezekiel and other ancient Jewish mystics, who contemplated the throne-chariot and the heavenly palaces,
'strove for a similar mystical knowledge'.[43]

Strugnell's observation that the chariot-throne passages in the *Songs*
lack the 'guided tour' type of description does not nullify the underlying mystical motif, as Schiffman thinks,[44] for not all Merkabah
mystical experiences necessarily hold the idea of angelic accompaniment or of heavenly ascent.[45] The community was constantly using the
tradition behind the book of Ezekiel to prove its Zadokite line of priesthood[46] and therefore it is natural that it also used Ezekiel's Merkabah

40.   Segal, *Paul the Convert*, p. 319 n. 50, argues for the transformation motif
as underlying the sect's belief of 'one company with the angels'.

41.   Maier, *Vom Kultur zur Gnosis*, p. 133.

42.   Newsom, *Sabbath Sacrifice*, p. 21, specifies the Sabbath whole-offering as
the time when the *Shabbat Shirot*, which contribute to the sense of liturgical
communion with the angels, were used as the quasi-mystical S*hirot*. This recalls the
Merkabah hymn used by the Merkabah mystic in the *Hekhalot* text.

43.   See Vermes, *Dead Sea Scrolls* (1995), p. 51.

44.   Schiffman, 'Merkavah Speculation', p. 19.

45.   That the Qumran community had believed in the angelic 'guided tour'
type of vision can be seen in another Qumran document 5Q15, which describes the
'New Jerusalem'. See F.G. Martínez, *Qumran and Apocalyptic: Studies on the
Aramaic Texts from Qumran* (Leiden: E.J. Brill, 1992), pp. 180-213, for the
Qumran provenance of this document.

46.   See B. Gärtner, *The Temple and the Community in Qumran and the New
Testament: A Comparative Study in the Temple Symbolism of the Qumran Texts*

vision to give the community an awareness of its divine call to constitute the 'true' priesthood. Despite the author's free use of Ezekiel, one can see a tendency to describe extensively the angels and other beings connected with the throne, by avoiding the anthropomorphic way of describing God's appearance (especially in 4Q286–287). For the priestly community in Qumran it is the angels who represent God's glory.[47]

Since the composition of all the *Shabbat Shirot* is dated to 50–1 BCE, they provide strong evidence for the likelihood that Merkabah mysticism was practised by the sectarian Jews at Qumran at the dawn of Christianity.[48] This finding is reinforced by the esoteric character of the Qumran writings, a brief study of which will enable us to understand one more dimension of Jewish mysticism that had been known in the first century.

The Esoteric Character of Qumran Writings
Scholem, in his attempt to trace the 'gnostic' elements in Judaism,[49] refers to the Qumran texts with the aim of finding a possible connection between these texts and later Jewish esotericism.[50] Although he is convinced that phrases such as 'the רזי פלא ("wondrous mysteries") of God' betray the esoteric teachings of the sectarians, he has not pursued his investigation further to illumine some of the phraseological and/or essential similarities between the Scrolls and the later Jewish sources of esoteric tradition. As the words μυστήριον ('mystery') and μυστικίσ-μος ('mysticism') have the same root, μύειν or μυεῖν, and, as 'Jewish

---

and the New Testament (SNTSMS, 1; Cambridge: Cambridge University Press, 1965), pp. 4-5, 14. G.J. Brooke, *Exegesis at Qumran* (Sheffield: JSOT Press, 1985), pp. 107, 334 n. 68, has demonstrated that the whole of Qumran literature echoes the thought of Ezekiel.

47.   Cf. J. Abelson, *The Immanence of God in Rabbinical Literature* (London: Macmillan, 1912), pp. 13-14, who observes that for a Jew, even in the Old Testament time, angels were a substitute for God in his close contact with humans.

48.   Gaster, *Scriptures*, pp. 15-18, calls the Qumranites 'a mystical community', because they were striving to achieve personal enlightenment in the solitary desert, but he is not aware of the underlying Merkabah mystical elements in their writings.

49.   By 'gnostic', Scholem means the religious tendencies that exhibit 'a mystical esotericism' for the elect based on illumination and the acquisition of a heavenly and divine knowledge (see Scholem, *Jewish Gnosticism* [1960], p. 1).

50.   Scholem, *Jewish Gnosticism* (1960), p. 3.

esotericism' can usefully replace 'Jewish mysticism',[51] a study of the
רז-motif in Qumran texts may illumine further the Jewish 'mystical'
tendency at Qumran.

The word רז frequently occurs in the *Hodayot* of Qumran as 'ein
häufiger Ausdruck für wunderbare Geheimnisse, die nur Gott zugäng-
lich machen kann'[52] (see 1QH 1.21; 2.13; 4.27, 28; 11.10; 13.2, 13;
1QM 14.14; 1QS 9.18; 9.5; etc.). The 'wondrous mysteries', according
to these passages, belong to God and it is he who alone can reveal them
(cf. Dan. 2.19, 22, 28-30, 47). There are in general two types of
mysteries: some are to be proclaimed to 'all the living' (e.g. the gra-
cious 'works of God' performed in human lives—1QH 4.29), and
others are to be concealed from outsiders and even from the untrained
initiates of the community (1QS 4.6; 9.17, 22).[53] The second type,
which is our interest, is called by Brown the 'Cosmic Mysteries',[54]
because the secrets are concerned with the divine order of creation. The
concept of רז in Qumran was developed from the idea of the ancient
prophets being introduced in their visions into the heavenly assembly
and there learning the secret divine plans for cosmic history.[55] Since no
one is righteous with God, no one could understand all his mysteries
(1QH 7.26-32; 12.19-20), in particular, the one who lives in flesh (1QH
13.13-14). But God has made known to all his favoured children (i.e.
his chosen ones) the mystery of his truth (1QH 9.9-10, where רז is in
parallel with סוד).

Reference to רז occurs in the sixth *Sabbath Song*, 4Q403 1.1.16-26
(= 4QSl.I.1.16-26),[56] which describes the fifth angel's (נשׂיאי רוש) praise
upon all who know the secrets of the most pure (ל]כו[ל]יודעי רזי
טהור[י]—טוהר—line 19). Strugnell, who takes טהורי טוהר as an angelic
title in the sense of 'the luminous celestial ones' or 'the pure ones of

51. See above, pp. 56-57.
52. '...a common expression for wonderful mysteries which God alone can
unveil'. Nötcher, commenting on 1QH 4.27, 28; quoted by M. Mansoor, *The
Thanksgiving Hymns* (Leiden: E.J. Brill, 1961), p. 128 n. 4.
53. See R.E. Brown, *The Semitic Background of the Term 'Mystery' in the
New Testament* (FBBS, 21; Philadelphia: Fortress Press, 1968), p. 25; Mansoor,
Thanksgiving Hymns, p. 106 n. 10.
54. Brown, *Semitic Background*, pp. 27-28.
55. See M.P. Horgan, *Pesharim: Qumran Interpretations of Biblical Books*
(Washington: Catholic Biblical Association, 1979), p. 237.
56. See the Hebrew text with English translation and commentary in Strugnell,
'Angelic Liturgy', pp. 322-34; and Schiffman, 'Merkavah Speculation', pp. 22-34.

the bright heaven', interprets these mysteries as those known by the
angels in the divine council (cf. 'the mysteries of the holy ones' in
1 En. 106.19).[57] In 1QM 14.14 'the wonderful mysteries on high' is in
apposition to 'the design of Thy glory' (Vermes's translation)[58] and
according to 1QH 13.13-14 God's glory and his name[59] are revealed in
creation, which is designated as the 'mysteries of His wisdom'. Two
factors need our attention here. (1) Both the readings, 'the mysteries of
Thy understanding' and 'to make known Thy glory' in 1QH 13.13, are
not corrupted and hence reliable; (2) the divine name and glory are
mentioned as secrets in the context of God's creation (see 1QH 13.8-
20). Name and glory are closely associated or even identified in the
expression אלוהותכה כבוד שם את ('the Glorious Name of your God' in
4Q286–287 MS B Frag. 1, line 8).[60] Thus the phrase 'secrets of the most
pure', to which the sixth *Sabbath Song* refers, denotes reasonably the
splendour of his glory as perceived by the angels in heaven. This will
explain why there is no clear description of the glory of God in the
Shabbat Shirot, even though it was the object of the angelic praise. It is
clear that the glory (and also the name) of God, the central focus in
Merkabah mysticism, was regarded as a 'secret' in Qumran.

The Qumran texts attest the fact that God reveals wondrous mysteries
through the right interpretation of the Scripture.[61] The psalmist's statement, 'Thou hast made me...an interpreter of knowledge by wondrous
secrets', clearly alludes to the Scripture as containing divine secrets
(1QH 2.13). The psalmist is presumably 'a man in an eminent leading

---

57.   Strugnell, 'Angelic Liturgy', pp. 325-26. For him טוהר means, as in
4QBerakot, uniquely 'heaven'.

58.   Vermes, *Dead Sea Scrolls* (1995), p. 140. Dupont-Sommer's version has:
'For Thy [glori]ous kingship is great, together with Thy marvellous Mysteries in
the heights [of heaven]' (see A. Dupont-Sommer, *The Essene Writings from
Qumran* [Oxford: Basil Blackwell, 1961], p. 191).

59.   Habermann's reading: הגדול שמכה בסוד in 1QH 13.14, followed by
Mansoor (see Mansoor, *Thanksgiving Hymns*, p. 179 n. 1). While Vermes, *Dead
Sea Scrolls* (1995), p. 228, renders it as 'the great design of Thy wisdom', Dupont-
Sommer, *Essene Writings*, p. 242, renders it, '[Thy] great secret of truth'.

60.   See Eisenman and Wise, *Scrolls Uncovered*, pp. 228, 230. Cf. Frag. 3,
Col. 1, line 7 (כבודכח שם את לברך).

61.   See J.D.G. Dunn, *Romans 9–16* (WBC, 38B; Dallas, TX: Word Books,
1988), p. 915; Brown, *Semitic Background*, p. 27 n. 88. This kind of secret may be
classified under Brown's 'Mysteries of the Sect's interpretation of the Law' (pp.
24-27).

position, possibly the teacher of righteouness himself'.[62] It is God who instructs his elect in his marvellous mysteries (רזי פלא) and shows his power by his wonderful secret counsels (סוד פלא) (1QH 4.27-28), which again refer to the interpretation of the Law (cf. 1QS 4.6).[63] No one is capable of understanding the divine mysteries unless God himself wills to make them known (1QH 10.2-5). If we understand 'esotericism' to mean 'a special attitude towards Scripture and the explication of its content',[64] then the Hymns and the *Pesher*-texts of Qumran provide one more evidence for the existence of the esoteric/mystical attitude in Qumran.

The word רז carries an eschatological connotation, when it is used in connection with the 'mysteries of iniquity' or 'sinful secrets', which now work against God's deeds (1QH 5.36; 1QM 14.9) and which will be annihilated at last when wickedness is banished by righteousness (1Q27). In 1QH 8.4-36 the term רז denotes the eschatological figure, a 'holy branch', which is in some way hidden with its mystery (רזו) sealed off. God is said to have fenced off the fruit of the branch (probably the Teacher of Righteousness—cf. CD 1.11) 'with the mystery of the mighty in strength and holy spirits'. God hid the Teacher from humans until the time when he would reveal to him his salvation (1QH 5.11-12). Thus in Qumran texts a person is spoken of as hidden and this idea was later applied to the concealment and the revelation of the Righteous One (*1 En.* 38.2-3) or the Son of Man (*1 En.* 48.6; 62.7-10) or the Messiah (*4 Ezra* 12.32; 13.26-52) who will judge the sinners.[65]

In sum, the רז passages in Qumran literature bring out the following elements as esoteric, which, at the same time, reflect a 'mystical' character: (1) the knowledge of the divine order of creation, hidden for an ordinary human being but revealed to the initiates; (2) the splendour of God's glory as perceived in the heavenly council and the name and glory of God in creation; (3) the right interpretation of the Scripture that is made known only to whom God wills; (4) and the whole system of evil that works against God now, but which will be dealt with by 'the Messiah' at the time when God will reveal his eschatological salvation to him.[66]

62. Mansoor, *Thanksgiving Hymns*, p. 106 n. 10.
63. See Brown, *Semitic Background*, p. 25.
64. Gruenwald, *Merkavah Mysticism*, p. 22.
65. See also Brown, *Semitic Background*, pp. 26-27.
66. There is another document of Qumran community which contains allusion

4QMessAr or 4Q534

Another document, purported to be written in Qumran at the end of the first century BCE,[67] which sheds additional light on Merkabah mysticism, is 4QMessAr.[68] Its main theme is the 'horoscope' of the royal Messiah, describing his hand, hair, thigh, knees, and his spiritual qualities such as wisdom and understanding. Both Scholem and Gruenwald have demonstrated that these physiognomic speculations and the speculations concerning one's palm (chiromancy) and forehead (metoposcopy) were in existence among the Merkabah mystics.[69] Gruenwald maintains that the esoteric traditions embodied in the Jewish physiognomic and chiromantic fragments are concerned with the measurements of God's body, which point back to the tradition at Qumran.[70] But, as our study below shows, it does not seem that the physiognomy and chiromancy had gained much ground in the first-century mystical thinking.

Conclusions

Our study shows that Ezekiel's vision of God's glory on the chariot had attained considerable attention as early as the second century BCE, when the Wisdom of ben Sira was written. It is possible that ben Sira's exhortation not to be preoccupied in matters beyond one's ability includes also the Merkabah mystical interest, which sought an ascent to heaven to see God and to know cosmological secrets.

The Qumran texts, which we have examined, give us some evidence that probably the practice of Merkabah mysticism was part of worship at Qumran. In the light of the *Hekhalot* literature we can identify the

---

to Merkabah mysticism and that is 11QMelch (see below, pp. 139-41).

67.　　See Martínez, *Qumran and Apocalyptic*, pp. 3-5 for the Aramaic text and English translation. Vermes shows reservations in accepting the messianic interpretation of this text. For him the text may also allude to the miraculous birth of Noah—see G. Vermes, *The Dead Sea Scrolls in English* (Sheffield: JSOT Press, 3rd edn, 1987), p. 305; *idem, Dead Sea Scrolls* (1995), p. 367; in favour of a messianic interpretation see Alexander, '3 (Hebrew Apocalypse of) Enoch', p. 250 and Martínez, *Qumran and Apocalyptic*, p. 22.

68.　　Vermes, who uses the siglum 4QMessAr in the third edition of *Dead Sea Scrolls* (p. 305) uses 4Q534 in the fourth edition (p. 367).

69.　　See Gruenwald, *Merkavah Mysticism*, p. 220 n. 11; *idem*, 'Further Jewish Physiognomic and Chiromantic Fragments', *Tarbiz* 40 (1971), pp. 301-19 (English summary on p. v).

70.　　Gruenwald, 'Physiognomic and Chiromantic Fragments', p. v.

following elements as 'mystical' in Qumran community.

1. The angelology, comprising descriptions of the fiery appearance of the angels, their glorious vestments, their division in ranks, their songs of praise to the divine chariot, their strong allegiance to the divine presence, and the worshipper's communion with the angels. The Qumranites believed that the angels who attend the chariot-throne of God represent for them the glory of God; hence the greater emphasis on angelology.

2. A quick reference to God as the glory and king who is seated on the royal chariot-throne, and as the one who dwells in the midst of the angelic priests; the streams of fire flow in his presence and he speaks in small still voice. An experience of heavenly ascent was evidently not foreign to the Qumranites.

3. Esotericism has taken different shapes in Qumran writings. The knowledge of God in his creation, the splendour of his glory, the right interpretation of Scripture, the eschatological judgment, and the physiognomic way of describing the royal Messiah were all treated by the Qumranites as esoteric and different aspects of mysticism.

Our analysis of three sabbath songs shows that in all probability the Qumran sect did practise 'mysticism' by contemplating Ezekiel's chariot-throne, particularly at the time of sabbath whole-offering, and that Ezekiel 1, 8 and 10 were freely used in the composition of the *Songs of Merkabah*. Though there may be some effort to worship God through an exegesis of these passages, what is striking is that they were used as 'vehicles for mystical trance experience'.[71] This means that the Merkabah mystical practice was current in Qumran from the first century BCE until at least 68 CE. The further discovery of the text of the twelfth *Sabbath Song* in Cave 11 and the Aramaic Levi document in Cave 4 containing the Merkabah vision of Levi indicates the wider influence of the Merkabah mystical practice among the Jewish sects. Now we can examine with confidence some of the Jewish and Christian writings that belong to the first century CE and see whether Merkabah mysticism was known and practised in the late-first-century Judaism and Christianity. If so, what were its salient features?

71. See C. Newsom, 'Merkabah Exegesis in the Qumran Sabbath Shirot', *JJS* 38 (1987), pp. 11-30 (15 n. 12).

Chapter 6

EVIDENCE OF MERKABAH MYSTICISM IN THE CHRISTIAN ERA

Evidence of Merkabah mystical practice can be found in three important traditions which describe the heavenly ascent of the key figures,
Paul, Isaiah and Moses, and which are commonly accepted as belonging to the first century CE. An analysis of the works that contain these
ascent-traditions is called for in order to understand the essence of
mysticism as practised at that time.

2 Corinthians 12

In the autobiographical statement of Paul (2 Cor. 12.1-4) we find some
evidence for the existence of the practice of an ascent to heaven, and
possibly that of Merkabah mysticism, even in the early part of the first
century CE. The fact that the Corinthian church was able to understand
the concepts of 'being caught up to the third heaven/Paradise', 'in the
body or out of the body' and 'hearing unutterable things' makes one to
think that the tradition concerning heavenly ascent is much older than
the mid-first century (55–58 CE), when 2 Corinthians was written.[1]

Establishing the points of connection between the Merkabah visions
described in Mishnah and Talmud and two of Paul's major visions
referred to in 2 Cor. 12.1-4, 8-9 and Acts 9.22, 26, Bowker has argued
that Paul's visions are based on Merkabah contemplation.[2] However,
Schäfer has advanced the thesis that despite the fact that Paul refers in 2
Cor. 12.1-4 to an 'ecstatic experience', it is impossible to see a form of
Merkabah mysticism underlying in it.[3] In contrast, Tabor, without

1.   The date 'fourteen years ago' brings Paul's ascent to around the year 40, a
clear indication of such a practice in the early part of the first century.
2.   Bowker, ' "Merkabah" Visions', pp. 157-73.
3.   Schäfer, 'New Testament and Hekhalot Literature', he also disproves the
proposed parallels between the experience of the four rabbis who entered into
Paradise and Paul's ascent to Paradise.

showing knowledge of Schäfer's work, argues that Paul's ascent in 2 Corinthians 12 fits in well, in its structure and content, with the vision of the Merkabah throne of God.[4] Segal promotes this view by stating that Paul is the only Jewish mystic to report his own mystical experiences and therefore that they are important evidence for the existence of first-century Jewish mysticism.[5] Therefore a brief exegetical investigation of 2 Cor. 12.1-4 may enable us to see whether or not any mystical tendency is reflected in his experience.

Paul classifies his experience of 'being caught up to the third heaven' with his visions (ὀπτασίαι) and revelations (ἀποκαλύψεις) and the context of 2 Corinthians 12 seems to suggest that through this experience he learned that true καύχησις lies in ἀσθένεια.[6] Noteworthy are the following aspects in this passage.

The Heavenly Ascent
That Paul had a *Himmelreise* is clear from the verb ἁρπαγέντα, which means 'a snatching-up' or 'being carried off', a key-word to denote an ascent to heaven in the apocalyptic and mystical literature. (cf. *Apoc. Abr.* 15.3-4; *1 En.* 70.1-2; 71.1; *Asc. Isa.* 6.10). The passive voice probably makes God the subject of the action. This means that the rapture became possible to Paul primarily through God's initiative, strictly speaking, 'in the power of Christ'.[7] This echoes the mystical visions received by 'righteous men' exclusively by divine influence at a particular point in their lives.

4.   J.D. Tabor, *Things Unutterable: Paul's Ascent to Paradise in its Greco-Roman, Judaic, and Early Christian Contexts* (New York: Lanham, 1986), pp. 113-27.

5.   Segal, *Paul the Convert*, pp. 34-71; Morray-Jones, 'Paradise Revisited. Part 1', pp. 177-217 and 'Paradise Revisited. Part 2', pp. 265-92, has vehemently argued that Paul's account of his ascent to Paradise, where he saw the enthroned and 'glorified' Christ, has its roots, like the Jewish *pardes* story, in the mystical tradition.

6.   The linkage of καύχησις to ἀσθένεια is the one that structurally binds the unit 2 Cor. 12.1-10—see R.P. Spittler, 'The Limits of Ecstasy: An Exegesis of 2 Corinthians 12:1-10', in G.F. Hawthorne (ed.), *Current Issues in Biblical and Patristic Interpretation: Studies in Honour of M.C. Tenney* (Grand Rapids: Eerdmans, 1975), pp. 259-66 (262).

7.   The phrase ἐν Χριστῷ may imply Paul's life lived in the power of Christ and thus he disclaims all credit for the glorious experience—see A. Plummer, *A Critical and Exegetical Commentary on the Second Epistle of St Paul to the Corinthians* (ICC; Edinburgh: T. & T. Clark, repr. 1925), p. 340.

An Ecstatic Experience

The expression, 'whether in the body or out of the body I do not know, God knows', surely indicates Paul's experience in terms of ecstasy, for in ecstasy normally the visionary's normal faculties are suspended in a trance-like state and therefore he is not sure of the mode of vision.[8] Such ecstatic experiences are given prime importance in Merkabah mystical literature. R. Nehunya b. Ha-Qanah, for example, by falling into an ecstatic trance, ascends to heaven to descend into the chariot. R. Ishmael had to bring him back from his Merkabah vision with a piece of cloth (*HR* 20.1, 3; *Synopse* §§225, 227).

An Esoteric Experience

Paul's experience in 2 Corinthians 12 is esoteric in character, which is clear from his use of the third person ('I know a man in Christ', 'this man') to describe his own experience (cf. v. 7). Paul preserves the 'secrecy' of the experience lest he boasts of it. In addition, the phrase ἄρρητα ῥήματα in v. 4 implies that the things that he heard should not be proclaimed.[9] It is 'hidden' not only because of its sacredness,[10] but also because of the possible abuse among the immature and 'untrained'. However, our inquiry as to whether or not Paul had Merkabah visions depends on the place where he was taken and thus an analysis of Paul's destination is called for.

The Destination

It is now generally agreed that Paul is speaking in 2 Cor. 12.1-4 of one and the same experience.[11] If so, the 'third heaven' in v. 2 and

8.   Cf. H. Wildberger, *Isaiah 1–12: A Commentary* (Minneapolis: Fortress Press, 1991), p. 260; Dunn, *Jesus and the Spirit*, p. 84.

9.   Although it is possible to understand the phrase as denoting 'words that are insufficient' or 'that are not able to be translated', as R. Martin shows, the following phrase ἃ οὐκ ἐξὸν ἀνθρώπῳ λαλῆσαι conveys the idea that 'a human being is not permitted to utter'—see R. Martin, *2 Corinthians* (WBC, 40; Waco, TX: Word Books, 1986), p. 405; Spittler, 'Limits of Ecstasy', p. 263; V.P. Furnish, *II Corinthians* (AB, 33; New York: Doubleday, 1984), p. 527. Cf. *Apoc. Abr.* 15.5-7, where Abraham, during his ascent, saw a great crowd of angels who were worshipping God by crying out words that were unknown to the patriarch.

10.   See Martin, *2 Corinthians*, p. 405.

11.   For terminological parallels between v. 2 and vv. 3-4, see Martin, *2 Corinthians*, p. 392, who concludes that both descriptions are of the same event. See also C.K. Barrett, *A Commentary on the Second Epistle to the Corinthians*

'Paradise' in v. 4 denote the same place (cf. *2 En*. 8.1-3; *Apoc. Mos.* 37.5). Tabor, on the basis of the parallel structure in vv. 2 and 4, sees it as a single journey reported in two stages and states that Paul was taken first to the third heaven, then to *Pardes* in the highest heaven.[12] However, no evidence exists to claim that *Pardes* was in the highest heaven. On the contrary, the two first-century documents, *Life of Adam and Eve* and *2 Enoch*, place *Pardes* in the third heaven (cf. *Apoc. Abr.* 21; *Apoc. Mos.* 37.5; 40.1). Moreover, after mentioning 'the third heaven' in v. 2, the corollary would be to say 'the highest heaven' or 'the seventh heaven', if Paul had wanted to refer in v. 4 to the place of his final stage. Martin has remarked that the repetition of his experience indicates merely *Stilempfinden*, a semitic device like a 'synthetic parallelism'.[13]

Does Paul's Ascent Include a Heavenly Vision?
Did Paul have a vision of God or Christ in Paradise? According to the *Life of Adam and Eve* 25, Adam saw in Paradise the Lord sitting on the chariot and *2 En*. 8.3 describes Paradise as a garden in which the Lord takes a walk (Rec. A) or in which he takes a rest (Rec. J).[14] Though Paradise was the abode of the righteous ones, the tradition that it was a place of God's presence was not completely absent in Jewish thinking, particularly in the first century of our era. 2 Corinthians 12 *prima facie* seems to attest Schäfer's view that Paul had an auditory experience rather than a vision.[15] There are, however, several factors that point to a vision of Christ given to Paul in Paradise and which Schäfer ignores.

1. Paul's reference to his ascent as a paradigm for his 'visions and revelations' suggests that it had contained both a vision and revelation.

2. The genitive κυρίου, which follows ὀπτασίας καὶ ἀποκαλύψεις, can be a subjective genitive (i.e. the visions granted by the Lord), but at the same time it can also be treated as an objective genitive, implying

(HNTC; New York: Harper & Row, 1973), p. 310; R.C.H. Lenski, *The Interpretation of St Paul's First and Second Epistles to the Corinthians* (Minneapolis: Augsburg, 1963), pp. 1293-94.

12.   Tabor, *Things Unutterable*, p. 115.

13.   Martin, *2 Corinthians*, p. 392.

14.   This argues against Schäfer who dichotomizes Paradise and garden, by saying that the term *pardes* in the story of the 'Four entered into *pardes*' means only 'garden' and not 'Paradise'—see Schäfer, 'New Testament and Hekhalot Literature', p. 26.

15.   Schäfer, 'New Testament and Hekhalot Literature', p. 23.

that the object of Paul's vision was Christ.[16] Paul's encounter with Christ regarding his weakness and Christ's comforting words, 'My grace is sufficient for you, for my power is made perfect in weakness' (v. 9), seem to reinforce our view that he had seen and encountered Christ in Paradise.

3. Paul ironically boasts of weakness, not only because it came 'as a *result* of this very privileged experience, namely the harassing angel of Satan (vv. 7-10)',[17] but also because Christ's power is perfectly manifested precisely in his weakness (v. 9). This idea is not far from what happens to the Merkabah mystics. We have seen how the visionaries became so weak that they immediately fell down at the vision of the Lord sitting on the throne (*1 En.* 14.14, 24; 71.2, 11; *2 En.* 21.2; 22.4). After this, the power of the enthroned deity touched them, in most cases through the angels, and transformed them and gave them the privilege of standing in close relationship with God. This must have happened to Paul also as it did in his vision of Jesus on the road to Damascus (Acts 9; 22; 26), which, according to Bowker, reflects the Merkabah vision of Ezekiel 1 and 2.[18] It is hard to accept that Paul did not see anything or anyone in Paradise, but only heard ἄρρητα ῥήματα. The idea that τὸ ἄρρητον may refer to God or his manifestation through the Logos or potencies (δυνάμεις) had been known at least in Hellenistic Judaism. According to Philo, God, τὸ ὄν, is ἄρρητον, but his name is known through his 'potencies' (*Rer. Div. Her.* 170; *Sacr.* 60). He says that it is the sacred Logos, which imparts τὰ ἄρρητα that are not allowed to reach the ears of the uninitiated (*Somn.* 1.191). Segal rightly holds that unlike Acts and Galatians 1, 2 Cor. 12.1-9 is a confessional description of a vision, which is both mystical and apocalyptic.[19]

16.   See Martin, *2 Corinthians*, p. 397; Dunn, *Jesus and the Spirit*, p. 414 n. 88. One can say that the vision of the Merkabah, the bearer of the divine presence, is transferred to Christ, the revelation of God.

17.   That is, in vv. 7-10 Paul speaks of his temptation to be elated by this extraordinary revelation and the resulting harassment from Satan which the Lord allows to remind him of his place (Tabor, *Things Unutterable*, p. 114).

18.   Bowker, ' "Merkabah" Visions', pp. 167-73. Morray-Jones's argument that the 'angel of Satan' is reminiscent of the demonic 'angels of destruction' who fight with Merkabah mystics such as Akiba ('Paradise Revisited. Part 2', pp. 282-83) does not do justice to Paul's experience. For the rabbi who was stricken (*nipga'*) did not manage to come down in peace; and God intervened in the struggle of Akiba with the angel to leave him. Both these experiences speak contrary to Paul's.

19.   Segal, *Paul the Convert*, p. 35; however, his argument for Paul's belief in

If Paul had thus seen God as revealed in Christ (cf. Gal. 1.15) once more in his ascent, then why did he prefer not to mention it? It seems that Paul's concern here is not so much for what he saw as for what he heard, for he was not prepared to be puffed up by his visions and thus to live on the same level as that of his opponents. Moreover, the things that he saw can hardly be explained and boasted about.

We have evidence in the coptic *Apocalypse of Paul* (second century CE), which describes Paul's heavenly journey after the pattern of Merkabah mystical visions, that 2 Cor. 12.2-4 was interpreted at an early period not only in the light of Ps. 68.19 but particularly in the light of Merkabah mysticism.[20]

Our study thus shows that the heavenly ascent of Paul in 2 Corinthians 12 does contain several features of Merkabah mysticism. If, as Scholem mentions, the esoteric doctrines, *Ma'aseh Merkabah* and *Ma'aseh Bereshit*, were already taught in pharisaic circles in the Second Temple period[21] or even earlier,[22] then why could not Paul, as a Pharisee, have practised Merkabah mysticism?

The Ascension of Isaiah

The Merkabah mystical interest that was current in the first century is also attested by another Jewish work, the *Ascension of Isaiah*, which shows a definite Christian influence in chs. 6–11, which describe Isaiah's throne-vision. According to Box, these chapters, as also 3.13–4.18, reflect the condition of the Church at the end of the first century and therefore can be dated to the late first century CE.[23] The following

'a body-to-body-identification with his heavenly savior' has no ground in any of the Jewish or Christian writings. Cf. Morray-Jones, 'Paradise Revisited. Part 2', pp. 265-92 for the thesis that Paul is describing in 2 Cor. 12 an ascent to heavenly temple and a Merkabah vision of the glorified Christ.

20.   See J.M. Scott, 'The Triumph of God', pp. 260-81, who shows that 2 Cor. 12.2-4 and 2 Cor. 2.14 are mutually interpretative and describe Paul's Merkabah experience, having their common link to the Ps. 67.19 LXX tradition. Cf. above, p. 61.

21.   See Scholem, *Major Trends*, p. 42; Rowland, 'The First Chapter of Ezekiel', pp. xxi-xxiii.

22.   See above, pp. 45, 50-53.

23.   G.H. Box, in R.H. Charles, *The Ascension of Isaiah* (London: SPCK, 1917), pp. ix-xi. Barton, 'Ascension of Isaiah', p. 781, upholds Charles's view that chs. 6–11, being one among the three constituents of *Asc. Isa.*, circulated independently as early as the first century. Even if we accept Knibb's view (M.A. Knibb,

features of Merkabah mysticism in this Jewish–Christian work are noteworthy.[24]

1. Isaiah was taken up through seven heavens by an angel who came down from the seventh heaven. The description that Isaiah's eyes were open although his lips were silent and that the spirit of his body was taken up although his breath remained in him shows that the prophet was in an ecstatic trance (6.11-12),[25] recalling the mystical experience of Nehunya b. Ha-Qanah in his trance (*HR* 15.1–22.2; *Synopse* §§198–236).

2. That the book exhibits an interest in knowing the heavenly world is clear from 6.15, which says that what Isaiah saw was 'not a vision of this world, but of the world that is hidden from man'.

3. The prophet saw a throne in each heaven and the one seated on it was the angel of that particular heaven in all his glory.[26] In each heaven there were angels both on the left and right side of the throne, singing praises to God's glory who is in the seventh heaven (7.17). So great was the glory of the one seated on the throne in every heaven that the visionary attempted to worship the enthroned one in the second heaven but was forbidden by the accompanying angel, because one can worship neither the throne nor the angel, but only him who is in the seventh heaven (7.21).

4. In the seventh heaven, which is the climax of Isaiah's vision, he could see a marvellous light and innumerable angels as well as all the righteous like Adam, Abel and Enoch, who, in their heavenly garments, looked like angels, standing there in great glory (9.6-9). Isaiah could even see God, who was 'standing' and whose glory surpassed that of all others. All the righteous and the angels worshipped him and sang

'Martyrdom and Ascension of Isaiah', *OTP*, II, pp. 143-76 [150]) that the vision of Isaiah belongs to the (early) second century CE, it falls within the period of the composition of John.

24.   For the Merkabah mystical elements detected in *Asc. Isa.*, see Gruenwald, *Merkavah Mysticism*, pp. 57-62.

25.   When his spirit was caught up into heaven, Isaiah could no longer see the men who were standing before him (*Asc. Isa.* 6.10).

26.   In the light of Jewish tradition that the angels cannot fold their legs and sit in heaven (see Gruenwald, *Merkavah Mysticism*, pp. 60, 66-67, esp. nn. 113 and 137; Alexander, 'Family of Caesar', pp. 291-92), we should presume that the glorious angel sitting in each heaven was a righteous man who had been transformed into an angel (cf. 7.22, where the guiding angel informs Isaiah that Isaiah's throne, along with his garments and crown, are set in the seventh heaven).

praises unto him (9.27-29, 41-42). Having been bidden by the accompanying angel, the visionary too joins these heavenly beings in worshipping and singing just as Abraham did in his ascent (*Apoc. Abr.* 17; cf. *1 En.* 71.11). Similarly, the Merkabah mystic joins in the seventh palace with all the heavenly beings singing praise and making music. Isaiah could indeed see the great glory (9.37); however, after seeing once, he could not look upon him afterwards, but he saw the righteous gazing intently upon the glory (9.39).[27]

5. Isaiah saw there Christ Jesus, who is known as the Lord as well as the Son (9.5, 14, 35). It is the Lord who permits the seer to enter into the seventh heaven (9.5). Along with him is the Holy Spirit, who is called 'a second angel' and who too is to be worshipped (9.36). The redemptive work of the Son by his descent to the earth in human form and then ascent back to heaven is revealed to the visionary saying that only after the accomplishment of his mission will the righteous sit on their thrones and wear their crowns (9.12-18).

6. As to Isaiah himself, the glory of his face was being transformed as he went up from heaven to heaven (7.25) until he was transformed into the likeness of the angels (9.30). We have observed above the transformation of the Merkabah visionary into the angelic likeness.[28]

7. The whole vision of Isaiah has an esoteric tone, for he describes his vision at the end only to King Hezekiah, to his son Josab, to the prophets and to the men who had been approved by the Spirit because of their righteous deeds. The secrets of heaven, which had been revealed to Isaiah, are not to be proclaimed to the public (6.16, 17; 11.36-40).

The Heavenly Ascent of Moses

The Exagoge
Meeks has convincingly demonstrated that in the early centuries of Christian era there was among some Jews a mystical preoccupation with the heavenly mysteries and that in the New Testament period Moses was regarded by them as one of the greatest prototypes of the

---

27.   Gruenwald, *Merkavah Mysticism*, p. 62, fails to notice this point, when he concludes that Isaiah could not see the great glory.

28.   Morray-Jones, 'Transformational Mysticism', pp. 11-15, argues that the mystic was transformed into the divine likeness, but most of his arguments only prove the transformation into angelic likeness.

mystic ascent to heaven.[29] By comparing Moses-tradition found in *Memar Marqah* with that found in the Jewish midrash *Gedulat Mosheh*, he concludes that the overlapping traditions and mutual influence of the Samaritan and Jewish *Haggadah* about Moses is the result of the fluid situation in Palestine, perhaps as early as the first century.[30] The tradition of Moses' ascent at Sinai and of his vision of 'a great throne' there goes back to the second century BCE when the *Exagoge* was written by a Jewish poet, Ezekiel. In this text Moses describes his dream thus:

> On Sinai's peak I saw what seemed a throne
> so great in size it touched the clouds of heaven.
> Upon it sat a man of noble mien,
> becrowned, and with a scepter in one hand
> while with the other he did beckon me.
> I made approach and stood before the throne.
> He handed o'er the scepter and he bade
> me mount the throne, and gave to me the crown;
> then he himself withdrew from off the throne.
> I gazed upon the whole earth round about;
> things under it, and high above the skies.
> Then at my feet a multitude of stars
> fell down, and I their number reckoned up.
> They passed by me like armed ranks of men.
> Then I in terror wakened from the dream.[31]

The whole dream describes how Moses will become God's vicegerent in the course of his vision of a 'man' on the throne. The Greek word φῶς used for the 'man' seems to suggest that the enthroned human figure was God, who gave to Moses his own throne and sceptre.[32] This recalls the Merkabah vision of Ezekiel 1; Daniel 7; *1 Enoch* 37–71; *T. Levi* 3–5; *2 Enoch* 22-33. As Van der Horst rightly argues, Ezekiel the dramatist found the literary form of a Merkabah vision quite suitable to express the idea of Moses as God's vicegerent. That Moses was

29.   See above, pp. 38-40.
30.   Meeks, *Prophet-King*, pp. 241-57.
31.   R.G. Robertson's translation (see his 'Ezekiel the Tragedian', *OTP*, II, pp. 803-19 [811-12]). See Meeks, *Prophet-King*, p. 148 n. 1 for the Greek rendering of the dream and its interpretation.
32.   See Meeks, *Prophet-King*, p. 148. In the Old Testament God and his words are identified as light (Pss. 36.10; 119.105, 130).

not considered as equal with God in glory is evident from Sir. 45.2: 'He made him equal in glory to the holy ones.'

The Liber Antiquitatum Biblicarum *(Pseudo-Philo)*
Another first-century Jewish work, the *Liber Antiquitatum Biblicarum* (*LAB*), which was wrongly ascribed to Philo,[33] makes reference to the ascent of Moses. It asserts that Moses, just before his death, had ascended to Mt Oreb and had a vision of the cosmos's secrets with a revelation of what measure of time has passed by and what remains before the last things (*LAB* 19.14-16). God reveals the secret in the words:

> Et dixit ad eum Dominus: ISTIC MEL, APEX MAGNUS, MOMENTI PLENI-TUDO, ET CIATI GUTTA, ET OMNIA complevit tempus. Quatuor enim semis transierunt, et duo semis supersunt (*LAB* 19.15).[34]

The phrase 'istic mel, apex magnus' is emended by M.R. James as 'stigma et apex manus' and thus his English translation reads:

> And the Lord said to him [i.e. Moses]: An instant, the topmost part of a hand, the fullness of a moment, and the drop of a cup. And the time hath fulfilled all. For $4\frac{1}{2}$ have passed by, and $2\frac{1}{2}$ remain.[35]

Wadsworth, however, rejects James's emendation and treats the Latin version of *LAB* 19.15 as damaged. He argues that the words 'istic mel, apex magnus' denote the 'mystical' (i.e. secret) name of Moses, Melchi/Melchiel, which has been used in association with the 'mystical' (i.e. hidden) message of God regarding the end-time and Moses' final glorification. He therefore recovers the reading as 'istic Mel[chiel Pontif] ex magnus', that is, 'This, O Melchiel, great priest, is but the turning of a balance, the drop of a cup'.[36] Two sides of the 'mystical' phenomenon

33. After a brief discussion on the date of the composition of *LAB*, Schürer concludes, 'All in all, a first century A.D. date is *opinio communis*', although it is impossible to state categorically whether it belongs to pre- or post-70 (Schürer, *Jewish People*, III.1, p. 329). See also M. Wadsworth, 'A New Pseudo-Philo', *JJS* 29 (1978), pp. 186-91 (188), and D.J. Harrington, 'Pseudo-Philo', *OTP*, II, pp. 297-377 (299), who argue for the first century as the probable date of the composition of *LAB*.

34. See M. Wadsworth, 'The Death of Moses and the Riddle of the End of Time in Pseudo-Philo', *JJS* 28 (1977), pp. 12-19 (14).

35. See M.R. James, *The Biblical Antiquities of Philo* (London: SPCK, 1917), p. 131; Harrington, 'Pseudo-Philo', p. 328 n. s.

36. See Wadsworth, 'Death of Moses', pp. 15-17. He also cites Goodenough,

may be noticed here: the revelation of the cosmological secrets to Moses, and God's bestowal of a secret name on him in his ascent to Mt Oreb before he was finally glorified.

The elements of Merkabah mysticism can be perceived in *LAB* in the vision given to Cenez, who, in his ecstatic state saw things unknown to him. James comments that the things that Cenez saw clearly resemble those that were seen by the prophet Ezekiel.[37] References to the flames (*LAB* 28.7), light (28.8), the forms of men walking to and fro (28.8 = Ezek. 1.5-10), a voice (28.8), and the man 'Adam', whose voice was heard (28.9—James's translation) are unmistakable indications of the influence of Ezekiel 1. Thus the work of Pseudo-Philo provides one more piece of evidence for the existence of the Merkabah-like visions in the first century CE.

Conclusions

Our investigation of three different traditions proves beyond doubt that the Merkabah mysticism had been known and practised in the first century of our era. These writings show that the major aspect of mysticism is an ascent to heaven to encounter God.

Paul, as a Jew, was familiar with Merkabah mysticism and most probably he himself was taken up to the third heaven/Paradise, where, as our study shows, he could have seen Christ, the revelation of God. The mystical interest of Christians is also reflected in *Ascension of Isaiah*, a Jewish work transformed by Christian adaptation in describing the heavenly visions of Isaiah. *Ascension of Isaiah* clearly mentions that Isaiah saw Christ in his glory and particularly his descent and ascent.

Meeks's study and the *LAB* indicate that the mystical tradition centred on Moses' ascent to God was alive in some Jewish circles. This is expressed in the *Exagoge* by distinctive use of the literary form of Merkabah visions. The Merkabah-like vision of Cenez, described in *LAB* 28, is another indication for the existence of the mystical practice based on Ezekiel's chariot vision.

who suggests that there was a tradition of a mystical Moses called Melchi, who exercised a priestly, mediating function in heaven and that his name had some relation to Melchizedek.

37.   James, *Biblical Antiquities*, p. 165 n. 6.

The practice of Merkabah mysticism in the first century is further confirmed by some of the apocalyptic writings of that period, to a study of which we now turn.

Chapter 7

THE APOCALYPTIC LITERATURE OF THE LATE FIRST CENTURY

Both apocalypticism and Merkabah mysticism share in common the ideas of an ascent to heaven, angels, and the revelation of the heavenly realm, though with different emphases. Therefore scholars have increasingly realized the value of apocalyptic to the study of Merkabah mysticism. Morray-Jones maintains that the vision of God's *kabod*, including the mystical practice of 'heavenly ascents' was inherited from apocalyptic circles,[1] although in apocalyptic the vision of God is nowhere regarded as an unqualified goal to be pursued as it is in Merkabah mysticism.[2] Gruenwald has successfully demonstrated the Merkabah mystical elements from some of the apocalyptic writings.[3] However, as we have indicated above, his study is inadequate and needs further exploration.[4] In this chapter, therefore, I will attempt to trace the Merkabah mystical aspects from six of the apocalyptic books usually thought to have been written in the late first century. This, in turn, will throw light on the extent to which Merkabah mysticism was in practice at the time of John.

1.   Morray-Jones, 'Paradise Revisited. Part 1', p. 184.
2.   See Michaelis, 'ὁράω', p. 339. Other points of different emphasis are brought out by Alexander ('3 [Hebrew Apocalypse of] Enoch', p. 235), according to whom the Merkabah texts concentrate more on the mysteries of heaven and on the description of God's throne than on the eschatological themes such as the last judgment, the resurrection of the dead, the messianic kingdom, and the world to come, all of which are the concerns of apocalyptic. He also observes that cosmology bulks larger in apocalyptic than in Merkabah mysticism, whereas the theurgic element is much more explicit in Merkabah mysticism than in the apocalyptic.
3.   Gruenwald, *Merkavah Mysticism*, pp. 29-72.
4.   See above, p. 54.

The Similitudes of Enoch (1 Enoch 37–71)[5]

1 Enoch 39

1 Enoch 39 is the first passage in the *Similitudes of Enoch* to describe Enoch's heavenly ascent, a major component of Merkabah mysticism. Enoch was carried off from the earth by whirlwinds and was set 'into the ultimate ends of the heavens' (39.3), whence he saw the faithful Israel dwelling with the holy angels (vv. 4 and 5), shining like the light of fire and praising the name of the Lord of the Spirits (vv. 6b-7). The angelic hymn is given by using terms from Isa. 6.3 and Ezek. 3.2 (MT). That Enoch is caught up in a Merkabah vision is confirmed by the following chapter (40.1-2), which portrays a multitude of angels standing before the 'glory of the Lord of the Spirits' (cf. Dan. 7.10). Enoch himself, in the course of his vision, blessed and praised the Lord and his face was 'transformed' at the sight of the heavenly realm (vv. 9-14). The mystic's participation in the heavenly hymn and his transformation to a heavenly being, as we have seen, is the result of a Merkabah mystical vision.

While it is implicit that Enoch had a vision of the Lord of the Spirits, it is explicit that he could see 'the Elect One' (39.6a). In the *Similitudes*, the Elect One is viewed not only in relation to virtue, 'righteousness' (39.6; 53.6), but also as the one who sits on the Throne of Glory to receive blessings and to render judgment (45.3; 51.3; 55.4; 61.8). The Elect One is identified with the Son of Man (48.6), who sits on the Throne of Glory (62.3; 68.29) and at least once he is mentioned on a par with the Messiah (52.4-9). His messianic function (ch. 49) echoes that of the figure in Isa. 11.5 and 42.1. The presence of a messianic figure is not foreign to the Merkabah tradition found in the *Hekhalot* literature (cf. *3 En.* 45).[6]

5. There is a consensus among scholars that the *Similitudes* belongs to the first century CE; see R.H. Charles, *The Book of Enoch or 1 Enoch* (Oxford: Clarendon Press, 1893), pp. 107-108; 113-15; J.H. Charlesworth, *The Pseudepigrapha and Modern Research With A Supplement* (Chico, CA: Scholars Press, 1981), p. 98; E. Isaac, '1 (Ethiopic Apocalypse of) Enoch', *OTP*, I, pp. 5-89 (7); A.Y. Collins, 'The "Son of Man" Tradition and the Book of Revelation', in J.H. Charlesworth (ed.), *The Messiah: Developments in Earliest Judaism and Christianity* (Minneapolis: Fortress Press, 1992), pp. 536-68 (564).

6. See Gruenwald, *Merkavah Mysticism*, pp. 38-39.

1 Enoch 47–48

The Merkabah vision is repeated to Enoch in an eschatological setting
(ch. 47). The seer had a vision of God, who is described as the ancient
of days,[7] sitting upon the throne of his glory and of his escorts standing
before him (47.3; cf. also 60.2-3). The books of the living were opened
before him and the righteous ones were filled with joy, because their
prayers were answered. The whole scene shows traces of influence of
the judgment scene in Daniel 7, indicating that Merkabah visions are
often closely tied up with the divine act of judgment. The man-like
figure was given a name and as God's Messiah he had been concealed
in his presence (48.2-7). I will discuss this figure below.

1 Enoch 71

Another passage that reflects Merkabah mystical influence is ch. 71, a
passage that poses textual problems. Gruenwald believes that *1 Enoch*
71 was added by the editor(s) as an appendix to the book of *Similitudes*,
since, for him, it is impossible for the author to describe Enoch's translation again in ch. 71 once he mentioned it in ch. 70.[8] However, it is
more likely that both chs. 70 and 71 describe in two stages the same
ascension experience of Enoch, at first to the place of the righteous
(possibly the Paradise) and then to the highest heavens. Therefore
ch. 71 may be integral to the *Book of Similitudes*.[9] The throne-vision
described in ch. 71 shows several features of Merkabah mysticism.

A Vision of God by Ascent to Heaven. Enoch ascended into the heavens
and saw God, the Head of Days, who existed with numerous angels and
archangels (71.1, 10-14). In all other visions, notably in *1 Enoch* 14,
God is portrayed as seated on the throne, and in 71.7-17 there is no
such clear picture, but it is implied in the reference to 'the Throne of
Glory' (v. 7) that is watched over by the heavenly beings. This implicit
reference may be due to the author's intention to emphasize the
dwelling of God with the multitude of angels and the Son of Man. By

7.   See Sparks (ed.), *The Apocryphal Old Testament*, p. 228 n.4.
8.   Gruenwald, *Merkavah Mysticism*, pp. 42-43.
9.   See M. Black, 'The Eschatology of the Similitudes of Enoch', *JTS* 3
(1952), pp. 1-10. Charles, *1 Enoch* (1893), pp. 183-84, who argued in his first edition of his commentary on *1 En.* that ch. 71 is a later addition, became convinced in
1912 that it belongs to the *Book of Similitudes*—see R.H. Charles, *The Book of
Enoch or 1 Enoch* (Oxford: Clarendon Press, 2nd edn, 1912), p. 142.

this time the tradition concerning the throne of God must have become so familiar that the author presumes that his readers will understand the expression, 'the Throne of His Glory'. His appearance, as in Dan. 7.9, shows human or even angelic form, for his head is described as white and pure like wool and his garment as indescribable (v. 10). The 'stream of fire' of Dan. 7.10 is replaced by the 'rivers full of living fire' or 'a circle of fire' in *1 En.* 71.6, recalling *Hekhalot* mysticism.

The Angels. On arrival into the heavens, Enoch at first saw the angels, walking upon the flames of fire. Their garments were white and the light of their faces looked like snow (vv. 1-2). The archangel, Michael, led Enoch into the heavenly and cosmological secrets until he took him up in the highest heaven (vv. 3-5). The angels were encircling and guarding the Throne of Glory and the house made up of crystals (vv. 7-13; cf. Ezek. 1.22). The angelic function of 'going in and out of' the house may imply the divine link between God and the universe established through the angels. If so, we have here a conceptual parallel with the vision of Jacob in Gen. 28.12-13, a passage that, according to Odeberg, gave rise to mystical speculation in Jewish circles, long before the Fourth Evangelist.[10]

The Visionary. Segal argues that the heavenly journey taken by Enoch's name, rather than by his soul (*1 En.* 70–71), reflects 'a level of mystical speculation that predates the importation of the platonic notion of a soul'.[11] Enoch fell upon his face before God with trembling and his spirit was transformed (v. 11). He began to praise and glorify God with a loud voice (cf. *Apoc. Abr.* 17 for the Merkabah hymn sung by the adept himself). The expressions, 'my spirit passed out of sight' in v. 1 and 'he carried off my spirit' in v. 5 are understood as referring to Enoch's translation into the heavenly realm.[12] Literally, however, they mean that his spirit was concealed, or vanished, or became extinguished.[13] Does this mean in any way that Enoch was deified before the face of God?[14] The passage does not seem to suggest this. If he had lost

10.   Odeberg, *Fourth Gospel*, pp. 33-40.
11.   Segal, *Paul the Convert*, p. 47.
12.   See M. Black, *The Book of Enoch or 1 Enoch* (Leiden: E.J. Brill, 1985), pp. 67, 251.
13.   See Isaac, '1 (Ethiopic Apocalypse of) Enoch', p. 49 nn. 71a and 71f.
14.   See Segal, *Paul the Convert*, pp. 45-46, who argues that exemplary men,

his identity, then the features of his further vision (vv. 5-17) and the transformation of his spirit in v. 11 will hold little sense. There would have been no need for the angel's promise to Enoch at the end of the vision (vv. 14-17).

The Son of Man. There is, however, one important feature that suggests to scholars such as Segal Enoch's merging with the divine. That is the use of the name 'Son of Man' in ch. 71. On the basis of the expression 'You are the Son of Man' in a verse that poses textual problems[15] and uncertain translation (*1 En.* 71.14), scholars have argued that Enoch was transformed into a heavenly figure, the Son of Man.[16] However, Segal has not persuasively proved the idea of deification in this passage. What he shows, instead, is the transformation of the adept into the angelic vicegerent of God.[17] Strictly speaking, both Casey and Segal could not successfully prove the deification/angelification of Enoch. They could only show that the Son of Man was not viewed as a title by first-century Jews. There are several factors that argue against the theory of deification.

First, it is not certain, as Segal himself notes,[18] whether *1 Enoch* 70–71 retells Enoch's ascent at the time of his earthly life or at the end of his life. If the ascent had taken place during his earthly life, as it seems so, then the idea of apotheosis can hardly be deduced from *1 Enoch* 71. Secondly, while in the second parable (46.3) the Son of Man is described as the author of righteousness, in 71.14-17 Enoch is

---

like Enoch in the *Similitudes*, can ascend to divinity by identification with or transformation into the enthroned figure.

15.   Isaac ('1 [Ethiopic Apocalypse of] Enoch', p. 50 n. 71) observes that one of the Ethiopic MSS ends ch. 71 in v. 12a and that the scribe has transposed to this place 78.8b–82.20. Appel argued that the passage in which the heavenly Son of Man had originally been mentioned in 71.13 has now been lost and therefore that later scribes made changes in the text to apply it to Enoch—see Charles, *1 Enoch* (1912), p. 144. In the absence of the original text of the *Book of Similitudes* it is difficult to evaluate any suggestion regarding the text.

16.   See Segal, *Paul the Convert*, pp. 45-46; M. Casey, *Son of Man: The Interpretation and Influence of Daniel 7* (London: SPCK, 1979), pp. 102-107; *idem*, 'The Use of the Term "Son of Man" in the Similitudes of Enoch', *JSJ* 7 (1976), pp. 11-29; cf. C. Rowland, *The Open Heaven: A Study of Apocalyptic in Judaism and Early Christianity* (London: SPCK, 1982), pp. 106-107.

17.   Segal, *Paul the Convert*, pp. 46-47.

18.   Segal, *Paul the Convert*, p. 47.

portrayed as the one who is governed by righteousness (cf. 71.16: 'righteousness never forsakes you'). In the third parable (60.10) Enoch is addressed as 'Son of Man' by the angel and the same vocative sense (cf. Isaac's translation) fits well also in 71.14. Thirdly, 46.1 clearly points to another person, who was with God and whose face looked both like a man and an angel and the expression 'This Son of Man, whom you have seen' (46.4) definitely differentiates him from the seer, Enoch. Therefore the expression 'Son of Man' in 71.14 does not prove Enoch's transformation into a divine or messianic figure. Who, then, is this Son of Man?

We have already noticed that the Son of Man in the *Similitudes* is the Elect One, the Messiah, who renders judgment on behalf of God by sitting on the Throne of Glory. The same idea is repeated in *1 Enoch* 48. He removes the mighty ones from their thrones and crushes the sinners (cf. 48.2, 6). The whole description in *1 Enoch* 46–48 is based on Dan. 7.9 and 13, a text that was used in some Merkabah mystical circles in the early second century to see God in his two manifestations, and which alerted the rabbis to the danger of what Segal calls the 'Two Powers in Heaven heresy'.[19]

God grants the Son of Man not only to sit on the Throne of Glory but also to be the object of worship for the rulers (62.3-10). His pre-existence is envisaged in his concealment in the presence of God's power from the beginning (62.7) and therefore he does not seem to be a man exalted to heaven.[20] Does the enthroned Son of Man denote 'a transference of the Throne of Glory from God to another figure', as Rowland has argued?[21] It does not seem to be a transference of God's throne to the Son of Man, for he is described as the one who was with God (46.1) or in the place where God was sitting (47.3–48.1); it was while the Lord of the Spirits was sitting upon the throne of his glory (62.2)[22] that the Son of Man sits on the throne to render judgment (62.5-16). It is

19.   See Segal, *Two Powers in Heaven: Early Rabbinic Reports about Christianity and Gnosticism* (Leiden: E.J. Brill, 1977), pp. 33-73; cf. below pp. 147-49. It should be noted that the Son of Man in the *Similitudes* is not 'one like a son of man', as we have it in Dan. 7.13.

20.   Against Rowland, *Open Heaven*, p. 104.

21.   Rowland, *Open Heaven*, p. 105.

22.   This reading is attested by all the known MSS (see Isaac, '1 [Ethiopic Apocalypse of] Enoch', p. 43 n. 62c); therefore it is a hasty conclusion, drawn by Rowland, *Open Heaven*, p. 105, that the title Lord of Spirits is never linked with the throne.

more likely that there is a delegation of power from God to the heavenly Son of Man to act as His vicegerent.[23]

Summary

Our study of the *Similitudes*, in retrospect, shows that, as early as the first century, there was a tradition in Judaism that righteous men could ascend to the highest heaven to see God on the throne. God is described primarily as the Head of Days or as the Lord of Spirits, whose appearance was more like a heavenly being, possibly angelic, with wings, head and garment. The angels were praising God and the Elect One and were guarding his throne. In particular, there were four chief angels, who were with God, and one of whom (Michael) revealed the cosmological secrets to Enoch. Thus one can see a fusion of two traditions in the *Similitudes*: apocalyptic and 'mystical'. Another individual appears in the throne-vision as the one who was with God and to whom God had granted to accept blessings and worship from kings and rulers. He seems to be a heavenly figure, because his face was like that of a human being and his countenance was full of grace like that of an angel. He is called the Son of Man, the pre-existent Messiah and God's vicegerent, who, under God's authority, will exercise justice by sitting on the Throne of Glory.

The Slavonic Book of Enoch (2 Enoch)

A major portion of the *Slavonic Book of Enoch* (*2 Enoch*) describes the ascent of Enoch through seven heavens finally to see the face of God and then his descent to earth for a period so that he might communicate the divine revelation to his generation. *2 Enoch* is usually dated to the late first century CE, although those, who find a Hebrew or Aramaic original, argue for a date earlier than 70 CE.[24] Therefore it reflects the

---

23.   My own observations here are confirmed by J.J. Collins, 'The Son of Man in First Century Judaism', *NTS* 38 (1992), pp. 448-66 (451-59), who argues that in *1 En.* 71.14 Enoch is not at all identified with the 'Son of Man' of his visions.

24.   Both Meshchersky and Sokolov have argued for a Hebrew version as underlying the Greek version of *2 Enoch*. This theory is accepted by Andersen because of the Semitisms in the text (F.I. Andersen, '2 [Slavonic Apocalypse of] Enoch', *OTP*, I, pp. 91-213 [94]). N. Schmidt, 'The Two-Recensions of Slavonic Enoch', *JAOS* 41 (1921), pp. 307-12, argues that the short recension is Palestinian. Therefore a date prior to 70 is possible (see Charlesworth, *Modern Research*, p. 104).

beliefs and practices of late-first-century Judaism, which could have formed a part of the background to the Gospel of John.

The Heavenly Ascent

2 En. 1a.1-6 can be viewed as a summary of *2 Enoch* 1–23: the Lord took Enoch to heaven in order to show him the sovereignty of God on the throne, who is surrounded by the heavenly armies and immeasurably shining light. Enoch's ascent to heaven took place by the guidance of the two angels who appeared to Enoch in human form (*2 En.* 1.3-5; cf. 19.1). They led him through seven heavens until he saw God at a distance in the seventh heaven. The entourage of two angels in Enoch's heavenly journey reflects the idea expressed in *HR* 17 (*Synopse* §§206–13) of the two angels who carry the Merkabah mystic from one palace to another. Even the concept of seven heavens was not foreign to the people of the first century (cf. *Apoc. Abr.* 19). Gruenwald has indicated that this concept has parallels not only in Jewish apocalyptic literature, but also in later Jewish mystical and cosmological writings.[25]

The Angels

The angels appear in *2 Enoch* primarily as ministering beings. Almost in all the seven heavens Enoch could see numerous angels assigned to different functions. Except in the second and fifth heavens, where there were rebellious and evil angels (chs. 7 and 18), in all other heavens the angels were, as 'armed troops', singing praises to God (chs. 17 and 19) and worshipping him (8.8 in both J and A). This is also true with the band of heavenly armies, which consisted of angels and archangels, assembled before the enthroned Lord (chs. 20 and 21 in both J and A).[26] The two angels who took Enoch up to heaven brought and placed him at the edge of the seventh heaven (21.2), whence the archangel (in J only) Gabriel carried and placed him in front of the face of the Lord (21.3–22.7). While Michael, the Lord's greatest archangel, anointed Enoch with oil and exchanged his clothes for the clothes of glory (22.6), another archangel, Vereveil, supplied Enoch with books and pen, and gave instruction in the deeds of the Lord in all his creation so that Enoch could write them down. The idea of the ministering angels,

25. Gruenwald, *Merkavah Mysticism*, p. 49 n. 72.
26. Cf. *T. Levi* 3.3, which places the heavenly armies in the second heaven; 4Q405 20.2-21-22.13-14 describe the angels as divided into 'mustered troops' and 1QM 3.1-6 as the 'eschatological troops for battle'.

who are divided into armies and camps according to their duties, occurs not merely in the *Hekhalot* texts, but also in the Qumran texts, which we have examined.[27]

Cosmology

The angelology in *2 Enoch* is linked with the cosmic dimension of the heavenly vision. In the first heaven Enoch could visualize the angels who govern the stars and the heavenly 'combinations' of the planets (ch. 4) and who guard the treasuries of the snow and the dew (chs. 5 and 6). The angels in the fourth heaven were going in front of the sun's chariot (11.4; J adds that the angels, having six wings, were in flaming fire), implying that they functioned as guides to the orderly movements of the luminaries. We should note that the teaching of the creation of the world, including the movements of the sun and the moon (chs. 11–17; 23–32; major parts of ch. 30 and chs. 31–32, however, are absent in A), always focuses on God and His wisdom in creating the world. The whole account of creation is full of divine secrets, which God will reveal only to the chosen ones (24.2-3). Enoch's heavenly journey was thus a tour of cosmic phenomena. This form of esoteric teaching falls in line with the *Ma'aseh Bereshit*, a study of which will lead one to know God, the 'hidden truth' behind creation. Gruenwald notices this fact when he states that the description of the cosmological, or astronomical, phenomena in *2 Enoch* always finds a basic interest in theosophical matters. In other words, everything in heaven ultimately leads the visionary to perceive the wisdom and lordship of God and thus the idea of seven heavens alludes to Merkabah mysticism.[28]

Paradise (פרדס)

2 Enoch locates Paradise in the third heaven, when it records that Enoch was brought up to the third heaven and placed in the midst of Paradise, an inconceivably pleasant and productive garden (8.1-2),

27. See H. Odeberg, *3 Enoch or the Hebrew Book of Enoch* (New York: Ktav, repr. 1973), I, pp. 147-70, for the extensive study of Angelology in *3 Enoch*. Cf. also M.A. Morgan (trans.), *Sepher Ha-Razim: The Book of the Mysteries* (Chico, CA: Scholars Press, 1983).

28. See above, pp. 83, 110-11. Gruenwald, *Merkavah Mysticism*, p. 49. Tabor, *Things Unutterable*, p. 96, states that there seems to be a line of 'theosophic' tradition and practice running from the oldest Enoch material through later *Hekhalot* literature.

prepared for the righteous as a place of reward (ch. 9) as well as the shelter of an eternal residence (65.10). Although *2 Enoch* does not provide direct evidence of the belief that Paradise was the dwelling-place of God whence he appeared to the visionary, it does not exclude the possibility of seeing God there, for in this garden the Lord takes a walk and finds rest under the tree of life (8.3).[29]

The Paradise-scene exhibits the presence of the angels (300 in number, according to J), who not only guard Paradise, but also worship God by singing unceasingly (*2 En.* 8.8; cf. chs. 17, 18 and particularly 20.3, 4 in J). We have already noticed in the Merkabah texts preserved in Qumran that the angelic hymn is an integral part of the throne-vision. *HR* 4 contains the hymns sung by the angels and even by the throne itself in praise of God. This 'mystical' tradition is reflected in *2 Enoch* and therefore, as Gruenwald rightly maintains, *2 Enoch* is already connected with the Merkabah lore.[30]

The Vision of God on the Throne

The key passage for our understanding of Merkabah mystical experience is chs. 20–39. It is in the seventh heaven that Enoch had a direct vision of God on the throne and this occurred to him in two phases: at first from a distance (20.3) and then closely in front of the face of the Lord (22.5-7). According to J, the throne of God is an 'exceedingly high throne' (20.3) and in A it is 'many-eyed and immovable' (1a.4). It is also 'the supremely great throne', not made by hands (22.2 both in A and J). This echoes Ezekiel 1, which describes the wheels of the throne-chariot as being full of eyes. Before seeing the Lord, however, Enoch saw a 'great light' with all the fiery armies of angels and archangels (20.1), which exhibits the biblical tradition that fire/light is the major component in divine manifestation (Exod. 19.18; Ezek. 1.4, 13, 27; and the MT of Ezek. 8.2 uses the word 'fire' in lieu of 'man' to denote the revelation of God). We have already observed that in the Merkabah mystical tradition fire/light plays a primary role. According to the *Hekhalot* texts, the object of the vision in the seventh palace is the appearance of God on the throne in human-like form and of fire/light.

29.   Even Gruenwald, *Merkavah Mysticism*, p. 50, who maintains that the word 'Paradise' in *2 En.* is not a *terminus technicus* for theosophical speculations, perceives a technical change in this direction in its use in 2 Cor. 12. He, however, supposes that 2 Cor. was written after *2 En.* was written, which is hard to maintain.

30.   Gruenwald, *Merkavah Mysticism*, p. 50.

The second phase of Enoch's vision of God was direct and definite (21.3–22.8). It focuses on God's face, which appeared strong, very glorious and terrible (22.1-2). The phrase 'the face of the Lord', which replaces Ezekiel's 'the glory of the Lord', occurs in this small passage seven times and it is said that the Lord, with his mouth, called Enoch (22.5). If we accept 'the clothes of my glory' as a possible original reading in 22.8, as Charles has maintained (but Vaillant gives *des vêtements de ma glorio* as a secondary reading), then it means 'the garments of God'[31] with which Enoch was clothed. In brief, Enoch was able to see God in human or angelic form. Although these references, in particular 39.6 ('I have seen the extent of the Lord, without measure and without analogy, who has no end'; cf. Vaillant's edition), echo the *Shi'ur Qomah* tradition, it would be hasty to conclude with Gruenwald that *2 En.* 39.6 may contain the first reference to the *Shi'ur Qomah* of God,[32] for whereas the *Shi'ur Qomah* is mainly concerned with the measurement of God's body, the Enoch passage is concerned with the *measureless* extent of God's body. The emphasis seems to be on God's anthropophany or angelophany as seen by the 'mystic'.

The Transformation and the Commissioning of Enoch

Both before and after seeing God, Enoch was terrified and he trembled (20.1; 21.2; cf. *1 En.* 14.13, 14, 24. However, in Isa. 6.5 and Ezek. 1.28 the visionary became terrified only after seeing God). His fall on his face (21.2; 22.4), his cry, 'Woe to me, my soul has departed from me from fear', and his search for the two angels for support (21.4) all point not merely to the frail nature of human beings before God, but also to the danger involved in seeing God face to face.[33] Despite the visionary's weakness and vulnerability, the fact that he was transformed into one of the heavenly beings remains a significant feature in the throne-vision of Enoch. He attains the prestigious position of standing before the face of the Lord forever (22.7; 36.3). His earthly garment was removed before he was anointed with the holy oil and clothed with the

31.   R.H. Charles, *The Book of the Secrets of Enoch* (Oxford: Clarendon Press, 1896), p. 28.

32.   See Gruenwald, *Merkavah Mysticism*, p. 213; cf. Rowland, *Open Heaven*, p. 85.

33.   See I. Chernus, 'Visions of God in Merkabah Mysticism', *JSJ* 13 (1982), pp. 123-46, for the idea of the possibility of seeing God in Merkabah mysticism under certain conditions and the dangers involved in such a vision.

clothes of God's glory (cf. A22.8 with J22.8), which, in the apocalyptic tradition, signify the eschatological clothes given to the righteous when they rise to the heavenly realm from the earth (cf. *1 En.* 62.15; 108.12; Rev. 3.4, 5, 18; 4.4; 6.11; 7.9, 13, 14; *4 Ezra* 2.39, 45; *Asc. Isa.* 9.9).

What kind of transformation was this? Does it imply the 'spiritualized' condition of the body, as Andersen maintains?[34] Is it apotheosis or apo-angelosis? The internal evidence seems to suggest the latter, for 22.10b states that Enoch, without any observable difference, became like one of the 'glorious ones', that is, the angelic beings (cf. 22.7), who themselves did obeisance to the Lord. The clothing of Enoch with the clothes of God's glory, therefore, should be viewed as his transformation into the glory of the angelic beings. In this light, Morray-Jones's thesis, as we have already noted, that the goal of the Jewish mystical endeavour is the 'transformation into the divine image or likeness' needs to be modified as the 'transformation into the likeness of the angelic beings'.[35] A tradition that was absorbed into *3 Enoch* 4–15 describes Enoch's final transformation into the angel Metatron, who himself, by bearing the very name of God, was occupying God's throne. We can infer that a similar tradition is already found in a first-century text such as *2 Enoch*.[36]

After Enoch was transformed into a heavenly/angelic being, the secrets of creation, which had been hidden even from the angels, were revealed to him (24.2, 3). The one who was initiated into these mysteries was commissioned by God to go down to earth in order to proclaim to his sons and his generation all that God had revealed to him from the lowest heaven up to God's throne (ch. 33). Enoch is given charge to perform this task on earth for 30 days and then to be taken back to remain in front of his face forever (ch. 36). The idea of the sending of divine agency was not new in the Jewish mystical tradition of the pre-Christian period (cf. also the throne-visions in Ezek. 1–2 and Isa. 6).

There is little doubt that the factors that we have examined above became central in the 'mystical' thinking of the leading Jewish rabbis

34.   See Andersen, '2 (Slavonic Apocalypse of) Enoch', p. 139 n. 22p.

35.   See Morray-Jones, 'Transformational Mysticism', p. 15; cf. above, p. 111 n. 28.

36.   P.S. Alexander, 'The Historical Setting of the Hebrew Book of Enoch', *JJS* 28 (1977), pp. 156-80 (160), argues that *2 En.* 22.8 is one of the texts that possibly provides a background to *3 En.* 3–15 and that there exists a historical link between the *Hekhalot* mystics and the circles that generated the Enoch tradition.

in Palestine. There is every reason, therefore, to suggest that Merkabah mysticism was integral to at least some important strands of first-century Jewish apocalyptic.

The Fourth Book of Ezra

Another important Jewish apocalyptic document, which is worth investigating for an understanding of the 'mystical' practice in first-century Judaism is the fourth book of Ezra. The chronological reference, 'In the thirtieth year after the destruction of our city' (3.1), shows that *4 Ezra* could have been composed about 100 CE. Box maintains that the eagle-vision (chs. 11–12) might have been composed either in the reign of Domitian (80–96 CE) or in the reign of Vespasian (69–79 CE) and that the 'Son of Man' vision (ch. 13) sometime before 70 CE.[37] The consensus is that *4 Ezra* was composed in the last decades of the first century CE,[38] which roughly coincides with the time when John emerged in written form.

Does 4 Ezra *Deny an Ascent to Heaven?*
Arguing that the last phrase of *4 Ezra* 4.8 should be read as 'I have not entered paradise', M.E. Stone suggests that this verse seems to deny the possibility of 'entering פרדס' to acquire a special knowledge from heaven, as it was claimed by the Jewish mystical tradition.[39] According to him, the absence of heavenly journeys, visions of the Throne of Glory, astronomical speculations and the like all seem to reflect the rejection of an esoteric and speculative knowledge.[40] Although Stone seems to accept the existence of the Merkabah type of mystical tradition at the time when *4 Ezra* was composed, his view that this apocalyptic book possibly rejects esoteric and speculative knowledge is to be questioned.

First of all Stone bases his view on comparatively later versions such

---

37.   See G.H. Box, *The Ezra-Apocalypse* (London: Pitman, 1912), pp. xxviii-xxxiii, 249, 286. J.M. Myers, *I and II Esdras* (AB; New York: Doubleday, 1974), pp. 129-30, holds that the implicit question posed in *4 Ezra* 3.20 as to why the evil heart is allowed to remain in man so that the law had no effect on his transformation was the besetting problem of first-century rabbis.

38.   See Charlesworth, *Modern Research*, p. 112.

39.   M.E. Stone, 'Paradise in 4 Ezra iv:8 and vii:36, viii:52', *JJS* 17 (1966), pp. 85-88.

40.   Stone, 'Paradise', p. 88.

as Armenian, Ethiopic (only two MSS), Latin, etc., ignoring the possibility that a Hebrew or Aramaic *Vorlage* may be behind them.[41] Metzger translates the same phrase in 4.8 as: 'Neither did I ever ascend into heaven'[42] and this does not prove in any way that *4 Ezra* opposes the heavenly ascent or any other forms of mystical speculation; it only shows the impossibility of ascending to heaven or entering the Paradise in human strength. One can see, however, several allusions in *4 Ezra* to heavenly journeys. For instance, the angelic guide and interpretation are mentioned in the narrative of dream visions. Reference to God's throne and glory is found in Ezra's prayer before he was taken up to heaven (8.19-22; cf. 14.49-50 in Syriac, which speaks of Ezra's ascent to heaven at the end of his mission). God's dwelling-place is described as the 'upper chambers in the air' (8.20). The plural form 'upper chambers' does not seem to mean the upper part of the two-storeyed world, as Myers has suggested,[43] but the heavenly palaces,[44] which became the focal point of contemplation in *Hekhalot* literature. God's throne and glory are placed in apposition and both are beyond human comprehension (8.21). Before the glory of the Lord stand the hosts of angels, who are changed to wind and fire in subjection to God's command (8.22). The heavenly picture one gets here recalls the throne-theophany of Ezekiel 1, 1 Kings 22, Isaiah 6, and *1 Enoch* 14. Though no particular heavenly vision is mentioned, the ideas of 'throne', 'glory' and 'angels' have been used as though the author possessed first-hand knowledge of the heavenly world. Therefore Stone's argument that *4 Ezra* rejects an ascent-motif is unacceptable.

The idea of the translation of the seer too is not absent in *4 Ezra*. The

41. H. Gunkel, B. Violet and G.H. Box, following J. Wellhausen, have argued for an Hebrew original—see Box, *Ezra-Apocalypse*, pp. xiii-xx; M. Dean-Otting, *Heavenly Journeys: A Study of the Motif in Hellenistic Jewish Literature* (JU, 8; Frankfurt: Peter Lang, 1984), p. 240 and p. 259 nn. 32, 33. Cf. B.M. Metzger, 'The Fourth Book of Ezra', *OTP*, I, pp. 517-59 (519-20). L. Gry has argued for an Aramaic original—see Dean-Otting, *Heavenly Journeys*, p. 259 n. 34. The fifth as well as the sixth visions of Ezra (chs. 11–13), which heavily depend on Dan. 7, could have been composed originally in Aramaic—see Myers, *Esdras*, pp. 118-19. Charlesworth, *Modern Research*, p. 112, observes that the original language is Semitic, either Hebrew or Aramaic.

42. Metzger, 'Fourth Book of Ezra', p. 530.

43. Myers, *Esdras*, p. 244.

44. Box, *Ezra-Apocalypse*, pp. 177-78 n. e, interprets 'the upper chambers in the air' as 'the heavenly paradise'.

place to which Ezra was 'caught up' is described as 'the place of those who are like him' (*4 Ezra* 14.49-50 in Syriac; cf. 2 Cor. 12.2-3). It is the place where he will live eternally, as the scribe of the divine Law, with God's Son and with those who are like himself (cf. 14.49-50 with 14.9). This suggests that Ezra was transformed into the likeness of the heavenly beings, as happened typically to the Merkabah mystic. However, the focus of the author of *4 Ezra* is not the throne-motif.

The Fifth and the Sixth Visions of Ezra

That the narratives of both the fifth (i.e. the eagle) and the sixth (i.e. the 'Son of Man') visions are influenced by Daniel 7 is known from the interpretation of the eagle-vision:

> The eagle which you saw coming up from the sea is the fourth kingdom which appeared in a vision to your brother Daniel. But it was not explained to him as I now explain or have explained it to you (*4 Ezra* 12.11-12).[45]

However, the author of *4 Ezra* reinterprets some of the key aspects found in Daniel's vision. The fourth beast in Dan. 7.7, for instance, symbolizes the Greek or Macedonian Empire, whereas in *4 Ezra* 11–12 the eagle (= Daniel's fourth kingdom) represents the Roman Empire (12.12). He does not use the symbol of a man-like figure either to represent the people of God or God the Most High. Instead, he uses the expression 'a lion-like creature' to symbolize the Messiah (cf. 11.37 with 12.32; cf. also Gen. 49.9). This shift may be because of the author's intention to highlight the function of the Messiah on earth in contrast to the function of the man-like figure of Daniel 7 in heaven. The Messiah is the one who had been kept by God (12.32) in his possession and in this sense it seems that the author of *4 Ezra* presents the Messiah as a heavenly figure.[46] Nevertheless, he will appear on earth from the posterity of David in order to deliver the 'remnant of God's people' and to make them joyful until the day of judgment (12.34). It is thus the vindication of Israel by God through his Messiah, which ultimately emerges as the main emphasis in the fifth vision.

---

45.   Metzger's translation. For terminological and conceptual parallels between *4 Ezra* 11–12 and Dan. 7 see Casey, *Son of Man*, pp. 122-24; Rowland, *Open Heaven*, p. 186.

46.   Myers, *Esdras*, pp. 294, 302, maintains that the messiah here is the pre-existent one as the clause 'reserved till the end of days' indicates. Box, *Ezra-Apocalypse*, p. 273 n. ss, comments that the heavenly Messiah is implied in 12.32.

Noteworthy is the fact that the man-like figure of Daniel 7 is interpreted as the messianic figure in *4 Ezra* 11–12. The same theme is repeated in ch. 13, which uses the word 'man'.

The sixth vision introduces in 13.3 *'ayk dmûtha dbarnasha*, 'one like the resemblance of a man', recalling Daniel's 'one like a son of man'. Though this expression in itself does not prove that the Son of Man was recognized as a title in Judaism, the vision as a whole demonstrates the author's use of Dan. 7.2, 13 (cf. *4 Ezra* 13.2-4, 25, 32). The symbol of 'a man-like figure', who flew with the clouds of heaven, is surely reminiscent of the 'one like a son of man' of Dan. 7.13, who was coming with the clouds of heaven. Although both *4 Ezra* 13 and Daniel 7 illuminate the vindication of the faithful Israel, in *4 Ezra* the 'man-like figure' denotes the Messiah, who is also known as 'God's son' (13.3, 26, 32, 52; cf. 7.28-29).

The act of 'coming up out of the heart of the sea' in *4 Ezra* 13 does not carry the sense of rivalry against God, as it does in Dan. 7.2, 3, but it may perhaps imply the hiddenness of the Son (13.52). Thus the author of *4 Ezra* used Daniel 7 freely and his freedom is also reflected in his fusion of Dan. 2.45 and Dan. 7.13 in *4 Ezra* 13.6, 7. Just as in Daniel 2 the stone, cut from a mountain by no human hands, stands for the heavenly kingdom which will overcome all the earthly kingdoms, so in *4 Ezra* 13 the mountain carved out without hands (i.e. Mt Zion) becomes the vehicle of the Messiah in his mission of bringing judgment on all rival nations. The whole episode becomes more sensible if only the man-like figure of *4 Ezra* is understood as a heavenly being.[47]

4 Ezra 11–13, then, reflects a belief current at the end of the first century, possibly even before 70 CE, in which the Danielic 'son of man' was identified with the pre-existent Messiah, who will lead God's people victoriously over hostile nations and bring salvation to them. Our analysis shows that the author of *4 Ezra* was familiar with the texts of throne-theophany, and that he could use Dan. 7.13, a text in which

---

47.   Rowland, *Open Heaven*, pp. 186-87, holds that as the man who comes up from the sea is merely a symbol of the Messiah, he cannot be regarded as a heavenly being. So also Casey, *Son of Man*, p. 124. However, the interpretation of the vision (13.52) makes it clear that the act of coming out of the sea denotes not so much the origin of the man as his hiddenness from human eyes. Further, the act of flying 'with the clouds of heaven', his supernatural voice and gaze (cf. Mic. 1.4; Judg. 16.15, where this is attributed to Yahweh), and his carving out a great mountain without hands (13.6; cf. v. 36), though symbolic, point to the man as a heavenly being.

'mystical' interest was developed as early as the second century CE, by identifying the 'son of man' with the pre-existent Messiah through whom God brought judgment on ungodly nations.

The Apocalypse of Abraham

The *Apocalypse of Abraham* is another Jewish text, composed after 70 CE,[48] which is purported to contain Merkabah mystical features and therefore falls within the scope of our investigation. Scholem comments on this book that it is 'a text that more closely resembles a Merkabah text than any other in Jewish apocalyptic literature'.[49] Therefore a study of the *Apocalypse of Abraham* will throw further light on the mystical practice seemingly prevalent in the late first century.

Preparation and the Angelic Guidance
Before Abraham was taken up to heaven, he had to prepare himself for 40 days by means of ascetic practices such as abstinence from every kind of food cooked by fire, from wine and from anointing himself with oil (*Apoc. Abr.* 9.7; cf. 12.1-2). This is precisely described in the *Hekhalot* literature as a means of attaining mystical experience.[50] Similarly, the heavenly ascent and the revelation of secrets by an angel, which are common motifs in the *Hekhalot* texts, occur also in the *Apocalypse of Abraham*, Abraham was taken up to heaven by the angel, Jaoel, who also revealed to him the heavenly secrets.

The Heavenly Vision
It was in the seventh heaven that the patriarch could see the throne of fire and hear the voice of God (*Apoc. Abr.* 18–19). Abraham's vision, found in ch. 18, reflects in several ways the chariot-vision of Ezekiel 1. The importance of this vision, as Gruenwald observes,[51] is twofold: (1) it contains the longest Merkabah hymn in the apocalyptic literature;

48.   R. Rubinkiewicz, 'Apocalypse of Abraham', *OTP*, I, pp. 681-705 (683), argues that *Apoc. Abr.* was composed sometime after 70 CE (because the author describes the destruction of Jerusalem in ch. 27) and before the middle of the second century. Charlesworth, *Modern Research*, p. 68, dates it to 80–100 CE, stating that it was written in a Semitic language.
49.   Scholem, *Jewish Gnosticism* (1960), p. 23.
50.   See above, pp. 81-82.
51.   Gruenwald, *Merkavah Mysticism*, p. 55.

and (2) it has a detailed description of the Throne of Glory.[52]

The Merkabah Hymn. In the vision of Abraham, the celestial song is recited not merely by the angels (15.5-7; cf. 18.3) and the four living creatures (18.3, 8, 11), but by the ascended one himself (ch. 17). Jaoel, who is the 'Singer of the Eternal One' (12.4), teaches celestial songs to the seer (17.4-7) and to the four living creatures (18.11). The song recited by Abraham unveils the nature of God and ends up with a prayer to reveal the 'promised secrets' (17.8-21). Prayers and hymns, recited both by the heavenly beings and the Merkabah visionary, occupy an important place in the *Hekhalot* tracts (e.g. *HR* 3–4, 7–10, 24–26). The terms that describe God's voice (i.e. 'like a voice of many waters, like a voice of the sea in its uproar'—17.1) have parallels in *HR* in descriptions of the sound of the hymn of praise, sung by the Throne of Glory to its king.[53] The heavenly hymn found in the *Apocalypse of Abraham* carries theurgic implications. It has the effect of protecting the visionary from all dangers that might befall him in his 'mystical' endeavour (cf. 17.2-7). *Ma'aseh Merkabah* contains hymns, which have the effect of rescuing the ascending seer.[54] It also descibes how the use of prayers with their magical names could protect the mystic, who descends to and ascends from Merkabah.[55]

The Throne-Vision. As the patriarch was still reciting the song, he saw under the fire 'a throne of fire' (18.1-3; cf. *1 En.* 71.5-7), around which were the 'many-eyed ones', that is, a band of angels reciting the song. Under the throne were stationed four living creatures and they too were singing.[56] Behind them was the chariot with fiery wheels and the wheels were full of eyes (18.12-14; cf. Ezek. 1.18). The throne is once

52.   See above, pp. 83 and 110-11 for the idea of the revelation of God's glory in the seventh heaven.

53.   See *Synopse* §§251, 411-12. Cf. Scholem, *Major Trends*, p. 61, p. 363 n. 60; *idem*, *Jewish Gnosticism* (1960), pp. 20-30, esp. p. 27.

54.   See Scholem, *Jewish Gnosticism* (1960), p. 110 §16; *Synopse* §569; Gruenwald, *Merkavah Mysticism*, pp. 102-104.

55.   Scholem, *Jewish Gnosticism* (1960), pp. 113-15, §§26-31; *Synopse* §§586-91.

56.   However, in Ezekiel's vision the four living creatures do not appear singing. Although the four faces of the *hayyot* in the *Apoc. Abr.* are the same as those of the *hayyot* in Ezek. 1.10, their six wings recall the six wings of the *Seraphim* in Isa. 6.2 rather than the four wings of those in Ezek. 1.6 and 10.12.

more mentioned as being above the wheels, but without any particular reference to any figure seated on the throne. Does this imply that the author intended to portray an empty throne? The other aspects of the vision argue against the concept of an empty throne. The 'voice' which came out of the fire was heard like the voice of 'a single man' (18.13, 14; cf. also 8.1; 9.1; 17.1). This points unmistakably to a tradition that had combined both Ezek. 1.26 ('likeness of a human form' on the throne) and Ezek. 1.28 ('the voice of one speaking', heard by the seer).[57] That the voice is the voice of God is clear from 8.1 and 9.3. Such an indirect reference to the one who is seated on the throne makes it improbable that the author had an empty throne in mind. Also, the expression, 'like the voice of a single man' to refer to God's voice makes it difficult to accept Rowland's thesis that the *Apocalypse of Abraham* excludes the anthropomorphism that plays a significant part, for example, in Ezek. 1.26-27.[58] Why, then, was the author reticent to make a plain reference to God in the throne-vision? What is the significance of the angel's statement: 'You will not look at him himself' (16.3)? Probably the *Apocalypse of Abraham* reflects another branch of Jewish tradition, which claimed that it is impossible to see God face to face, albeit one can see his throne-glory and hear his voice, and that the angels are the best intermediaries in a heavenly ascent to see his glory.[59]

No doubt, the whole Merkabah vision in the *Apocalypse of Abraham* is designed after Ezekiel's chariot-vision. The element of fire, for example, attains significance in this vision. The throne is not only encircled by fire (cf. *1 En.* 71.6), but is itself called 'a throne of fire' and the Mighty One came down from heaven in 'a stream of fire' to call Abraham (8.1; 17.1; 19.1). Fire itself is surrounded by 'an indescribable light'(18.13) and the fire, light, dew and the multitudes of angels, which are on the seventh firmament are collectively known as 'a host of the invisible glory', which is above the living creatures (19.4).[60] It can be said that 'God revealed Himself by Himself' (cf. 7.12) to Abraham

57.   G.H. Box, *The Apocalypse of Abraham* (London: SPCK, 1918), p. 63 n. 6.
58.   Rowland, 'The Visions of God', pp. 151-54.
59.   See Gruenwald, *Merkavah Mysticism*, pp. 93-96, for the controversy that existed among the Tannaim as to whether it is possible to see God and, if so, when and under what conditions.
60.   See above p. 90 for the idea that the angels who attend God's throne constitute his glory.

by this vision—a remarkable feature of Merkabah mysticism. This is confirmed by one more aspect of Merkabah mysticism, that is, the vision of a principal angel who bears the name of God to which we now turn.

The Angel, Jaoel

The angel, Jaoel, who bears God's 'ineffable name', is sent by God to escort Abraham in the latter's ascent to heaven (10.3-8). Gruenwald has already shown the points of contact between the Jaoel-narrative and the mystical experience described in *Hekhalot* and Midrashic literatures.[61] However, an important subject, which has direct bearing on the 'mystical' experience of first-century Judaism, remains to be discussed. Rowland argues that the bearing of God's name by Jaoel shows an interest in an exalted angelic figure with divine attributes in the place of the anthropomorphic description of God in Merkabah visions such as in Ezekiel 1 and *1 Enoch* 14.[62] Does this mean that Jaoel can be identified with the human-like figure of Merkabah mystical visions? Is he the manifestation of God? Since there are at least two factors that seem to point in this direction, they need careful analysis.

The name Jaoel is a combination of the three root-letters of the Tetragrammaton with an ending 'el' (i.e. YHW-el). The angel introduces himself as 'a power through the medium of his ineffable name in me' (10.3, 8) and this name was conferred on him by God himself (10.8). It is noteworthy that God also is addressed as Jaoel in Abraham's song (17.13), although this divine title is not attested either in the Bible or in any liturgy. This indeed makes Jaoel the highest of all the angels and archangels in status, but it is not certain whether by virtue of God's name he could be considered as the exalted angel with divine attributes, as Rowland maintains, or as 'second only to God Himself', as Box maintains.[63] In the throne-vision of Abraham (ch. 18) Jaoel is described neither as a *synthronos* nor as a figure who was occupying the throne of Ezek. 1.26, as Segal supposes,[64] but as the one who teaches 'the song of peace' to the adept and to the living creatures. He himself knelt down and worshipped the Eternal One, when his 'voice' came to Abraham (17.2). His main function seems to be to

61.   Gruenwald, *Merkavah Mysticism*, pp. 52-55.
62.   Rowland, 'The Visions of God', pp. 153-54.
63.   Box, *Apocalypse of Abraham*, p. xxxv.
64.   Cf. Segal, *Paul the Convert*, p. 42.

escort the patriarch and to preserve him from dangers when they ascend to the throne of God. The bestowal of the divine name on the angel Jaoel, then, seems to be no more than the bestowal of divine authority on God's vicegerent[65] (cf. *1 En.* 48.3 for the Son of Man who was given a name to carry out the divine will).

Jaoel appeared to Abraham 'in the likeness of a man' (*Apoc. Abr.* 10.4) and this recalls Daniel's 'one like a son of man' (Dan. 7.13) and the appearance of two angelic figures in Dan. 8.15; 10.5, 18. The first two descriptions in *Apoc. Abr.* 11.2 (i.e. the appearance of his body looked like sapphire and that of his face like chrysolite) parallel, albeit not exactly, the first two aspects of the description of the angel's body in Dan. 10.6. The hair of Jaoel's head, which appears like snow, reflects the appearance of the Son of Man in Rev. 1.14. But the clothing of Jaoel seems to be purple in colour (11.3), while that of God in Dan. 7.9 is white as snow. The description of Jaoel's 'turban' (*kidaris*) and of the golden staff in his right hand resembles that of the figures in Rev. 19.12 and Rev. 1.16 respectively. The reference to 'a rainbow' is reminiscent of the rainbow that qualifies the brightness round about the divine throne in Ezek. 1.28. Despite these parallels with Merkabah visions, there appears no real affinity between Jaoel and the Son of Man of Daniel 7 except that both are described as man-like figures. Resemblance with the Son of Man of Rev. 1.14 at only one point is insufficient to prove that Jaoel was the Son of Man, who came to be recognized as a kind of 'second God' alongside God the Most High. The apparent similarities with Ezekiel 1 and Rev. 1.14 can only show that the angel Jaoel is a heavenly figure, who had close association with the 'invisible glory' and who, by bearing God's name, functioned as his vicegerent. It does not seem that Jaoel appears as a substitute for the anthropomorphic deity of the Merkabah visions.

Summary
Our investigation shows that the *Apocalypse of Abraham* contains the key aspects of Merkabah mysticism (the seer's preparation before ascent, the heavenly hymns, the vision of God on the throne, fire/light around the throne, the retinue of angels, and God's vicegerent) and that the author has liberally used Ezekiel 1 by making alterations to suit his

---

65.   See above, p. 83, for the *Hekhalot* idea that bearing God's name does not make the angels equal with God either in status or in divinity. Cf. Exod. 23.21; 11QMelch describes Melchizedek bearing God's name.

own situation and purpose. As in the Qumran texts, in the *Apocalypse of Abraham* also the angelic mediation needed to see God's glory is stressed. This apocalyptic text, then, provides further proof for our thesis that Merkabah mysticism had been known and practised at the end of the first century CE.

The Testament of Abraham

The experience of an ascent to heaven and seeing heavenly thrones by Abraham is described in a unique way in the *Testament of Abraham*, another Palestinian apocalyptic document,[66] the tradition of which probably goes back to the first half of the first century CE.[67] This document, as we have it now, exists in two recensions, A and B.

The Heavenly Ascent and the Vision of Abraham

At the request of Abraham, the archangel Michael took him up on a chariot of *Cherubim* to heaven, whence Abraham saw the world and everything that was happening in it (A10). However, this vision of all created things is not the same as the *Ma'aseh Bereshit*, for what the patriarch saw in the world was human works, both good and evil, rather than the created order of the universe.

It does not seem that Abraham had a direct access to the divine presence to see God. Any communication is made through the archangel alone. When he entered the first gate in heaven, he saw two ways: one, being narrow, led to life and another, being broad, led to destruction (A11). Outside these two gates he could see a man seated on a 'golden throne' (A11.4) or the 'throne of great glory' (B8.5). The man on the throne is interpreted as Adam, the first-formed (ὁ πρωτόπλαστος Ἀδαμ). He does not hold the function of giving judgment, as the enthroned human figures do in other throne-visions (cf. Dan. 7.9-14;

66. The tour of earth, the views of judgment, heaven, hell, afterlife, etc., are apocalyptic elements in *T. Abr.*—see E.P. Sanders, 'Testament of Abraham', *OTP*, I, pp. 871-902 (879).

67. See G.H. Box, *The Testament of Abraham* (London: SPCK, 1927), pp. xxviii-xxix. Rowland, *Open Heaven*, p. 107, argues that the fact that the book exists in a variety of different recensions is probably a strong indication of its antiquity, i.e. written round about the beginning of the Christian era. Sanders, 'Testament of Abraham', p. 875, suggests a date of c. 100 CE, plus or minus 25 years. Charlesworth, *Modern Research*, p. 70, accepts this date, but says that the exact date is debatable.

1 En. 62.3, 7-10; *T. Abr.* A12.11), but he weeps for those who enter through the broad gate and rejoices for those who enter through the narrow gate (A11.6-12). Apart from the description of the throne of Adam as 'the throne of great glory' in B8.5 (in Rec. A it is Adam who is described as adorned in glory—A11.8-9), there is nothing to suggest that what Abraham saw was the throne of God, as in Ezek. 1.26. Also, the term 'glory' in this context means the glory given to Adam and not the glory of the Lord himself.

Between the two gates Abraham saw another throne with the appearance of terrifying crystal and flashing like fire (A12.4; but the parallel B10–11 to A12–13 does not contain any reference to this throne). The wondrous man who was sitting on this throne was Abel, the son of Adam (A13.2-3). He looked like a son of God, as bright as the sun, holding the task of judging and sentencing the human souls according to their deeds recorded in the book kept before him. There appears at least two similarities between this throne-vision and the one found in *1 Enoch* 14, which is rightly described by Gruenwald as containing 'a model vision of Merkabah mysticism':[68] The appearance of the throne of Abel as 'terrifying crystal', which resembles the crystal-like appearance of God's throne in *1 En.* 14.18 (cf. Ezek. 1.22), and the flashing fire from the throne, which parallels the 'streams of flaming fire' that issue from beneath the throne of God in *1 En.* 14.19 (cf. Ezek. 1.4, 13, 27). The brightness of Abel as the sun resembles the shining gown of the Great Glory in *1 En.* 14.20 and of the shining face of the son of man in Rev. 1.16.

Do these parallels, then, indicate the manifestation of God on the throne in the form of Abel? Or does this prove that the throne of God has been separated from God himself and linked with Abel, as Rowland has postulated?[69] This seems to be unlikely. Indeed there are some parallels between the throne-theophany of Ezekiel 1 and that of *Testament of Abraham* 12, but there are also some differences. There is no reference, for instance, to the retinue of angels around the throne or to its movement, although mention is made of the two angelic scribes who were standing on both sides of the table before the throne, a 'light-bearing' angel in front of the table and a 'fiery angel' (A12.7-18).

Although in both Ezekiel 1 and *Testament of Abraham* the human figures appear on the throne, in the former it is the appearance of the

68. Gruenwald, *Merkavah Mysticism*, p. 36.
69. Rowland, *Open Heaven*, p. 108.

man-like figure, while in the latter it is the man himself. The task of the man-like figures in other throne-theophanies has not exclusively been to effect judgment, but to reveal the heavenly and cosmological secrets and, in particular, to commission the visionary for the divine work (see Ezek. 1–2; Isa. 6.1-9; 1 Kgs 22.19-23; *1 En.* 14–15; *2 En.* 22–55; *Apoc. Abr.* 18–32). The judgment of Abel is only the first stage of the threefold judgment, anticipating the final judgment to be held by God when he comes, and therefore even the sentence passed by Abel could be superseded by intercession (*T. Abr.* 14.5-9). The divine chariot (i.e. the chariot of *Cherubim*) does not serve as the vehicle of God in his manifestation, instead, as the vehicle of the visionary in his ascent (A10.1). These differences make it clear that Abel's throne is not identical with God's throne, albeit a heavenly one. Abel's supreme authority to give judgment is the outcome of God's delegation of his power to a human being rather than to a heavenly being (e.g. *1 En.* 62), for the author's conviction is that 'every man is judged by man' (A13.3). In the heavenly realm what Abraham saw was not the throne on which the glory of God was manifested, but the throne on which God's representative was sitting to execute divine judgment. This indicates neither the throne-manifestation of God nor the separation of God from his own throne. There is no clue that the ascended visionary mistook the human figures on the thrones for God. The idea that a man represents God and executes judgment recalls the Merkabah mystical visions found in the *Similitudes* and *4 Ezra* as well as the esoteric doctrine of Qumran community. We can examine here one more Qumran document that points in this direction, 11QMelch.

11QMelch
In 11QMelch the chief angel, Melchizedek, as *'elohim* and *'el*, exercises judgment on behalf of God. Horton observes that in Qumran the word *'elohim* is not used often as a name for God.[70] Noll has argued that since Melchizedek is clearly a Michael-like figure, we may conjecture that the word-play with *'elohim* and *'el* is the product of speculation on Melchizedek's exoteric name, Michael.[71] However, the name

---

70.   F.L. Horton, *The Melchizedek Tradition: A Critical Examination of the Sources to the Fifth Century AD and in the Epistle to the Hebrews* (SNTSMS, 30; Cambridge: Cambridge University Press, 1976), pp. 76-77.
71.   S.F. Noll, 'Angelology in the Qumran Texts' (PhD Thesis, University of Manchester, 1979), pp. 65-66.

'el in the psalm cited in 11QMelch (Ps. 7.8) suggests God as the agent of judgment and in the *Shabbat Shirot* the name *'elohim*, rather than *'el*, is used for the angels. It seems, then, that Melchizedek, as the highest archangel and God's vicegerent, who was bearing God's name (cf. Exod. 23.20; *Apoc. Abr.* 10.6-8; 17.13), sat on the throne of God (cf. Horton's translation of line 11) to exercise judgment against his enemies. Alexander has drawn parallels between the heavenly Melchizedek and Metatron, noting that both hold exalted positions among the angels and that both are heavenly judges (see *3 En.* 16.1 for Metatron functioning as the judge by sitting on the throne in the seventh palace).[72] We should add that just like Melchizedek, Metatron also bears God's name in the mystical tradition of Judaism.[73] It is, however, noteworthy that the name Metatron occurs at the earliest only in *Re'uyoth Yehezkel*, which belongs to the third or the fourth century CE and in which Metatron is found as a secret name of Michael. Alexander, who sees a striking resemblance between Metatron and Michael, maintains that Metatron in *3 Enoch* embodies three major and originally independent figures: Enoch, Yahoel/Lesser YHWH, and Michael/Metatron.[74]

Now the resemblance between the Melchizedek of Qumran and the Metatron of the *Hekhalot* text is quite striking, for Michael is the exoteric name both for Melchizedek and Metatron and both these figures carry most of the attributes of Michael.[75] Scholem has pointed out that the traditions about the secret names of angels, including the ascribed divinity because of that, which are found in the *Hekhalot* books and *Re'uyoth Yehezkel*, are but a continuation of the tradition of the Essenes of the first century CE.[76] If so, the origin of the name Metatron may be traced back in the Melchizedek tradition of Qumran. This means that the idea of an exalted angel exercising judgment by

72. Alexander, '3 (Hebrew Apocalypse of) Enoch', p. 250.

73. See *3 En.* 48d.1; 3.2; and *Re'uyoth Yehezkel* states, 'Mitatron, like the name of the Power...like the name of the Creator of the world' (cited in Alexander, 'Historical Setting', p. 164).

74. Alexander, 'Historical Setting', pp. 161-67.

75. See Alexander, 'Historical Setting', p. 163; for functional similarities between Melchizedek and Michael see Newsom, *Sabbath Sacrifice*, p. 37; cf. Vermes, *Dead Sea Scrolls* (1995), p. 360. However, some essential differences between Melchizedek and Michael are found in the *War Scroll*—see Horton, *Melchizedek Tradition*, p. 81.

76. Scholem, *Jewish Gnosticism* (1960), p. 48.

bearing God's name, which was inherent in *Hekhalot* mysticism, is already found in 11QMelch. In the *Similitudes* the same function is assigned to the Son of Man, but in *Testament of Abraham* 12 to a man like Abel.

Final Observations
This brings us to the conclusion that the *Testament of Abraham* is another indication that the 'mystical' feature of the heavenly journey, which includes the angelic entourage and a knowledge of the heavenly secrets, had already been known in first-century Palestinian Judaism. Also the idea of God's delegation of his authority to a man, who sits on the Throne of Glory, reflects the Merkabah mystical tradition. Both James and Sanders have argued for the Christian influence in *Testament of Abraham*, particularly on chs. 10–14, which describe the ascension of Abraham's soul to heaven.[77] If so, it may well indicate the interest prevailed among Jews and Christians alike in heavenly ascents and mysteries. This is confirmed by the apocalypse that originated in Christian circles to which we now turn.

The Book of Revelation

Gruenwald argues that although the Book of Revelation took its final shape some 20 years after the destruction of the temple, its Merkabah material is typical of the Jewish apocalyptic books before the destruction.[78] The Merkabah mystical aspects in this apocalypse can be examined in two phases: the idea of Son of Man and the throne-vision.

The Idea of Son of Man
An epiphany of 'one like a son of man (ὅμοιον υἱὸν ἀνθρώπου)' occurs in a vision to John when he was ἐν πνεύματι (Rev. 1.9–3.22). Is this Son of Man the same heavenly being as the one in the *Similitudes*? Or possibly the Son of Man whom we meet in the Synoptic Gospels? Or is he the same man-like figure of Dan. 7.13? Can he be the man-like figure, who constitutes the Glory of God in the Merkabah vision of

77.   See M.R. James, *The Testament of Abraham* (Cambridge: Cambridge University Press, 1892), pp. 50-55 for phraseological and ideological parallels with Christian writings. Sanders, 'Testament of Abraham', pp. 872-73, 879, finds Christian interpolations in at least three places (A11.2, 10-11; 13.3; B8).
78.   Gruenwald, *Merkavah Mysticism*, p. 62.

Ezekiel 1? Since these texts were largely used in the Jewish mystical circles, a study of the son of man of Revelation 1 will throw light on the relationship of this figure to the Merkabah mystical practice in the first century, particularly among Christians.

The Son of Man: His Form and Function. The risen Jesus appears as one like a son of man, clothed with a long robe and with a golden girdle round his breast (Rev. 1.13). This recalls the angel of Dan. 10.5, who had been clothed in linen and whose loins were girded with gold of Uphaz. A.Y. Collins argues that the man clothed in linen (ἐνδεδυκὼς ποδήρη in OG) in Ezek. 9.2, who symbolizes a priestly angel, forms a closer parallel to Rev. 1.13 (both robe and girdle are the garb of the high-priest in Exod. 28.4; 39.29), although Dan. 10.5 also has influenced Rev. 1.13.[79] She further suggests that the angelic attribute, ὅμοιον υἱὸν ἀνθρώπου, is based on the angelic character of the figure in Dan. 7.13.[80] Moreover, his eyes which were like a flame of fire (= Dan. 10.6), his feet which were like burnished bronze (= Dan. 10.5, 6; Ezek. 1.7; *Apoc. Zeph.* 6.12) and his face which was like the sun shining in full strength (= *2 En.* 1.5; *Apoc. Zeph.* 6.11) all indicate that the man-like figure of Rev. 1.12-16 assumes angelic form in his revelation.[81]

Although the 'one like a son of man' assumes angelic form, there are several aspects that show that he was much bound up with God, particularly with the Throne of Glory that appears in Merkabah visions.

1. The Son of Man resembles the priestly angel of Ezek. 9.2 in being clothed with a long robe (ἐνδεδυμένον ποδήρη—Rev. 1.13). But the resemblance can be accounted for by the close association of both the figures with the one seated on the throne in Merkabah mystical visions (cf. Ezek. 9.2 with Ezek. 10.1-2, 6-8).

2. The head and the hair of the Son of Man were as white wool, white as snow (Rev. 1.14—λευκαὶ ὡς ἔριον λευκὸν ὡς χιών) and this echoes the appearance of the raiment (λευκὸν ὡσεὶ χιών) and of the hair (ὡσεὶ ἔριον καθαρόν) of the Ancient of Days who was seated on

79.   A.Y. Collins, ' "Son of Man" Tradition', p. 548.
80.   A.Y. Collins, ' "Son of Man" Tradition', p. 550.
81.   See P.R. Carrell, 'Jesus and the Angels: The Influence of Angelology on the Christology of the Apocalypse of John' (PhD Thesis, University of Durham, 1993), who argues that Jesus, in Rev. 1.13-16, 14.14 and 19.11-16, is adopting temporarily the angelic form, though he is not an angel.

the throne in Dan. 7.9 LXX (cf. *1 En.* 71.10).

3. The description of the eyes of the Son of Man resembles that of the eyes of the angel in Dan. 10.6. However, whereas Dan. 10.6 uses the expression ὡσεὶ λαμπάδες πυρός ('as lamps of fire'), Rev. 1.14 uses ὡς φλὸξ πυρός ('like a flame of fire'). Strictly speaking, the eyes of the Son of Man resemble the appearance of God's throne in Dan. 7.9 LXX, where ὡσεὶ φλὸξ πυρός qualifies the throne of God.[82]

4. The voice of the Son of Man was like the sound of many waters (ὡς φωνὴ ὑδάτων πολλῶν—Rev. 1.15), recalling the sound of the wings of the *hayyot* (Ezek. 1.24 LXX: ὡς φωνὴν ὕδατος πολλοῦ) and that of the coming of the glory of God (Ezek. 43.2 LXX: ὡς φωνὴ διπλασιαζόντων πολλῶν) more than the words of the angel in Dan. 10.6, which are ὡς φωνὴ ὄχλου.

5. The description of the face of the Son of Man as shining like the sun (Rev. 1.16) recalls the wheels of God's throne and the gown of the 'Great Glory', which are described in *1 En.* 14.18, 20 as shining like a sun (cf. in *T. Abr.* A12.5 Abel, who is seated on the throne, appears as bright as the sun).

Thus one can see that the apocalyptist has drawn materials not only from Dan. 7.9, but also from Ezek. 1.7, 24; 9.2; 43.2; Dan. 7.13; 10.5-6; *Apoc. Zeph.* 6.12; and *1 En.* 14.18, 20—passages that show influence of the Merkabah mystical tradition. No doubt, there is a strange fusion of theophany and angelophany in the christophany of Revelation 1.[83] What does this fusion show? It shows that the author as well as his readers were familiar with current Merkabah mystical tradition, particularly as it was used in Qumran. Since the expressions that describe the glory are applied in the *Shabbat Shirot* to the angels who attend the chariot throne, Newsom is right in maintaining that in the Merkabah visions of Qumran the attendant angels constitute the visible appearance of the glory.[84] Precisely this angelic role in Merkabah mysticism is fulfilled by the Son of Man in Revelation 1: he constitutes the visible appearance of the glory of God. The use of the 'I am' formula, the prerogative of Yahweh, by the Son of Man and his acceptance of worship in Rev. 1.17 (cf. Isa. 44.6) indicate his divine attributes. The double function of the angels who attend God's throne, priestly and military, which we have observed in the twelfth Sabbath

82.   See also Carrell, 'Jesus and the Angels', pp. 190-92.
83.   Cf. Carrell, 'Jesus and the Angels', p. 199.
84.   Newsom, *Sabbath Sacrifice*, p. 233. Cf. 4Q405 22.5-6.

Song, is also fulfilled by the Son of Man in Revelation 1. His garments of long robe and chest band (Rev. 1.13) indicate his priestly function and the sharp two-edged sword that issues from his mouth (Rev. 1.16) marks his military function as the Messiah (cf. *4 Ezra* 13.9-13; *1 En.* 62.2).

If the appearance of the Son of Man is the epiphany of an angelomorphic being,[85] it is not because he is an angel, but because he, in his angelic form and function, represents and constitutes the very glory of the enthroned God, and hence the use of Merkabah texts which we have shown above.[86] It is not improbable, then, that the Son of Man, the manifestation of God's glory, by undertaking temporarily an angelic form and function, was temporarily separated from the divine throne to reveal heavenly mysteries.[87] The Merkabah mystical aspect is also envisaged in the commissioning of the seer by the Son of Man so that he might write and proclaim God's words to the seven churches (Rev. 1.19; cf. Ezek. 2.8–3.11; Isa. 6.8, 9) and Rowland rightly identifies the vision in Revelation 1 as 'John's call vision'.[88]

The Son of Man Seated on the Cloud. The expression ὅμοιον υἱὸν ἀνθρώπου also occurs in Rev. 14.14. Casey argues that Rev. 14.14 does not depend on Dan. 7.13 and that the 'one like a son of man' is an angelic figure, who obeys the command of another angel, performing a function similar to his (14.15-19).[89] However, it is likely that the word ὅμοιος, as an equivalent of ὡς, translates the Aramaic כ of Dan. 7.13.[90] Moreover, the coming of the Son of Man on a white cloud and his golden crown, which symbolizes his kingship and dominion, betray the influence of Dan. 7.13-14. The sickle for the harvest alludes to Joel 4.13 (3.13 in RSV), where God is the agent of both harvest and vin-

85. Cf. Carrell, 'Jesus and the Angels', pp. 199-200.

86. Cf. A. Farrer, *The Revelation of St John the Divine* (Oxford: Clarendon Press, 1964), pp. 66-67, who maintains that in Rev. 1.13-16 John gathers the features of glory from the composite figure of divine majesty in Ezek. 1.26 and from the great angel in Dan. 10.

87. Cf. Carrell, 'Jesus and the Angels', pp. 212, 243, 277.

88. C. Rowland, 'The Vision of the Risen Christ in Rev. i.13ff.: The Debt of an Early Christology to an Aspect of Jewish Angelology', *JTS* 31 (1980), pp. 1-11 (11).

89. Casey, *Son of Man*, pp. 148-49.

90. See A.Y. Collins, '"Son of Man" Tradition', pp. 566-67.

tage.[91] The whole notion of harvest by the Son of Man is embodied in the synoptic tradition, Mt. 24.30-31 and Mk 4.29, which seems to underlie Rev. 14.14-16.

However, the question is: why is ὅμοιος υἱὸς ἀνθρώπου depicted as seated on the cloud (ἐπὶ τὴν νεφέλην), whereas in Dan. 7.13 he comes with the clouds (μετὰ τῶν νεφελῶν) and in *4 Ezra* 13.3 he flies with the clouds of heaven? The author's intention is probably to picture the Son of Man as the representative of God, if not an identification with him, in executing his judgment. Just like the throne which is the seat of God, the one who renders judgment, in Dan. 7.9, so also a cloud is the seat of the man-like figure in Rev. 14.14 (cf. *1 En.* 62.2-16, etc., where the Son of Man sits on the Throne of Glory beside God to execute judgment). The act of sitting on the cloud does not allow us to see the Son of Man as an angel. Wherever the author really means an angel, he is careful to use the term ἄγγελος or ἄλλος ἄγγελος, but he uses the expression ὅμοιος υἱὸς ἀνθρώπου to denote a unique heavenly being, who, as a human in an angelic form, exhibits divine features. Although there is an allusion to the synoptic Son of Man, the man-like figure who appears in Merkabah mystical visions gives a better background for understanding the Son of Man in Revelation, which presents him as the one who represents God's glory and function. Thus it is clear that first-century Christians identified the risen Jesus with the Danielic Son of Man who, like the man-like figure in Merkabah mysticism, manifests God *sui generis* by incorporating both human and angelic forms.

The Throne-Vision

Another aspect of Merkabah mysticism is envisaged in the throne-vision described in Revelation 4–5. The vision of John, the apocalyptist, of an open door in heaven (4.1), implies the first stage of his entry into heaven (cf. *T. Levi* 5.1; *Asc. Isa.* 6.6). The instruction ἀνάβα ὧδε given by the voice and the seer's 'being in the Spirit at once' imply his heavenly ascent.[92] After this he had a vision of God seated on the throne, which recalls the chariot-vision of Ezekiel after the heavens were opened (Ezek. 1.1; cf. Rev. 19.11). Though we can infer that the

91. A.Y. Collins, ' "Son of Man" Tradition', pp. 564-67.
92. R.H. Charles, *A Critical and Exegetical Commentary on the Revelation of St John* (2 vols.; ICC; Edinburgh: T. & T. Clark, 1920), I, pp. 22, 111, comments that the phrase ἐγενόμην ἐν πνεύματι denotes the ecstatic condition into which the seer has fallen.

trumpet-like voice (cf. 1.10) belongs to an angel, it is not clear whether the visionary was led by an angel or was caught up into heaven like Paul.[93]

In his ecstatic trance the apocalyptist saw a throne in heaven with one seated on it (4.2). In the light of 7.15, 15.5-8 and 16.17 we can maintain that this vision took place in the temple (*T. Levi* 5.1; 18.6; Isa. 6.1). This is the same as the idea that God appears from his holy palace (היכל) (cf. Ps. 11.4)—an idea that later gave rise to the Jewish *Hekhalot* literature. God's appearance on the throne was in the form of light, as bright as jasper and cornelian, rather than in human/angelic form, and around the throne was a rainbow, which constitutes a part of God's glory in Ezek. 1.28. The elements of the flashes of lightning, the peals of thunder, and the torches of fire, which are connected with the throne in 4.5 echo the theophany described in Ezek. 1.4, 27-28; Dan. 7.9, 10; *1 En.* 14.11, 17 and Exod. 19.16. We have already observed that the fiery appearance of God was treated as one of the major aspects of Jewish mysticism in the *Hekhalot* literature. The appearance of the crystal-like sea of glass before the throne seems to be the author's adaptation of Ezekiel's crystal-like firmament, which supports the throne of God (Ezek. 1.22-26; 10.1). The plural 'thrones', assigned to the 24 elders, around the throne of God recall the 'thrones' of the heavenly assize in Dan. 7.9. Arguing that the 24 elders are the righteous ones, who, as part of their eschatological reward, had the privilege of sitting in the presence of God, Gruenwald finds here an allusion to the mystical tradition centred on Metatron, who was sitting on the throne of Glory and was mistaken by Elisha b. 'Avuya as another power equal to God (*b. Ḥag.* 15a; *3 En.* 16).[94]

The four living creatures, which appear in the Merkabah vision of Ezek. 1.3-25, are mentioned in Rev. 4.6-8 too. That they were full of eyes recalls the *Ofannim* of the chariot in Ezek. 1.18; 10.12. The six wings of these *hayyot*, however, recall the six-winged *Seraphim* of Isa. 6.2, and the singing of heavenly beings such as the *Cherubim* and *Seraphim* (Isa. 6.3; *2 En.* 21.1; cf. *1 En.* 71.7; 14.23) is transferred to the *hayyot* in Revelation (4.8).[95]

---

93.   Gruenwald, *Merkavah Mysticism*, p. 64, finds a similarity between Paul's ascent and John's ascent.

94.   Gruenwald, *Merkavah Mysticism*, p. 66.

95.   Cf. above p. 83 for trisagion (or *Qedusha*) as an integral part of Merkabah mysticism.

While God is the object of worship and veneration in Revelation 4, another figure, the Lamb (ἀρνίον), appears in Revelation 5 as the one who is standing between the thrones ('in the midst of the throne' in 7.17) and who too was considered worthy to receive the glory and blessing due to God (cf. 7.9-12). His mission is described in the pattern of that of Ezekiel, which followed his Merkabah vision (cf. Rev. 5.1-7 with Ezek. 2.9–3.3). The Lamb, symbolizing Davidic Messiah,[96] appears as inseparable from the throne of God in the Christian apocalyptic tradition (7.9-17; cf. the risen Jesus sitting on the throne of his Father in 3.21; also 22.1 'the throne of God and of the Lamb'). The seven eyes of Christ, being reminiscent of the seven eyes of Yahweh which run through the whole earth (Zech. 4.10), indicate that he shares the omniscience as well as the omnipotence of God.[97] This recalls the Son of Man of the *Similitudes*, who sat on the Throne of Glory as God's unique vizier.

It seems, then, that by the end of the first century some of the Jews and Christians alike, particularly those who took great interest in the mystical speculation based on Ezekiel 1 and Daniel 7, did not hesitate to ascribe the glory and honour due to God alone to the messianic figure (whether by the name Son of Man or Lamb), because he was God's agent in a unique way.

'Two Powers in Heaven' Heresy

The close link between the idea that the Son of Man was primarily God's revelation, having divine status and authority, and Merkabah mysticism has been thoughtfully brought out by Segal in his study of the so-called ' "Two Powers in Heaven" Heresy'.[98] He finds in two *Mekilta* passages and in *Pek. R. Piska* 21, which insist on the two

96.   Cf. the title 'the Lion of the tribe of Judah, the Root of David' (5.5; cf. Gen. 49.9; *4 Ezra* 12.31-32). In *T. Jos.* 19.8 a lion, presumably from Judah, assists the Messiah, the 'conquering lamb'.

97.   Charles, *Revelation*, I, p. 143.

98.   See Segal, *Two Powers*, pp. 33-59; *idem, Rebecca's Children: Judaism and Christianity in the Roman World* (Cambridge, MA: Harvard University Press, 1986), pp. 151-58. Segal, however, is not sure as to when the heresy was explicitly named 'Two Powers in Heaven'. All he can say is that, since the interpretation of the plural 'thrones' in Dan. 7.9 in terms of God's mercy and justice belongs to the tannaitic period, the original heresy is probably older than the second century CE (*Two Powers*, p. 53).

manifestations of the one God, Yahweh, an attempt on the part of certain rabbis to defend their monotheistic faith against such statement as 'There are two powers in heaven' (cf. *3 En.* 16; *b. Ḥag.* 14b). The *Mekilta* passages show that some Jews understood the plural 'thrones' in Dan. 7.9 as implying two divine figures with equal authority, which, according to certain rabbis, is the mark of 'two powers in heaven' heresy. These rabbis attempted to insist that only one God was sitting on the throne, by citing Dan. 7.10, which has a singular pronoun, and Exod. 24.10-11.[99] These two passages, according to Segal, indicate the 'proto-merkabah mystics' as one of the alleged heretical groups.[100] This is confirmed by our observation that the root of the Metatron tradition, which has reference to 'two powers in heaven' (*3 En.* 16), goes back to the first century when the traditions concerning Enoch, Yahoel and Melchizedek were alive in Palestinian Judaism. The idea of a principal angel, who played a divine role by bearing God's name, suggested to the rabbis a creature of God participating in God's divinity and thus posed a threat to their long-cherished monotheistic faith. In this sense, not merely Dan. 7.9-10, but also Ezek. 1.26-27 could have contributed to the upsurge of the 'two powers' misconception.

Segal produces evidence from Hellenistic mystical and apocalyptic Judaism (e.g. Philo) and the New Testament to prove the presence of a kind of 'two powers' heresy even in the first century, mainly in the binitarian nature of Christianity (i.e. emphasizing Christ and the Father as God) and in its exaltation/glorification Christology developed from the Son of Man tradition.[101] He also points out that the Fourth Gospel, which claims the equality of Jesus, the Son of God, with God, reflects the 'two powers' tradition.[102] Our analysis of the Son of Man passages in Revelation proves beyond doubt that the risen Jesus was believed by Christians to be the Danielic Son of Man, who exhibits divine prerogatives and authority in a unique way.[103] It is possible, then, that those

---

99. The talmudic tradition shows that R. Akiba (50–135 CE) interpreted the Son of Man of Dan. 7 as the figure (for him, David) who had been enthroned next to God, but that later, as other rabbis objected to such an interpretation, he (or his students) agreed that the heavenly thrones symbolize the two aspects of God's providence, his mercy and his justice, which implies 'one God in two hypostases'—see Segal, *Two Powers*, pp. 48-49.

100. Segal, *Two Powers*, p. 60.

101. Segal, *Two Powers*, pp. 7, 24, 70, 205-19.

102. Segal, *Two Powers*, pp. 213-17.

103. Although Segal, *Two Powers*, pp. 212-13, cites Rev. 19.11-16; 22.12-13

who had great interest in Merkabah mystical visions in both Judaism and Christianity in the first century can hardly be excluded from the tradition that paved the way to the full-blown 'two powers in heaven' apostasy later in the second or the third century CE.

Conclusions

The six apocalyptic texts, which we have examined, show that Merkabah mysticism is integral in various degrees to the apocalyptic visions current in the first century CE. Almost all of them reflect an interest in heavenly ascent. The experience of seeing God's glory on the throne, angelic entourage, heavenly hymn, worship with the angels in heaven, the transformation and the commissioning of the visionary, etc., are embodied in the apocalyptic visions that we have analysed. The most significant aspect of Merkabah mysticism found in apocalyptic is the delegation of God's power either to an exalted human being (e.g. Abel) or to a chief angel (e.g. Melchizedek and Jaoel) or to a unique heavenly figure, the Son of Man to act as his vicegerent in judgment.

The figure, the Son of Man, appears in the *Similitudes* and *4 Ezra* as God's Messiah and Son. In the *Similitudes* he appears to sit on the Throne of Glory on a par with God and to receive worship and praise. However, in the Christian apocalypse the Son of Man is portrayed as the manifestation of the glory of the enthroned God, recalling the appearance of God's glory in Merkabah mysticism. This tendency in mystical circles attests Segal's theory of 'two powers in heaven' heresy, against which some rabbis in the second century had to react in order to safeguard Jewish monotheism. Whether or not Merkabah mysticism can be viewed as an inner-Jewish development of pre-70 apocalyptic (Alexander), definitely most of the elements of Merkabah mysticism are already present in pre- and post-70 apocalyptic.

Therefore the apocalyptic literature not only enables us to ascertain the character of the earliest meditation on Ezekiel (Rowland), but also provides sound evidence to our thesis that Merkabah mysticism was current among both Jews and Christians in the late first century.

for Christians' identification of Christ with God, he has not examined Rev. 1.13-14; 14.14 for that purpose.

Chapter 8

THE YOHANAN BEN ZAKKAI TRADITION

Scholars such as Scholem, Urbach, Bowker, Neusner, Goldberg, Rowland and Gruenwald[1] have argued that Merkabah mystical praxis had its root in Palestinian Judaism even before 70 CE and that it continued in the religious life of the early tannaitic rabbis, R. Yohanan b. Zakkai and his pupils, even after 70. Since Yohanan was a contemporary of John, an investigation of the available sources on Yohanan, will enable us to know the mystical beliefs commonly held at the time of John.

The primary evidence for the possible mystical experience attributed to Yohanan and his school is the Merkabah exposition delivered by one of his disciples, Eleazar b. 'Arakh. The story is recorded in four different versions, as found in *Mekilta deRabbi Simeon b. Yohai* (M), *t. Ḥag.* 2.1 (T), *y. Ḥag.* 2.1 (PT), and *b. Ḥag.* 14b (BT). The Hebrew version of all these sources is synoptically published by Bowker[2] and its English translation, with minor variations, is rendered by Morray-Jones.[3] The content of the story of Eleazar's exposition can be grasped by determining the possible original version and by undertaking a synoptic

---

1. Scholem, *Major Trends*, p. 41; E.E. Urbach, 'Ha-Masorot 'al Torat ha-Sod bi-Tequfat ha-Tannaim', in A. Altmann (ed.), *Studies in Mysticism and Religion: Presented to G.G. Scholem on his Seventieth Birthday* (Jerusalem: Magnes Press, 1967), pp. 2-11; Bowker, ' "Merkabah" Visions', pp. 157-73; Neusner, *Life of Yohanan ben Zakkai*, pp. 134-42; A. Goldberg, 'Der Vortrag des Ma'asse Merkawa: Eine Vermutung zur frühen Merkawamystik', *Judaica* 29 (1973), pp. 9-12; Rowland, 'The First Chapter of Ezekiel', pp. v-vi, 88-151, 239-72; *idem, Open Heaven*, pp. 282-83, 303-305; Gruenwald, *Merkavah Mysticism*, pp. vii, 73-86.

2. Bowker, ' "Merkabah" Visions', pp. 192-96.

3. Morray-Jones, 'Talmudic Tradition', pp. 229(a)-229(l); cf. the synoptic study of this story by J. Neusner, 'The Development of the Merkavah Tradition', *JSJ* 2 (1971), pp. 149-60. See also Rowland, *Open Heaven*, pp. 284-88, 295.

study of all the four versions of the story to the extent that it lies within
the scope of our inquiry.

The Mekilta Version of the Yohanan Tradition

Bowker, followed by Rowland, argues that while T preserves the early
structural form through which the traditions were transmitted, M represents the earliest sequence of the Yohanan/Eleazar tradition and even
the original content of the tradition as a whole.[4] Gruenwald, overlook-
ing M, argues for 'a common source' from which PT and BT drew
materials, T being their abbreviation.[5] However, he does not give any
more details about the existence of such a common source. Both
Halperin and Morray-Jones, on the other hand, have argued for M as
the original version.[6] This seems to be more probable, not only because
of its description of Yohanan's dismounting as taking place after he
saw the fire, but also because of the absence of the Mishnaic restriction
(*m. Ḥag.* 2.1) in the beginning of M. It would have been easier to add
the story into the 'mystical collection' with a cap of mishnaic restriction than to omit the restriction from the original, while all the other
three versions are retaining it.[7] Therefore I quote below only the M
version, as given by Bowker (pp. 160-63), in the light of which I will
discuss the other three versions of the Merkabah exposition of Eleazar.
The terms that are bracketed appear in other lines in M, but they form a
parallel with other versions in those particular lines. The lines that contain no reading in M are marked with dots or a space is left.

1	ומעשה ברבן	5	החמור	9	בן ערד תלמידו	
2	יוחנן בן זכאי	6		10	מהלך אחריו	
3	שהיה רוכב על	7	ויוצא מירושלם	11	אמר לו ר׳	
4		8	ור׳ אלעזר	12	שנה לי פרק אחד	

4.   Bowker, ' "Merkabah" Visions', pp. 161, 165-66. Neusner, 'Development',
pp. 158-59, who first accepted M as original, later on argued for the priority of T
version—see Halperin, *Merkabah*, p. 119 n. 52.

5.   Gruenwald, *Merkavah Mysticism*, pp. 84, 86.

6.   See Halperin, *Merkabah*, p. 127; Morray-Jones, 'Talmudic Tradition', pp.
231-64.

7.   However, both Bowker, ' "Merkabah" Visions', p. 160 (lines 1-20), and
Neusner, 'Development', pp. 149-50, have included this part in their rendering of
M. Whereas Bowker has acknowledged it as Epstein's 'hypothetical reconstruction', Neusner treats it as part of M—see Bowker, ' "Merkabah" Visions', p. 160
n. 1; Halperin, *Merkabah*, p. 113 n. 3.

13	במעשה מרכבה	27		91	רבן יוחנן בן זכי
14	אמר לו לא כך	28	(ירד מהחמור)	92	שהייתה האש
15	שניתי לכם	29	(רבן יוחנן בן זכי)	93	מלהטת מכל סביביו
16		...		94	ירד מהחמור
17	אלא במרכבה	44	היה ר׳ אלעזר בן ערד		...
a	ביחיד	45	דורש	99	ונשקו
18	אלא אם כן היה	46–47		100	ואמר לו
19	חכם ומבין	48	(ירד מהחמור)	101	ר׳ אלעזר בן ערך
20	מדעתו אמר לו	49	(רבן יחנן בן זכי)	102	אשרי יולדתך
21		...			...
22		61	עד שהייתה האש	121	אשריך
23	אם לאיו תן לי	...		122	אברהם אביון
24	רשות שאומר	74	מלהטת מכל סביביו	123	אזה
25	לעניך	...		124	יצא מחלציך
26		90	כיון שראה		

Although the original story lacks lines 1-20, in M the expression ירד מהחמור (line 94) shows that both Yohanan and Eleazar were undertaking a journey and the term דורש in line 45 indicates the exposition given by Eleazar before Yohanan. However, the issue arising is: did Yohanan and Eleazar undergo mystical experience in the sense that they had a vision of God's glory?

The Merkabah Mystical Experience

Claiming the M version as primary, Halperin argues that the story attributed to the disciples of Yohanan is basically exegetical, without an ecstatic visionary experience.[8] According to him, the Merkabah tradition based on Eleazar's story is rooted in a cycle of miraculous legends, and set in a narrative framework in order to exemplify Eleazar as a 'scholar'; and the supernatural phenomena such as fire, angels, earthquake, rainbow and the *bat qol* reflect more the Sinai revelation, but only secondarily Ezekiel's Merkabah.[9] Halperin's views are rightly challenged by Morray-Jones who argues that Eleazar's story attests 'the two way interaction between speculative exegesis and visionary mysticism', which is present in the apocalyptic and *Hekhalot* mysticism as well as in the early Christian literature.[10] He has also proved that

---

8.   Halperin, *Merkabah*, p. 139.
9.   Halperin, *Merkabah*, pp. 128-33; cf. also *idem*, *Faces*, pp. 15-19.
10.   Morray-Jones, 'Talmudic Tradition', pp. 22-29.

references to 'fire', 'rainbow' (as Halperin also accepts) and 'the sum-
mer month of Tammuz' (in the second story in BT) reflect primarily
Ezekiel's Merkabah vision. Apart from these, the following factors
make it more probable that Yohanan and his disciple underwent the
experience of seeing God's glory.

1. The addition of more supernatural elements and more disciples of
Yohanan in both the Talmuds without uniformity suggests that the
original story of Eleazar later led to various speculations both in Palestine and Babylon. Therefore it is misleading to use these later developments to prove Sinai influence on the original Merkabah story of
Yohanan's disciples.

2. The fire, which encircles Eleazar (סביביו), proves more the fiery
character of God's manifestation, as Halperin admits,[11] than its link
with Sinai tradition. The resemblance with the 'sinaitic' phenomena
shows only the common element of divine presence inherent in both
Eleazar's story and the Sinai theophany and therefore does not
necessarily point to an influence of one tradition upon another. One
cannot deny, however, the connection that occurred with Sinai tradition
at a later stage (cf. Yohanan's dream about reclining on Mt Sinai in
BT). But such a link with Sinai as well as the two rabbinic anecdotes
cited by Urbach (*y. Ḥag.* 2.1; *Lev. R.* 16.4)[12] betray a deliberate attempt
in some rabbinic circles to suppress the Merkabah exposition by sub-
stituting the less dangerous narrative of Sinai manifestation. Moreover,
the שהייתה האש מלהטת מכל סביביו of lines 92-93 in Eleazar's story lies
in closer parallel to the סביב כמראה־אש בית־לה and the כמראה־אש ונגה
לו סביב of Ezek. 1.27 than to the Sinai narrative.

3. 'The glory of our father who is in heaven' (בכבוד אביו שבשמים) in
lines 111-12 of T has replaced all supernatural elements of other versions. This means that for T these elements are the symbols of the
divine glory, which in fact is the climax of the Merkabah vision in
Ezekiel 1.[13] The fact that it is the glory of God that is expounded (דרש)
and perceived (ידע) indicates that both the exposition and the perception of the Merkabah go together.[14] Moreover, PT links the idea of

---

11. Halperin, *Merkabah*, p. 129.

12. Halperin, *Merkabah*, p. 129.

13. Rowland, 'The First Chapter of Ezekiel', p. xvii, rightly treats lines 111-12
of T as a basis for Merkabah mysticism.

14. Morray-Jones, 'Paradise Revisited. Part 1', pp. 187-88, argues that the

'glory' with that of God as creator in its expression, 'I should hear the Glory of my Creator' (lines 53-54). This makes it probable that Eleazar's story was traditionally accepted, at least in Palestine, as a form of 'mystical' teaching, consisting both of *Ma'aseh Bereshit* (seeing God's glory in creation) and *Ma'aseh Merkabah* (seeing God's glory in Merkabah vision).

4. Halperin, by viewing Yohanan's act of dismounting from the ass and of wrapping himself up (T and BT—1.51) in the light of R. Jonathan's dismounting described in *Gen. R.* 32.10, *Deut. R.* 3.6 and *Song R.* 4.4, infers that it implies no more than Yohanan putting himself 'literally and figuratively' on the student's level and therefore that no Merkabah vision is involved.[15] However, Halperin has ignored the context in which the verb נתעטף is used in both the stories. Whereas in Eleazar's story it is used in connection with the exposition of the Scripture (or Merkabah), it is used in Jonathan's story in the context of the response given to a Samaritan who had defied the sanctity of Jerusalem. In a discourse such as Eleazar's, as Halperin himself admits,[16] it is reasonable to understand that in the 'wrapping oneself up' a vision of divine presence is implied, for the wrapping is to avoid gazing upon the enthroned God.[17] Therefore Yohanan's dismounting and wrapping himself up was a preparation on his part for the vision of the divine glory.

5. Halperin also argues that the esoteric doctrine asciated with Ezekiel 1 was developed only through the public exegesis of Ezekiel's vision in the Synagogue of second-century Palestine and that the stories of Merkabah expositions, leading to the actual 'manifestations' of the glory, were soon ascribed to the disciples of Yohanan.[18] He derives this conclusion by concentrating mainly on the literary evidence that belongs to the late tannaitic and amoraic periods. He has looked back into pre-Christian writings, including the Angelic Liturgy of Qumran, merely to trace out the Merkabah mystical elements that later became inherent in rabbinic literature. His study, however, misses even the crux of Merkabah mysticism: seeing God in his glory. His presuppositions have led him to analyse, among Christian documents, only Revelation,

original notion of דעת indicates a 'visionary-mystical experience' and 'esoteric knowledge'.

15. Halperin, *Merkabah*, pp. 126-27.
16. Halperin, *Merkabah*, p. 125.
17. See Isa. 6.2; *1 En.* 14.19, 21.
18. Halperin, *Merkabah*, pp. 179-83; *idem, Faces*, pp. 15-18.

ignoring such important witness as 2 Corinthians 12. After an inquiry into the apocalyptic literature to trace the earliest form of Merkabah exegesis, Halperin proceeds to the synagogue tradition of the second century, without paying enough attention to the first-century Jewish tradition. His scepticism is also reflected in his study of 4QS1 fragments, when he expresses the impossibility of understanding the second fragment because of its broken condition.[19] In the light of the newly published Qumran fragments, which substantially point to the community's Merkabah mystical practice, Halperin's study of the earliest Merkabah tradition can be substantially discounted.

Did Yohanan Practise Merkabah Mysticism?

Morray-Jones, though tracing the 'esoteric visionary mystical tradition' as early as the tannaitic period, does not accept that Yohanan himself had undergone a visionary-mystical experience based on Ezekiel 1. He assumes that Yohanan, by becoming suspicious of such experiences, 'denied its legitimacy'. By the second century CE, argues Morray-Jones, the Merkabah stories were linked with Sinai tradition and then attributed to Yohanan in order to win popular acceptance of the mystical practices of the rabbis such as Hanina b. Dosa and Eliezer b. Hyracanus.[20] He cites *b. Suk.* 28a, *ARN* (A) 6 and 13, and the story of the healing of Yohanan's son by Hanina b. Dosa to prove that Yohanan was not a practising ecstatic. According to him, some of the Tannaim had inherited the 'thaumaturgic ability' from sources other than Yohanan.[21]

Such views do not, however, take into account how the esoteric teachings were normally communicated in Jewish schools. Alexander has shown that 'mysticism', as a secret doctrine in Palestinian Judaism, was communicated by an established master to the inner circle of his pupils, who would form a 'mystical conventicle' round him.[22] It is also unclear why disciples such as Eleazar and Eliezer, who possessed

19. Halperin, *Faces*, pp. 49-54. However, he concedes that the language used in this fragment resembles that of Ezekiel's Merkabah and of the *Hekhalot*.
20. Morray-Jones, 'Talmudic Tradition', pp. 282-307.
21. Morray-Jones, 'Talmudic Tradition', p. 285.
22. Alexander, 'Historical Setting', pp. 168-69. Cohen, *Shi'ur Qomah*, p. 3, indicates that one mystic's experiences served as 'the mediative spring-board for others' mystic journeys'.

thaumaturgic ability, should seek to prove their ability of seeing
Merkabah visions before a master who denied its legitimacy or who
himself had not known an ecstatic experience. The text in *b. Suk.* 28a
clearly indicates that Yohanan did not neglect *Ma'aseh Merkabah*
('great matters').[23] Hanina's posture of 'putting his head between his
knees' does not necessarily indicate the ecstatic trance of the *Hekhalot*
mystics, as Morray-Jones assumes[24] (cf. 1 Kgs 18.42b).

Morray-Jones cites the two versions of the expositions of Eliezer b.
Hyracanus that were delivered for the approval of Yohanan (*ARN* [A] 6
and 13; *Gen. R.* 42.1).[25] After omitting what he supposes to be the
redactional materials, he reconstructs the original form of the story,
which portrays Yohanan as the one who kissed Eliezer, when he realized his wrong judgment on the latter's ability to discourse on the
Torah.[26] He fails to ask, however, whether such an intuitive ecstatic
experience of an 'ignorant country lad' has precedence in any other
rabbinic writings, or, at least, in the protocol for the admission of disciples to the school at Yavneh. What Morray-Jones calls the 'scornful
challenge' posed by the Yavnean rabbis against Eliezer, the newcomer,
to discourse on the Torah speaks contrary to Yohanan's conviction that
his disciples should *qualify* themselves for the study of Torah, as no
one can *inherit* knowledge of it.[27] Yohanan's address to Eliezer, 'Master, you have taught me the truth' does not exhibit either Eliezer's supe-
riority or Yohanan's lack of ecstatic ability, as Morray-Jones argues,[28]
but it simply illustrates Yohanan's willingness to learn even from his
pupils.[29]

Morray-Jones also indicates that Yohanan's name is not mentioned
in the *Hekhalot* texts save in an alternative reading of MS M40 of *HR*

23. Although this may be a later addition, as Neusner thinks (observed by
Morray-Jones, 'Talmudic Tradition', p. 284 n. 2), Neusner does not prove that
Yohanan was not a practising Merkabah mystic.
24. Morray-Jones, 'Talmudic Tradition', pp. 285-86.
25. Morray-Jones, 'Talmudic Tradition', pp. 286-92.
26. Morray-Jones, 'Talmudic Tradition', p. 295.
27. See Neusner, *Life of Yohanan ben Zakkai*, pp. 97-117, for Yohanan's
friendly relationship with his disciples and Eliezer's faithfulness to Yohanan until
the latter's death. Note especially Yohanan calling Simeon b. Natanel, an ignorant
man, an 'oasis in the desert' (p. 109).
28. Morray-Jones, 'Talmudic Tradition', pp. 293-94.
29. Neusner, *Life of Yohanan ben Zakkai*, p. 105, shows that Yohanan adopted
'pedagogical technique' in his teaching.

14.3, while the names of ten sages are mentioned.[30] However, it is only natural for the *Hekhalot* texts, which preserve the idea of heavenly ascent as a major technique in 'mystical' experience, to ignore the experiences of the Yavnean rabbis who did not put much stress on an ascent to heaven. Further, at a time when the *Hekhalot* literature was compiled, it would probably have been felt unnecessary to focus more on first-century rabbis such as Yohanan or Eleazar than on the leading rabbis of the second century.

There exists no convincing proof, then, to assure us that Yohanan was a stranger to Merkabah visionary experience. Why then does there exist no written document about Yohanan's mystical practice? The occasion when Yohanan started his school in Yavneh is probably important to answer this question. He chose Yavneh to make it a religious centre to revive Judaism at a time when the temple had been destroyed leaving little hope for cultic worship. This was indeed a time of humiliation and persecution particulary for the rabbis such as Yohanan. At a time when their political power had diminished and their identity was being threatened, their mystical visions, if at all divulged, would have easily been ridiculed. P.S. Alexander makes a similar observation for the *Hekhalot* mystics. According to him, had the visions of the mystics told plainly, the Roman emperor and his officials would probably have dismissed them as the inventions of 'deluded fanatics who had lost touch with reality'.[31] The same socio-political reason

can be attributed to the secrecy of Yohanan's experience as well. As Neusner indicates, the content of the esoteric speculation was kept secret in Yohanan's day[32] and this tendency accounts for the lack of literary evidence for Yohanan's practice. In fact, Yohanan considered ethics and mysticism to be correlated by arguing that a heavenly vision of the Almighty should lead the pious to 'seek a true perception of the Godhead in all the concrete imagery of the astral mysticism of the day'.[33] He emphasized love and social involvement of the mystics even

---

30. Morray-Jones, 'Talmudic Tradition', pp. 298-99; similarly Halperin, *Merkabah*, p. 139.

31. See Alexander, 'Family of Caesar', pp. 296-97.

32. Neusner, *Life of Yohanan ben Zakkai*, p. 137. Biram, 'Ma'aseh Bereshit; Ma'aseh Merkabah', p. 236, holds that Yohanan refused to discuss the secret doctrine even in the presence of a single person, although he was its founder.

33. Neusner, *Life of Yohanan ben Zakkai*, pp. 141-42.

though they were in a powerless and oppressed condition. This has value in our time too!

Conclusions

We can conclude, then, that Yohanan and his school did practise Merkabah mysticism by means of Merkabah exegesis. There is no reason to doubt that Yohanan himself was a practising mystic. The transmission of the story of Merkabah exposition to the other disciples of Yohanan and the appearance of several versions in the process of transmission show no less than the growing interest of the Palestinian and Babylonian rabbis in such a practice even from the first century CE. Thus, at the time of John some leading rabbis of Judaism practised mysticism in the sense of 'seeing God's glory', by expounding the passages on Ezekiel's chariot and they did not separate mysticism from ethics.

Chapter 9

THE INFLUENCE OF KEY PASSAGES FROM SCRIPTURE

Our investigation thus far has revealed that in the pre- and post-Christian periods there was a growing interest, both as individuals and as a community, in Merkabah visionary experience and that such an experience is very much bound up with biblical texts, particularly with Ezekiel 1, Isaiah 6 and Daniel 7. A study of these passages, then, will enable us to understand to what extent the Merkabah mystical features known in the first century had their roots in Scripture.

The Merkabah Mystical Elements in Ezekiel

Ezekiel 1 contains the vision of God, as seen by Ezekiel, possibly in 593 BCE, when a state of hopelessness regarding freedom and of fear of total alienation from God was prevailing among the Jews, particularly in Jerusalem.[1] The two expressions, 'the heavens were opened' and 'I saw visions of God', in Ezek. 1.1 emphasize the divine origin and hence the supernatural nature of Ezekiel's vision. We can list below the major components of the vision, which later came to be regarded as 'mystical' in Judaism.

The Living Creatures (חיות)
The glory of the enthroned God is described from the bottom of the throne-chariot upwards, beginning from the four living creatures (*hayyot*), which have semi-human and semi-nonhuman forms (Ezek. 1.4) and which are identified with the *Cherubim* in Ezekiel 10. Each of these supernatural beings has four wings, two of which touch the wing of another creature, while two cover their bodies (Ezek. 1.6, 11, 23). Unlike in Isa. 6.2-3, where the movements of the wings of the *Seraphim*

1.   See W. Eichrodt, *Ezekiel: A Commentary* (London: SCM Press, 1970), pp. 52-54.

are directly linked with their singing of the glory of Yahweh, in Ezekiel 1 the moving of the wings leads the creatures to go forward with an audible sound bearing the divine throne (Ezek. 1.12, 24; cf. 10.19).[2]

Does this sound denote the praise and blessing offered by the creatures to the enthroned one (cf. Isa. 6.3; *Targ. Ezek.* 1.24b)? The MT, however, does not seem to suggest this. Like Ezek. 3.12, 1.24 too speaks only of an 'unpersönlichen Geräusch der Bewegung' (a 'sound of the movement of an impersonal being').[3] Also, Ezek. 10.5, an interpretative addition to Ezek. 10.3b, compares the sound of the wings of the *Cherubim* to the voice of God, and Ezek. 43.2, the reminiscence of the theophany by the River Chebar (43.3), applies the 'sound of many waters' to the 'sound' of the coming of God's glory. Therefore the קוֹל of the wings cannot be understood as praise. By the time when the *Similitudes* was written, or even earlier in Qumran texts, the *Cherubim* and *Seraphim*, along with the *Ofannim*, came to be classified as angelic beings (*1 En.* 61.10; 71.7; cf. also *2 En.* 21; *T. Adam* 4; 4Q403 1.2.15; 4Q405 20.2-21-22.3, 7-9). Therefore the *hayyot/Cherubim* play an angelic role, though it was not recognized at the time when Ezekiel was written. The appearance of coals of fire, which move like torches to and fro in the midst of the *hayyot* (Ezek. 1.13; cf. 10.2, 6-7), probably indicates God's presence (cf. Ezek. 1.27), for the movement of the fire enables the movement of the *hayyot* (Ezek. 1.14).

The living creatures in Ezekiel 1 and the *Cherubim* in Ezekiel 10 are bearing the throne of God (cf. Ps. 18.10) and moving, most probably, towards the prophet himself (Ezek. 1.28b–3.12).[4] In the then historical situation, both in Palestine and Babylon, the vision of the enthroned Yahweh, as borne by the four living creatures, would convey the message that it is Yahweh, more than the four chief deities of Babylon, who is the king, the one who controls human history at all times and circumstances.[5]

2.   The קוֹל of the wings is compared to three different kinds of sounds: (1) it was like the sound of many waters, which is surely reminiscent of Ezek. 43.2 (so also argues Zimmerli, *Ezechiel*, I, p. 69); (2) it was like the voice of the Almighty, a comparison that is not found in the LXX, but which might be the influence of Ezek. 10.5; (3) it was like the sound of a host, i.e. the noise of a military camp (מחנה), which is also missing in the LXX, but which appears in a clumsy way in Ezek. 43.2 LXX.

3.   Zimmerli, *Ezechiel*, I, pp. 68-69.
4.   Zimmerli, *Ezechiel*, I, p. 54.
5.   See W.H. Brownlee, *Ezekiel 1–19* (WBC, 28; Waco, TX: Word Books,

The Wheels (אופנים)

The term אופנים in Ezek. 1.15-21 and 10.15-17 stands for the chariot (מרכבה). The brightness of the wheels appeared like the 'gleaming of a chrysolite' (כעין תרשיש), a precious stone (cf. Ezek. 10.9b) that resembles the 'gleaming bronze' (כעין חשמל) of Ezek. 1.27. Each wheel stood beside each creature and went in any direction without turning to either side (Ezek. 1.17), but following the front wheel (cf. Ezek. 10.11).[6] The wheels, being full of eyes round about, moved in perfect unison (Ezek. 1.18-19).

Halperin argues that Ezek. 10.9-17 shows in two stages the development of the angelological conception of the אופנים: the literal 'wheels' receding and being replaced by an angelic class, the *Ofannim*.[7] Though *prima facie* it seems likely, a careful exegesis of 10.11-14 does not support this view.[8] If Ezek. 10.9-17 marks the development of the angelological interpretation, how is it that the tradition is untraceable after Ezekiel 10, even in the book of Watchers (*1 En.* 1–36), where one could expect it because of the high importance there is to angelology? One can still see a clear distinction between the *Ofannim* and the angels in 4Q405 20.2-21-22.9. Ezekiel 1, the *Vorlage* of Ezek. 10.9-17 (Halperin), however, reflects a fixed tradition in which the *Ofannim* are no more than the chariot's wheels, which are fully governed and guided by the רוח (1.20).

1986), pp. 11-12; H.F. Fuchs, *Ezekiel 1–24* (Die Neue Echter Bibel; Würzburg: Echter Verlag, 1984), pp. 24-25.

6.	D.J. Halperin, 'The Exegetical Character of Ezek. x. 9-17', *VT* 26 (1976), pp. 129-41 (138), prefers here the literal meaning 'head' for הראש. However, the following verb along with the preposition (אחריו ילכו = 'they walked behind it') makes this sense impossible, for no one can follow the head unless the term is understood as a leading figure or object. Halperin is led to favour this meaning by his presupposition that אופנים are already conceived as angels in Ezek. 10.

7.	Halperin, 'Ezek. x. 9-17', pp. 129-41.

8.	For Halperin, Ezek. 10.12 refers to the flesh and the limbs of the *Ofannim*. But in fact it distinctly classifies *Ofannim* with גב, בשר and יד. If the author had perceived these limbs as belonging to the *Ofannim*, it would be irrelevant for him to place the *Ofannim* in the same category as the limbs. Strictly speaking, v. 13, which emphasizes the identity of גלגל with the *Ofannim*, is important in the whole argument, but Halperin dismisses it as secondary material added later (see pp. 130, 131 n. 6, 132; similarly, Zimmerli, *Ezechiel*, I, p. 203).

The Glory of God on the Throne

The author reaches the climax of his vision in 1.26-28, where he describes 'the appearance of the likeness of a human form (דמות כמראה אדם)' on the throne that rests upon the firmament, over the heads of the living creatures. The expression, 'Such was the appearance of the likeness of the glory of the Lord', in v. 28 is, according to Brownlee, 'a one-sentence summary of what the prophet saw'.[9] Though this is true in a broader sense, it seems that the focus lies primarily on the likeness of אדם as the 'image' of Yahweh's glory, for the parallel account of the theophany (8.2-4) highlights דמות כמראה איש rather than the throne-chariot.[10] The man-like figure in 1.26, then, is no one but the revelation of God to the prophet (cf. מראות אלהים in 1.1).

The MT uses the word אדם in 1.26 in contrast to the איש of 8.2. The *Targum of Ezekiel* renders 1.26b as: 'and above the likeness of the throne there was the likeness of the appearance of Adam, above it from on high', thus retaining the word אדם without translating it. Levey argues that the *Targum of Ezekiel* bears evidence of the redactive hand of Yohanan b. Zakkai with strong allusions to Merkabah mysticism, because he notices messianic activism being replaced by Merkabah mysticism in the *Targum of Ezekiel*.[11] If Merkabah mysticism is inherent in the *Targum of Ezekiel*, then the deliberate use of the term 'Adam', with its accompanying phrase, דמות כמראה, for the manifestation of God,[12] must bear special significance in the mystical tradition of the first century CE, the period of our interest.

The man-like figure is surrounded by two degrees of light: the upper part of his loins shone with the 'gleaming *hashmal*', which itself is enclosed by fire, and the lower part with the appearance of fire (1.27; cf. 1.4 and 8.2). The encircling fire symbolizes the 'brightness' or 'radiance' of his glory, recalling the manifestation of the majesty of Yahweh

9.   Brownlee, *Ezekiel 1–19*, p. 15; H.D. Preuss, 'דְּמָה/דְּמוּת', in *ThWAT*, II, col. 274, states, '1.28 stellt als Schlußvers von Kap 1'.

10.   G. Fohrer argues that the expression, 'This was the appearance of the likeness of the glory of the Lord' in 1.28 refers only to the דמות כמראה אדם of v. 26 and not to the whole vision of the throne-chariot (see C. Colpe, 'ὁ υἱὸς τοῦ ἀνθρώπου', *TDNT*, VIII, p. 418 n. 151); cf. Rowland, *Open Heaven*, p. 97.

11.   S.H. Levey, *The Targum of Ezekiel* (ArBib, 13; Edinburgh: T. & T. Clark, 1987), pp. 2-5, esp. p. 4.

12.   Levey, *Targum of Ezekiel*, p. 7, maintains that the figure, Adam, had been associated with the celestial temple and the throne of the deity in the circles from which the *Targum of Ezekiel* originated.

in the wilderness story (Exod. 16.7; 24.16-18; 29.43; 40.34-35; etc.). Thus Ezek. 1.26-28 describes how God, who is seated on the throne with fire encircling him, reveals himself in the likeness of the appearance of a man. The use of the generic term 'Adam', in the context of divine revelation, may imply God's identification with his people who were in bondage and suffering at the time of Ezekiel and his closeness to save them. The description of the enthroned God, manifested in the likeness of man, gave rise in varying degrees to mystical speculation, particularly in the first century CE, as we have observed above. Gruenwald grasps the crux of Jewish mysticism when he claims that the mystical visions in the Scripture are those visions in which God appears to man in a man-like form and seated upon a throne.[13]

Yahweh's self-revelation in אדם כמראה דמות also has an esoteric overtone, for his name is not mentioned either in 1.26 or in 1.28c which refers to the voice 'of the one who spoke'. The reason, according to Zimmerli, is to preserve the mystery of the deity hidden in the manifestation of his glory.[14] This means that even the prophet could see God only as far as he was revealed in אדם כמראה דמות rather than the whole deity, otherwise he would die (cf. Exod. 33.20). We have already noticed the esoteric implication of the chariot exposition in the restriction imposed on the common people (*m. Hag.* 2.1), for in the early rabbinic period Ezekiel 1 was considered as a passage that communicates 'one of the most profound secrets of Judaism, the mystery of God himself', which was the pillar of Jewish mysticism.[15]

Interestingly enough, Ezekiel 10, without mentioning the figure seated upon the throne (cf. 9.3), makes reference instead to a 'man clothed in linen' (9.11–10.1). This figure, in all probability, is a priestly angel,[16] whose priestly aspect qualifies him 'to enter among the cherubs and handle the heavenly fire blazing among them' (10.7). It is not clear why the author refers to a man, who does not hold equal status with the figure in Ezek. 1.26.[17] Does this tendency reflect the beginning of the

---

13. Gruenwald, *Merkavah Mysticism*, p. 31. Cf. Scholem, *Jewish Gnosticism* (1960), p. 36; Fossum, 'Jewish-Christian Christology', p. 260.

14. Zimmerli, *Ezechiel*, I, p. 70.

15. Rowland, *Open Heaven*, p. 277.

16. See above, p. 142.

17. Rowland, *Open Heaven*, p. 96, supposes that the separation between the human figure and the throne is already perceived in Ezek. 8; cf. *idem*, 'Vision of the Risen Christ', pp. 1-11.

process in which anthropomorphism was giving way to angelomor-phism?[18] It does not seem so, for the presence of the man-like figure of Ezek. 1.26 is implied in 10.2 (note the expression ויאמר אל־האיש, the subject being יהוה as in 9.4) and even the glory of the Lord is still active (10.4). One can see, however, reticence in later traditions to-wards the anthropomorphic way of describing God.

The Prophetic Commission

The manifestation of God did not remain for Ezekiel as merely an ecstatic visionary experience, but it also brought to the visionary a new responsibility to proclaim the words of judgment to the people of Israel at large and to his fellow exiles in particular. He was sent in his status as בן אדם, an ordinary human being who was equipped, in his weak-ness and frailty, by the רוח. Haag argues that in Ezekiel the translation 'Son of Man' should be avoided, for 'man' is the only possible ren-dering.[19] This argument, however, overlooks the context in which the expression בן אדם has been used in Ezek. 2.1. If there is any theolog-ical significance at all in the term אדם in 1.26 and if the throne-vision and commission go hand in hand (cf. Isa. 6; Acts 9.3-22; 22.6-21; 26.12-23),[20] then there must be a special significance in the use of the phrase בן אדם as well.[21] It denotes a man of mortal nature, but who was empowered by the רוח for a special task. He became the 'sent one', 'an ambassador' for God,[22] who received divine authority to proclaim God's word to the people. That is, Ezekiel was sent not as בן בוזי (see 1.3), which would have made him no more than an ordinary man incapable for the divine mission, but as בן אדם who was made capable by God's word (2.8-10) and the Spirit. The one who had a vision of אדם became בן אדם.[23]

18.   Cf. Rowland, 'The Visions of God', pp. 137-54.

19.   H. Haag, 'בֶּן אָדָם', *TDOT*, II, pp. 159-165 (163); Brownlee, *Ezekiel 1–19*, pp. 25-26.

20.   For Zimmerli, *Ezechiel*, I, p. 35, Ezek. 1, without the commissioning speech in Ezek. 2–3, 'bleibt in torso'.

21.   *Targ. Ps.-J. Ezek.* uses in Ezek. 2.1 the phrase *bar 'adam* rather than *bar 'enasha*, whereas it translates *'adam* in Ezek. 1.10 into *'enasha*—see R.D. Kimḥi's comment cited by Levey, *Targum of Ezekiel*, p. 7.

22.   See G. von Rad, *Old Testament Theology. II. The Theology of Israel's Prophetic Traditions* (ET; London: SCM Press, 1965), p. 223.

23.   H.W. Hines, 'The Prophet as Mystic', *AJSL* 40 (1923–24), pp. 37-71,

Some Observations

Four important factors in relation to Merkabah mysticism emerge here. First, the key aspects such as the heavenly ascent, the angelic entourage and praise, which dominated the mystical thinking of the rabbis in the first and second century CE, are absent in Ezekiel's vision. Secondly, the opening of heaven here implies the descent of God by the River Chebar, for the prophet sees a wheel *on the earth* (Ezek. 1.15). Thirdly, although there is no explicit reference in Ezekiel's chariot-vision to the angels, the *hayyot* and the *Cherubim* clearly point to the angelic groups. There is also an oblique reference to an angelic being in his priestly attire in Ezekiel 9–10. Fourthly, as the phrase דמות כבוד־יהוה in 1.28 primarily points to דמות כמראה אדם in 1.26, one can see in Ezekiel 1 a strong sense of anthropomorphism in describing God. However, in the development of the theophany tradition there was some reticence to describe God in anthropomorphic terms, for in Ezekiel 10 this figure is not explicitly mentioned, although one can hear him speaking (10.2).

The Merkabah Mystical Elements in Isaiah 6

The closest parallel to Ezekiel's Merkabah vision is Isaiah's *Berufungs-vision* that is recorded in Isaiah 6. John clearly refers to this passage in Jn 12.41-42 and therefore it is imperative for us to have a brief study of the vision in Isaiah 6 so that we might find out the salient features of Merkabah vision that can be traced back even to the pre-exilic period.

The Vision of God on the Throne

King Uzziah's death marked the end of the period of peace and fertility in Judah and Isaiah had to proclaim Yahweh's message of judgment under the new king, Ahaz, and in new circumstances. It was also a time when Israel had been weakened by the rising power of Assyria.[24] It is at this point that Isaiah saw אדני sitting upon a throne.[25] In its historical situation, this vision may mean that Yahweh, as king, determines the

---

calls Ezekiel a 'mystic' precisely because he had seen or heard God and had been illumined by him.

24.   For a detailed historical situation of the late eighth century BCE see O. Kaiser, *Isaiah 1–12: A Commentary* (London: SCM Press, 1972), pp. 2-5; E.J. Young, *The Book of Isaiah* (3 vols.; Grand Rapids: Eerdmans, 1965), I, pp. 9-21.

25.   O. Eissfeldt, 'אדני אָדוֹן', *TDOT*, I, pp. 59-72 (71), shows that the term אדני can refer no more than to Yahweh himself.

events in human history by calling and dismissing nations.[26] The phrase
יֹשֵׁב עַל־כִּסֵּא specifies Yahweh's kingly rule and the following phrase
רָם וְנִשָּׂא reinforces this idea by emphasizing his sovereignty over all
circumstances. What is implicit here is explicitly mentioned in v. 5 by
saying that the prophet's eyes have seen the king, who is the Lord of
the heavenly army. The image of Yahweh as king portrays not only his
sovereignty, but also the standard of *his relationship with human
beings*. Kaiser highlights the latter aspect by saying that God, as king,
can demand obedience and the loyalty of vassals from his worshippers,
ensuring them of his protection.[27] It is probable that the prophet
intended his audience, in the wake of a decaying situation in Judah,
both politically and religiously, to know that Yahweh's kingship is
permanent and therefore that he, having been sent by him, holds continuously divine authority in his mission. The goal of *Hekhalot* mysticism, 'gazing at the King in His beauty' seems to have originated from
this prophetic tradition.

The prophet's sense of terror and awe, which is expressed in his
words, 'Woe is me! For I am lost' and his affirmation that his eyes have
seen the Lord (6.5) presuppose that he really experienced a *visio
externa* ('an actual external vision').[28] However, the question arises
how the actual perception of God would have been possible to Isaiah
against the Hebrew conviction that no one can survive the vision of
God (cf. Exod. 33.20; 19.21; Judg. 6.22-23; 13.22; Gen. 32.30; Jn 1.18;
1 Tim. 6.16). Although the prophet does not give a visual sketch of
Yahweh,[29] references to 'sitting' on the throne and to his 'robe', which
filled the temple, imply some physical form, possibly a human form, in
which Yahweh manifested himself. Young rightly comments that it is
not the essence of God that Isaiah saw, but a manifestation of his glory
in human form, adapted to the capabilities of the finite creature.[30]

26.   See J.D.W. Watts, *Isaiah 1–33* (WBC, 24; Waco, TX: Word Books,
1985), p. lv.
27.   Kaiser, *Isaiah 1–12*, p. 80. Y. Gitay, *Isaiah and his Audience: The Structure and Meaning of Isaiah 1–12* (Assen: Van Gorcum, 1991), p. 124, maintains
that 'seeing God' is to do with one's relationship with the fearful God.
28.   Wildberger, *Isaiah 1–12*, p. 260; cf. Kaiser, *Isaiah 1–12*, p. 74.
29.   See Wildberger, *Isaiah 1–12*, p. 261.
30.   See Young, *Isaiah*, I, pp. 235-36. He also speaks (pp. 245-46) of two
aspects of God's glory: God's 'essential glory' (i.e. that glory that he has in and of
himself as God) and his 'declarative glory' (i.e. the glory that he has displayed in
the created universe).

The temple (היכל) is described as the place of God's manifestation in Isaiah's vision. Wildberger comments that in the light of 1 Kgs 22.19 and Ezek. 1.1 it is more likely that the heavenly dwelling-place is meant here.[31] His argument, however, overlooks the fact that both in 1 Kings 22 and Ezekiel 1 Yahweh manifests himself on earth and that there is no indication that the prophets ascended to heaven. The היכל is described as בית ('house') in 6.4, a term that is generally applied to the Jerusalem temple (cf. Isa. 56.7; Jer. 7.11). It is more probable that Isaiah saw the Lord in the holy place of the Jerusalem temple,[32] which implies the descent of the deity. Although Isaiah 6 describes the manifestation of God in terms of his descent to the 'divine palace' on earth, later in the apocalyptic and mystical traditions the divine manifestation was linked with the ascent of the privileged men to heaven.

The Seraphim
The six-winged *Seraphim* are mentioned as standing above the throne (6.2), unlike the four living creatures of Ezek. 1.22, 26, which are positioned below the throne of God. These groups of heavenly beings cannot be identical, for, apart from their positions, there are marked differences in their structure and function. For example, the *Seraphim* of Isaiah 6 have six wings each unlike the *hayyot* of Ezekiel 1 which have four wings each. The *hayyot* do not sing praising the enthroned God as the *Seraphim* do. Also, the *Seraphim* do not hold the function of protecting the deity/king like the two figures, which were commonly believed in the ancient Near East to accompany the deity in order to protect him.[33] The *Seraphim* of Isaiah 6 exhibit personal qualities, possessing human organs, speech and understanding. If we accept Isaiah's vision as that of a heavenly council, then the *Seraphim* can imply a group of the 'host of heaven' (cf. 1 Kgs 22.19), the praising and serving angels.

The Heavenly Hymn
Although the expression 'the Glory of the Lord' does not occur in Isaiah's theophany, one can see an implicit reference to it in the

31.   Wildberger, *Isaiah 1–12*, p. 262; Young, *Isaiah*, I, p. 237 n. 8.
32.   The word היכל means not simply '(royal) palace', but also the entire building of the temple (1 Sam. 1.9) and, in particular, the inner sanctuary (1 Kgs 6.17; Pss. 5.8; 79.1; 138.2).
33.   See Wildberger, *Isaiah 1–12*, p. 263; Young, *Isaiah*, I, p. 239.

trisagion of the *Seraphim*, which exalts God's holiness and glory (6.3). Whereas קדוש signifies God's inner nature, the divine perfection that separates God from his creation, his כבוד points to his revealed nature, the glory, which is revealed in the created universe (see Pss. 19.1; 89.6a; 97.6).[34] Thus the song of praise contains both the theological and the cosmological dimension of God's glory and we recall again that these two aspects are embedded in the two branches of study of Jewish mysticism: *Ma'aseh Merkabah* and *Ma'aseh Bereshit* respectively.

Fire

As in Ezekiel 1, in the throne-vision of Isaiah 6 'fire' also plays an important role, but mainly as cleansing agent. The terms עשן ('smoke') in Isa. 6.4 and רצפה ('burning coal') of the altar in Isa. 6.6 present fire as an integral part of the divine presence. The shaking of the mountains (cf. the shaking of the foundations of the threshold in Isa. 6.4) and the clouds of smoke had already been known in Jewish circles as major components of theophany (cf. Exod. 19.9, 18; 24.15-18.; Judg. 5.4-5; 1 Kgs 8.10). Therefore Procksch's view that the smoke is the condensed breath of those singing praises[35] is unacceptable in a theophany narrative such as this. The focus intended by the prophet in the whole scene is the enthroned God in his self-revelation rather than the praise of the *Seraphim*. Isaiah's guilt is taken away and sins are forgiven and thus his life is transformed by the symbolic touch of his mouth with the fire taken from the altar. In this way the fire of God equips the prophet for divine mission.

The Divine Commission

As in Ezekiel's chariot-vision, in Isaiah 6 too God's commissioning of the visionary follows vision. This is implied in the words, לך ואמרת ('go and speak'—Isa. 6.9), although Israel will respond to the message with a harsh rejection. The act of sending occurs, unlike in Ezekiel, in the form of a dialogue between God and Isaiah. The setting seems to be the heavenly council,[36] in which a decision to send Isaiah to the people

---

34.   Thus Procksch—see Wildberger, *Isaiah 1–12*, p. 266; Watts, *Isaiah 1–33*, p. 74.

35.   See Wildberger, *Isaiah 1–12*, p. 268. Procksch's view ignores the קול הקורא ('The voice of him who called'), which caused the shaking of the threshold and the smoke.

36.   Cf. 1 Kgs 22.19-23; Job 1.6-12; 2.1-6; Zech. 3.1-5; see Watts, *Isaiah 1–33*, p. 72.

had already been taken. Therefore, to detach theophany from divine commissioning, whether the visionary actively responds as Isaiah or passively submits as Ezekiel, is to miss the kernel of the throne-vision.

Daniel's Vision in Daniel 7 and Merkabah Mysticism

The book of Daniel, one of the apocalypses of the second century BCE, describes the vision of God's throne and the heavenly assize in 7.9-14 without any reference to a heavenly ascent. We have already noticed the importance that this text had held both among the so-called 'pre-Merkabah mystics' and the midrashic rabbis in the development of the 'two powers in heaven' apostasy as well as in defence against it.[37] Scholars such as Bowman, Feuillet, Black and Rowland,[38] have argued for a literary and theological connection between Ezekiel 1 and Dan. 7.9-14. An inquiry into Dan. 7.9-14, then, will throw further light on the key aspects of Merkabah mysticism practised at the time of John.

Daniel's vision in ch. 7 reflects the historical situation of the Jews during the rule of Babylonia, Media, Persia and Greece, particularly referring to the rule of Antiochus Epiphanes, who is identified as the 'little horn' (7.8, 24, 25).[39] The author of Daniel 7 refers to the wicked deeds of Antiochus as war against the law-abiding Jews (7.20, 21) and his blasphemy against God (7.25). In this historical context the judgment of God is revealed to Daniel in a vision, according to which the 'fourth beast' and the 'little horn' will be destroyed, but the pious Jews will be vindicated.

37. See above, pp. 147-49.
38. J. Bowman, 'The Background of the Term "Son of Man"', *ExpTim* 59 (1947-48), pp. 238-88 (285); M. Black, 'The Throne-Theophany Prophetic Commission and the "Son of Man": A Study in Tradition History', in R. Hamerton-Kelly and R. Scroggs (eds.), *Jews, Greeks and Christians: Religious Cultures in Late Antiquity* (Festschrift W.D. Davies; Leiden: E.J. Brill, 1976), pp. 57-73; Rowland, *Open Heaven*, p. 55. Feuillet's position is cited by Black, 'Throne-Theophany', pp. 60-61.
39. See Casey, *Son of Man*, pp. 19-22; however, following the author of *4 Ezra* (*4 Ezra* 12.11-12), R.H. Charles, *A Critical and Exegetical Commentary on the Book of Daniel* (Oxford: Clarendon Press, 1929), pp. 169-72, argues that undoubtedly the fourth kingdom stands for Rome; against this interpretation see N.W. Porteous, *Daniel: A Commentary* (London: SCM Press, 1965), pp. 103-104.

The Throne-Vision

Daniel's vision takes the form of a Merkabah vision. At the judgment thrones were placed and the 'ancient of days' took his seat (Dan. 7.9). The plural 'thrones' can possibly express the idea that the heavenly powers or 'the angelic assessors' take part with God in the act of judgment (cf. Ps. 122.5; also Rev. 4.4-11).[40] Whether the judgment takes place on earth (so argues Casey) or in heaven (so argues Hartman and this seems more probable in the light of Job 1 and Ps. 82),[41] the scene illuminates the manifestation of God by using traditional materials from 1 Kgs 22.19-23, Isaiah 6 and Ezekiel 1. He is the king of history, but at the same time judge of all. The seer does not undertake an ascent to heaven, but has the vision on earth.

Seeing God

The one who is seated on the throne is called עתיק יומין (7.9), which literally means 'one aged in days', that is, an aged being.[42] This expression underlines two important factors: God's action in time and his anthropomorphic mode of revelation. It is true, as Charles thinks, that the expression 'ancient of days' may not in itself indicate a human being, but the following references to his raiment and hair betray clear anthropomorphism in the description of God.[43] Thus God is revealed to Daniel in human terms, as the one who himself is involved in human affairs.

According to Rowland, one of the distinguishing features of the view of history in apocalyptic is 'the belief that the whole course of history is under God's control and conforms to the plan laid down by God before the foundation of the world'.[44] Exactly this is envisaged in the throne-vision of Daniel 7. While God rules as king even at the time of fierce

40.   See Charles, *Daniel*, p. 181. J.A. Montgomery, *A Critical and Exegetical Commentary on the Book of Daniel* (Edinburgh: T. & T. Clark, 1927), p. 296, comments that the 'thrones' constitute the 'judicial bench'.

41.   Casey, *Son of Man*, pp. 17-18, 22-23, 29; L.F. Hartman and A.A. Di Lella, *The Book of Daniel* (AB, 23; New York: Doubleday, 1977), p. 217.

42.   Charles, *Daniel*, p. 181; Montgomery, *Daniel*, p. 297. Hartman (Hartman and Di Lella, *Daniel*, p. 206) renders 'one advanced in days', i.e. an old man. NEB renders, 'one ancient in years'.

43.   Charles, *Daniel*, p. 181; Rowland, *Open Heaven*, p. 105. Cf. Gen. 24.1 for the corresponding Hebrew phrase בא בימים used in connection with Abraham's life.

44.   Rowland, *Open Heaven*, p. 90.

persecution of his people, his sovereignty over human affairs has been in existence even before the foundation of the world, because he is the 'ancient of days'. It is little wonder, then, that the idea of God's kingship and sovereignty, embedded in the throne-vision, was dominant in the 'mystical' thought of the Jews, who were also experiencing similar kind of humiliation, especially after 70.

The description that his raiment was white as snow and that the hair of his head was like pure wool hints at the human form of God (cf. *1 En.* 14.20; 71.10). Apart from these, there is no direct reference to the physical features of the 'ancient of days' in Daniel 7. In the light of the divine manifestation mentioned in Ezek. 1.26 and Isa. 6.1, we can argue that Dan. 7.9 too, although יְקָרא (= Hebrew כבוד) does not occur, depicts the glory of Yahweh revealed in a man-like figure who was sitting upon the throne.[45]

The Appearance of Fire

That Daniel could see the 'Glory of God' is confirmed by the statements: 'His throne was fiery flames, its wheels were burning fire. A stream of fire issued and came forth from him' (Dan. 7.9c, 10a). In biblical tradition 'fire' and 'glory' synonymously refer to Yahweh (cf. Zech. 2.9—RSV 2.5).[46] The proper element of deity, as Montgomery comments, is fire with its effluence of light (cf. Exod. 3.2; Deut. 4.24; 33.2) and the stream of fire that comes forth from the divine presence denotes the irresistibility of the divine energy in judgment (cf. Pss. 50.3; 97.3).[47] In fact the destruction of the 'beast', the hostile empire, by divine fire leads to the dominion of God's people (Dan. 7.11-14). The flaming throne, the fiery wheels and a stream of fire recall the Merkabah visions of Ezek. 1.13-14, 26-28; 10.2; and *1 En.* 14.18-22.

The Retinue of Angels

In almost all throne-visions God is not pictured as appearing alone, but

---

45.   Scholem holds that since God does not in himself possess a physical form, he takes up a form, which can be known as the 'glory', in order to reveal himself to human beings and this glory is called *guf ha-Shekhinah* ('the body of the Divine Presence')—as shown by Chernus, 'Visions of God', p. 143; Fossum, 'Jewish–Christian Christology', p. 262.

46.   T.N.D. Mettinger, *The Dethronement of Sabaoth: Studies in the Shem and Kabod Theologies* (ConBOT, 18; Lund: C.W.K. Gleerup, 1982), pp. 110-11, observes that in Zechariah 'light' symbolizes the presence of God as *kabod*.

47.   Montgomery, *Daniel*, p. 298.

always as accompanied by numerous heavenly beings, in particular angels. This is all the more true when he renders judgment (Ps. 82.1). The tradition that millions of angels are standing around the throne of God to serve him was current both in the second century BCE (e.g. *1 En.* 1.9; 14.22) and the first century CE (e.g. *1 En.* 40.1; 71.8, 13; Rev. 5.11). Dan. 7.10 too reflects such a tradition, when it states, 'A thousand thousands served him, and ten thousand times ten thousand stood before him'.

The One Like a Son of Man

Most scholars believe that the enigmatic human appearance of God in Ezek. 1.26, being an angel (cf. Exod. 23.20-21), is directly related to the 'one like a Son of Man' (אנש כבר) of Dan. 7.13, who too has angelic form (cf. both in Dan. 8.15 and 10.16 the angelophany is described in anthropomorphic terms).[48] Did the author of Daniel 7 identify the 'Son of Man' in any sense with the man-like figure of Ezek. 1.26? Is his appearance the mark of angelophany or theophany or both? A closer study of the 'Son of Man' is called for.

The passage shows that the 'one like a Son of Man', who represents the people of God in receiving dominion, comes with the clouds and that, in contrast, the beasts, which symbolize the kings/kingdoms alien to God, rise up from the sea. Therefore the Son of Man is, in all probability, merely a symbolic being, who represents the people of the Most High, just like the four beasts represent four different kingdoms (Dan. 7.18, 22, 25, 27).[49] Those who do not view the Son of Man as a

48.   See N. Schmidt, 'The Son of Man in the Book of Daniel', *JBL* 19 (1900), pp. 22-28; J.J. Collins, 'The Son of Man and the Saints of the Most High in the Book of Daniel', *JBL* 93 (1974), pp. 50-66; Segal, *Paul the Convert*, p. 41; Rowland, 'Vision of the Risen Christ', pp. 1-11, esp. 1-3; *idem, Open Heaven*, pp. 94-104, 182, where Rowland argues that the Son of Man in Dan. 7 is a divine figure/exalted angel, probably Gabriel; so also J. Fossum, *The Name of God and the Angel of the Lord: Samaritan and Jewish Concepts of Intermediation and the Origin of Gnosticism* (WUNT, 36; Tübingen: J.C.B. Mohr [Paul Siebeck], 1985), p. 279 n. 61. M. Barker, *The Great Angel: A Study of Israel's Second God* (London: SPCK, 1992), p. 38, identifies the Son of Man with an unnamed angel, Yahweh. For identification of the Son of Man with Michael, see Rowland, *Open Heaven*, p. 476 n. 47. In contrast, however, Procksch maintains that the man who comes with the clouds of heaven is connected with that of the coming of the 'glory of Yahweh' in Ezek. 1.26—see von Rad, *Old Testament Theology*, II, p. 312 n. 27.

49.   M.D. Hooker, *The Son of Man in Mark: A Study of the Background of the*

symbolic being have proposed either a ditheistic theory or a 'bifurca-
tion of God' theory,[50] although there is no ground in Daniel 7 to favour
these views. Caragounis rightly argues that the 'one like a Son of Man'
in 7.13 is a symbolic figure in human form which can be perceived
from the preposition כ, but his observation that he symbolizes a non-
human reality is ill-founded.[51] Caragounis mainly emphasizes that
Daniel's vision involves two divine beings, one in the form of an old
man and another as 'a *son* of a/the man' (emphasis his).[52] Some of his
major findings need careful examination.

According to Caragounis, the 'one like a Son of Man' can hardly be
identified with the 'saints of the Most High' and the RSV mistranslates
the Aramaic מלכותה as 'their kingdom' and לה יפלחון וישתמעון as
'...shall serve and obey them' in v. 27, while the verse actually refers
to the Most High (in singular) rather than to the saints (in plural).[53] The
main problem in Caragounis's approach is that he interprets the original
Aramaic and the LXX versions of Dan. 7.27 in the light of the later text,
Theodotion (Θ), arguing that the earlier form of Θ goes back to pre-
Christian times. This leads him to conclude that the expression לעם
קדישׁי in 7.27b is 'really awkward' and that the term עם in the Aramaic
text and λαῷ in the LXX are later insertions.[54] However, this raises the
question: would a later scribe make the original smooth rendering awkward? Even if we take away עם from the Aramaic, the expressions 'his
kingdom' and 'all dominions shall serve and obey him' will not refer to
the Most High (whom Caragounis identifies as the 'one like a Son of
Man'), but to חיותא רביעיתא ('the fourth beast') of v. 23, for the term
'his dominion' in v. 26 refers back to that of the fourth beast and the
term עליונין never occurs either in nominative or in accusative to make
him the object of veneration, but in constructive state. It is more

Son of Man and its Use in St Mark's Gospel (London: SPCK, 1967), p. 27, finds the
Son of Man as symbolizing the people of the Most High both in their suffering and
vindication. Cf. Casey, *Son of Man*, pp. 27-28.

50.   Rowland, *Open Heaven*, pp. 94-113, argues that Dan. 7.13-14 is the result
of the separation of the divine functions from the figure on the throne to another
divine figure. Against this, see the substantial criticism posed by Hurtado, *One
God*, pp. 85-90.

51.   C.C. Caragounis, *The Son of Man: Vision and Interpretation* (Tübingen:
J.C.B. Mohr [Paul Siebeck], 1986), p. 61.

52.   Caragounis, *Son of Man*, pp. 61-81.

53.   Caragounis, *Son of Man*, pp. 63-67.

54.   Caragounis, *Son of Man*, pp. 64-65.

sensible, then, to retain the Aramaic as the original and the RSV rightly follows it.

Caragounis argues that if the 'Son of Man' is understood as the saints on earth, the clouds are inappropriate as a means for transportation. For him the appearance of the 'Son of Man' with the clouds of heaven implies that he is the 'Most High' or the 'Exalted One'.[55] He is right in accepting that the clouds are the mark of theophany. This, however, does not make the 'Son of Man' the Most High, but it only shows that he is a heavenly being in contrast to the four beasts that arose out of the sea. One cannot ignore the idea implied in the text that the man-like figure represents not only the saints of the Most High, but also, as a heavenly being, God himself.[56]

Arguing that Dan. 7.14 and 7.27 are not exactly parallels, Caragounis maintains that the identification of the 'Son of Man' with the saints of the Most High is the result of an uncritical equation of v. 14 with the whole of v. 27.[57] However, it is inappropriate to expect complete parallel between a vision and its interpretation. One needs to look at the underlying common motif in them. The words מלכות and שלטן are used interchangeably in both verses and 'the greatness (רבותא) of the kingdoms under the whole heaven' in v. 27a paraphrases the word 'glory' (יקר) in v. 14. Since these verses complement each other, the differences cannot be treated as a ground to disprove the role of the 'Son of Man' as representing the saints of the Most High.

It is impossible to find evidence in Dan. 7.22 for two different entities: one the Ancient One and another the 'Most High', as Caragounis believes. According to him, the oft-repeated עליא in the Aramaic sections of Daniel refers to the Ancient One, whereas the double plural word עליונין, which is spoken in relation to the saints, denotes the 'Son of Man'.[58] This implies for Caragounis that the 'Son of Man' of Daniel 7 is another God higher than the Ancient of Days, who is only עליא.[59] In the vision, however, the 'Son of Man' clearly plays a subordinate role to the Ancient of Days, as his function of 'receiving' the kingdom shows (v. 14). Moreover, he himself is brought and presented before

55.   Caragounis, *Son of Man*, pp. 72, 76.
56.   Cf. above, pp. 144-45.
57.   Caragounis, *Son of Man*, pp. 72-73.
58.   Caragounis, *Son of Man*, pp. 74-75.
59.   But Caragounis, *Son of Man*, p. 78, also refers to the seniority (in age?) of the Ancient of Days.

the Ancient of Days (קדמוהי in v. 13 = Hebrew לפני = 'before him'), just as a human visionary is brought before God in apocalyptic/mystical visions.[60] The word עליונין is a 'unique, Hebraizing word', corresponding to the Aramaic עליא[61] and the added plural is no more than the 'plural of eminence', which intensifies the idea of the singular.[62] This means that Caragounis's ditheistic view is highly questionable. His argument that the author of Daniel has drawn from Ezekiel's דמות כמראה אדם to describe the 'one like a Son of Man' also seems improbable, though he is right in maintaining that the Supreme Being on the throne (7.9-10) is reminiscent of Ezekiel's theophany.[63]

Rowland, as we have noticed above, has argued that Dan. 7.13-14 points to the final stage of the gradual separation of the human figure from his throne (Ezek. 1.26), which had already taken place in Ezek. 8.2, in order to function as an agent of the divine purpose.[64] But the text itself suggests that the 'Son of Man' is the symbol of the saints of the Most High, who receive the kingdom from God so that all nations should serve them. Moreover, the kingly status and glory is given to this figure by the will of God and he (the people) would rule on God's behalf. In this sense the Son of Man also represents God as his chief agent.[65] This observation makes Rowland's idea of the splitting-off of the deity altogether unacceptable. Moreover, the heavenly scene in Daniel 7 does not picture an empty throne to argue for the separation of the man-like figure from the throne and the Son of Man is not described as 'sharing' the kingdom and dominion with the Ancient of Days, but they are delivered to him.

The Son of Man in Daniel 7 does not seem to symbolize such angels

---

60. One cannot agree, therefore, with Caragounis (*Son of Man*, pp. 73-74), that the escort of the 'Son of Man' to the very presence of God is to take his seat on one of the thrones beside him. A similar view is also expressed by Fossum, *Name of God*, p. 279 n. 61.

61. Montgomery, *Daniel*, p. 307.

62. See A.B. Davidson, *Hebrew Syntax* (Edinburgh: T. & T. Clark, 3rd edn, repr. 1954), §16(c); cf. E. Kautzsch (ed.), *Gesenius' Hebrew Grammar* (Oxford: Clarendon Press, 2nd edn, 1910), §124q for the significance of the plural of two nouns.

63. Caragounis, *Son of Man*, p. 78.

64. Rowland, 'Vision of the Risen Christ', pp. 5-11; *idem*, *Open Heaven*, pp. 96-98.

65. See Hurtado, *One God*, p. 71.

as Gabriel or Michael,[66] for no angelic being is shown as coming to God with the clouds of heaven and as being presented to him in the divine council. Unlike the angelic beings mentioned in Daniel 8 and 10, the man-like figure in Daniel 7 symbolizes a unique chief agent, the saints of the Most High, who will act on God's behalf so that he will become the object of honour and glory for all peoples and nations.[67]

Nevertheless, Dan. 7.13 LXX (OG) reads: ὡς υἱὸς ἀνθρώπου ἤρχετο, καὶ ὡς παλαιὸς ἡμερῶν παρῆν, καὶ οἱ παρεστηκότες παρῆσαν αὐτῷ.[68] The reading is found only in two LXX MSS of Daniel: the *Codex Chisianus* (MS 88) and the incomplete Chester Beaty Papyrus codex 967, which, being one of the earliest copies of parts of the LXX, belongs to the late second or early third century CE.[69] This reading cannot be dismissed as a scribal error,[70] for even if ὡς can possibly be treated as the corruption of ἕως, the alteration of τοῦ παλαιοῦ to παλαιός and the omission of the article cannot be considered as corruption.[71] Does this prove that there was a tradition that *identified* the Danielic Son of Man with the Ancient of Days? Carrell argues that the particle ὡς does not allow us to identify the Son of Man with the Ancient of Days just like the first ὡς does not identify the Son of Man with a particular son of man.[72] However, ὡς in this case, having been combined with a substantive (i.e. παλαιὸς ἡμερῶν), takes the place of the substantive itself.[73] In this sense the Son of Man in the OG is

66. See above, p. 172 n. 48.
67. See Hurtado, *One God*, pp. 17-23, 71-90 for the pre-Christian idea of an exalted figure/heavenly being who can act as God's chief agent.
68. 'He came as a son of man and as the ancient of days was present, and the bystanders were present with him.' For the translation of the full verse see A.Y. Collins, 'The "Son of Man" Tradition', p. 555.
69. See D.E. Aune, 'Christian Prophecy and the Messianic Status of Jesus', in J.H. Charlesworth (ed.), *The Messiah: Developments in Earliest Judaism and Christianity* (Minneapolis: Fortress Press, 1992), pp. 404-22 (421); cf. H.R. Balz, *Methodische Probleme der neutestamentlichen Christologie* (WMANT, 25; Neukirchen–Vluyn: Neukirchener Verlag, 1967), p. 69 n. 6.
70. Thus maintains Montgomery, *Daniel*, p. 304; A.Y. Collins, 'The "Son of Man" Tradition', p. 555, supposes that the error should have occurred in the second century or earlier.
71. See F.F. Bruce, 'The Oldest Greek Version of Daniel', *OTS* 20 (1977), pp. 25-26.
72. Carrell, 'Jesus and the Angels', pp. 63-64.
73. See W. Bauer, W.F. Arndt and F.W. Gingrich, *A Greek–English Lexicon of the New Testament and Other Early Christian Literature* (Chicago: University of

pictured as identical with the Ancient of Days. However, it seems that the scope of this identity is only limited, that is, in appearance or manifestation (παρῆν) and in majesty or glory (οἱ παρεστηκότες παρῆσαν αὐτῷ). That is, the Son of Man in Dan. 7.13 LXX (OG) is identical with the Ancient of Days in the sense that he represents or manifests the latter's kingly glory and authority (cf. Dan. 7.14 LXX [OG]). The same picture has emerged in our analysis of Rev. 1.14, which describes the 'one like a Son of Man' as the one who represents God's kingly glory on earth.[74] This means that the tradition that identified the Son of Man with the Ancient of Days in his representative and revelatory role goes back to first-century Christians who had mystical interests.[75] However, the possibility that some Jews, probably from a 'mystical' circle, interpreted Dan. 7.9 as early as the second century CE in terms of two divinities points to the involvement of the Jews as well. The evidence for the divine status of the 'Son of Man' in the *Similitudes* and in the book of Revelation indicates the first century CE as the date for the existence of such a belief.[76]

J. Lust, defending the LXX reading as the correct one, argues that it presents a theology that corresponds to the one in Ezekiel's visions, which may be considered as its source.[77] This indeed confirms our view that the recognition of the 'one like a Son of Man' as the Ancient of Days in glory was made primarily by the Jews and Christians who had 'mystical' interest in the first/second century, the period in which John was written.

Conclusions

The scriptural passages, Ezekiel 1, Isaiah 6 and Dan. 7.9-14, which we have examined, do not seem to stress an ascent to heaven to see God in his glory, as the *Hekhalot* mystics later practised. Instead, they bring the manifestation of God down to earth. The prophets such as Ezekiel,

Chicago Press, rev. 2nd edn, 1979), p. 897, s.v. II.3a(a).

74. See above, pp. 141-45.

75. See Caragounis, *Son of Man*, p. 62. Bruce, 'The Oldest Greek Version', p. 26, rightly argues for the Christian origin of this tradition; Segal, *Two Powers*, p. 7, suggests that Christians were included in the list of *minim* because of their binitarian faith.

76. Cf. J.J. Collins, 'Son of Man in First Century Judaism', pp. 448-66.

77. J. Lust, 'Daniel 7,13 and the Septuagint', *ETL* 54 (1978), pp. 63-69; similarly, Aune, 'Christian Prophecy', p. 421 n. 64.

Isaiah and Daniel had the experience of 'seeing' God's glory as seated upon the throne in human-like form. God is accompanied by numerous angelic beings, particularly by the *hayyot*, *Cherubim* and *Seraphim*, which minister unto him. 'Fire', the effluence of light, which shines around the man-like figure, plays a vital role in all the three chariot-visions. It appears as the source of transformation of the life of the prophet (Isa. 6.6-7) and of destruction of the enemies of God and of his people in judgment (Dan. 7.11). In Isaiah's vision the *Seraphim* sing hymns praising the holiness and the glory of the one seated on the throne.

Judgment seems an integral part of Merkabah visions. Both Ezekiel and Isaiah, for whom the Merkabah vision was also their *Berufungs-vision*, are sent as God's agents to the people to proclaim the words of judgment. Daniel's vision pictures God not only as king, but more explicitly as judge, who offers 'salvation' to the saints of the Most High and 'destruction' to the hostile kingdom. In all three visions God's salvation and judgment are mediated by a human agency: whereas in Ezekiel and Isaiah the prophet himself becomes the bearer of divine judgment, in Daniel dominion is given to the 'one like a Son of Man', who does not seem to be an angel or an exalted human, but a unique heavenly figure who represents the people of God. However, by the late first century, he was recognized by some Jews and Christians, who had been engaged in Merkabah mystical practice, as the manifestation of God's glory and majesty. Thus the root of the tradition about the Son of Man goes back to Ezek. 1.26 and Isa. 6.1.

In sum, we should note that all major elements of Merkabah mysticism found in the *Hekhalot* literature, except the heavenly ascent, occur in the biblical texts that we have examined. No doubt, these texts became the sources of inspiration in developing the mystical doctrine in Palestinian Judaism. The idea of heavenly ascent in Merkabah mysticism is perhaps the outcome of the conflation of these Merkabah visions with apocalyptic visions.

Chapter 10

CONCLUSION (FOR PART II)

Our inquiry into some of the Jewish writings, both apocalyptic and non-apocalyptic, indicates unmistakably that Ezekiel 1, Isaiah 6 and Daniel 7 had a strong influence in the religious thought of many Jews and Christians in Palestine, particularly of those who had 'mystical' interest. The main reason for such an interest is perhaps a sincere longing for closeness to God, which was probably instigated by the calamity in 70 CE. At a time when God was thought of being far from apprehension, both before and after the destruction of the Jerusalem temple, it is little wonder that Ezekiel 1 attained prime importance, for it not only reflected the same historical situation as that which existed after 70, but also supplied a relevant source for an experience of 'seeing God's glory' in human terms. Such an experience was later called 'Merkabah mysticism'. We have traced the major elements of this experience in all the writings that we have examined. A display of these elements in a tabular form will give us a better understanding of Merkabah mysticism as it was practised in the late first century when John was written.

Motif	Non-apocalyptic	Apocalyptic	Christian
1. An ascent to heaven	Moses Tradition, *LAB*	*Sim. En.; 2 En.; Apoc. Abr.; T. Abr.*	Rev. 4; *Asc. Isa.*; 2 Cor. 12
2. The descent of God's glory	Ezek. 1; Isa. 6; Yohanan tradition	----------	Rev. 1; *Asc. Isa.*
3. Chariot-throne	Ezek. 1; Isa. 6; Dan. 7; Qumran texts	*Sim. En.; 2 En.; Apoc. Abr.; T. Abr.*	Rev. 4; *Asc. Isa.*

4. God's self-revelation	Ezek. 1 (man-like, glory); Isa. 6 (the Lord); Dan. 7 (the Ancient of Days); Yohanan (the glory); Qumran (glory & king)	*Sim. En.* (Head of Days, the Lord of the Spirits); *2 En.* (the Lord); *Apoc. Abr.* (the Eternal One)	Rev. 4 (human); 2 Cor. 12 (Christ); *Asc. Isa.* 9 (the Great Glory)
5. Streams of fire/light	Ezek. 1; Isa. 6; Dan. 7; Yohanan; Qumran	*Sim. En.*; *2 En.*; *Apoc. Abr.*	Rev. 1; 4
6. Retinue of angels	- *do* -	- *do* -	Rev.; *Asc. Isa.*
7. One like a man or Son of Man	Ezek. 1; Dan. 7	*Sim. En.*; *4 Ez.*	Rev. 1; 14
8. God's judgment	Ezek. 1; Isa. 6; Dan. 7; 11QMelch	*Sim. En.*; *4 Ez.*; *T. Abr.*	Rev. 14
9. Cosmological/heavenly secrets	Dan. 7; Qumran; *LAB*; Sir.	*Sim. En.*; *2 En.*; *T. Abr.*; *Apoc. Abr.*	2 Cor. 12; Rev.; *Asc. Isa.*
10. Transformation of the visionary	Isa. 6 (transformed human life)	*Sim. En.*; *2 En*	*Asc. Isa.*
11. Sent on mission	Ezek. 1–2; Isa. 6	*2 En.*; *Apoc. Abr.*	Rev. 1

12. Apart from these, our study has also thrown light on what is called 'the communal mysticism' that was practised particularly in Qumran community during worship, when its members realized together a sense of union with the angels in heavenly worship.

13. We are also convinced that the mystical idea involved in the *Ma'aseh Bereshit* was already alive in the first century CE and that it revealed God by his name, 'I am/I will be there'. The Qumranites believed that God's name and his glory are revealed in creation.

14. The early traditions of both the *Ma'aseh Bereshit* and the *Ma'aseh Merkabah* were considered esoteric in the sense that they contain the secrets of God which are revealed, at least in part, to the initiates, but not to those who would misunderstand them.

These 14 aspects of Palestinian mysticism, which can primarily be known as 'Merkabah mysticism', can be treated as a definition of 'mysticism'. What, among these, are the most significant for understanding the Gospel of John? Does John become more meaningful if we read it against the background of the Palestinian Jewish mysticism of the late first century CE? In what way is John addressing

those who had been preoccupied with 'mystical' interests? Does he
share their concerns? Does he polemize or persuade them? In short,
how was his mystical teaching, if any, relevant to the people of his
time? An analysis of these issues is our major concern in the following
pages.

Part III

'MYSTICISM' IN THE GOSPEL OF JOHN

Chapter 11

INTRODUCTION (TO PART III)

We have noticed that a major deficiency in the study of Johannine mysticism, undertaken so far, is the failure to perform critical and exegetical study of John by placing it in its religio-historical context. The result is that scholars, who have attempted to trace mystical elements in John, have tended to adopt either the *unio mystica* view or the *communio mystica* view uncritically in one form or the other. Therefore, before we investigate John to find out whether or not it contains 'mystical' elements, we should remind ourselves of the key aspects that were considered as 'mystical' in the late first century CE when John, as per common consensus, was written.

Mystical Currents at the Time of John

Hellenistic Mysticism

Hellenistic mysticism is concerned with the experience of an individual's union with God, which is possible for a person if he cleanses himself from the irrational torments of matter and if the Logos (i.e. reason) is built up in him. Knowledge of God is to be attained by 'beholding the beauty of the Good and thereby becoming a god (ἀποθεωθῆναι)'. 'Mysticism', as the *Hermetica* describe, denotes an experience of 'cosmic consciousness', that is, an apprehension of God by comprehending within oneself all sensory perceptions of created things, by imagining oneself to be everywhere at once, and by making oneself like God.

At the dissolution of the body a person mounts upward and enters into God (θεωθῆναι). Because a person is thus deified, he or she also becomes immortal (ἀθάνατος). The mystical ascent is also expressed in terms of God filling a great basin with νοῦς and sending it down to earth; people should dip themselves in this basin, recognizing the purpose of their existence and believing that they shall ascend to him who sent the basin down.

Hellenistic-Jewish Mysticism as in Philo

The essence of Philo's mysticism is 'to see God as he is revealed' and even as he is in himself. God can be envisaged only through God just as light is to be known through light. He reveals himself in his δυναμεῖς, but supremely through his λόγος. Philo holds that a vision of God is possible in human mind rather than to one's physical eyes. According to him, a person can have union with God and can have a vision of God by union with Sophia (= the Logos), the divine force and life.

The 'mystical' ascent to God is possible only after severance from the world of mortality. For Philo, under the guidance of the Scripture the mind can be led to ascend to the divine. Philo's mysticism resembles Hellenistic mysticism in its claim that God dwells within individual souls. It is through Moses, the *mystagogue*, that the initiates are initiated into the mysteries of God.

Palestinian Jewish Mysticism

We have observed that Palestinian mysticism in the first century was mainly based on the explication of Ezekiel 1 and therefore that it is known as Merkabah mysticism. We have listed 14 elements, that are interrelated, as the main features of the Merkabah mystical practice.[1] We also have noticed that a Jewish background provides the best key for understanding John and that in spite of the newly published Qumran documents sufficient attention has not been given to a study of John against the background of Jewish mysticism.[2] Therefore I attempt here to trace out the mystical elements in John, if any, by using the 14 features of the Palestinian Jewish mysticism, as a definition of 'mysticism', but at the same time by comparing my findings, wherever necessary, with the mystical ideas found in the *Hermetica* and in Philonic writings. This, in turn, will show us whether or not the Gospel of John is a mystical document. If it is, we will also know the nature and purpose of Johannine mysticism.

---

1. See Chapter 10.
2. See above, pp. 42-44.

Chapter 12

THE ASCENT-MOTIF IN JOHN

One of the leading ideas in first-century mysticism, both in Palestinian and Hellenistic Judaism, is the experience of an ascent to heaven to apprehend God.[1] For Meeks the descent–ascent of Jesus is fundamental among the special patterns of language used in John.[2] An inquiry into the ascent-motif of John will enable us to see whether or not John is in any way associated with the mystical belief of his time.

The Ascent and Descent of the Angels

John 1.51
The first reference to ascent–descent occurs in 1.51, which depicts the angels as ascending and descending upon the Son of Man:

καὶ λέγει αὐτῷ, Ἀμὴν ἀμὴν λέγω ὑμῖν, ὄψεσθε τὸν οὐρανὸν ἀνεῳγότα καὶ τοὺς ἀγγέλους τοῦ Θεοῦ ἀναβαίνοντας καὶ καταβαίνοντας
ἐπὶ τὸν υἱὸν τοῦ ἀνθρώπου.

This verse forms the climax of the call of the disciples (1.35-51). The idea of 'seeing' plays a vital role in the whole narrative and probably 1.50-51 should also be understood with an emphasis on 'seeing'.[3] When Nathanael came at first to Jesus, he acknowledged that Jesus is ὁ

---

1.   See A.F. Segal, 'Heavenly Ascent in Hellenistic Judaism, Early Christianity and their Environment', *ANRW*, II, 23.2 (1980), pp. 1352-89 (1334-76) for the heavenly ascent motif recurring in the Hellenistic, Hellenistic-Jewish and New Testament writings.

2.   W.A. Meeks, 'The Man from Heaven in Johannine Sectarianism', *JBL* 91 (1972), pp. 44-72 (44); cf. G.C. Nicholson, *Death as Departure: The Johannine Descent–Ascent Schema* (SBLDS, 63; Chico, CA: Scholars Press, 1983), esp. pp. 10, 19, 21-74.

3.   Cf. E. Haenchen, *John* (2 vols.; Hermeneia; Philadelphia: Fortress Press, ET 1984), I, p. 166.

υἱὸς τοῦ Θεοῦ and βασιλεὺς τοῦ Ἰσραήλ (1.47-49).[4] Jesus, by perceiving that his disciples need a clear understanding of who he is, promises them in 1.51 a greater vision. The expression τὸν οὐρανὸν ἀνεῳγότα also indicates that Jesus' followers will experience a heavenly and hence revelatory vision. Does it denote literally an opened heaven? What is the significance of the ascent and descent of the angels? If the expressions deployed in 1.51 are images for the actual experience, as Cadman suggests,[5] what then is this experience?

Higgins argues that the idea of the heaven opened is reminiscent of Stephen's vision in Acts 7.56.[6] Lindars, however, dismisses this parallel as merely coincidental.[7] Borsch has argued for a link with the 'opening of heaven' at the baptism of Jesus in Mk 1.10.[8] But, except for the idea of the opened heaven, there is no conceptual parallel between 1.51 and Mk 1.10. Definitely 1.32-33 refers to Jesus' baptism, but this does not guarantee that 1.51 too is modelled on the baptism tradition. Higgins also finds an indirect reference in 1.51 to the statement: 'Hereafter you will see (ἀπ' ἄρτι ὄψεσθε) the Son of Man seated at the right hand of Power, and coming on the clouds of heaven' (Mt. 26.64 = Mk 14.62).[9] Although the Antiochian and Alexandrian traditions follow this interpretation,[10] the ideas of the opened heaven and of the angelophany, which dominate 1.51, are absent in Mt. 26.64 and therefore it is insufficient to bring out the full sense of 1.51. Similarly,

4.   Brown, *Community of the Beloved Disciple*, pp. 25-26, identifies these confessions, which were made in the initial stage of the disciples' call, as belonging to a 'low' Christology.

5.   So W.H. Cadman, *The Open Heaven: The Revelation of God in the Johannine Sayings of Jesus* (Oxford: Basil Blackwell, 1969), p. 26.

6.   A.J.B. Higgins, *Jesus and the Son of Man* (London: Lutterworth, 1964), p. 157; R. Maddox, 'The Function of the Son of Man in the Gospel of John', in R.J. Banks (ed.), *Reconciliation and Hope: New Testament Essays on Atonement and Eschatology* (Festschrift L.L. Morris; Exeter: Paternoster Press, 1974), pp. 186-204 (190).

7.   B. Lindars, 'The Son of Man in the Theology of John', in *idem, Jesus Son of Man: A Fresh Examination of the Son of Man Sayings in the Gospels in the Light of Recent Research* (London: SPCK, 1983), pp. 147-53, 218-21 (148).

8.   F.H. Borsch, *The Son of Man in Myth and History* (London: SCM Press, 1967), pp. 278-79; cf. Lindars, 'The Son of the Man in the Theology of John', p. 218 n. 5. Against this position, see F.J. Moloney, *The Johannine Son of Man* (Biblioteca di scienze Religiose, 14; Rome: Las, 1978), p. 39.

9.   Higgins, *Jesus*, p. 157.

10.   Cf. the variant reading of 1.51 which places ἀπ' ἄρτι before ὄψεσθε.

the connection between 1.51 and Mt. 25.31 to argue for the motif of enthronement-on-the-cross in 1.51 is 'tenuous'.[11]

Bultmann comments that the verb ὁράω is used in John for both heavenly and earthly revelation.[12] If so, Ezek. 1.1, ἠνοίχθησαν οἱ οὐρανοὶ, καὶ ἴδον ὁράσεις Θεοῦ (LXX), which speaks of the divine revelation accompanied by the movements of the heavenly beings, can be considered as a passage that gives the most relevant background for the phrase ὄψεσθε τὸν οὐρανὸν ἀνεῳγότα.[13] In view of many other usages of Ezekiel in John,[14] the influence of Ezekiel's chariot-vision on 1.51 is not improbable. E. Kinniburgh's argument against the background of Ezek. 1.1 saying that there is no reference in 1.51 to the vision of God or of the Son of Man[15] is largely based on the superficial reading of 1.51. 3 Macc. 6.18, which she quotes to support her argument that the opening of the heavens is for the descent of the angels, in fact speaks more of the revelation of the face of God, without any reference to the *ascent* of the angels. If we interpret the verse against the background of Ezekiel's vision, does this mean that the disciples are assured of a vision of the glory of God? A careful analysis of the remaining part of 1.51 will make it clear.

John 1.51b

1.51b:

τοὺς ἀγγέλους τοῦ Θεοῦ ἀναβαίνοντας καὶ καταβαίνοντας επὶ τὸν υἱὸν τοῦ ἀνθρώπου.

Gen. 28.12b (LXX):

καὶ οἱ ἄγγελοι τοῦ Θεοῦ ἀνέβαινον καὶ κατέβαινον ἐπ᾽ αὐτῆς.

11. So Moloney, *Son of Man*, p. 40.
12. Bultmann, *John: A Commentary*, p. 69 n. 2; Michaelis, 'ὁραω', pp. 361-66.
13. See G. Quispel, 'Nathanael und der Menschensohn (Joh 1.51)', *ZNW* 47 (1956), pp. 281-83 (283); E.M. Sidebottom, *The Christ of the Fourth Gospel in the Light of First-Century Thought* (London: SPCK, 1961), p. 76, argues that the Baptism versions, both in the Synoptics and John, reflect the language of Ezek. 1.1. So also Rowland sees in the opening of heaven recorded in the baptism narratives of all three Gospels a clear allusion to Ezek. 1.1—see Rowland, 'Apocalyptic, the Poor', p. 507.
14. See Sidebottom, *Christ of the Fourth Gospel*, pp. 73-78 for parallels between Ezekiel and John.
15. E. Kinniburgh, 'The Johannine "Son of Man"', *TU*, IV (1968), pp. 64-71 (65).

The parallelism between these verses shows that John has used Gen. 28.12 in 1.51b and therefore Genesis 28 may throw some light on 1.51b. The replacement of the ἐπ' αὐτῆς (i.e. κλίμαξ) of Gen. 28.12 by ἐπὶ τὸν υἱὸν τοῦ ἀνθρώπου needs our attention. In view of the fact that there is no trace either in the MT or in the LXX of Gen. 28.12, that the ascent–descent of the angels took place on Jacob, it is impossible to accept Burney's thesis that בו in Gen. 28.12 can mean 'on him' (i.e. on Jacob).[16] The Jacob of Genesis 28 has essential parallel with Nathanael rather than with the Son of Man. Similarly, the *Prayer of Joseph*, which Ashton uses to interpret 1.51, does not form a real parallel to the ascent–descent of the angels on the Son of Man and eventually he ends up demonstrating only the dissimilarities between John and the *Prayer of Joseph*.[17]

Odeberg understands 1.51 in the light of *Ber. R.* 68.18, as interpreted by R. Hiyya and R. Yannai (*Tanḥ.* 38a), and the Jewish mystical tradition which linked Gen. 28.12 with Isa. 49.3. On this background, argues Odeberg, 1.51 shows that through the ascending and descending angels a union was established between the celestial appearance, the δόξα of Christ, and his appearance in flesh.[18] Such a union, which is possible only in the Son of Man in whom also the believers are included, is *eo ipso* a communion with the Father under the aspect of ἀνάβασις, and a revelation of the Father under the aspect of κατάβασις (cf. 14.9-10).[19] That is, 1.51 has mystical connotation in the sense that it speaks of the φανέρωσις of Christ's δόξα on earth and that it promises the believers that they will have an experience of entering into the spiritual reality similar to that of the ascending and descending angels of God on earthly man.[20] Though Odeberg's central thesis that 1.51 portrays the φανέρωσις of Christ's glory, which echoes the first-century Merkabah mysticism, is right, his method of interpretation is not without problem. Primarily, we can hardly interpret 1.51 in the light of a rabbinic

16.   C.F. Burney, *The Aramaic Origin of the Fourth Gospel* (Oxford: Clarendon Press, 1922), pp. 115-17.

17.   Ashton, *Understanding*, pp. 345-46. J.Z. Smith, 'Prayer of Joseph', *OTP*, II, pp. 699-714 (711), holds that *Pr. Jos.*, in its present form, remains a tantalizing fragment that has left no discernible impact on subsequent literature.

18.   Odeberg, *Fourth Gospel*, pp. 35-42, esp. pp. 35-36.

19.   Odeberg, *Fourth Gospel*, pp. 36-40; cf. Dodd, *Interpretation*, pp. 246-47.

20.   Odeberg, *Fourth Gospel*, p. 40.

Midrash that belongs to the third century CE.[21] Moreover, it is not clear
how the ascent and the descent of the angels *upon* the Son of Man can
stand for the believers' experience of entering *into* the spiritual reality.
Odeberg's idea of 'inclusiveness' in the Son of Man does not complement John's emphasis on 'believing' and the subsequent ethical responsibility of Jesus' followers.[22]

Rowland suggests that John has used Gen. 28.12 as well as its interpretation found in *Gen. R.* 68.12 and in particular in the four versions
of the Palestinian Targum.[23] According to him, the features (איקונין) of
Jacob are set on the Throne of Glory; the angels who escorted Jacob
from his father's house ascend to heaven to tell the angels there about it
and, as a result, the angels came down from heaven to see in Jacob the
same form found in the heavenly throne, for this was a divine secret
hidden even from the angels (cf. *1 En.* 14.21; 1 Pet. 1.12). Viewed thus,
argues Rowland, 1.51 portrays the Son of Man as the one who discloses
the very nature of God, his *kabod*, and in this sense the Johannine Jesus
is the embodiment of the mystery of God.[24] Rowland's argument for
the apocalyptic element in 1.51 actually speaks for the presence of
Merkabah mysticism inasmuch as the Son of Man is understood as the
revelation of God's glory. However, this approach too suffers the same
defect as that of Odeberg. What evidence is there to convince us that
the tradition found in the Palestinian *Targum of Genesis* 28 was alive at
the time of John?—an issue of which Rowland himself is aware.[25] It is
irrelevant to argue, as Rowland does, that in the light of 14.28 the ἐπὶ
τὸν υἱὸν τοῦ ἀνθρώπου of 1.51 should be taken only with κατα-

21.   See Higgins, *Jesus*, p. 159; Barrett, *John*, p. 187, finds even Philo's
interpretation of the ladder (*Somn.* 1.133-35) irrelevant to interpret 1.51.

22.   Schnackenburg, *St John*, I, p. 321, argues that the 'inclusive' nature of
mysticism contradicts the Johannine soteriology, which always calls for faith in
Jesus and attachment to him. Bultmann, *John: A Commentary*, p. 105 n. 3, accepts
Odeberg's mystical interpretation of 1.51 by using *Ber. R.* 68.18, but rejects the
inclusive sense.

23.   C. Rowland, 'John 1.51, Jewish Apocalyptic and Targumic Tradition',
NTS 30 (1984), pp. 498-507.

24.   Rowland, 'Targumic Tradition', pp. 500-504.

25.   Rowland, 'Targumic Tradition', p. 502. J.H. Neyrey, 'The Jacob Allusions in John 1:51', *CBQ* 44 (1982), pp. 586-605 (604), argues that due to the non-
existence of the midrashic traditions of Gen. 28.12 in the first century, they cannot
be used to interpret 1.51.

βαίνοντας, and not with ἀναβαίνοντας;[26] for, unlike 14.28, 1.51b is a
quotation from a biblical text and therefore the ὑπάγω καὶ ἔρχομαι
πρὸς ὑμᾶς of 14.28 cannot serve as the Johannine pattern for the
ἀναβαίνοντας καὶ καταβαίνοντας ἐπὶ τὸν υἱὸν τοῦ ἀνθρώπου of
1.51. Strictly speaking, it is unnecessary to use either the rabbinic or the
targumic texts, but we should examine the biblical text itself for
understanding 1.51.

The Significance of the Son of Man and the Angels
None of the scholars whom we have observed above could bring out
the real significance of 1.51, for they did not give equal attention to
Ezekiel 1 and Genesis 28. If the opening of heaven implies a heavenly
vision, what then is its content? It is natural to treat the accusative τοὺς
ἀγγέλους as the object of the promised vision in 1.51. But if John's
concern was with the angels, then why did not he mention them later in
the Gospel?[27] In Genesis 28 the vision of Yahweh to Jacob and the
means of communication with him are emphasized more than the
ascent–descent of the angels. So also in 1.51b the activity of the angels
takes place on the Son of Man and therefore he is 'vitally but indirectly
important'.[28] Gen. 28.12-17 contains two major aspects: the stairway
(סלם)[29] from the earth to heaven (v. 12) and God's self-manifestation to
Jacob on earth (vv. 13-17).[30] The סלם makes the intercourse between
heaven and earth possible. In 1.51 there is no reference to the סלם or to
the presence of Yahweh, but both are embodied in the Son of Man. By
using Gen. 28.12-17, John seems to say that Jesus is the way to the
Father (cf. 14.6) as well as the very presence of God on earth (1.14, 18;

26. Rowland, 'Targumic Tradition', p. 505.
27. Jn 5.4, which refers to ἄγγελος κυρίου, has no support in reliable MSS.
There is no particular angelology in 12.29.
28. Kinniburgh, 'Johannine "Son of Man"', p. 65. Both M. Black, *An
Aramaic Approach to the Gospels and Acts* (Oxford: Clarendon Press, 2nd edn,
1954), p. 85 and Neyrey, 'Jacob Allusions', p. 599, argue that the figure, Son of
Man, is the focus in 1.51.
29. סלם in Gen. 28.12 means not a 'ladder', but an 'ascent' or 'stairway', i.e.
a 'piled-up construction which reaches from earth to heaven'—see C. Westermann,
Genesis 12–36: A Commentary (Minneapolis: Augsburg, ET 1985), p. 454; G. von
Rad, *Genesis: A Commentary* (London: SCM Press, ET 1961), p. 279.
30. עליו in Gen. 28.13 means that the Lord stood 'before him (i.e. Jacob)' or
'opposite to him', and not 'upon the stairway'—Westermann, *Genesis 12–36*, p.
455. Cf. the marginal reading in RSV: 'beside him'.

14.9, 10).[31] In the Son of Man, the real communion with God and communication between heaven and earth is possible, for he is the revelation of his glory. In the light of an allusion to Ezekiel's throne-vision, it
appears that John replaces not only Jacob's ladder and Yahweh with the
Son of Man, but also Ezekiel's throne on which the prophet saw the
glory of God. In other words, the visions of Jacob and Ezekiel are
reinterpreted by John in terms of a person, Jesus the Son of Man. Our
analysis below further confirms the use of the Merkabah mystical
tradition in 1.51.

Quispel argues that in 1.51 a vision of the glorified Christ, similar to
the one mentioned in 12.41, is promised and that this is due to the
influence of an esoteric tradition, based on such theophanies as in
Ezekiel 1 and Isaiah 6, which existed in Palestine in the first century.[32]
His suggestion that behind the ἀναβαίνειν καὶ καταβαίνειν lies the
Hebrew ירד, the technical term used in Merkabah mysticism,[33] implies
that the angels symbolize the mystics who ascend and descend. This is
improbable. However, his suggestion that the vision of the Son of Man
in 1.51 corresponds to the *Offenbarungsgestalt* (i.e. the *kabod*) of God,
described in Ezek. 1.26 and Isa. 6.1,[34] is acceptable in the light of the
glory-motif developed in John. This confirms Rowland's thesis that the
Son of Man in 1.51 exhibits the very nature of God, his *kabod*. Thus
John seems to use in 1.51 the language and the idea drawn from the
Merkabah mysticism of his time, and therefore the title, Son of Man,
alludes not so much to the synoptic Son of Man as to the apocalyptic/
mystical Son of Man.[35] By presenting the Son of Man as the 'mystical
way' to God and as the revelation of God's glory, John alludes to the
heavenly journey undertaken by Merkabah mystics to see God. For him
it is faith in Jesus as the Christ that could make the invisible God
visible rather than a journey to heaven. That is why the promise for a
great vision to Jesus' followers (cf. the plural ὄψεσθε) is given when
the disciples confessed him as the Christ obviously in an imperfect
sense.

The role of the ascending and descending angels in this revelatory

31.   Cf. the phrase ἐγώ εἰμι found in Gen. 28.13 is applied to Jesus in John.
32.   Quispel, 'Nathanael', pp. 281-83.
33.   Quispel, 'Nathanael', p. 283.
34.   Quispel, 'Nathanael', p. 282.
35.   The idea that the Son of Man represents and manifests God's glory was
familiar in the Christian apocalyptic/mystical circles—see above, pp. 141-45.

act, then, can be no other than that of the angels who surround the throne of God, serving him and thus adding to his glory. The angels in 1.51, as Bühner puts it, symbolize the epiphany of the heavenly glory hidden in the earthly Jesus and, as ministers of God, their movements symbolize the *Verkehr* between heaven and earth.[36] Therefore there is a possibility now of seeing the heavenly glory and of having communion with God *on the basis of* (ἐπί + acc.) what Jesus will accomplish by his death and exaltation. This experience, which is essentially the same as Merkabah mysticism, is for John μεῖζω τούτων. It also proves that the phrase ἐπὶ τὸν υἱὸν ἀνθρώπου denotes primarily the historical Jesus in whom the divine glory was seen here on earth (see 1.14; 2.11; 12.23-24; cf. 12.27 with 13.31-32), although a similar vision in the re-ascended Son of Man is not thereby ruled out.[37] The supreme revelation of God is possible in the risen Jesus even on earth (cf. 20.28) as well as in heaven (17.24).[38] The future epiphany is after all the continuation of the present epiphany.

John combines in 1.51 the mystical text, Ezek. 1.1, 26, with Gen. 28.12 probably to confront the current mystical belief.[39] As the possibility of seeing the heavenly glory in the Son of Man and of having communion with God is available even here on earth, for John there is

36. Bühner, *Der Gesandte*, pp. 391-92. The angels in the *Hekhalot* literature became figures who provide the link between the mysteries of heaven and the apprehension of the one who descends to the Merkabah (see Elior, 'Mysticism, Magic, and Angelology', p. 27).

37. For the view that the promised vision in 1.51 is that of the re-ascended Son of Man who was crucified and returned to glory, see J.W. Pryor, 'The Johannine Son of Man and the Descent–Ascent Motif', *JETS* 34 (1991), pp. 341-51 (342); W. Loader, *The Christology of the Fourth Gospel: Structures and Issues* (BEvT, 23; Frankfurt: Peter Lang, rev. edn, 1992), pp. 119-20; Neyrey, 'Jacob Allusions', pp. 589-91, 597-601. Some scholars, however, confine the revelation of the heavenly reality only to the earthly life and death of Jesus—see Kinniburgh, 'Johannine "Son of Man"', pp. 64-65; Moloney, *Son of Man*, pp. 38-40; Lindars, 'The Son of Man in the Theology of John', p. 149; Rowland, 'Targumic Tradition', pp. 504-506; M. Pamment, 'The Son of Man in the Fourth Gospel', *JTS* 36 (1985), pp. 56-66 (62-64).

38. S.S. Smalley, 'The Johannine Son of Man Sayings', *NTS* 15 (1968–69), pp. 278-301 (288), holds that the Son of Man saying in 1.51 refers both to his earthly ministry (historical) and to his exalted position (eternal).

39. Gen. 28.12 is one of the visionary texts that was combined in the *Haggadah* with Dan. 7 and Ezek. 1, the primary texts used in Merkabah mysticism—see Dahl, 'Johannine Church', p. 136.

no need to ascend to heaven to see God. In this sense 1.51 is a polemic against the claims of Merkabah mystics of his time as well as a call for a greater vision in Jesus. If Dodd's argument that the dominant idea in Jn 2.1–4.42 is the inauguration of a new order of life for humankind through the incarnation of the Logos by replacing the old order of religion is correct,[40] then it is most probable that John has the same replacement idea also in 1.51 which may serve as the preamble for the whole Gospel in general and for chs. 2–4 in particular.[41] That is, John polemizes by replacing the current mystical practice centred on the chariot-throne by a mystical vision of God in Jesus, and more particularly on the cross of Jesus.[42] It is perhaps impossible to appreciate fully John's approach of polemics at this stage. However, our study below makes it more clear.

The Descent of the Son of Man

The idea of heavenly ascent is expressed in a paradoxical tone in 3.13-15 with another reference to the Son of Man. This passage is a part of Jesus' dialogue with Nicodemus, which begins with a reference to Jesus' heavenly origin (3.2), proceeds to describe the means of 'seeing' and 'entering' the kingdom of God (3.3-8) and, after confirming the

---

40.   See Dodd, *Interpretation*, pp. 297-317. Cf. R.H. Lightfoot, *St John's Gospel: A Commentary* (ed. C.F. Evans; Oxford: Clarendon Press, 1956), pp. 107-35, who treats 1.19–2.11 as one unit and 2.12–4.54 as the projection of new order over against the old. 1.51 then is inseparable from chs. 2–4.

41.   Cf. Bultmann, *John: A Commentary*, p. 106, who comments that 1.51 promises to Jesus' disciples the vision in faith of Jesus' δόξα in all that he does. Haenchen, *John*, I, p. 166, sees 1.51 as pointing to the continuous relationship Jesus has with the Father during his earthly sojourn. For John, effective revelation of God's glory lies on the cross of Jesus. As Carson (*John*, p. 165) comments, it is Jesus' death/exaltation that provides Nathanael and the other disciples the most powerful fulfilment of the promise in 1.51 (cf. 8.28). Schnackenburg, *St John*, I, p. 322, maintains that 1.51 contains the first words of revelation on the Son of Man which are then followed by others that develop the theology of the Son of Man. Therefore the saying in 1.51 can fully be understood only in conjunction with the motif of revelation found in John as a whole (see also below, pp. 210, 236 and p. 242 nn. 124, 125). In this sense, the shadow of the cross is to be seen in the Son of Man saying in 1.51, though not explicitly mentioned.

42.   It is noteworthy that cross is foreshadowed in 1.19–12.50, for the Son of Man who performs signs is the Christ who was exalted and glorified through the cross—see Dodd, *Interpretation*, pp. 383-89, esp. p. 383.

heavenly origin and authority of Jesus in 3.11, explains in 3.13-15 how this heavenly experience becomes possible.

John 3.13

καὶ οὐδεὶς ἀναβέβηκεν εἰς τὸν οὐρανὸν εἰ μὴ ὁ ἐκ τοῦ οὐράνου καταβάς, ὁ υἱὸς τοῦ ἀνθρώπου.

The polemic purpose of John has been detected in this verse by some scholars. Whereas Odeberg, Dahl and Dunn find a polemic note against the practice of Merkabah mysticism,[43] Borgen and Meeks have argued for a polemic against the mystical practice centred on Moses' ascent.[44] At any rate, 3.13 gives a clear evidence for the current belief that some persons claimed that they ascended to heaven and received revelations to make known to the world below. Before we explore the background against which 3.13 can be read, we should note the main emphasis of this verse.

Seeing an ascent–descent–return pattern in 3.13, Borgen argues that according to 3.13, Moses at Mt Sinai and others did not ascend to heaven to be installed in an office of glory, but Jesus, the Son of Man, had been installed in office before his descent (in the incarnation).[45] Although Borgen is aware of the problem involved in this interpretation that the pre-existent Son of Man did not ascend from earth, he justifies himself by arguing that the word ἀναβέβηκεν functions on two levels: that of human beings and that of a divine being, and that in Jewish thought the concept of 'ascent into heaven' can refer to a heavenly being, God, and his enthronement (cf. 1 Sam. 2.10-11; Pss. 47.6; 68.19; Dan. 7.13-14; Philo, *Sacr.* 8-10).[46] This has led him to argue that the εἰ μή clause in 3.13, similar to 6.46 and 17.12, should take up the verb ἀναβέβηκεν from the main clause. Thus 3.13 can be read as:

καὶ οὐδεὶς ἀναβέβηκεν εἰς τὸν οὐρανὸν εἰ μὴ ὁ ἐκ τοῦ οὐρανοῦ καταβάς, ὁ υἱὸς τοῦ ἀνθρώπου, (οὗτος ἀναβέβηκεν εἰς τὸν οὐρανόν).[47]

43. See above pp. 34, 36 and 41.
44. P. Borgen, 'The Son of Man Saying in John 3:13-14', in *idem, Philo, John, and Paul: New Perspectives on Judaism and Early Christianity* (BJS, 131; Atlanta: Scholars Press, 1987), pp. 103-20 (104-109); Meeks, *Prophet-King*, pp. 297-301.
45. Borgen, 'Son of Man Saying', pp. 107-109.
46. Borgen, 'Son of Man Saying', pp. 105-12.
47. Borgen, 'Son of Man Saying', pp. 107-108.

Borgen seems to lay more emphasis on the word ἀναβέβηκεν than the passage warrants. The concern of the passage is 'bearing witness' in terms of τὰ ἐπίγεια to what one has seen in heaven (3.11-12). This means that Jesus' dialogue is still focusing on earthly things and therefore that ὁ ἐκ τοῦ οὐράνου καταβάς is likely to be emphasized. Moreover, 3.13 can hardly be understood in the light of 17.12 and 6.46, for the construction of the εἰ μή clause in 3.13b differs from that in 17.12b and in 6.46b and c.

17.12b	6.46b and c
εἰ μὴ ὁ υἱὸς τῆς ἀπωλείας...	εἰ μὴ ὁ ὢν παρὰ τοῦ θεοῦ, οὗτος ἑώρα-
(ἀπώλετο)	κεν τὸν πατέρα.

17.12b contains no prepositional phrase and in 6.46 the prepositional phrase παρὰ τοῦ θεοῦ appears after ὁ ὤν, whereas in 3.13 the prepositional phrase ἐκ τοῦ οὐρανοῦ is placed between ὁ and καταβάς. This means, by emphasizing the heavenly origin of the Son of Man, 3.13 rules out the necessity for him of an ascent to heaven like other exalted human figures, for he is already ἐκ τοῦ οὐρανοῦ and ἄνωθεν ἐρχόμενος (3.31). This is confirmed by the antithetic position of ὁ καταβάς to ἀναβέβηκεν, an element that is missing in 17.12 and 6.46. Even if we read the verb of the main clause in the εἰ μή clause also (cf. 6.46; 17.12; Mt. 12.4; Lk. 4.27), this cannot shift the emphasis in 3.13 from the descent of the Son of Man to his ascent. As Borgen himself observes, the concept of the Sinaitic ascent and descent is changed into the idea of descent and ascent.[48] But his view that John intended to put the pre-existent ascent first and then the descent can hardly be entertained.[49]

What does the word καταβάς mean in 3.13? Odeberg holds that under the aspect of κατάβασις Jesus, the celestial man, who appeared in flesh, is a revelation of the Father.[50] Bultmann argues that the coming down of Jesus from heaven is to deliver the message (or knowledge)

48. Borgen, 'Son of Man Saying', p. 105. Bultmann, *John: A Commentary*, p. 150 n. 2, comments that as the text stands the ἀναβαίνειν does not precede the καταβαίνειν but rather the reverse.

49. Borgen, 'Son of Man Saying', p. 104. Failure to consider the above-mentioned factors has led Pryor to argue that it is the ascension motif, not the descent, that draws out the Son of Man terminology in John, particularly in 3.13— see Pryor, 'Johannine Son of Man', pp. 346-51.

50. Odeberg, *Fourth Gospel*, p. 36.

entrusted to him by the Father.[51] Barrett identifies ὁ καταβάς as referring to the incarnation, stating that the Son of Man descends from heaven to earth to convey the ἐπουράνια to humans.[52] That is, according to 3.13, the pre-existent Son of Man entered the human history as a human (cf. 'The Logos became σάρξ' in 1.14) in whom God can be perceived. For even in his earthly life the oneness with the Father has continued and this is another important aspect of Jesus' descent.[53] The descent of the Son of Man to the earth to become a human is not just to impart knowledge, but to make 'the encounter of the creator with his creature'[54] possible by revealing the glory of the creator himself. On what background, then, can 3.13 be meaningfully understood?

The Background of John 3.13

We have noticed that in Hellenistic mysticism there is no clear descent–ascent motif. The nearest parallel may be found in God sending the basin of νοῦς down with a herald so that people might dip themselves into the νοῦς and believe that they shall ascend to God. However, in John, the one who descends is the Son of Man, a personal being (like the Son of God who is sent). As the interaction with God is possible here on earth because of his descent, there is no hint in 3.13 of the believers' ascent to heaven or of their deification. Moreover, *CH* 4.4 does not refer to the ascent as actual practice but only as a mental belief in future ascent. Although for Philo, too, mystical ascent is essential to see God, the soul in its ascent only knows that he is incapable of being seen. The soul, according to Philo, can ascend only when it is freed from the bonds of matter through ascetic practice.[55] Moreover, he does not clearly indicate the descent of a heavenly messenger except to mention the sending of Moses to the earthly sphere (*Sacr.* 8–10). Again, the idea of incarnation of a heavenly being is not so explicit as we have it in John.

51. Bultmann, *John: A Commentary*, pp. 150-51.
52. Barrett, *John*, pp. 212-13; cf. Bernard, *St John*, I, pp. 111-12; Moloney, *Son of Man*, p. 122; Nicholson, *Death as Departure*, p. 97 and p. 185 n. 77.
53. See M.L. Appold, *The Oneness Motif in the Fourth Gospel: Motif Analysis and Exegetical Probe into the Theology of John* (WUNT, 2.1; Tübingen: J.C.B. Mohr [Paul Siebeck], 1976), *passim*; Nicholson, *Death as Departure*, pp. 10, 62.
54. The 'incarnation' as defined by Käsemann—see Haenchen, *John*, I, p. 297; cf. Dunn, *Christology*, p. 262, who rightly stresses the notion of divine revelation involved in the incarnation.
55. See above, pp. 72-73, 76.

Ruckstuhl argues that the Man (= God's son) pre-existed as the Wisdom of God before he *became* the Son of Man to reveal heavenly secrets on earth and to make the hidden God visible and approachable.[56] Though there is no evidence in John to accept that 3.13 speaks of the descent of the Man to *become* the Son of Man,[57] Ruckstuhl's suggestion of the Wisdom background for John's descent–ascent motif points in the right direction (cf. *1 En.* 42.1-2; cf. Wis. 9.17-18; Sir. 24.1-12). However, the word ὁ καταβάς does not occur in the sense of incarnation even in Wisdom tradition.

According to Burkett, the question in Prov. 30.4, 'Who has ascended to heaven and come down?', expects the answer, 'No one except God', for God in the Old Testament has on numerous occasions either ascended to heaven or descended from heaven, and in 3.13 Jesus substitutes 'no one except the Son of the Man', interpreting the repeated ascent/descent of God as his own.[58] Prov. 30.4, like Deut. 30.12, Bar. 3.29 and Rom. 10.6-8, stresses the inability of any human to ascend to heaven and come down, without expecting an answer, 'No one except God'. Even though this is the picture one gets in 3.13a, Prov. 30.4 speaks of only ascent–descent of humans rather than the descent–ascent of the Son of the Man. Moreover, the aorist καταβάς in 3.13b denotes not a repeated action, but an action performed once and for all. Even the term ὅταν in 9.5 does not convey a repeated action of Jesus to come to the world, as Burkett argues,[59] but, in the light of 9.4, it refers to the transitory nature of Jesus' earthly life (RSV aptly translates 'as long as'). In fact Prov. 30.4 is only a sarcastic statement without having God as the subject and the name 'Ithiel' in Prov. 30.1 is a personal name (cf. Neh. 11.7) with four possible meanings, and the meaning 'with me is God' is only one of them.[60] Burkett's interpretation of 3.13 depends

56.   E. Ruckstuhl, 'Abstieg und Erhöhung des johanneischen Menschensohns', in R. Pesch and R. Schnackenburg (eds.), *Jesus und der Menschensohn* (Festschrift A. Vögtle; Freiburg: Herder, 1975), pp. 314-41 (329, 334-35).

57.   Against this view, see Nicholson, *Death as Departure*, pp. 185-86 n. 77.

58.   D. Burkett, *The Son of the Man in the Gospel of John* (JSNTSup, 56; Sheffield: JSOT Press, 1991), pp. 47-50, 85-87. Cf. also Ruckstuhl, 'Abstieg', p. 327 and Sidebottom, *Christ of the Fourth Gospel*, pp. 120, 123, 206. Burkett, *Son of the Man*, pp. 51-75, 169-71, argues that the Johannine title the 'Son of (the) Man' comes from Prov. 30.1, 'the Man' being God, and the 'son' called 'Ithiel' (i.e. 'God with me'). Thus, for Burkett, the Son of the Man is the Son of God.

59.   Burkett, *Son of the Man*, p. 86.

60.   C.H. Toy, *A Critical and Exegetical Commentary on the Book of Proverbs*

entirely on his translation of Prov. 30.1-4 that is 'based on the consonants of the Hebrew text, emended slightly in v. 1 following the LXX'.[61]
This raises these issues: Why should v. 1 alone be emended? Why
should the LXX be followed only in part, while keeping the consonants
of the Hebrew text? Since his translation does not do justice either to
the Hebrew text or to the LXX, his suggested background of Prov. 30.1-
4 is inadequate to interpret 3.13.

The approach, which takes first-century Jewish thought seriously, is
particularly relevant to interpret 3.13.[62] Not all 'ascent' stories,
including the apocalyptic ascent tradition,[63] form direct parallel with
3.13. Meeks, for example, has denied the dependence of 3.13 on Moses
traditions because of its notion of Jesus' paradoxical enthronement and
the descent–ascent pattern, but argues for a polemic against Moses-
centred piety.[64] However, the terms οὐδεὶς and εἰς τὸν οὐρανόν in
3.13a do not allow us to think of 3.13 as a polemic directed against
Moses' ascent alone. Odeberg has strongly argued his case that 3.13 is
directed not against the theory of the descent of the divine among
human, but against some theory of an ascent into heaven, particularly
against the coarser form of Merkabah mysticism current at the time of
John.[65] We have noticed above how the traditions of Merkabah-like
visions and heavenly ascents attributed to Moses, to Enoch and to
Abraham were in circulation in Palestine in the first century.[66] It is

(ICC; Edinburgh: T. & T. Clark, 1899), pp. 519, 521. According to Toy, in Prov.
30.4 God is not the subject as the sequence 'ascended...descended' (the starting
point being the earth) shows. R.B.Y. Scott, *Proverbs–Ecclesiastes* (AB, 18; New
York: Doubleday, 1965), p. 176, translates the term 'Ithiel' as 'There is no God'.

61.   Burkett, *Son of the Man*, p. 51. Evans, *Word and Glory*, pp. 94-99,
commends Burkett's study in general, but questions his conclusion that הגבר 'the
Man' refers to God.

62.   See M. de Jonge, 'Nicodemus and Jesus: Some Observations on
Misunderstanding and Understanding in the Fourth Gospel, *BJRL* 53 (1970–71),
pp. 337-59 (352); Dunn, 'Let John Be John', pp. 310-25.

63.   Bühner, *Der Gesandte*, pp. 378-83, argues for a polemic in 3.12-13, 31-36
against the apocalyptic ascent tradition.

64.   Meeks, *Prophet-King*, p. 297; cf. de Jonge, 'Nicodemus and Jesus',
p. 353.

65.   Odeberg, *Fourth Gospel*, pp. 72-73, 89, 94-98; see also Dunn, 'Let John
Be John', pp. 326-27; Meeks, 'Man from Heaven', p. 52; Bultmann, *John: A
Commentary*, p. 150 n. 1.

66.   Cf. Segal, 'Heavenly Ascent', pp. 1352-89, who has drawn a useful
picture of the heavenly journeys described in Jewish documents, Philo and

possible that John refutes the claims of the Merkabah mystics that they made heavenly ascents to see God's glory. Even the very use of the term ὁ υἱὸς τοῦ ἀνθρώπου in 3.13 recalls the man-like figure who appears in mystical visions (Ezek. 1.26; Dan. 7.9, 13).[67] We have seen that 3.13 emphasizes the descent of the Son of Man and the descent-motif is not far away from the early form of Merkabah mysticism. In the Merkabah visions of Ezekiel 1, Isaiah 6, and of Yohanan's school, the descent of the deity for the sake of self-manifestation is presupposed.[68] However, κατάβασις in terms of incarnation is missing also in Merkabah mystical visions. It seems that while John is refuting the Merkabah mystical belief of an ascent to heaven to see the throne of God, he enriches the idea of the descent of God's glory in human-like form with his own doctrine of incarnation. That is, for John the place where one can see the divine glory and can have communion with God is no more the throne as held by the Merkabah mystics of his time, but in the incarnate life of the Son of Man (cf. 1.14).

It is possible, then, that 3.13 is a polemic directed primarily against Merkabah mystics who were familiar with the idea of an ascent to heaven and of the descent of the deity to reveal himself in an anthropomorphic form. It is natural that such mystics could have understood John's statement: 'No one has ascended to heaven but he who descended from heaven, the Son of Man (who is in heaven).'[69] However, John's doctrine of descent–ascent is fully governed by the descent of the Son of Man from heaven to earth by incarnation to reveal the

---

Gnosticism. See also C.H. Talbert, 'The Myth of a Descending-Ascending Redeemer in Mediterranean Antiquity', *NTS* 22 (1976), pp. 418-40.

67.   See Rev. 1.13-16 for the human/angelic appearance of the Son of Man in a mystical vision.

68.   The wheels, which bear the throne of God, were seen by Ezekiel on earth (Ezek. 1.15, 19, 21; cf. 3.22-23). Probably Isaiah saw the enthroned Lord in Jerusalem temple. In the Yohanan tradition, 'fire', which symbolizes God's self-manifestation, encircles Eleazar.

69.   Burkett, *Son of the Man*, p. 81, however, denies any such polemic, by arguing that there is no evidence that Nicodemus and his fellow Jews were claiming visionary knowledge of heavenly secrets or that they were in danger of accepting other than Jesus as the revealer of such secrets. However, the reference to Jesus' origin as ἀπὸ θεοῦ (3.2) and the very subject of the dialogue, τὰ ἐπουράνια, make it probable that Nicodemus himself, as John presents the encounter, had a desire to know more of the heavenly secrets, particularly of God's kingdom. Burkett thus takes up a position that is contrary to John's argument (cf. 3.10-12).

heavenly realities, in particular God in his kingly glory. In view of the replacement-motif envisaged specifically in chs. 2–4,[70] it seems likely that John replaces in 3.13 the Jewish throne-mysticism with the mystical experience that has become possible in Jesus, the Son of Man. Although the descent–ascent schema falls in close parallel with Wisdom tradition, the related idea of seeing God on earth in the Son of Man directly reflects the Merkabah mystical belief of John's time. However, the thought does not end up here, but it continues in 3.14-15 an analysis of which I undertake on pp. 203-206. Our observation that John seems not only to polemize, but also to proclaim the gospel by using the same mystical tradition becomes clear in the idea of birth ἄνωθεν which John presents as the requirement for Merkabah-like visions, as we see below.

Birth ἄνωθεν *and the Kingdom of God*
We have noticed that ascetic practices, prayers and fasts were adopted as necessary preparations by Merkabah mystics to make a heavenly journey. The rationale behind this is that the one who aspires to see God should avoid fleshy deeds.[71] For John, however, the fleshy deeds can be put off not by an ascetic kind of life, but by the birth from above (3.3), that is, by a life transformed by the Spirit (cf. 3.5, 8).[72] Odeberg

---

70. John uses the phrase κατὰ τὸν καθαρισμὸν τῶν Ἰουδαίων in 2.6 with the purpose of showing how the Jewish rite of purification is superseded by the life of truth given by Jesus Christ (see Dodd, *Interpretation*, p. 299; Carson, *John*, p. 173). The Johannine Jesus indicates that he, in his person, replaces the temple, the dwelling place of God, and the whole worship pattern of Jews and Samaritans (2.13-22; 4.19-26) (see especially Dodd, *Interpretation*, pp. 300-303; Carson, *John*, pp. 180-84; Brown, *John*, I, p. 180; J.R. Wohlgemut, 'Where Does God Dwell? A Commentary on John 2:13-22', *Direction* 22 [1993], pp. 87-93). Barrett, *John*, pp. 195-97, who observes that 2.13–4.54 forms a whole, comments that John develops his main theme that in Christ the eternal purposes of God, as expressed in Judaism, is fulfilled. However, fulfilment involves replacement of the old order of religious life with the new and spiritual order. It is noteworthy that the events mentioned in chs. 2–4, or even afterwards, are placed within the context of the death and resurrection of Jesus Christ, thereby foreshadowing the cross, the climax of the revelation of God's glory in Jesus (see Dodd, *Interpretation*, pp. 300-303; Wohlgemut, 'Where Does God Dwell?', pp. 87-93). See also above, p. 194.

71. See W.C. Grese, '"Unless One is Born Again": The Use of a Heavenly Journey in John 3', *JBL* 107 (1988), pp. 677-93 (684-85).

72. Since John uses the same word with the meaning 'from above' in 3.31 and 19.11, 23, possibly the same is primarily meant in 3.3 too. However, in view of his

asserts that the entrance into the celestial world is conditioned by the birth from above.[73] This is in accordance with the principle that like can only be known by like: the heavenly kingdom, being spiritual by nature (cf. 4.24; 6.63; 8.21, 23), can be experienced only by those who have replaced the flesh with the spirit.[74]

The idea of ἐκ πνεύματος γεννᾶσθαι in 3.3, 5, 6, 8 is reminiscent of the ἐκ θεοῦ ἐγεννήθησαν of 1.13,[75] suggesting that those who are born of the Spirit are those who receive the Logos and believe in his name. Thus, the experience of new birth for John comes ἐκ θεοῦ, rather than ἐν θεῷ as in Hellenistic mysticism,[76] and is theo- and christo-centric. Dodd remarks that this effectively dissociates Johannine sense of rebirth from all mythological notions of divine generation such as were current in Hellenistic circles.[77] In John's view, only the Son of Man, whose abode was 'above', can offer new birth to those who believe in him. What is the relevance of the kingdom of God in this context?

There are two dimensions of God's kingdom in Jewish thought: God sitting on the throne as king (1 Kgs 22.19; Ps. 103.19; Isa. 6.1; Ezek. 1.26; etc.) and the eternal, resurrection life which will be enjoyed in his kingdom at the end time (cf. Dan. 2.44; 7.14, 27; 12.1-3).[78] It is God's kingship that is emphasized in 3.3, 5, for 3.1-15 is largely concerned with the revelation of the 'above' that is available in the Son of Man now on earth. Schnackenburg rightly suggests that in Johannine perspective the 'kingdom of God' implies 'the heavenly realm on high to which the divine envoy leads (cf. 14.3; 12.26; 17.24)'.[79] The author does not use the phrase any further, because, for him, God's kingship has given way to Christ's kingship, culminating in his enthronement on

---

tendency to pun on words and to present heavenly matters through earthly images, the meaning 'again' is also implied; for the birth from above is essentially a born-again experience. This, however, was misunderstood by Nicodemus as a second birth in flesh—cf. Bultmann, *John: A Commentary*, p. 135 n. 1.

73. Odeberg, *Fourth Gospel*, pp. 70-71.

74. Grese, '"Unless One is Born Again"', p. 685. Cf. Philo's φωτί φῶς in *Praem. Poen.* 46.

75. See Dodd, *Interpretation*, p. 305.

76. See above, p. 67.

77. Dodd, *Interpretation*, p. 305.

78. See Carson, *John*, p. 188.

79. Schnackenburg, *St John*, I, pp. 366-77; cf. J.C.O. O'Neill, 'The Kingdom of God', *NovT* 35 (1993), pp. 130-41 (134), argues that only if the word 'kingdom' is understood as a house or city or land can one speak of 'entering' the kingdom.

the cross (cf. 1.49; 6.15; 12.13; 18.36; 19.10-11).[80] We can reasonably conclude that ' "seeing" and "entering" the kingdom of God' means seeing and entering the heavenly realm by faith in and through the Son of Man, to see God as king and to experience the heavenly realities, including eternal life.[81] Thus, for John a vision of God's kingly glory and participation in the heavenly world, for which the Merkabah mystics were aspiring, some even by an ascent to heaven, is possible here on earth for those who are born of the Spirit by believing in Jesus. Still the questions arise: in what manner does the Son of Man reveal God as king and make the encounter with God possible? Is God revealed as seated on the throne? Is he accompanied by the angels, as in Merkabah visions? An analysis of 3.14-15 is called for to clarify these issues.

John 3.14-15

Καὶ καθὼς Μωϋσῆς ὕψωσεν τὸν ὄφιν ἐν τῇ ἐρήμῳ, οὕτως ὑψωθῆναι δεῖ τὸν υἱὸν τοῦ ἀνθρώπου, ἵνα πᾶς ὁ πιστεύων ἐν αὐτῷ ἔχῃ ζωὴν αἰώνιον.

The key word to explain 3.14-15 is the passive form of ὑψοῦν. Some scholars argue that ὑψοῦν in 3.14 primarily means the lifting-up of Jesus on the cross, although his exaltation follows afterwards.[82] Some others find the main emphasis as lying on the lifting-up of Jesus to heaven, although the lifting-up took place by means of crucifixion.[83] Some argue that both Jesus' death and his return to heaven are equally accommodated in 3.14.[84] According to Odeberg, ὑψωθῆναι, denoting

80. See below, pp. 236-43.
81. See Meeks, 'Man from Heaven', pp. 52-53, who argues that both 'seeing' and 'entering' the kingdom of God refer to a *Himmelreise* tradition. The kingdom of God was conceived in the late first century as the self-revelation of God or as God in his activity (see below, pp. 237-38).
82. Bernard, *St John*, I, pp. 113-14, and II, pp. 303, 442; Brown, *John*, I, pp. 145-46; Barrett, *John*, p. 214; Schnackenburg, *St John*, I, pp. 396-97; Ruckstuhl, 'Abstieg', pp. 331-33; Moloney, *Son of Man*, pp. 60-65; W. Thüsing, *Die Erhöhung und Verherrlichung Jesu im Johannesevangelium* (NTAbh, 21; Münster: Aschendorff, 2nd edn, 1970), pp. 3-12, 301-302.
83. Dodd, *Interpretation*, pp. 247, 307, 375-79; Bultmann, *John: A Commentary*, p. 152 n. 4, p. 350; Nicholson, *Death as Departure*, pp. 98-103; Pryor, 'Johannine Son of Man', p. 350.
84. G.R. Beasley-Murray, *Gospel of Life: Theology in the Fourth Gospel*

the glorification of the Son of Man after his death, refers to a spiritual experience of 'mystical union' with the believer, in which the Son of Man is elevated and gazed upon by the believer, who, in such experience, ascends upwards to the δόξα, the 'image' of the heavenly Son of Man.[85] Those who argue for Jesus' final ascent as implied in 3.14 interpret it in the light of the ὑψωθήσεται καὶ δοξασθήσεται of Isa. 52.13 and of the ὑψοῦν of Acts 2.33 and 5.31. However, their arguments do not take into account the main arguments posed by Meeks and Moloney who find the prime reference as to crucifixion.

The passages, Acts 2.33, 5.31 and Phil. 2.9, which use ὑψοῦν, clearly mention that they mean Jesus' exaltation to heaven rather than leaving it ambiguous. Although ὑψωθῆναι and δοξασθῆναι occur in Isa. 52.13, the subsequent verses (14-15) and almost the whole of Isaiah 53 make it clear that the servant's glory lies in his vicarious suffering and death. Loader finds in 8.21-24 and 12.31 a shift of emphasis from crucifixion to Jesus' return to the Father.[86] But the point at issue in 8.21-24 is not where Jesus is returning to, but who Jesus is (cf. v. 25). The twice-repeated particle νῦν in 12.31 and the evangelist's gloss in 12.33 show that Jesus' death on the cross is implied by the verb ὑψοῦν in 12.32, 34. The fact that it was 'the Jews' who will exalt the Son of Man (8.28) makes it very clear that the evangelist meant primarily crucifixion by using the verb ὑψοῦν in his Gospel.[87]

The use of Num. 21.8, 9 in 3.14 reinforces this: Moses set (θές in Num. 21.8 LXX and ἔστησεν in v. 9) a brazen serpent upon a signal-staff (σημείον) by God's command so that the one who is bitten by a serpent might find life (ζήν) when he looks on (ἐπιβλέπειν) it. Likewise, it is God's salvific plan (δεῖ) that he should lift up (ὑψοῦν) the Son of Man so that the one who believes (πιστεῖν) might have eternal life (ζωὴν αἰώνιον). Thus, the ὑψωθῆναι of 3.14 should be understood in terms of the θές and ἔστησεν of Num. 21.8, 9 and hence this can only mean the placement of the Son of Man on the cross rather than his ascension to the Father. Even a reference to the vicarious

(Peabody, MA: Hendrickson, 1991), pp. 49-50; Loader, *Christology*, pp. 115-18.

85. Odeberg, *Fourth Gospel*, pp. 99-100, 109-13.

86. Loader, *Christology*, p. 117.

87. See J. Riedl, 'Wenn ihr den Menschensohn erhöht habt, werdet ihr erkennen (Joh 8, 28)', in R. Pesch and R. Schnackenburg (eds.), *Jesus und der Menschensohn* (Festschrift A. Vögtle; Freiburg: Herder, 1975), p. 360.

nature of the death of the Son of Man as underlying 3.14-15 has been detected by A.T. Hanson.[88]

Another important change made by John, while using Num. 21.8, 9, is that the act of looking (ἰδών and ἐπιβλέπων) upon the brazen serpent is described in 3.15 as believing (πιστεύων) in the Son of Man. Though, as we will see below, 'seeing' is not fully identified with 'believing' in John, at least 'seeing' is in most cases implied in 'believing' (1.50-51; 2.11; 9.37-38; 20.8, 29; etc.).[89] That is, the one who sees the glorified Son of Man on the cross and believes in him will have eternal life. In other words, in John's 'believing in the Son of Man', 'beholding his glory' on the cross is presupposed.[90] The purpose of lifting up the Son of Man on the cross, according to 3.14-15, is to reveal his glory (or name) and those who behold it and believe in the Son of Man attain eternal life. This is indeed the μείζω τούτων promised in 1.50. The promise of everlasting life is made to Enoch who had seen God's glory on the throne in *2 En.* 22.7. It is probable that John uses in 3.13-15 the core of Merkabah mysticism and reinterprets it by saying that a vision of God's glory is available in Jesus' death on the cross.[91] That is, for John, the divine glory is revealed not on the heavenly throne with the angelic entourage, but on the earthly throne, the cross (cf. Col. 2.15), being surrounded by hostile forces. The cryptic allusion to cross found in 1.51; 2.1-11, 13-22; 3.13; 4.20-26 is made clear in 3.14-15! These passages suggest that the Jewish throne-mysticism is herewith transformed into cross-centred mysticism in John. Broadly speaking, the Christ of John is the bearer of God's glory and the Son of Man who fulfils the mystical goal of the seekers. But what is distinctive in John is his presentation of *cross* as the throne on which the Son of Man reveals God's eternal glory and therefore it seems likely that John replaces throne-mysticism with cross-mysticism.

---

88. A.T. Hanson, *The Prophetic Gospel: A Study of John and the Old Testament* (Edinburgh: T. & T. Clark, 1991), p. 49.

89. G.L. Phillips, 'Faith and Vision in the Fourth Gospel', in F.L. Cross (ed.), *Studies in the Fourth Gospel* (London: Mowbray, 1957), pp. 83-96 (91-92), indicates that πιστεύειν is the crown and consummation of 'seeing'.

90. Cf. 1.12, where believing 'in his Name' is emphasized. For John, 'name' is identified with Jesus' 'glory' (cf. 17.6, 11, 12, 26 with 17.5, 22, 24); cf. *Targ. Num.* 21.8 identifies the act of beholding the brazen serpent with that of directing one's heart to 'the Name of the Word of the Lord'.

91. See also below, pp. 227-30.

According to Num. 21.8-9, as Wis. 16.5-12 has it, the people were saved not by turning to the brazen serpent (i.e. the thing that was beheld), but by 'turning towards' God (Wis. 16.7), who sent his mercy (v. 10) or his Word (v.12) to heal them. John seems to apply this passage to Christ, by saying that the divine life is attainable only by turning to the Son of Man, in whose crucifixion the love, mercy and glory of God are to be seen. Thus John uses the current mystical belief, perhaps tying it with Wisdom tradition, as a vehicle to present God's redemptive love revealed in Jesus (cf. 3.16-17 with 3.13-15) rather than just polemizing against it. If 'polemic' alone was his purpose, then the addition of 3.15-21 would be irrelevant.

The Ascent of the Son of Man

Among several Johannine passages that speak of Jesus' ascent to heaven, 6.62 refers directly to the ascent of the Son of Man and therefore a study of this passage will enhance our understanding of the ascent-motif in John.

John 6.62

> ἐάν οὖν θεωρῆτε τὸν υἱὸν τοῦ ἀνθρώπου ἀναβαίνοντα ὅπου ἦν τὸ πρότερον...

The focus of our study will be on: what did the evangelist mean by ἀναβαίνοντα? What are its implications, if any? Is it in any way related to the current mystical tradition? After drawing the attention of his readers to the pre-existence and the κατάβασις of the Son of Man in 3.13, John refers in 6.62 to the ascent of the Son of Man to the place where he was before (πρότερον).

Meeks indicates that as the Fourth Gospel progresses, more and more emphasis is placed on the ascent which contains such independent motifs as 'being lifted up', 'misunderstanding', 'heavenly dwellings' and 'mutual indwelling'.[92] This emphasis is anticipated in 6.62. Moloney undermines the idea of Jesus' ascent to heaven in 6.62, when he argues that 6.62, being a polemic against the popular idea of the heavenly ascent, shows that there was no need for Jesus to 'ascend' because his origin itself has been with God and therefore that Jesus'

---

92.   Meeks, 'Man from Heaven', pp. 62-66.

revelation on earth is true.[93] However, Moloney ignores that 6.62 poses a 'hypothetical' statement without attempting to give a full picture of Jesus' ascension to heaven. Though hypothetical, it alludes to 'some occurrence by which a revelation of high importance' will be given by virtue of the ascension of the Son of Man.[94] The idea of revelation in 6.62 is expressed by John on a different scale. In the light of 6.35-58, the subject of the offence (cf. 6.61) is Jesus' descent from heaven (i.e. incarnation) and the necessity to eat his flesh (i.e. the act of coming to and believing in the Word-become-flesh which was sacrificed on the cross for the life of the world;[95] cf. 6.42, 52). The point in 6.62 is that if Jesus' 'disciples' do not believe (6.64) but take offence at the life-giving effect of his incarnation and death, they can scarcely believe his ascension, which will exhibit even greater glory—the glory that he had in heaven with God (17.5)—and hence that they will stumble even more (cf. 3.12).[96]

Nevertheless, the phrase ἀναβαίνοντα ὅπου ἦν τὸ πρότερον, like 3.13, presupposes the pre-existence and the descent of the Son of Man prior to his ascent to heavenly glory. Bühner argues that the ascent–descent of the Son of Man is based on the rabbinic connection of prophet and angel and on Moses tradition.[97] He also suggests that whereas the ascension aspect has the background of Enoch tradition, the descent aspect echoes 11QMelch and the *Prayer of Joseph*.[98] Bühner's argument does not do enough justice to the heavenly origin of

93.   Moloney, *Son of Man*, pp. 121-23.

94.   Cadman, *Open Heaven*, p. 90.

95.   See J.D.G. Dunn, 'John VI: A Eucharistic Discourse?', *NTS* 17 (1970–71), pp. 328-38 (331, 333); Beasley-Murray, *Gospel of Life*, p. 97.

96.   B.F. Westcott, *The Gospel According to St John* (London: John Murray, 1882), p. 109, and Barrett, *John*, p. 303, mention an interpretation which suggests that the offence is caused by the death of Jesus, the first part of ascension and that it is removed by his heavenly ascension. However, John nowhere seems to mean directly Jesus' suffering and death by the term ἀναβαίνειν. If John anticipated the removal of offence, then the separation of πολλοὶ μαθηταί would be inexplicable. The verb ἀναβαίνω, among other verbs, primarily implies Jesus' ascent to heaven, although it is used eight times with geographical sense (see Nicholson, *Death as Departure*, p. 58).

97.   Bühner, *Der Gesandte*, pp. 425-29.

98.   Bühner, *Der Gesandte*, pp. 426-27. Similarly Ashton finds in John's descent–ascent pattern a fusion of two mythologies: angelic and mystical—Ashton, *Understanding*, pp. 353-56.

the Son of Man and to the interrelated Son of God Christology of John's Gospel.[99] His argument also does not take into consideration the idea of revelation and incarnation, and the other independent motifs connected with Jesus' ascent. Viewed thus, the descent–ascent of the Son of Man can hardly be fitted even with the descent–ascent of the angels, who came down to earth with an entirely different mission from that of the Son of Man.

Nevertheless, Bühner's view that the ascent, descent and the lifting-up of the Son of Man can be understood exclusively from the Christian apocalyptic and Jewish esoteric traditions[100] fits in well with the histor-ical context of late-first-century Judaism, which shows traces of interest in mystical ascents and descents. Borgen rightly maintains that in his presentation of theophanic ideas John reflects especially the early Merkabah mysticism.[101] Against the current claims for a 'mystical' ascent to heaven, John seems to proclaim that divine glory can be actually seen not in the ascent–descent of the patriarchs and prophets or of angels, but in the descent–ascent of the Son of Man. The mystical ascent is possible for John only by the descent of the Son of Man. This polemic and proclamative tendency of John is clearly perceived in two main themes related to Jesus' ascent: heavenly journey and heavenly dwellings.

The Heavenly Journey
The language used for Jesus' ascent, such as ἀναβαίνω, ἔρχομαι, μεταβαίνω, ὑπάγω, πορεύομαι and ἀπέρχομαι,[102] betray the influence of the *Himmelreise*, believed to be undertaken by some prominent figures in the first century. John describes the heavenly journey of Jesus as 'going to the Father' from the world just as he came to the world from God (13.1, 3; 17.11, 13), though it was misunderstood by the Jews and Peter, among the disciples, as referring to a physical journey (cf. 7.35; 13.37).

The heavenly journey of Jesus paves the way for the future ascent of the disciples[103] and this idea is brought out in an esoteric way.[104] The

99. See Dunn, 'Let John Be John', p. 329.
100. Bühner, *Der Gesandte*, p. 425.
101. Borgen, *Bread from Heaven*, pp. 2-3, 177. See also above, p. 37.
102. See Nicholson, *Death as Departure*, p. 58, for the list of verses that imply Jesus' ascent or return to the Father.
103. Meeks, 'Man from Heaven', p. 65.

misunderstanding of the riddle, 'Where I am going you cannot come' (7.33-34; 13.33) helps the evangelist to bring out this idea. Jesus' reply to Peter's inquiry, ου δύνασαί μοι νῦν ἀκολουθῆσαι, ἀκολουθήσεις δὲ ὕστερον (13.36b), clearly shows the possibility for his disciples to go to the Father by means of Jesus. Meeks correctly observes that the term ἀκολουθήσεις does not mean in this context either imitating Jesus or accepting a similar fate of dying on the cross, but 'it is to go *by means of him*'.[105] This is reinforced by two important Johannine ideas: Jesus is the way (ὁδός) to the Father (14.6) and the door (θύρα) by means of which the sheep enter (10.7, 9). It seems probable, then, that John uses the esoteric/mystical tradition of his time to describe how one can undertake a heavenly journey to see God and to experience heavenly life. However, he makes two important alterations: (1) he treats an angelic guide as non-essential for a heavenly journey of Jesus' followers, because the one who descended from above made open a permanent way to the Father;[106] (2) the privilege of making a heavenly ascent is no more confined to those who fulfil all the commandments including certain dietary laws, but to anyone who follows Jesus and thus there is a shift in identifying the 'insiders'.[107]

The fact that the disciples can follow Jesus not now but afterwards (13.36b) argues against Odeberg's mystical interpretation of 6.62 that the believers are fully absorbed in the divine reality by an ἀνάβασις in the Son,[108] for there is no reference in 6.62 to the union of the believer in the ascent of the Son of Man to God. This is further confirmed by the use of the present tense ἀναβαίνω, 'I am in the process of ascending', in 20.17.[109] Beasley-Murray's rendering, 'I am on my way' brings out the full significance of Jesus' ascent. For John, Jesus is the way to the Father (14.6), but his disciples can come to the Father only after the

104. Cf. Nicholson, *Death as Departure*, p. 60.

105. Meeks, 'Man from Heaven', p. 65.

106. See below, pp. 253, 267 for the notion that in John the angelic function is transferred to the role of the paraclete.

107. Cf. Meeks, 'Man from Heaven', pp. 69-70 for the idea that John's ascent–descent motif gave a social identity to the believers and made them 'insiders'.

108. Odeberg, *Fourth Gospel*, pp. 259-60, 267-69.

109. G.R. Beasley-Murray, *John* (WBC, 36; Dallas: Word Books, 1987), p. 377; Schnackenburg, *St John*, III, p. 319. Both these scholars cite F. Blass, A. Debrunner and R.W. Funk, *A Greek Grammar of the New Testament and Other Early Christian Literature* (Chicago: University of Chicago Press, 1961), §323.3 for the futuristic use of the present.

Father's will is accomplished through the death, resurrection and ascension of the Son of Man. In this sense the ascension of Jesus paves way for his followers to ascend to heaven.

The Heavenly Dwellings

The heavenly journey of Jesus is directly connected with heavenly dwellings (μοναί), another important aspect of Merkabah mysticism. Jesus' 'going to the Father' is to prepare for his disciples a τόπος in the οἰκία of his Father, which has many rooms (μοναί πολλαί); then he will come again to take them and make them dwell there with himself (14.2-3). McCaffrey has argued that the word τόπος in 14.2-3 technically means the heavenly temple (cf. 4.20; 11.48)[110] and Segovia understands it as the temple for the disciples in 'the world above'.[111] If so, Jesus is promising them that he will take them to the heavenly temple where the glory of God dwells and which too is his own dwelling (14.3). That is, it is the glory of Jesus that dwells in the heavenly sanctuary and which will be beheld by the disciples (17.24). Thus, Jesus is not only the ὁδός (or *mystagogue*) to the Father, but he himself is the manifestation of God in the Father's house—an idea embedded also in 1.51.

P.S. Alexander argues that the reference to God's οἰκία with its μοναὶ πολλαί in 14.2 recalls the Merkabah traditions about God's heavenly 'palaces' and 'dwellings' with their many 'chambers'.[112] We have also observed in the Jewish mystical texts that in the chambers of the palace of the seventh heaven the glory of God can be seen. This gives us further evidence for the presence of Merkabah mystical elements in John by means of which the evangelist interacts with those who had known and/or practised Merkabah mysticism. The mystical notion is also obvious in the use of the term οἰκία, which in John means also 'household' rather than just 'building' (4.53; 8.35).[113] The

110.   McCaffrey, *The House with Many Rooms*, pp. 185-92; he also observes (pp. 177-84) that the οἰκία of 14.2 refers to the heavenly temple as well as to the family relationship with the Father (cf. 8.35).

111.   F.F. Segovia, *The Farewell of the Word* (Minneapolis: Fortress Press, 1991), p. 83 n. 46.

112.   See Alexander, '3 (Hebrew Apocalypse of) Enoch', p. 247.

113.   See R.H. Gundry, 'In my Father's House are many μοναί', *ZNW* 58 (1967), pp. 68-72 (71). However, McCaffrey, *The House with Many Rooms*, pp. 178-79, suggests that the idea of 'building' also cannot be excluded.

expression 'my Father's house' implies that God is the Father whose household is the followers of Jesus, the τέκνα θεοῦ (1.12).[114] Thus Jesus' ascent to the Father makes a way for his followers to be admitted into God's family in heaven. The expressions, τοὺς ἀδελφούς μου and πρὸς τὸν πατέρα μου καὶ πατέρα ὑμῶν καὶ θεόν μου καὶ θεὸν ὑμῶν, used by the risen Jesus at the point of his ascension to the Father (20.17) reveal that the disciples have now equal privilege with Jesus in the family of God. This has close parallel with Merkabah tradition, according to which the mystic is transformed into one among the angels, who constitute 'the celestial family' or 'his household in the height' (*3 En.* 12.5). This also echoes the 'communal mysticism' of Qumran by which the worshippers enjoyed a sense of union with the angels in heaven before the Throne of Glory. The mystical union with the angels is transferred in John to the 'mystical' union with the angelomorphic Son of Man[115] by means of Jesus' ascent, not in the sense of absorption in him but in the sense of sharing the same relationship with God.[116]

Conclusions

We have examined the ascent-motif in John on three interrelated levels: the ascent and descent of the angels, the descent of the Son of Man, and the ascent of the Son of Man.

John mentions the ascent and descent of the angels in 1.51 without making any further significant reference to them in the Gospel. The reference in 1.51 is due to John's use of Gen. 28.12. Since the angels are ascending and descending upon the Son of Man, who replaces the stairway and the presence of Yahweh of Genesis 28, he is the primary focus in the promised vision. For John the real sense of Jesus' messiahship and sonship lies in perceiving him as the Son of Man in his double role: he is the way to have communion with God and at the same time he himself is the revelation of God's glory. John brings out this idea by uniquely combining Ezek. 1.1 and Gen. 28.12, thus recalling the appearance of God's glory in Merkabah mysticism. For him the

114. The 'house' in the world above exclusively belongs to Jesus' followers— see Segovia, *Farewell*, p. 82 n. 45.

115. Note that the Christophany of the risen Jesus in Rev. 1.13-16 is described in terms of angelomorphism.

116. Cf. Schnackenburg, *St John*, III, p. 320; Beasley-Murray, *John*, p. 378.

Merkabah vision is meaningfully possible not by an ascent to heaven, but in Jesus, the Son of Man, here on earth. The importance of the ascending and descending angels in this revelatory act, then, is twofold: they represent the angels who radiate God's glory by surrounding his throne and serving him; and they symbolize the communication with God which has become possible on the basis of the life and work of the Son of Man on earth.

The same concern for Merkabah visions in the Son of Man is brought out in the unique descent-theology of John in 3.13-15. The expression 'No one has ascended into heaven' clearly betrays the implicit polemic purpose of the evangelist directed primarily against the Merkabah mystics of his time. However, he also proclaims to them the descent of the Son of Man from heaven in order to convey the ἐπουράνια to humans as well as to reveal God's kingly glory uniquely in his exaltation (or enthronement) on the cross. John stresses the need for overcoming the deeds of the flesh, not by ascetic practices as followed by the Merkabah mystics, but by a life transformed by the Spirit, before one can 'see' and 'enter' the kingly realm of God. This new birth is ἐκ θεοῦ rather than ἐν θεῷ as in Hellenistic mysticism and is to be experienced by believing in the Son of Man, for he alone has seen and known the heavenly realities as they are. Thus, for John, a vision of God's kingly glory and the knowledge of the heavenly world, which were thought by the mystics to be attainable by an ascent to heaven, is possible here on earth in the Son of Man. For it is the Son of Man who manifested God's glory, not by being seated on the throne with an angelic entourage, but by being 'lifted up' on the cross where he was surrounded by his adversaries. In John, then, the cross, which is the throne of the Son of Man, becomes paradoxically the locus of divine glory, replacing the chariot-throne of Jewish mysticism.

The descent of the Son of Man in John is followed by the ascent of the Son of Man, which is described mainly in terms of 'departure from the world' and 'going to the Father'. John 6.62 clearly shows how faith in the incarnational life of Jesus decides one's faith in his ascension. The glory that was revealed in the earthly life of the Son of Man will be more splendid in his ascent to heavenly glory and therefore unbelief in his ascent, by taking offence at his descent, will only lead to a greater offence. What radically distinguishes the Johannine ascent-motif from the ascents ascribed to the patriarchs, prophets and angels is not merely the descent of the Son of Man from heaven, but also two, among other, main motifs connected with Jesus' ascent: the heavenly journey of Jesus' disciples and their dwelling with the Father in the heavenly temple as his household (14.2-3).

Jesus' ascension has paved the way for them to be taken up with Jesus to the chambers of God, to live in communion with the Father and to behold his glory as revealed in Jesus. Thus, for John, Jesus is not only the ὁδός, but also the *mystagogue* to the Father. The experience of mystical ascent with Jesus to the heavenly temple is possible only for those who believe in Jesus' incarnation, death, and ascension to the Father. Others can grasp neither the place to which the Son of Man ascends nor its implications. Thus John's ascent-motif, flavoured with esotericism, reflects the 'communal mysticism' of Qumran. However, for John, communion with God is possible through Christ rather than by angelic mediation. Although the ascension of Jesus unites him as a family with his followers in the heavenly dwellings, there is no trace of their deification. John seems to use the terms and concepts that were familiar in the Merkabah mystical circles, and to persuade those who took interest in mystical ascent to believe in the descent–ascent of the Son of Man. Because it is in the Son of Man that the divine glory can be perceived, the Johannine Son of Man represents the human-like figure in whom God manifested himself in Merkabah visions. In brief, by means of the ascent-motif John polemizes, proclaims and persuades the people of his day by reinterpreting the contemporary mystical belief in terms of the person and function of Jesus, the Son of Man.

Chapter 13

A VISION OF GOD ON THE THRONE

We have recognized that the main concern of Merkabah mysticism is
'to see God in his glory and as a human-like figure, seated on the throne
as king'. In Chapter 12 we focused on the descent–ascent of the Son of
Man in whose earthly life, death and ascension God's glory is revealed
and by believing in whom one can enter the heavenly realm to see the
kingly glory of God. Such a portrayal of the Son of Man betrays the
influence of the one like a Son of Man known in the apocalyptic/
mystical circles. In this chapter I will examine whether there is a distinctive emphasis in John on the experience of seeing God in his kingly
majesty. For this purpose this study concentrates on three major motifs
in John: 'seeing', 'glory', and 'king'.

The Idea of 'Seeing'

The frequent usage of the verbs ὁράω, θεωρέω, θεάομαι, βλέπω,
ἐμβλέπω and the cognate words in John[1] shows that the idea of 'seeing'
is one of the dominant Johannine themes. The Hebrew word צפה is distinctively used in the *Hekhalot* literature for 'beholding' the Merkabah[2]
and the LXX translates this word often by using ὁράω (e.g. 1 Sam. 4.13;
Isa. 21.6; 52.8; Ezek. 33.6; Hab. 2.1). In the *HR* the words ראה (ὁράω
or εἶδον in the LXX) and הסתכל (the hithpael of סכל), which means the
same as the Greek θεάομαι and θεωρέω,[3] are frequently used to denote

---

1.   See Michaelis, 'ὁράω', pp. 340, 345.
2.   See P. Schäfer, *Konkordenz zur Hekhalot Literatur* (2 vols.; Tübingen:
J.C.B. Mohr [Paul Siebeck], 1988), II, p. 573.
3.   See M. Jastrow, *A Dictionary of Targumim, the Talmud Babli and
Yerushalmi, and the Midrashic Literature* (2 vols.; New York: Choreb, 1926), I,
pp. 990-91; E.A. Abbott, *Johannine Vocabulary* (London: A. & C. Black, 1905),
§§1598, 1604.

the mystic's vision of God on the throne. The *Hermetica* describe the mystical vision of God by using the term θεάσασθαι or θεασάμενος (*CH* 10.5, 6). Therefore a study particularly of the use of the verbs ὁράω, θεάομαι and θεωρέω is called for.

The Idea Conveyed by ὁράω

John uses ὁράω, in its aorist, perfect and future forms, mainly having either God or Jesus as the object of 'seeing'. He insists that no one has ever seen (ἑώρακεν) God except the only Son, who had been in perfect communion with the Father, and therefore who could make him known (1.18). The emphatic position of οὗτος in 6.46 confirms that it is Jesus alone who has perceived God in his capacity as the one who continuously (ὁ ὤν) and closely (παρὰ τοῦ θεοῦ) exists with the Father. Since the invisible God is revealed in a unique way by the μονογενὴς υἱός by virtue of his intimate love and unity with the Father,[4] the possibility of knowing God is inherent in one's fellowship with Jesus so that the one who has seen Jesus has also seen the Father (14.9). The term ἐξηγήσατο in 1.18 can mean 'to declare' God by means of his Word, which, for the Jews, was the Law, but for John is Jesus, who spoke and acted in history.[5] This means that the mystical vision, for John, is not attainable within oneself, as the *Hermetica* hold,[6] nor by climbing up to heaven, as some Jewish mystics believed, but in the life and work of Jesus enacted in human history.

If God is visible in Jesus, what sort of vision is it? What does John exactly mean by ὁράω? This term has different connotations, depending upon the tense and the contexts. It means 'to know' in the sense of 'learning' (ὄψεσθε in 1.39; ἴδε in 1.46, 7.52, 11.34; cf. 14.9 for the synonymous use of the verbs γινώσκω and ὁράω), 'to experience' (3.36—ὄψεται), 'to participate in the messianic age of salvation' (8.56—ἴδῃ), 'to speak to' (12.21—ἰδεῖν) or also 'to have a prophetic

---

4.   The phrase ὁ ὤν εἰς τὸν κόλπον means a perfect communion with the Father; it denotes the intimate love and unity that exist between the Father and the Son (cf. Bultmann, *John: A Commentary*, pp. 82-83; T.L. Brodie, *The Gospel According to John* (New York: Oxford University Press, 1993), p. 145.

5.   See B. Lindars, *The Gospel of John* (NCBC; London: Oliphants, 1977), p. 100; F. Mussner, *The Historical Jesus in the Gospel of St John* (Freiburg: Herder; London: Burns & Oates, 1967), pp. 18-23; Haenchen, *John*, I, p. 127.

6.   See above, pp. 64-65; cf. Sanford, *Mystical Christianity*, pp. 1-12.

vision' (12.41—εἶδεν; cf. Isa. 6.1, 5), etc.[7] The ὄψη of 1.50 and 11.40
indicates 'experiencing' the divine glory disclosed to the followers of
Jesus (cf. 1.14; 2.11) and the ὄψεσθε of 1.51 implies, as noticed above,
a vision of God's glory and communication with him in the Son of Man
(cf. 9.35-38). The possibility of perceiving (ἰδεῖν) God in his kingly
glory in the heavenly realm is envisaged in 3.3, 5 for those who have
been born ἄνωθεν. Again, the possibility to encounter Jesus in faith,
probably by means of the Holy Spirit, is known from 16.16-17, 19
(ὄψεσθε and θεωρεῖτε). 'Seeing' in the sense of encountering the risen
Jesus, and in him God, repeatedly occurs in the Easter Narrative (20.18,
20, 25, 29; cf. 20.28). ὁράω occurs also in connection with an eyewitness to the revelation of divine glory on the cross (19.35) and to the
appearance of the risen Jesus (20.8). Again, the perception of God in
Jesus Christ is described in the context of his death on the cross and
resurrection.

This survey shows that the Johannine ὁράω means 'seeing' on two
levels: the first level refers to physical sight, particularly of Jesus (cf.
1.33, 39, 46; 4.45; 5.6; 6.22, 24; 7.52; 12.9) and this is also true with
seeing signs, which in itself is insufficient for deeper faith or insight
(2.23-25; 4.48; 6.14, 30); the second level signifies a 'seeing' with a
higher degree of understanding, making relationship possible (1.50-51;
3.3; 9.37-38; 11.40; 12.21, 41; 20.25, 27-29). The same two-stage
process of 'seeing' underlies John's use of θεωρεῖν.

The Idea Conveyed by θεάομαι and θεωρέω
It is only in 1.14 that the aorist ἐθεασάμεθα is used with τὴν δόξαν
αὐτοῦ as the object. This witnessing statement of the Church, as
Michaelis states, indicates 'the unique impression' made by the seeing,
in which the element of eyewitness cannot be ruled out.[8] As it is a col-
lective witness, the meaning 'to contemplate', with a theatrical notion
of spectacle,[9] fits in 1.14. Mussner shows that ἐθεασάμεθα primarily
means 'a historical eyewitness' and also 'a seeing by faith'.[10] With the

7.   See Michaelis, 'ὁράω', pp. 341-43 n. 147; Schnackenburg, *St John*, II,
p. 222.
8.   Michaelis, 'ὁράω', p. 345.
9.   Abbott, *Johannine Vocabulary*, §1604.
10.   Mussner, *Historical Jesus*, pp. 18-19. O. Cullmann, *Early Christian Worship* (London: SCM Press, 1953), p. 45, finds in 1.14; 6.40; 14.19 an interplay of

same double sense the word ἐθεασάμεθα appears in 1 Jn 1.1 also.[11] Thus, one can see a fusion of two levels of 'seeing' in John's ἐθεασάμεθα: eyewitness and a deeper insight.

θεωρέω, on the other hand, means 'to behold', implying a rudimentary stage of 'seeing' spiritual truth, or 'to look with concentration', without having a deeper perception.[12] However, John himself places θεωρέω in parallel with γεύομαι (= to taste, experience) in 8.51, 53 and therefore for him it carries a much deeper sense than a rudimentary stage of 'seeing'. He seems to use θεωρέω to denote a vision of God in the life and work of Jesus:

ὁ θεωρῶν ἐμὲ θεωρεῖ τὸν πέμψαντά με (12.45).

John portrays this central theme on two interrelated levels. At first, θεωρέω denotes 'perceiving' Jesus at a superficial level, through which one may or may not attain an intensive understanding. For instance, the perception (θεωρῶ) of Jesus as the prophet at first gradually led the Samaritan woman to see Jesus as the Christ (4.19, 29). Peter could only see (θεωρεῖ) the burial materials in Jesus' tomb, but could not appreciate the significance of resurrection (20.6, 9; cf. 20.12, 14). Similarly, seeing signs at the first stage is not helpful to constitute full faith[13] (cf. 2.23; 6.2, 29, where θεωρεῖν is used). Secondly, θεωρέω denotes a 'closer fellowship' with Jesus. That is, although Jesus' departure will hinder his fellowship with his disciples, they will 'see' (θεωρεῖτε) him again in the ἄλλος παράκλητος (14.19; 16.19; cf. 16.16, where ὄψεσθε is used). With this kind of intensive seeing goes the eschatological seeing of his glory in heaven (17.24—θεωρῶσιν). This glory is identical with God's glory (17.5, 22; cf. 1 Jn 3.2). The eschatological 'seeing' mentioned in 17.24, then, implies a direct vision of God's glory in Jesus and having communion with him.

Hearing, Seeing, Believing and Witnessing
A true 'seeing', for John, is preceded by 'hearing' and followed by 'believing' and 'witnessing'. A typical example is John's call narrative

'seeing with the eyes' and 'seeing in faith' (i.e. spiritual seeing), which is the characteristic of John.

11.   Brown, *John*, I, pp. 502-503, finds in 1 Jn 1.1 a progression from ὁρᾶν to θεάσθαι.

12.   Phillips, 'Faith and Vision', pp. 84-85.

13.   Cf. Brown, *John*, I, p. 502.

(1.29-51), according to which the early disciples come to see Jesus by hearing the testimony of the Baptist (1.29-39), believe in him that he is the Messiah, and witness to their friends (1.39-49; see also 1.14; 1.34; 19.35 for 'seeing' that is followed by 'witnessing'). F. Hahn argues that the initial level of seeing comes by 'hearing', which could lead to a 'concrete seeing' of the works of the Son[14] (cf. 2.11). In contrast, if the initial 'seeing' of Jesus is based on signs, it fails to bring a genuine faith (e.g. 2.23-25; 3.9-11; 6.14-15, 41, 60, 64; 12.37).[15] That there can be no real 'seeing' without 'believing' is attested by 2.11, 23; 6.40; 12.44-45; 14.7, 9; 20.8, 26-29 and hence Phillips calls faith 'the consummation of the whole process of seeing and understanding'.[16]

The Relevant Background of Johannine 'Seeing'
In sum, we should say that the Johannine 'seeing', particularly when θεάομαι and ὁράω are used, portrays two levels of perceiving Jesus: (1) to see at a superficial level, either by seeing signs or by hearing a testimony; and (2) to perceive spiritually and intelligibly, which leads one to the commitment of faith to Christ and to testify about him. The second level of 'seeing' makes communion with God in Jesus possible both now and in future (cf. 17.24). Philo too speaks of the possibility of 'seeing' (ὁράω) God in the Logos, but does not think of it as a historical person with whom fellowship is possible.[17] Although he probably speaks of two levels of seeing God, at first through the Logos and then God as he is in himself, he presents this only at the philosophical level. At some points he denies the possibility of having a direct vision of God except for Abraham and Moses.[18] Sometimes Philo means 'deification of the holy soul' by referring to a vision of God

---

14. F. Hahn, 'Sehen und Glauben im Johannesevangelium', in H. Baltensweiler and Bo Reicke (eds.), *Neue Testament und Geschichte: Historisches Geschehen und Deutung im Neuen Testament* (Festschrift O. Cullmann; Tübingen: J.C.B. Mohr [Paul Siebeck], 1972), pp. 125-41 (127-30). Michaelis, 'ὁράω', pp. 361-62, calls this a 'further seeing', the decision that is taken in encounter with Jesus and which is also a turning to faith.

15. See C. Koester, 'Hearing, Seeing, and Believing in the Gospel of John', *Bib* 70 (1989), pp. 327-48; Cullmann, *Christian Worship*, pp. 41-46.

16. Phillips, 'Faith and Vision', pp. 85-86. However, for John, 'believing' is possible even without 'seeing' with physical eyes (20.29).

17. See below, pp. 293-94 and 297.

18. See *Leg. All.* 3.102; *Quaest. in Gen.* 4.4.

(*Quaest. in Exod.* 2.39-40), which is quite foreign to the Johannine concept of 'seeing'. Moreover, as Michaelis observes, the eschatological aspect of 'seeing' is not found in Philo's writings.[19] In spite of the common factor in Philo and John that God is perceivable through the Logos, the essential differences between them do not give the clue that John has used the Philonic concept of ὁράω or of θεωρέω.

The word θεάομαι occurs in the *Hermetica* (*CH* 10.5, 6) to indicate 'beholding the Good', but it affirms that humans are too weak to see that sight and also such a vision will never allow a person to live on earth. A vision is possible in one's mind but not to one's eyes (*CH* 13.13) and that too by 'drawing his soul up out of the body' and transforming him into a god. Thus the *Hermetica* nullify the possibility of seeing God here on earth. Even to behold him in the other world one needs to train the soul in this life by rigorous means (cf. *Stob.* 6.18-19). Ultimately the seeker could only say, 'I see that I am the All'. Such an ambiguity is altogether missing in John. Although the idea of bearing witness to a vision of Poimandres occurs in *CH* 1.26-28, the two degrees of 'seeing' God in his glory along with the idea of witnessing remind us of the Merkabah vision and make it probable that John is more closely influenced by the mystical tradition of Judaism.

The Glory-Motif

Having grasped the Johannine concept of 'seeing', it is proper for us to study the Johannine passages which contain δόξα (19 times) and δοξάζω (23 times),[20] to ascertain whether or not John's understanding of 'glory' is in any way related to the idea of glory that had been known in Merkabah mystical circles. Apart from the seven references where δόξα is used in John in a non-theological sense, it is used predominantly to refer to the glory of God or the glory of Christ.

19.   Michaelis, 'ὁράω', p. 334. The future ὄψομαι occurs only in *Leg. All.* 2.5; 3.56 and that too without containing any mystical or theological significance.

20.   W.R. Cook, 'The "Glory" Motif in the Johannine Corpus', *JETS* 27 (1984), pp. 291-97, holds that 'Glory' is a basic theme of John; P.E. Robertson, 'Glory in the Fourth Gospel', *TheolEduc* 38 (1988), pp. 121-31; W. Nicol, *The Sêmeia in the Fourth Gospel* (NovTSup, 32; Leiden: E.J. Brill, 1972), p. 125; and E. Käsemann, *The Testament of Jesus: A Study of the Gospel of John in the Light of Chapter 17* (London: SCM Press, ET 1968), p. 7.

The δόξα *of God*

There are two references that speak clearly of the glory of God:

11.4   αὕτη ἡ ἀσθένεια οὐκ ἔστιν προς θάνατον ἀλλ᾽ ὑπὲρ τῆς δόξης τοῦ
          θεοῦ, ἵνα δοξασθῇ ὁ υἱὸς τοῦ θεοῦ δι᾽ αὐτῆς.
11.40   οὐκ εἶπόν σοι ὅτι ἐὰν πιστεύσῃς ὄψῃ τὴν δόξαν τοῦ θεοῦ;

Brückner thinks that the δόξα of God here means the revelation of his greatness, uniqueness or splendour.[21] Following Kittel, Bratcher demonstrates the aptness of the meaning 'divine nature' or 'God-likeness' in John.[22] Such meanings, however, raise the question: what are the main characteristics of that divine nature that are revealed? Surely the exact sense needs to be decided in the light of the context. As the expression 'the δόξα of God' occurs in 11.4, 40 in relation to bringing Lazarus back to life, it may indicate 'God's saving power'[23] or 'God's love' expressed in his generosity to restore life.[24]

John 11.4 also shows that Lazarus's illness provides an occasion upon which proleptically God may bestow glory upon his Son,[25] which means that the glory of the one equals the glory of the other. This divine glory is shared with Jesus even in his pre-existent state (17.5, 22, 24). Since God has given his glory to Jesus because he loved him (17.24b), the δόξα in these passages implies the 'eternal relationship of love' that exists between the Father and the Son[26] and it becomes visible by the obedience of the Son in doing the Father's will on earth (17.4). Caird identifies the glory of God that is shared from all eternity by the Logos as 'God's essential worth, greatness, power, majesty, everything in him which calls forth man's adoring reverence'.[27] In other words, the δόξα of God is the 'radiance of God's many-

21.   K. Brückner, 'A Word Study of *Doxazo* in the Gospel of John', *NOT* 2 (1988), pp. 41-46 (42).
22.   R.G. Bratcher, 'What does "Glory" mean in Relation to Jesus? Translating *doxa* and *doxazo* in John', *BT* 42 (1991), pp. 401-408 (407-408); cf. G. Kittel, 'δόξα', in *TDNT*, II, pp. 232-55 (237).
23.   Bratcher, 'What does "Glory" mean?', p. 407.
24.   See M. Pamment, 'The Meaning of *doxa* in the Fourth Gospel', *ZNW* 74 (1983), pp. 12-16 (14-15), though she denies the meaning 'the splendour and power of God' for the Johannine δόξα.
25.   Barrett, *John*, p. 390.
26.   Barrett, *John*, p. 514.
27.   G.B. Caird, 'The Glory of God in the Fourth Gospel: An Exercise in Biblical Semantics', *NTS* 15 (1968–69), pp. 265-77 (269, 272).

splendoured character'.[28] However, John shows particular interest in 'God's love, generosity and saving power', which were revealed on earth in Jesus. This is the idea that underlies the word δόξα in 1.14, a study of which will illumine further the glory-motif of John.

The δόξα of Jesus

John 1.14. The first reference to the δόξα of Jesus occurs in 1.14:

> Καὶ ὁ λόγος σὰρξ ἐγένετο καὶ ἐσκήνωσεν ἐν ἡμῖν, καὶ ἐθεασάμεθα τὴν δόξαν αὐτοῦ, δόξαν ὡς μονογενοῦς παρὰ πατρός, πλήρης χάριτος καὶ ἀληθείας.

Before we attempt to find out any possible tradition that might have influenced John in 1.14, we should note at least three important factors in this verse.

First, δόξα in 1.14 should be understood within the framework of divine revelation, as the terms, ὁ λόγος σὰρξ ἐγένετο and ἐθεασάμεθα show. Bultmann suggests that the δόξα (of the Revealer) consists in what he is as Revealer for humankind, though he does not give enough attention to the content of revelation.[29] The glory came to be seen by faith precisely in the λόγος σὰρξ γενόμενος.[30] That is, it is the vision of the pre-existent Logos, which is possible neither in one's imagination (i.e. a mystical trance) nor within oneself, as Sanford claims,[31] but in a human. It is God taking up the 'weakness and transitoriness of the human condition'[32] and expressing himself from within it.[33] We have noticed that the appearance of divine glory in a human-like figure was the core of Merkabah contemplation in the late first century. John would have been aware of the existing mystical tradition, which itself had drawn materials from such biblical texts as Ezekiel 1, Isaiah 6 and Daniel 7. It also recalls the angelomorphic Son of Man, who possesses divine prerogatives and bears his glory (Rev. 1.13-16; 14.14). However, *for John, God's glory is manifested not in a human-like form, but in a historical person.*

28. Cook, 'The "Glory" Motif', pp. 292, 297.
29. Bultmann, *John: A Commentary*, pp. 68, 71; cf. p. 13 n. 1.
30. Bultmann, *John: A Commentary*, pp. 69-70.
31. Sanford, *Mystical Christianity*, pp. 8-9, 16-17.
32. See McCaffrey, *The House with Many Rooms*, p. 223; cf. Schnackenburg, *St John*, I, p. 267.
33. See H.U. von Balthasar, *The Glory of the Lord: A Theological Aesthetics.* I. *Seeing the Form* (Edinburgh: T. & T. Clark, 1982), pp. 435-62, esp. p. 459.

Secondly, as we have already indicated, the δόξα of the incarnate Word is the δόξα of God the Father. Since it was granted by the Father to his only Son (μονογενής), it is of the same essence with him.[34] The term ἐσκήνωσεν, alluding to the Hebrew שכן ('to dwell') and משכן ('tabernacle'), confirms that the glory of the Son is no less than the *Shekinah*, the visible manifestation of God (Exod. 24.16; 40.34-35; 1 Kgs 8.10-11). More specifically, according to John, it is the divine attributes of mercy or grace (ἔλεος or χάρις) and faithfulness to the covenant relationship with his people (ἀλήθεια)[35] that constitutes the revealed glory of God. Though πλήρης, which is indeclinable when followed by a genitive, refers to αὐτοῦ (i.e. μονογενής) in the phrase τὴν δόξαν αὐτοῦ, the whole phrase πλήρης χάριτος καὶ ἀληθείας indicates the nature of God's goodness which is his glory (cf. Exod. 33.18-19 with Exod. 34.5-7, where ואמת חסד constitutes God's glory, his goodness).

Thirdly, the testimony, ἐθεασάμεθα τὴν δόξαν αὐτοῦ, presupposes a sense of hiddenness, which was divulged to John and his associates. Bultmann rightly recognizes that the revelation is present in a peculiar *hiddenness*, for one can see the δόξα exclusively in the σάρξ rather than *alongside* the σάρξ or *through* the σάρξ.[36] The human life of Jesus, for John, is the arena in which God's glory can be encountered and this fact is not often appreciated by everyone. Carson remarks that there is a hiddenness to the display of glory in the incarnate Word in the sense that only those who have faith 'see' it in such events as Jesus' signs, his death and exaltation.[37] According to 2.11, only his disciples could perceive the glory manifested through the miracle. Martha had to believe in Jesus that he himself is the resurrection and life before she could see God's glory behind the performed miracle (11.25-28, 40,

34.	Cf. Westcott, *St John*, p. 12; in itself μονογενής means 'only of its kind' or 'unique', but when used in relation to a πατήρ, it means 'only son'—see Dodd, *Interpretation*, p. 305 n. 1; Barrett, *John*, p. 166.

35.	The Hebrew ואמת חסד is rendered in the LXX by ἔλεος καὶ ἀλήθεια and John prefers to use χάρις instead of ἔλεος probably to emphasize δόξα as the gift of God (Hoskyns, *Fourth Gospel*, p. 150) or as the covenant love of God (Brown, *John*, I, pp. 14, 34-35; Lindars, *John*, p. 95; Beasley-Murray, *John*, p. 14). The word ἀλήθεια denotes the faithfulness of God to his covenant which was expressed by the sending of his son (Schnackenburg, *St John*, II, p. 228).

36.	Bultmann, *John: A Commentary*, pp. 63-64.

37.	Carson, *John*, p. 130; M.M. Thompson, *The Humanity of Jesus in the Fourth Gospel* (Philadelphia: Fortress Press, 1988), pp. 118-19.

45-46). In both cases the crowd could see no more than the miracles. This clearly shows the esoteric tendency embedded in the Johannine δόξα theme, according to which the δόξα is both the manifestation and the concealment of God.[38] Mussner calls this paradox the 'mystery' of the historical Jesus—the mystery being the fact that in the historical Jesus the eyes of faith see 'the bringer of salvation, the λόγος τῆς ζωῆς'.[39] Also, there is a hiddenness in God's self-manifestation itself in the sense that what humans can see in the σάρξ is God's glory only to a limited degree insofar as it is revealed in Jesus, for σάρξ denotes the human mode of being which is 'earth bound (3.6), transient and perishable (6.63)'[40] and in short, human limitedness. The same limited apprehension of God is implied in the manifestation of God's glory in human-like form in Merkabah visions.

Many scholars have interpreted δόξα in 1.14 against the background of Exodus tradition (cf. Exod. 16.10; 24.16; 33.18-23; 40.34; Deut. 5.24). Carson, for instance, states that the glory revealed to Moses, displaying that divine goodness characterized by grace and truth, was the very same glory John and his friends saw in the Word-made-flesh.[41] Evans insists that the incarnation of the Logos cannot be correctly understood without a comparison and contrast with Moses and the Sinai covenant.[42] Undoubtedly John has used the terms and ideas of the Sinai covenant. However, we must be aware of at least three key aspects of John that are missing in the Sinai tradition.

1. The emphatic ἐθεασάμεθα of 1.14c is missing in the Sinai theophany. The idea of 'seeing' God's glory has less significance, in fact is prohibited, than the idea of 'hearing' his words (Exod. 19.21; 20.18-19; 33.20-23; Deut. 4.12, 15) and thus the Sinai tradition stresses an auditory, non-visual experience.[43] What the people could see were thunderings, lightnings and fire (Exod. 20.18; 24.17) or, at the most,

38. For John's esoteric tendency see below pp. 301-10. For the idea that God is hidden but at the same time revealed to the Merkabah mystic see Schäfer, *Der verborgene und offenbare Gott, passim*.

39. Mussner, *Historical Jesus*, pp. 21-23.

40. Schnackenburg, *St John*, I, p. 267; cf. von Balthasar, *The Glory of the Lord*, I, p. 458.

41. Carson, *John*, p. 129; cf. Brown, *John*, I, pp. 34-35; Beasley-Murray, *John*, p. 14.

42. Evans, *Word and Glory*, p. 81; see also pp. 79-83 for an echo of Exodus tradition in 1.14-18.

43. See Mettinger, *Dethronement*, p. 46.

something like a sapphire stone under his feet (Exod. 24.10).

2. The manifestation of God's glory in human-like form, described by John, has no importance in Exodus tradition, although Moses had a glimpse of God's back (Exod. 33.23).

3. For John, as we will see below, the glory revealed in Jesus is God's kingly glory (cf. Ps. 29.9-10; Isa. 6.1-3; Ezek. 1.26-28) based on Father–Son relationship and such a royal and filial connotation is precisely missing in the Sinai theophany.

These important differences show that the Exodus story is insufficient to interpret the revelatory character of the Johannine δόξα. Some scholars understand the term δόξα in 1.14 in the light of other biblical passages where כבוד occurs (e.g. 1 Kgs 8.11; Isa. 60.1; etc.).[44] In fact 12.41, another key passage in the glory-motif, recalls Isaiah's vision. Even Evans finally concludes, 'The incarnate Word then reveals the Father, something that parallels but goes beyond the role of Moses'.[45] Philo uses the word δόξα in *Quaest. in Exod.* 2.45 (an interpretation of Exod. 24.16a) to refer to God's self-revelation but without any connotation of 'seeing' the glory.[46] In the *Hermetica* δόξα never occurs as the object of the mystical visions of God. John's understanding of δόξα as God's kingly glory that was 'seen' in human form echoes the Merkabah texts, based on Ezek. 1.26-28 and Isa. 6.1-5, and therefore Merkabah mysticism provides a more acceptable background for understanding δόξα in 1.14. Our study below reinforces this.

John 12.41

> ταῦτα εἶπεν Ἰσαΐας, ὅτι εἶδεν τὴν δόξαν αὐτοῦ, καὶ ἐλάλησεν περὶ αὐτοῦ.

John places this verse in the context of the inability of the crowd to see the glory of Jesus because of their unbelief in him, although Jesus had performed τοσαῦτα σημεῖα (12.37). After citing Isa. 6.10 in 12.40,

---

44. See Westcott, *St John*, p. 12; Lindars, *John*, p. 95; Carson, *John*, p. 128. Schnackenburg, *St John*, I, p. 269, uses both the Exodus and temple-glory traditions to interpret 1.14.

45. Evans, *Word and Glory*, p. 83.

46. The word δόξα is interpreted in *Spec. Leg.* 1.45 as δυνάμεις and in *Spec. Leg.* 1.46 Philo avoids any reference to δόξα, preferring to use the term δυνάμεις. In *Quaest. in Exod.* 2.107 he uses δόξα with the meaning 'human praise' or 'opinion'.

probably with an allusion to Isa. 52.13 as well,[47] he states that Isaiah said this because he saw his glory and spoke of him, obviously pointing to Isaiah's vision seen in the temple (cf. Isa. 6.3). The key question is: whose glory does John refer to, that of Jesus or of God, by the pronoun αὐτοῦ? Although Harris presumes that 12.41 speaks of the 'glory of God',[48] almost all commentators agree that John portrays Isaiah as having seen the glory of Jesus, the Christ.[49] The terms αὐτοῦ and περὶ αὐτοῦ in 12.41 recall the αὐτοῦ and the εἰς αὐτόν of 12.37, and also anticipate the εἰς αὐτόν of 12.42, pronouns that unmistakably point to Jesus.

That Isaiah saw the glory of the pre-existent Christ is confirmed by John's presentation of the Logos-Son who was πρὸς τὸν θεόν and who was θεός (1.1). Moses wrote of Christ, the Logos-Son, even before the latter's incarnation (5.46) and Abraham did see the messianic time (8.56; cf. *4 Ezra* 3.14), whether in the birth of Isaac or on the day when God made a covenant with him is difficult to ascertain. John's interest in the pre-existence of Christ is reflected also in 8.58: πρὶν Ἀβραὰμ γενέσθαι ἐγὼ εἰμί (cf. 3.13; 6.62). For John the Scripture *in toto* bears witness to Christ (5.39, 46) and Isaiah 6 is not an exception to this.[50] The vision of Yahweh's glory in Isaiah 6 is interpreted in 12.41 as a vision of Christ; the Lord, sitting upon the throne, is identified not only with the pre-existent *Logos asarkos*, but also with the Logos, incarnate and crucified.[51] John believes that Jesus had possessed the divine glory even in his pre-existent state (17.5), that he displayed the same glory on earth (17.4, 22; 1.14; 2.11; 11.4, 40), and that he will receive the same glory in his ascension to the Father (17.1, 5, 24). Therefore the term εἶδεν τὴν δόξαν αὐτοῦ does not pose a prophetic view of the future

47.   Cf. C.A. Evans, *To See and Not Perceive: Isaiah 6.9-10 in Early Jewish and Christian Interpretation* (JSOTSup, 64; Sheffield: JSOT Press, 1989), pp. 132-33.

48.   J.R. Harris, 'Traces of Targumism in the New Testament', *ExpTim* 32 (1920–21), pp. 373-76 (375).

49.   Presumably because of the difficulty involved in the claim that Isaiah, a prophet who belongs to the eighth/seventh century BCE, saw Jesus' glory, a few MSS, particularly the Caesarean witnesses, have modified αὐτοῦ to τοῦ θεοῦ.

50.   See Dahl, 'Johannine Church', pp. 130-36; Borgen, *Bread from Heaven*, pp. 151, 175.

51.   Cf. Dahl, 'Johannine Church', pp. 131-32.

glory of Jesus, as Hoskyns and Bultmann have argued,[52] but it combines the past, present and the future into one event, stating that Jesus is the manifestation of God's eternal glory.

Young argues that even before John wrote 12.41, the prophet Isaiah and his book had become the source of considerable speculation among the Jews, particularly in apocalyptic circles.[53] However, he does not show any awareness of the influence of Isaiah 6 in Merkabah mysticism. Dahl finds the wording of 12.41 as close to that of *Targum of Isaiah*, which speaks of 'the glory of Yahweh' (6.1) and 'the glory of the Shekinah of Yahweh' (6.3), but observes that the idea in 12.41 is akin to that of *Ascension of Isaiah*, which describes Isaiah's vision of the descent and ascent of Jesus.[54] The precise relation of 12.41 to *Ascension of Isaiah* is unknown except that both reflect the main feature of Merkabah mysticism: seeing God's glory, in *Ascension of Isaiah* 'the Great glory' and in 12.41 'Christ's glory'. However, the roots of both the texts go back to Isaiah 6, an important text in Merkabah mysticism (cf. 12.40, where Isa. 6 is used). If so, 12.41 strengthens our case that behind the Fourth Gospel stands Merkabah mystical speculation. John, having been influenced by it, drives his point home that any direct vision of God is impossible (1.18; 5.37; 6.46), but that God can be seen in his glory only in the person and work of Jesus (cf. 14.9). If so, it seems that John reinterprets the current mystical visions, as claimed by the Palestinian Jews, in terms of the events in the life of Jesus. In this sense Dahl is right in seeing a polemic note directed against a piety that made the patriarchs and prophets heroes of mystical visions of the heavenly world.[55] In view of the same tendency that marks the ascent-motif of John, it is not surprising to see a polemic in 12.41 too. However, here also John not only polemizes, but particularly calls for faith in the Logos incarnate and crucified, by proclaiming that the divine glory can be seen in him alone.

52.   Hoskyns, *Fourth Gospel*, p. 428; Bultmann, *John: A Commentary*, p. 453 n. 4.

53.   F.W. Young, 'A Study of the Relation of Isaiah to the Fourth Gospel', *ZNW* 46 (1955), pp. 215-40 (216-21).

54.   Dahl, 'Johannine Church', pp. 131-32.

55.   Dahl, 'Johannine Church', pp. 141-42.

The Use of δοξάζω *in John*

John's theme of δόξα attains further significance by the verb δοξάζω, which clarifies the primary means by which Jesus' glory was revealed. There are several references in John that indicate that δοξάζω, both in its passive and active forms, primarily points to Jesus' death on the cross, the supreme moment when his glory was revealed. For example, the expression ἐλήλυθεν ἡ ὥρα ἵνα δοξασθῇ ὁ υἱὸς τοῦ ἀνθρώπου (12.23), which is followed by a reference to the imagery of the death of a grain of wheat, clearly refers to Jesus' death (cf. 12.32-33; 13.31). However, Loader argues that 12.23 in its context is associated with the mission theme and that the primary reference here is Jesus' returning to the glory of the Father.[56] But 12.24-25 does not support this argument. Loader's citation of Lindars, Schnackenburg, Nicholson and Beasley-Murray in support of his view is ill-founded.[57] All these scholars uniformly argue that the hour of glorification in 12.23 relates to Jesus' arrest and death.[58] Although Loader firmly states that the glorification texts are not referring to glory on the cross but to the heavenly glory,[59] he concludes paradoxically that both the glory revealed by signs and the heavenly glory interpret the death of Jesus.[60] It is true that Jesus' glorification in 13.1 and 17.1, 5 primarily points to his return to the heavenly glory. But whereas in 13.1 the word δοξάζω does not occur, in 17.1 the aorist δόξασόν does not exclude Jesus' passion and death.[61] The idea of Jesus glorifying the Father in terms of ἐπὶ τῆς γῆς τὸ ἔργον τελειώσας (17.4) implies his death on the cross (cf. 19.28, 30). Of course, after the cross, the task of glorifying Jesus will be carried out by the Holy Spirit (16.14) and by the Church (14.13; 15.8; 17.10), but

56. Loader, *Christology*, p. 109.

57. Loader, *Christology*, p. 250 n. 113.

58. Lindars, *John*, p. 427, connects the hour with Jesus' arrest, but affirms that it *anticipates* his heavenly glory. For Schnackenburg, *St John*, II, pp. 382-83, Jesus' final aim in his glorification is the giving of life to all believers, though he finds a reference to the future glory of Jesus in 17.5. Nicholson, *Death as Departure*, p. 153, conceives the hour of glorification in 12.23 as the hour of his departure, i.e. his death. For Beasley-Murray, *John*, p. 211, glorification is connected with Jesus' death, although it *includes* his return to the Father in 13.31-32; 17.1, 5.

59. Loader, *Christology*, p. 110.

60. Loader, *Christology*, p. 115. He concedes that death is the means whereby the Son returns to the Father's glory.

61. See Barrett, *John*, p. 502; Käsemann, *Testament of Jesus*, p. 19.

even this glorification is because of Jesus' passion and death.[62] Although δοξάζω does contain the future sense of going to the Father (13.32; 17.5), which is ignored by Pamment for whom δοξάζω refers exclusively to Jesus' death on a cross,[63] it is Jesus' death that is mainly in focus. For the fruit-bearing largely depends on the falling-down and dying of the grain, which figuratively indicates the death of the Son of Man (12.23-24). It is imperative, however, to avoid the two extreme interpretations: one indicating only the return to the glory of the Father as glorification and the other pointing exclusively to Jesus' death. Käsemann's balanced view that John portrays the divine glory as visible in Jesus' humiliation and that it is in the hour of passion and death (i.e. glorification) that Jesus leaves the world and returns to the Father does justice to the Johannine passages on δοξάζω.[64] In other words, cross for John is the focal point of the glorification of Jesus Christ.

If glorification ultimately lies on the cross of Christ, the moot question is: what does the verb δοξάζω actually mean? Notable in this connection is Caird's analysis of this verb in 13.31:

νῦν ἐδοξάσθη ὁ υἱὸς τοῦ ἀνθρώπου καὶ ὁ θεὸς ἐδοξάσθη ἐν αὐτῷ.[65]

Caird treats the ἐδοξάσθη of v. 31a as a true passive, implying that in the cross, regarded as already accomplished, God is to glorify Jesus in his role as Son of Man. But he infers that if the Johannine Jesus is already one with the Father (10.37-38; 14.11), then his glorification cannot be for himself, but for those whom he, as Son of Man, the inclusive representative, would draw to himself after being lifted up (12.32).[66] The ἐδοξάσθη of v. 31b, according to him, as a translation of the Hebrew niphal וְנִכְבַּד carries an intransitive sense, meaning God's act of manifesting his glory in the Son of Man, with ἐν having natural 'local sense'. Thus the meaning of 13.31 will be: 'Now the Son of Man has been endowed with glory, and God has revealed his glory in him.'[67]

---

62. Cf. Moloney, *Son of Man*, p. 178; McCaffrey, *The House with Many Rooms*, p. 146.

63. Pamment, 'Meaning of *doxa*', pp. 13-14.

64. Käsemann, *Testament of Jesus*, pp. 12-13, 19. He regards John as the first Christian who has presented the earthly life of Jesus as the inbreaking of the heavenly glory.

65. Caird, 'Glory of God', pp. 265-77.

66. Caird, 'Glory of God', pp. 269-70.

67. Caird, 'Glory of God', pp. 270-71. Caird shows evidence from the LXX

Since this meaning coincides with the central thought running through John, it is to be preferred. He also justly maintains that those who see the glory of Jesus see the glory of God, for in Jesus' works of mercy and life-giving (1.4; 5.26) God himself was working (5.17; 14.9-11; cf. 10.38; 11.4).[68]

That the revelation of God's glory in Jesus is emphasized in 13.31-32 is clear from the five times repeated verb δοξάζω, three times in aorist passive and twice in future indicative.[69] If we take ἐδοξάσθη as the ingressive aorist, as seems likely,[70] then the idea of revelation is presented in 13.31-32 in two dimensions: present and future. The glory of God is revealed in Jesus' life and ministry (2.11; 11.4, 40; 17.4), that is, in his act of loving obedience, exemplified in the washing of the disciples' feet (13.1-17) and culminating in his death on the cross (12.23-29; 17.1, 4), which is also his exaltation (3.14; 8.28; 12.32).[71] The terms δοξάσει and εὐθύς link 13.31-32 not only with 13.33, where Jesus speaks of his impending (μικρός) departure to the Father through his death, but also with the next three chapters which focus on the appearance of his glory in resurrection and in his coming back as ἄλλος παράκλητος to dwell with his own, although the same glory is visible in the crucifixion itself.[72] As we have noticed above, these present and future aspects of the revelation of God's glory point back to the past, when Jesus had the same glory in his pre-existence with the Father (17.5, 24). This pre-existent glory is the same as the one that was

and from the natural occurrences of analogy in languages for such an understanding of the Greek passive (pp. 273-77).

68.   Caird, 'Glory of God', pp. 272-73. Schnackenburg's criticism of Caird's position and his understanding of 13.31 as denoting mutual glorification (Schnackenburg, *St John*, III, pp. 51-52) do not sufficiently bring out the meaning of δοξάζω either in the passive or in the active.

69.   εἰ ὁ θεὸς ἐδοξάσθη ἐν αὐτῷ in 13.32a is accepted, though with some reservation, by the Editorial Committee of the United Bible Society's Greek New Testament as part of the original reading—see B.M. Metzger, *A Textual Commentary on the Greek New Testament* (Stuttgart: United Bible Societies, corrected edn, 1975), p. 242.

70.   See McCaffrey, *The House with Many Rooms*, p. 146.

71.   Cf. Pamment, 'Meaning of *doxa*', p. 14; Käsemann, *Testament of Jesus*, pp. 10-20; J.D.G. Dunn, 'The Washing of the Disciples' Feet in John 13.1-20', *ZNW* 61 (1970), pp. 246-52, demonstrates that Jesus' washing of the feet of the disciples is the σημεῖον which symbolizes his glorification.

72.   Cf. Barrett, *John*, p. 451.

revealed to Isaiah (cf. 12.41) and subsequently to Ezekiel (Ezek. 1.26-
28) and Daniel (Dan. 7.9-10, 13-14)—the texts that later occupied
central place in Merkabah mysticism. The revelation of God's glory in
the Son of Man is also reminiscent of the same vision described in
Revelation 1. No doubt, John is presenting the possibility of seeing
God's glory, for which the Merkabah mystics of his time were yearning, in the earthly activity of Jesus, culminating in his death on the
cross, which obviously replaces the throne of Merkabah visions.

There are three more elements that directly link John's glory-motif
with the Jewish mysticism of the first century.

A Community Affair

Seeing Jesus' glory is described by John as a community affair, which
is clear from the plural ἐθεασάμεθα of 1.14. We have observed that
Jesus' glory can be perceived deeply only by his followers, whether
eyewitnesses or the Church later on. In 17.24 seeing the glory of Jesus
in heaven is portrayed as the goal of the community. Moreover, δόξα is
the gift given by Jesus to his followers that they might be enabled to
have unity with one another (17.22). That is, δόξα seems to imply the
divine life imparted to Jesus' disciples to enable them to relate with one
another in love. Lindars justly comments that John thinks of the glory
of Jesus in 17.22 as a matter of 'relationship' between the members of
the believing community.[73] This relationship is nothing but the expression of the intimate personal relationship that exists between Father and
Son (cf. the phrase καθὼς ἡμεῖς). This echoes not only the transformation of the Merkabah mystic into the heavenly glory, but also the so-
called 'communal mysticism' of Qumran in which the worshippers, in
the vision of the throne of glory, realized a sense of union with the
angels in heaven as well as with one another. Dodd's description of
worship as nothing but the acknowledgment of God's glory in the person of Jesus Christ[74] is in effect not far away from the Merkabah
mystical experience. Bühner points out that since the Johannine community had seen Christ with the eyes of mystical admiration (*mystische
Verehrung*), it has portrayed Christ as the one who mediates the mysti-

73.   Lindars, *John*, p. 530.
74.   C.H. Dodd, 'The Prologue to the Fourth Gospel and Christian Worship',
in F.L. Cross (ed.), *Studies in the Fourth Gospel* (London: Mowbray, 1957), pp. 9-
22.

cal vision of God.[75] If so, it is probable that the 'Johannine' community, as a 'mystical community', used to see God's glory in Jesus Christ also at the time of worship, just like the Qumranites had a vision of the Merkabah in their worship.[76] At any rate, the Johannine idea of 'seeing God's glory' in Jesus has Merkabah mystical vision as its background, inviting those who had great interest in such visions to believe in Christ in order to see God's glory with deeper appreciation and to be transformed by the same glory.

The ὄνομα of God

Another important mystical feature reflected in John is the identification of the δόξα of God with his name (ὄνομα). This is shown by the verb φανερόω, which takes up both ὄνομα and δόξα as objects (17.6; 2.11; cf. 7.4; 9.3). This means that both ὄνομα and δόξα are used by John to indicate the self-revelation of God.[77] The future γνωρίσω in 17.26, which may mean 'I will continue to make it known'[78] (cf. Ps. 21.23 LXX), implies that the revelation of the name that took place in the earthly life of Jesus will continue to take place in the supreme sacrifice on the cross.[79] The same idea, as we have seen, is reflected also in δόξα.

The manifestation of the name is the same as the glorification of the Father (cf. 17.4 and 17.6) and the same manifestation both in the past and in future coincides with the continuous glorification of his name (cf. ἐδόξασα καὶ πάλιν δοξάσω [τὸ ὄνομα] in 12.28b). While 17.11, 12 describe the name of the Father as given by him to Jesus by using the verb δεδώκας, 17.22 describes the glory similarly by using the same verb.[80] Both the ὄνομα and the δόξα of God are given to the disciples to fulfil the same purpose that they may be one (cf. 17.22 and

75.　Bühner, *Der Gesandte*, p. 49. Note that the word *Verehrung* carries also the sense of worship.

76.　For similarities between Qumran and the 'Johannine' community see R.A. Culpepper, *The Johannine School: An Evaluation of the Johannine-School Hypothesis Based on an Investigation of the Nature of Ancient Schools* (SBLDS, 26; Missoula, MT: Scholars Press, 1975), pp. 145, 170.

77.　The verb γνωρίζω in 17.26, being the synonym of the φανερόω in 17.6, expresses the revelatory nature of the ὄνομα of God through Jesus.

78.　Brown, *John*, I, pp. 768, 773.

79.　See F.F. Bruce, *The Gospel of John* (Grand Rapids: Eerdmans, repr. 1992), p. 337.

80.　Cf. Bultmann, *John: A Commentary*, p. 515.

17.26). Bultmann rightly suggests that it makes no difference whether one says that Jesus reveals the name of God or that he reveals his own δόξα.[81]

The identification of ὄνομα and δόξα is unknown both to Philo and to the author of the *Hermetica*. In contrast, we find the same identification in the Qumran texts which mark God's name and glory as the 'mysteries of his wisdom' that are revealed in creation.[82] Both ὄνομα and δόξα show mystical features not only because they were treated as esoteric containing the secrets of God, but also because they were revealed in creation, which echoes the *Ma'aseh Bereshit*, another source of contemplation in first-century Jewish mysticism. The association of the Johannine ὄνομα with creation is envisaged in two ways: at first, the name in John can be identified with God's word uttered in creation, that is, יהי (= 'Let it be there') or אהיה (= 'I am/I will be there'), which emphasizes God's presence and his activity among the people; for John this name has been manifested in the Logos/Son,[83] who, by using the ἐγώ εἰμι formula,[84] displayed God's presence among the people. Secondly, the name is closely associated with the new world of God and with ζωή. For the phrase ἐν ἐκείνῃ τῇ ἡμέρᾳ (16.23a, 26), which refers to the eschatological time, is closely linked with God's answering of prayers in Jesus' name and the resulting joy of the disciples (16.24);[85] and the name of Jesus in 16.23-24 is figuratively attached with the genesis of a life (16.20-22) by the link-word χαρά.[86] Similarly, the

81.   Bultmann, *John: A Commentary*, p. 498. Against J. Marsh, *The Gospel of St John* (London: Penguin, repr. 1988), p. 563, for whom to manifest the name is not quite the same as to glorify the Father.

82.   See above, p. 100. For the revelation of God's glory in creation through the Logos see below, pp. 283-84, 294-95. Morray-Jones, 'Transformational Mysticism', pp. 3-19, argues that the equation 'Glory = Power = Name = Word' is both ancient and widespread, particularly in Merkabah mystical circles.

83.   Hayward, 'Holy Name', pp. 28-29; Fossum, *Name of God*, pp. 248, 255-56 n. 32, argues that both 'Name' (the Tetragrammaton) and the 'Logos' are the same in the prologue of John. But for Barrett, *John*, p. 505, they are closely related in 17.6, but not identical.

84.   Brown, *John*, I, pp. 11, 533-38 and *John*, II, pp. 754-56, suggests that the revealed name is ἐγώ εἰμι.

85.   H. Bietenhard, 'ὄνομα', *TDNT*, V, pp. 242-83 (272), argues that in Jesus is fulfilled the Jewish expectation that the new world of God will bring the revelation of his name. Cf. Dodd, *Interpretation*, p. 96.

86.   Cf. also the ἵνα…ζωὴν ἔχητε ἐν τῷ ὀνόματι αὐτοῦ of 20.31.

Johannine δόξα too is nothing but the ζωή that was inherent in the λόγος (1.1-4, 14). The identification of God's glory and his name is not foreign to Merkabah tradition also. Mettinger has convincingly shown that the *kabod* in Ezekiel's throne-vision functions as the name of God, which was familiar in the Deuteronomistic circles.[87] The idea that God's glory was revealed to Moses in terms of his name was also famil-iar in the mystical tradition centred on Moses (cf. Exod. 3.13-14; 6.2-3; and 33.18-19; 34.5-6).[88]

In short, John's use of δόξα shows the influence of Merkabah mysti-cism, the early form of *Ma'aseh Bereshit*, and possibly also the Moses-centred mysticism by its essential parallel with ὄνομα, since, for him, δόξα is the revelation of God's name.

The King-Motif in John[89]

We have noticed that seeing the glory of God in Jesus both on earth and in heaven is one of the dominant motifs in John. This constant empha-sis, along with the reference to the experience of being transformed by the same glory, takes us to the heart of Merkabah mysticism, which, in all probability, has influenced the evangelist in presenting the Gospel to the people of his day. It remains yet to be explored whether John por-trays God as the enthroned king, another motif inseparable from the idea of 'seeing his glory' in Merkabah mysticism, and to this we now turn.

Jesus as King
Nathanael's Confession. First and foremost, it is Jesus who is portrayed as king in John. We have learned that when Nathanael confessed Jesus as ὁ υἱὸς τοῦ θεοῦ, σὺ βασιλεὺς εἶ τοῦ Ἰσραήλ (1.49), Jesus qualified these titles by promising that the disciples would see the glory of God and would have communion with him in the Son of Man.[90] Thus John defines Jesus' kingship in terms of ὁ υἱὸς τοῦ ἀνθρώπου, by stressing the earthly presence of the king of Israel, in which he enjoys continual

87. Mettinger, *Dethronement*, pp. 107-108, 122-23.
88. See Meeks, *Prophet-King*, pp. 286-91.
89. I am grateful to the editors of *Tyndale Bulletin* for their kind permission to reproduce in this section most of the materials used in my article, 'Jesus the King, Merkabah Mysticism and the Gospel of John', *TynBul* 47 (1996), pp. 349-66.
90. See above, pp. 188-94.

communion with the Father and reveals his δόξα.[91]

Entry into Jerusalem. The same idea of seeing the king of Israel in the right perspective dominates the event of Jesus' entry into Jerusalem (12.12-19). In contrast to the public understanding that Jesus is the messianic king in the sense of the political deliverer of Jewish nationalism, John insists that the glory of this king is exhibited in such a humility that he made a young ass (ὀνάριον) as his throne. This is clear from his placement of the event of finding an ass and riding on it *after* the crowd's acclamation (12.13-14). The use of Zech. 9.9-10 in 12.15 depicts the 'lowly' king as the deliverer of Israel and the bringer of peace to the whole earth.[92] The echoes of Zeph. 3.14-17 and Isa. 35.4 in 12.13-15 describe Jesus as king who offers peace and salvation to his people and judgment to their enemies. By using the phrase, 'Fear not...' in the place of Zechariah's 'Rejoice greatly...', John contrasts the Caesar-related kingship that caused fear in Pilate (19.8) with the realm of the one who sits on a donkey.[93] For John, Jesus' authority as king, then, is not of this world (cf. 18.36).

John maintains that the glorification of Jesus through his death and resurrection was a necessary condition for understanding the royal significance of Jesus' entry into Jerusalem (12.16). This is reinforced by a reference to the sign of the raising of Lazarus from death in the entry narrative (12.17, 18), indicating that the enthusiastic crowds should see a greater sign of Jesus' death and resurrection, in whose light alone the glory of his kingship can clearly be perceived. This means that the glory of Jesus as king, which was effectively manifested in his death and resurrection, is already present in his riding on the young ass. Therefore John found it appropriate to link the entry-narrative with a plain reference to the glorification of the Son of Man by his death and resurrection (cf. 12.23-24, 32-33).[94] By means of the entry-

91.   Bultmann, *John: A Commentary*, p. 107.

92.   Appold's observation that the humility motif, which occurs in Mt. 21.5, is 'deleted' by John (Appold, *Oneness Motif*, p. 77 n. 1) is ill-founded. Although John does not use the word πραΰς of Zech. 9.9, the expression καθήμενος ἐπὶ πῶλον ὄνου in his brief citation sufficiently shows the humble nature of Jesus' kingship.

93.   Brodie, *John*, p. 410.

94.   The terms such as ἑορτής (12.12 and 12.20), ὁ ὄχλος (12.12, 17, 18 and 12.29, 34) and δοξασθῆναι (12.16 and 12.23, 28), and the universalistic overtone of 12.19 link the Entry-pericope with 12.20-26 and 12.27-36.

narrative, John seeks to lead the readers to understand the significance of Jesus' humiliating, but victorious, death, in which is revealed his kingly glory. The different nature of Jesus' kingship from the world's expectations is also envisaged in 6.14-15.

A Reference to Jesus as Prophet and King in 6.14-15. By treating the ὁ προφήτης of 6.14 and the βασιλεύς of 6.15 as identical, Meeks argues that 6.14-15 identifies Jesus as prophet-king like Moses and that Jesus does not deny that he is a king but denies only the time and the manner in which people tried to make him king.[95] However, it is doubtful whether 6.14 and 6.15 convey the same idea, for in no other place does John identify the titles ὁ προφήτης and βασιλεύς, not even in the Passion Narrative where Jesus accepts the title βασιλεύς. In fact ὁ προφήτης is not at all used as a final title for Jesus and, as de Jonge points out, wherever this title occurs, eventually other titles such as the Christ, the Son of Man and the Son of God supersede it (see 4.19, 25-26; 6.14, 32-51; 7.40-43; 9.17, 35-38).[96] It is also likely that there is a break of thought between v. 14 and v. 15.[97] If after the sign the people had really recognized Jesus as the prophet promised by Moses in Deut. 18.15, 18, it is unthinkable how they could make a new demand to perform a sign (6.30-31).[98] The statement in 6.14 seems to be a confession not aroused by a deeper understanding of Jesus and his words, but by an excitement of having eaten their fill (cf. 6.26) and therefore represents inadequate faith.

Those who saw Jesus as 'the prophet' were prepared to seize him by force and make him king. Strachan argues that Jesus was in danger of being regarded as a kind of Theudas, who was said to be a prophet and who attempted to mount a political uprising in c. 43–44 CE (cf. Acts 5.36) and that in order to avoid such a messianic rising did Jesus withdraw to the mountain.[99] Does this mean that the Johannine Jesus

95. Meeks, *Prophet-King*, pp. 87-91, 99.
96. De Jonge, *Stranger from Heaven*, pp. 50-66; Dunn, *Christology*, p. 141, holds that John is moving beyond the more limiting confines of a prophet-Christology in view of his very high Son of God Christology.
97. Appold, *Oneness Motif*, p. 77.
98. See Schnackenburg, *St John*, II, pp. 18-19.
99. R.H. Strachan, *The Fourth Gospel: Its Significance and Environment* (London: SCM Press, rev. 3rd edn, repr. 1946), p. 180; cf. Josephus, *Ant.* 20.51. See also C.H. Dodd, *Historical Tradition in the Fourth Gospel* (Cambridge:

accepted that he is a king but denied only the means by which he was about to be made king? If the notion of the messianic claimants was in the evangelist's mind in 6.14-15, as it seems probable by the use of the term ὁ ἐρχόμενος, then it is likely that for John Jesus rejected in this context the very title 'king'. Because he *is* already a king (cf. 18.37), there was no necessity for any one *to make* him king.[100] In view of the fact that Jesus accepts in other places (1.49; 12.13-15; 18.36-37) that he is βασιλεύς, all we can say is that the term 'king' in 6.15 anticipates Jesus' confession before Pilate that his kingship is not of this world.

Summary
Clearly John portrays Jesus as king, who reveals his kingly glory in a humble manner as seated on a donkey, and such a kingship can fully be grasped only in the light of Jesus' death and resurrection. As it does not seem that his kingship is described in terms of the prophet like Moses in Deut. 18.15-19, we can scarcely understand Jesus' kingly glory on the background of Moses tradition, as Meeks has postulated. Moreover, Moses made a mystical ascent to Sinai where he *was made* king, whereas the Johannine Jesus *is* king by the very fact that he has continual communion with the Father. The idea of the revelation of his kingly glory makes Merkabah mysticism as the most likely background for understanding Jesus as king in John. However, in contrast to the mystical visions, John seems to paint Jesus as king in his lowliness, enthroned on a humble animal and supremely on the cross. How can we perceive Jesus' kingly glory on the cross? To answer this question we will examine the idea of kingship in the Passion Narrative.

Jesus' Kingship is God's Kingship: A Portrayal in the Trial-Narrative
The title βασιλεύς plays a key role in the Johannine trial narrative.[101] C. Panackel states that the revelation of Jesus as king is 'the only unequivocal and direct self-revelation of Jesus' in the trial-narrative of

Cambridge University Press, 1965), p. 214; Beasley-Murray, *John*, pp. 88-89.
    100. De Jonge, *Stranger from Heaven*, p. 58.
    101. See D. Hill, ' "My Kingdom is not of this World" (John 18.36): Conflict and Christian Existence in the World According to the Fourth Gospel', *IBS* 9 (1987), pp. 54-62 (55), for whom Christ's kingship that culminates in his enthronement on the cross is the thread that binds together the entire Passion story, particularly the trial-narrative.

John.[102] Like the Synoptists, John also begins the dialogue between Pilate and Jesus with a reference to Jesus' kingship (18.33) and then defines it at first negatively: ἡ βασιλεία ἡ ἐμὴ οὐκ ἔστιν ἐκ τοῦ κόσμου τούτου (18.36). In view of the preposition ἐκ, the τοῦ κόσμου must be taken as the genitive of origin and thus the implication is that Jesus' kingship derives not from the world, but from God (cf. 8.23 where οὐκ...ἐκ τοῦ κόσμου τούτου is in apposition to ἐκ τῶν ἄνω).[103] Since Jesus' kingship originates precisely from the place of his own origin, that is, from God (cf. 8.42; 3.31), his kingly glory is the same as God's kingly glory. Therefore there is no need for the βασιλεία to be *established*, for example, by using military strategies, as earthly kingdoms are established (cf. 18.36b). This idea appears to state that the kingly glory of God, with which Merkabah mysticism is concerned, has become visible in Jesus, his Son. Further investigation confirms this.

By showing the compositional parallels between the βασιλεία of God in 3.3, 5 and that of Jesus in 18.36, Hengel justly argues that the kingly rule of God, which is the subject of Jesus' dialogue with Nicodemus, is identical with the kingly rule of Christ, which is emphasized in Jesus' encounter with Pilate, and that in the place of the synoptic kingdom of God there emerges in John the βασιλεία of his Son, the Christ.[104] However, Schnackenburg maintains that John's description of the βασιλεία of Jesus does not indicate the heavenly realm as the βασιλεία τοῦ θεοῦ of 3.3, 5 does.[105] But Chilton has convincingly shown that in the first century, particularly in the school of Yohanan ben Zakkai, the kingdom of God was conceived more as the self-revelation of God himself (i.e. *regnum dei deus est*).[106] He argues that Jesus and Yohanan shared a then current kingdom vocabulary,

---

102.   C. Panackel, ΙΔΟΥ Ο ΑΝΘΡΩΠΟΣ *(Jn 19, 5b): An Exegetico-Theological Study of the Text in the Light of the Use of the Term* ΑΝΘΡΩΠΟΣ *Designating Jesus in the Fourth Gospel* (Rome: Pontificia Università Gregoriana, 1988), p. 334.

103.   Cf. Meeks, *Prophet-King*, p. 63; Beasley-Murray, *John*, p. 331. Also the word ἐντεῦθεν (= 'from here') in 18.36c makes this sense possible.

104.   M. Hengel, 'Reich Christi, Reich Gottes und Weltreich im Johannesevangelium', in M. Hengel and A.M. Schwerner (eds.), *Königsherrschaft Gottes und himmlischer Kult im Judentum, Urchristentum und in der hellenischen Welt* (Tübingen: J.C.B. Mohr [Paul Siebeck], 1991), pp. 163-84 (176-79).

105.   Schnackenburg, *St John*, III, p. 249.

106.   B.D. Chilton, 'Regnum Dei Deus Est', in *idem, Targumic Approaches to the Gospels: Essays in the Mutual Definition of Judaism and Christianity* (New York: Lanham, 1986), pp. 99-107, esp. pp. 101-105.

preserved in the New Testament and the Targums, and that by the term 'kingdom of God' Jesus meant that God is active among us.[107] I have argued above that Yohanan and his school were practising Merkabah mysticism in which the kingship of God played a key role.[108] It is plausible, then, that John could have used the same mystical notion in his presentation of the βασιλεία τοῦ θεοῦ and of the βασιλεία of Jesus to convince the Jews who had great interest in Merkabah mysticism that God had revealed himself as king in his Son, Jesus Christ, and was active among them.

The unity between the kingship of the Father and that of the Son is clearly known in John's daring interpretation of Isaiah's vision of God-on-the-throne as a vision of Christ's glory (12.41). God could exercise his kingship in the world by sending his Son into the world (3.16; 1 Jn 4.9-10) and that is why the kingship of Christ functions so well 'in this world' even when it is 'unworldly'.[109] That is, the kingship of Christ is grounded in the pre-existence of the Son with the Father in the heavenly realm. This is known from two expressions in 18.37: εἰς τοῦτο γεγέννημαι and εἰς τοῦτο ἐλήλυθα, in which τοῦτο refers back to the βασιλεία and βασιλεύς of 18.36-37. It is in Jesus' earthly life that we can see him as king.

The βασιλεύς is further qualified by ἵνα μαρτυρήσω τῇ ἀληθείᾳ (18.37). Meeks rightly suggests that this statement shows Jesus' kingship as consisting in his mission of testifying to the truth.[110] ἀλήθεία in John denotes not an intellectual phenomenon, but 'the eternal reality that is beyond and above the phenomena of the world' and, in particular, the eternal kingdom of God, the origin of all human authority (19.11).[111] It is precisely this eternal reality that presents itself to humankind in incarnate form[112] either for salvation or for judgment, depending upon the response one yields to the truth (cf. 3.31-36; see 8.14, 16, where μαρτυρία and κρίσις are paralleled).

107. Chilton, 'Regnum Dei', pp. 101, 105.
108. See Chapter 8.
109. See Hengel, 'Reich Christi', p. 169. De Jonge, *Stranger from Heaven*, pp. 46-69, shows that the reinterpretation of Jesus' kingship is given in John in terms of divine sonship, i.e. in terms of the unique relationship between the Father and the Son.
110. Meeks, *Prophet-King*, p. 65.
111. Barrett, *John*, p. 537; Dodd, *Interpretation*, p. 176.
112. Cf. Haenchen, *John*, II, p. 180.

The idea of bearing witness to the truth is supplemented by John with the words 'Every one who is of the truth hears my voice' (18.37b), referring to those who will obey the words spoken by the king. That is, the one who has seen Jesus as king is ἐκ τῆς ἀληθείας and only that person can obey the eternal reality that is revealed through the witness borne by the king. But Pilate, being the representative of the earthly kingdom is wholly unable to perceive the kingship of Jesus and hence does not even grasp what the truth is. Suggesting a parallel here with the shepherd–sheep imagery in which the sheep hear the shepherd's voice (10.3) and with the prophet like Moses whom the people of Israel should heed (Deut. 18.15), Meeks argues that the kingship of Jesus, the Good Shepherd, is redefined in the Fourth Gospel in terms of the mission of the prophet.[113] Undoubtedly shepherd and king are parallel terms (cf. Ezek. 37.24; Zech. 11.6), but the idea of hearing his voice cannot be confined to the Mosaic prophet alone. The phrase ἀκούει μου τῆς φωνῆς should be interpreted not in isolation, but in its context of the revelation of Jesus' kingship and of his witness to the eternal reality. Viewed thus, the closest parallel to the idea of hearing his voice lies in Merkabah mystical visions. When Isaiah saw the Lord in his kingly glory, he heard his voice (ἤκουσα τῆς φωνῆς κυρίου) and obeyed (Isa. 6.8). Similarly, Ezekiel, in his chariot-vision, heard the voice of the one seated on the throne (ἤκουσα φωνὴν λαλοῦντος in Ezek. 1.28 and ἤκουον αὐτοῦ λαλοῦντος in Ezek. 2.2; cf. also Ezek. 3.12; 10.5; 43.6; *1 En.* 15.1; *Apoc. Abr.* 18.14; 19.1; Rev. 1.10, 12-16, 19-20).

The Merkabah tradition also refers to the witness borne to the people by the one who saw God as king and this witness carried the offer of salvation or judgment (i.e. condemnation), depending upon the hearers' response.[114] Although the idea of bearing witness to the divine secrets is found in the mystical tradition centred on Moses,[115] the idea of kingship based on Father–Son relationship and that of king–judge are not so explicit in Moses-centred mysticism. There is a possibility that even Moses' vision is described in the *Exagoge* by using the literary form of a Merkabah vision.[116] It is more probable that John used the Merkabah

113. Meeks, *Prophet-King*, pp. 66-67.
114. Apart from the throne-visions of Isaiah, Ezekiel and Daniel, see *2 En.* 33-39; *4 Ezra* 15–16.
115. Meeks, *Prophet-King*, pp. 301-307.
116. See P.W. van der Horst, 'Moses' Throne Vision in Ezekiel the Dramatist',

mystical notion to convey the message to his fellow-Jews that the same God, who is claimed by the mystics to have appeared as king on the throne, has now been revealed on earth as king in the incarnate life of his Son, Jesus Christ, particularly, as shown below, on the cross. Just as the kingly appearance of God involves judgment in terms either of salvation or of destruction, so too God's kingship, revealed in Jesus, involves judgment. Therefore John was not hesitant to identify the kingship of Jesus with that of God.

The Johannine idea that the kingship of Jesus is the same as the king-ship of God is reinforced by the title υἱὸς θεοῦ used in the trial-narrative. At the point in which the Jews cannot accept the Man, deprived of worldly power, as their king, they attempt to divert the focus to Jesus' claim that he is the Son of God, that is, the one equal to God, a claim that deserves only the death penalty (19.7; cf. 5.18).[117] However, the Johannine trial proceeding stresses repeatedly the claim 'king' (19.12, 14, 15, 19, 21-22), thereby giving a hint once more that Jesus is king who has a filial relation and equality with God (cf. 1.49 with 1.14, 18). That Jesus' kingship is based on his intimate unity with God is envisaged by the parallelism between the υἱὸν θεοῦ ἑαυτὸν ἐποίησεν of 19.7 and the ὁ βασιλέα ἑαυτὸν ποιῶν of 19.12. The same idea is implied in Pilate's increased fear of Jesus' divine sonship and in his question, 'πόθεν εἶ σύ...', expecting an answer, 'ἄνωθεν' (cf. 19.9, 11).[118] For John, if God is king, Jesus also is king and it is impossible to see God in his kingly glory without seeing his Son also in his kingly glory,[119] which, in contrast to human expectations, is manifested in the Son's suffering and death, an offence to 'the Jews'. Thus, the kingship

---

JJS 34 (1983), pp. 21-29. See also above p. 113.

117. The anarthrous υἱὸς θεοῦ does not make Jesus less than equal with God. The omission may indicate either the familiarity of the title (Bernard, *St John*, II, p. 618) or its qualitative use (Barrett, *John*, p. 542).

118. The word μᾶλλον in 19.8 means 'even more, now more than ever' (see Bauer, Arndt and Gingrich, *Greek–English Lexicon*, p. 489), not 'instead' (see D. Rensberger, 'The Politics of John: The Trial of Jesus in the Fourth Gospel', *JBL* 103 [1984], pp. 395-411 [405]), which is possible only when μᾶλλον is followed by a negative (Bauer, Arndt and Gingrich, *Greek–English Lexicon*, s.v. 3a). Pilate's previous fear at Jesus' statement about his kingship is implied in his ignoring the statement by asking 'What is truth?'—see Schnackenburg, *St John*, III, p. 260.

119. God's task of restoring his creation is undertaken by the enthroned king on the cross and in this sense too the unity between Jesus' kingship and that of the Father is exhibited—see Hengel, 'Reich Christi', pp. 166, 172, 179.

of Jesus, which paradoxically holds together the concept of the Son of Man and that of the Son of God, was hard to be grasped for the Jews of John's time, partly because of their association with the mystical practice that focused purely on the heavenly glory of the king. The equality between Jesus' kingship and God's kingship based on the Father–Son relationship is missing in the mystical tradition of Moses, as we have already observed above.

If the kingship of Jesus is one with that of God, one can ask: where is the throne on which Jesus appeared? Is Jesus described in John as the king surrounded by the angels? A further study of the Johannine Passion Narrative will shed some light on these questions.

Jesus as King in his Paradoxical Exaltation. Meeks suggests that John declares Jesus as king in his 'paradoxical exaltation' throughout the trial proceedings, which is clear from his account of the mocking of Jesus by the soldiers as 'King of the Jews' in the early part of the trial (19.1-3).[120] This mockery occurs as the ironic investiture and coronation of Jesus,[121] for after this Jesus is presented before the Jews with a purple robe and a crown of thorns by two parallel proclamations: ἰδοὺ ὁ ἄνθρωπος (19.5) and ἴδε ὁ βασιλεὺς ὑμῶν (19.14). That is, as J. Suggit points out, the man whom Pilate presents is clad in the symbols of kingship and suffering.[122] These proclamations have a revelatory connotation, for they emphasize dramatically the experience of 'seeing' Jesus as the man (cf. 4.29; 7.46; 8.40) and at the same time as the king of the Jews. Painter shows that prior to Jesus' death, the nature of his kingship was being revealed in the Son of Man sayings and that after ch. 13, he is referred to as king 12 times without using the title 'Son of Man'.[123] If so, the parallel use of ἄνθρωπος and βασιλεύς can ironically indicate that Jesus is king as the Son of Man rather than as

120. Meeks, *Prophet-King*, p. 69; cf. Mt. 27.26-31; Mk 15.15-20, where the mocking of the soldiers as 'King of the Jews' is recorded after Pilate delivered Jesus to be crucified.

121. Moloney, *Son of Man*, pp. 204-205.

122. See J. Suggit, 'John 19⁵: "Behold the Man" ', *ExpTim* 94 (1983), pp. 333-34 (334). Suggit shows that purple robe signifies the clothing of glory (cf. *Targ. Ps.-J.* Gen. 3.7), prosperity (cf. Lk. 16.19), and reward (cf. Dan. 5.29), apart from its use of the robe of priests.

123. J. Painter, 'The Enigmatic Johannine Son of Man', in F. van Segbroeck *et. al.* (eds.), *The Four Gospels 1992* (3 vols.; Feststrift F. Neirynck; Leuven: Leuven University Press, 1992), III, p. 1881.

the messianic eschatological king, as Meeks suggests.[124] Thus, the *ecce homo* evokes for perceptive readers the heavenly vision promised in 1.51, where we have detected the mystical idea of seeing God's glory in the Son of Man.[125]

However, the Jews were unable to perceive this paradoxical element embodied in the *ecce homo*. As they could hardly accept the man-in-humiliation who claims to be their king, they rejected the revelation of his kingship and cried out on both occasions the same slogan: σταύρωσον αὐτόν (19.6, 15).[126] The revelation of the king as the man in his blood-stained appearance confirms our earlier observation that the kingly glory of Jesus is to be seen in the suffering and death of the Son of Man (cf. 18.32). Thus the kingship and the glorification of Jesus are skilfully interwoven by John in the two proclamations: 'Behold the man!' and 'Behold your king!'

The revelation of Jesus' glory equally as man and king recalls Merkabah mystical visions in which God, as king, used to reveal his glory in human-like form. But John probably interprets the current mystical idea to proclaim that the kingly glory of God has now appeared in time and space in Jesus, who was lifted up on the cross in utter shame and humiliation. Jesus, for John, displays his kingly glory not only by being enthroned on the cross, but also by being surrounded by the hostile forces rather than by the angels as in Merkabah mystical visions. That the cross is the throne from which the divine king reigns is supremely demonstrated by the irrevocable title, ὁ βασιλεὺς τῶν Ἰουδαίων, written on the cross possibly as a mark of Pilate's final verdict (19.19-22). Therefore Meeks is right in calling ὁ ἄνθρωπος and

---

124. Meeks, *Prophet-King*, pp. 70-72, uses Zech. 6.12 LXX and Num. 24.17 LXX in support of this conclusion; but Barrett, *John*, p. 541, doubts a direct reference to Zech. 6.12. Suggit, 'John 19⁵', p. 333, argues that Pilate's two statements, 'Behold the man' and 'Behold your king' have the same meaning, fulfilling the vision promised in 1.50 and indicating that true kingship and true humanity will be revealed on the cross (cf. 1.49-51, where the same two titles, King and the Son of Man, occur).

125. P.D. Duke, *Irony in the Fourth Gospel* (Atlanta: John Knox Press, 1985), pp. 89, 107; cf. Panackel, ΙΔΟΥ Ο ΑΝΘΡΩΠΟΣ, pp. 336-37; Moloney, *Son of Man*, pp. 205-206, argues that the promise of 1.51; 3.14; 6.27, 53 and 8.28 becomes real in the *ecce homo* scene; cf. Suggit, 'John 19⁵', p. 333.

126. Whereas the act of crucifixion is emphasized in 19.6, the act of removing Jesus from the scene is emphasized in 19.15.

ὁ βασιλεύς 'the throne names'.[127] This reinforces our finding that John replaces the throne of Merkabah mysticism with the cross, the seat on which the Son of Man supremely reveals his glory.

Jesus, the Man/King, is also the Judge. John portrays the crucified king also as the bearer of judgment to the world (cf. 12.31; 16.11), for the king's μαρτυρία to the truth exposes the moral condition of the people and judges them either for salvation or for condemnation, depending on their response to the truth (18.37; 3.19-21). Ashton argues that judgment is the most important theological motif in the trial sequence, for by bringing Jesus to trial and sentencing him to death, the Jews were actually passing judgment on themselves.[128]

Not only the verb μαρτυρήσω (18.37), but also ἐκάθισεν (19.13) reveals the crucified king as judge. Scholars have pointed out that ἐκάθισεν can be understood either transitively or intransitively. If taken intransitively, the sense is that it was Pilate who sat upon the βῆμα; but if treated transitively, then the sense is that Pilate made Jesus to sit on the βῆμα with the motive of persuading the Jews to acknowledge him as their king-judge and thereby of testing their loyalty to Caesar. Though good cases can be made in favour of both interpretations,[129] the arguments favouring the transitive sense, which A. von Harnack suggested in 1893, seem stronger, as shown below, and hence preferable.

1. It is true that in the Matthaean parallel it is Pilate who is seated on the βῆμα (Mt. 27.19). However, John uses the active ἐκάθισεν, rather than the middle καθημένος, and links it with the verb ἤγαγεν. Thus for John ὁ Πιλᾶτος is the subject and τὸν Ἰησοῦν is the object of the verb ἐκάθισεν.[130]

---

127. Meeks, *Prophet-King*, pp. 69-78. Cf. Col. 2.15; Justin, *Apol.* 1.41 and *idem, Dial.* 73.1; *Ep. Bar.* 8.5 for the idea that Jesus rules from the cross.

128. Ashton, *Understanding*, pp. 226-29.

129. In favour of intransitive sense, see Ashton, *Understanding*, p. 228 n. 41; Bultmann, *John: A Commentary*, p. 664 n. 2; Beasley-Murray, *John*, p. 341. Those who argue for the transitive sense are Meeks, *Prophet-King*, pp. 73-76; Haenchen, *John*, II, p. 183; Brown, *John*, II, pp. 880-81; de la Potterie as shown by Meeks, *Prophet-King*, pp. 74-76, and de Jonge, *Stranger from Heaven*, p. 76 n. 74; Brodie, *John*, pp. 538-39. Barrett, *John*, p. 544, suggests that in the light of John's tendency to play on words of double meaning, both meanings are implied.

130. In 12.14 ἐκάθισεν has intransitive sense, but there ὁ Ἰησοῦς is clearly

2. The transitive sense gives a good sequence to Pilate's first declaration, ἰδοὺ ὁ ἄνθρωπος, for at first Pilate introduces Jesus with his crown of thorns and purple robe (19.5), but when he knows that Jesus claimed to be the Son of God, he becomes more fearful and seeks to release him (19.7-12). Such a reverence would have led Pilate to make a final attempt to show Jesus as the King of the Jews and this time by making him sit on the throne of judgment. Thus John gives a dramatic force to Pilate's words, ἴδε ὁ βασιλεὺς ὑμῶν (19.14).[131]

3. The transitive sense seems relevant to the context in which the identification of Jesus as king becomes a crucial issue and the Roman ruler firmly accepts Jesus as the King of the Jews (cf. 19.12, 14, 15, 19, 21-22).

4. The cry of the Jews by the words, ἆρον ἆρον, in addition to σταύρωσον αὐτόν in 19.15, stresses the idea of 'lifting up' obviously from the throne of judgment.

It is clear that John uses traditional materials with the christological purpose of showing that Jesus is king, who brings salvation and judgment to humans by his witness to the heavenly reality. The idea that the Son has been granted authority to judge because he is υἱὸς ἀνθρώπου has already been mentioned by John in 5.27 and there is little wonder that the same idea is applied to the crucified man and king. This echoes the Merkabah mystical visions, Daniel 7 in particular, which portray the offer of salvation and judgment by the human-like figure seated on the throne. John brings such a vision to earth, proclaiming that God's kingship is indeed revealed in Jesus of Nazareth and that his glory lies in his utter humiliation and death. The arguments posed by Dodd, Rensberger and Hengel for the political situation of the late first century for understanding the Johannine trial-narrative[132] do not adequately explain the recurring key concepts such as the revelation of Jesus' glory as king, the oneness of the kingship of God and that of Jesus, and the king's mission of bearing witness to the truth and thereby bringing salvation and condemnation. Therefore along with the political context, the religio-historical context of the late first century should also be taken into account. Viewed thus, the mystical speculation centred on

mentioned as the subject. Similarly, the participle καθίσας in 8.2 has Ἰησοῦς as the subject (cf. 8.1).

131. Barrett, *John*, p. 544.

132. Dodd, *Tradition*, pp. 112-20; Rensberger, 'Politics of John', pp. 395-411; Hengel, 'Reich Christi', pp. 166-67, 170-84.

Ezekiel's chariot emerges as the more relevant context to explain the polemical tendency of John, for it is the Merkabah tradition that aroused an interest in the minds of some Jews to see God in his kingly glory, to bear witness to what they had seen and to ascribe the task of judgment to a human figure seated on the throne.

Conclusions

From our analysis of the Johannine 'seeing', 'glory' and 'king', it becomes conspicuous that John gives a picture of an enthroned God who makes himself visible in Jesus. He underlines two levels of 'seeing': (1) to see with the physical eyes, either by hearing a testimony or by seeing signs; and (2) to perceive spiritually and intelligibly, leading one to the commitment of faith to Christ and to bear witness to that vision. By using the verbs ὁράω, θεάομαι and θεωρέω primarily in connection with seeing God or Jesus, John affirms that God in his glory can be seen only in the earthly life of Jesus rather than within oneself or by ascending to heaven, as some mystics were claiming. For it is Jesus alone who has perceived God, by having perfect communion with the Father.

The same idea is intensified by John's use of the δόξα theme, which seems doubly important for him because of his use of both δόξα and δοξάζω to denote divine revelation in Jesus. By using the word δόξα with the meaning 'God's many-splendoured character' in general and 'God's love' or 'his saving power' in particular, John proclaims that God's glory is manifested supremely, though not solely, in Jesus' death on the cross which too was his glorification/exaltation. For him the glory of Jesus equals the glory of God, for Jesus was possessing God's glory even in his pre-existent state and precisely this glory was seen by Isaiah in his vision. The same glory was seen by the 'Johannine' community in the Logos incarnate and was testified to. This glory was granted as a gift to the believers to practise love and unity with one another. They will behold the very same glory in heaven at the end-time.

In view of the fact that the idea of 'seeing' and a vision of the *kingly* glory of God in his Son do not attain significance in Sinai tradition, it would be improper to try to understand John's δόξα-motif in the light of Sinai tradition alone. We have observed that the appearance of the divine glory on the throne in human-like form was the major concern of

Merkabah contemplation in the late first century. John would have easily inclined to draw materials from the Merkabah texts such as Ezekiel 1, Isaiah 6 and Daniel 7 in addition to other biblical texts, including Exodus tradition. The clear allusion to Isaiah 6 in 12.40-41 supports this. Further, John's identification of δόξα with God's ὄνομα provides further evidence that possibly John had in mind Merkabah mysticism, the early form of *Ma'aseh Bereshit* and also the mystical tradition centred on Moses. Thus, John could meaningfully encounter those who had known or practised mysticism with the message that God's glory can be perceived not on the heavenly throne, but here on earth upon the cross and that the name that was revealed in creation and to Moses is now made known in the Logos incarnate and crucified.

What John has asserted in his δόξα-motif is substantially the same in his βασιλεύς-motif. For him Jesus, as ὁ ἄνθρωπος, is king who, without holding worldly power, reigns, and even judges, from the cross. Therefore Jesus' kingship can rightly be grasped only in the light of his death and resurrection, which are anticipated in his entry into Jerusalem riding on a young ass. Jesus' kingship is in perfect unity with God's kingship and hence there was no need to *make* him king, as, for example, Moses was made a prophet-king. This means that in Jesus God himself is revealed as king. As king, Jesus came into the world to bear witness to the eternal reality and to render judgment-salvation for those who acknowledge the revelation of God's kingship in Jesus, but condemnation for those who reject it.

Unlike the glory-motif, however, the king-motif shows no influence of Moses tradition. Although the mission of bearing witness is parallel to the mission of any prophet like Moses, the Johannine ideas such as the already existing unity of kingship between God and Jesus, the revelatory nature of Jesus' kingship, and the judgment involved are absent in the Moses-centred piety or in the political situation of the first century, but are present in Merkabah mystical visions. However, the heavenly emphasis of kingship, which is common in Merkabah mystical visions, is replaced by John with the more accessible nature of Jesus' kingship here on earth. For John, Jesus is enthroned as king and judge not on the heavenly throne, surrounded by the angels, but on the cross surrounded by hostile forces. This gives us another clue for the use of Merkabah mysticism by John, who probably attempts to convince his readers that the yearnings of the Merkabah mystics can be fulfilled only by 'seeing' Jesus as king, though radically in a different way: on the cross. Thus the replacement-motif which we have grasped in the early part of John's Gospel seems to continue to the latter part too.

Chapter 14

THE 'SENDING OF THE SON' IN JOHN

In the previous two chapters we have seen that John seems to write his Gospel, as one of his purposes, for the benefit of a group of Jews who had great interest in the mystical practice centred on Ezekiel's chariot-throne and that this he does by replacing (or reinterpreting) what is known as the throne-mysticism of Palestinian Judaism with the cross-mysticism, that is, the mystical experience of seeing in Jesus Christ God's glory that was most powerfully displayed on his cross. We have also observed that one mark of Jesus' kingship is his coming into the world to bear witness to the truth. A regularly recurring feature in most of the Merkabah visions, as understood and practised in the first century, is the commissioning of the visionary by God to go back to the people and bear witness to what he had seen and heard. In John the idea of bearing witness belongs to a larger spectrum of the sending-motif. Moreover, we have seen that scholars such as Preiss, Borgen, Meeks, Bühner and Ashton have proposed some form of Jewish mystical or apocalyptic tradition as background for understanding the idea of 'sending', which, according to some scholars, occupies central place in Johannine Christology.[1] If so, it is worth examining the theme of 'sending' to see whether or not John contains any kind of mystical features.

1.   See R. Bultmann, 'Die Bedeutung der neuerschlossenen mandäischen und manichäischen Quellen für das Verständnis des Johannesevangeliums', *ZNW* 24 (1925), pp. 104-109; Borgen, 'God's Agent', p. 137; M. Theobald, *Die Fleisch-werdung des Logos* (Münster: Aschendorf, 1988), p. 376; G.R. Beasley-Murray, 'The Mission of the Logos-Son', in F. van Segbroeck *et al.* (eds.), *The Four Gospels 1992* (3 vols.; Festschrift F. Neirynck; Leuven: Leuven University Press, 1992), III, pp. 1855-68 (1855).

Revelation by 'Sending'

Like other themes, which we have examined above, the theme of 'sending' also contributes mainly to John's idea of revelation. Haenchen maintains that the central message of John is that, although God and his dealings with humans are completely hidden (1.18; 5.37; 6.46), the knowledge of God is possible if only he sends someone to the world with such knowledge and that Jesus is the emissary sent by the Father precisely to make the hidden God known.[2] Jesus could manifest God, because he came from God (ὁ ὢν παρὰ τοῦ θεοῦ—6.46; 7.29; ἐκ τῶν ἄνω—8.23); he alone had seen the Father (6.46; cf. 3.11, 32); and as μονογενὴς υἱός he had been in the bosom of the Father (1.18; 3.16).

These ideas attain further emphasis in John by the terms πέμπειν, ἀποστέλλειν, ὁ πέμψας με and ὁ πέμψας με πατήρ. These terms sufficiently show that, for John, Jesus was sent in his status as God's Son, which enabled him to have an intimate and continued relationship with God and to mediate the vision of God (cf. 12.45; 14.9). The coming of the Son is from heaven and to do the Father's will on earth (4.34; 5.30; 6.38-39). This, however, does not make the Son one who has an independent will from the Father, for he can do nothing of his own accord (ἀφ' ἑαυτοῦ οὐδὲν—5.19, 30). Does this mean that the Son lived like a puppet in the hands of God? No! For John there was complete identity of will and life between Jesus and the Father who sent him, because they indwell one another (5.26; 10.30; 14.10-11). Therefore Jesus speaks not his own words, but those of the Father (3.34; 7.16; 8.26, 38, 40; 14.10, 24; 17.8) and performs not his own works, but those of the sender (4.34; 5.17, 19-27, 30, 36; 8.28; 14.10; 17.4, 14). In and through the agent, the sender himself speaks and acts (cf. ὁ δὲ πατὴρ ἐν ἐμοί μένων ποιεῖ τὰ ἔργα αὐτοῦ—14.10),[3] and thus is revealed, unlike the earthly envoy-model in which the sender is normally far off from the agent.

This revelatory nature of Jesus' mission incomparably exceeds the authority and purpose of any human agency, including the mission of Moses. In the mystical tradition centred on Moses he is enthroned as king of Israel during his ascent up Mt Sinai and becomes the mediator

2. E. Haenchen, 'Der Vater der mich gesandt hat', *NTS* 9 (1962–63), pp. 208-16 (210). See Beasley-Murray, *Gospel of Life*, pp. 16-17; and *idem*, 'Logos-Son', p. 1856, for the English rendering of this view of Haenchen.

3. Haenchen, 'Der Vater der mich gesandt hat', pp. 210-11.

of all kinds of heavenly secrets.[4] We have already noticed that Moses tradition does not give an exact parallel to the Johannine theme of revelation. What the ascendent 'saw', according to Meeks, is cosmic and political events as well as cosmological details.[5] But John presents Jesus as the one who had seen the Father and his works and he is sent to reveal precisely the same God by doing the same works. Such a revelation echoes Merkabah mysticism in which God becomes visible as much as he can be seen in the human-like figure on the throne. The one who is commissioned, after having such a vision, can testify to the vision of God, but he himself cannot reveal God. The mission of Jesus, however, is unique in that due to his oneness with the Father, God becomes visible and accessible in him.

The Revealed Glory in the Mission of the Son

The primary evidence for the authenticity of Jesus' mission as received from the Father is that he ultimately brings glory to the one who sent him:

> ὁ ἀφ' ἑαυτοῦ λαλῶν τὴν δόξαν τὴν ἰδίαν ζητεῖ· ὁ δὲ ζητῶν τὴν δόξαν τοῦ πέμψαντος αὐτὸν οὗτος ἀληθής ἐστιν καὶ ἀδικία ἐν αὐτῷ οὐκ ἔστιν (7.18).

If Jesus were simply speaking his own words, then he would naturally seek his own δόξα, but since he seeks the δόξα of God through his word and work, he is proved to be the divine emissary who is as truthful (ἀληθής) as God is (cf. 3.33; 8.26, where God is described as ἀληθής). The word δόξα in the phrase ὁ δὲ ζητῶν τὴν δόξαν τοῦ πέμψαντος αὐτὸν (7.18b) is taken by some commentators to have the sense of earthly 'praise' or 'honour', as it has in 5.41, 44; 7.18a.[6] However, in 5.41, 44 the word denotes the δόξα received by human beings from one another and therefore the natural connotation is human 'praise' and 'honour'; whereas in 7.18 the adversative conjunction δέ makes a contrast between 'his own glory' (τὴν δόξαν τὴν ἰδίαν, i.e. Jesus' honour as a human being) and 'the glory of him who sent him'. God can hardly be honoured in the same measure as a human is

---

4. Meeks, *Prophet-King*, pp. 206, 215.

5. W.A. Meeks, 'Moses as God and King', in J. Neusner (ed.), *Religions in Antiquity: Essays in Memory of E.R. Goodenough* (NumSup, 14; Leiden: E.J. Brill, 1968), pp. 367-70.

6. See Schnackenburg, *St John*, II, p. 133; Brown, *John*, II, p. 312; Barrett, *John*, p. 318; Bultmann, *John: A Commentary*, p. 275.

honoured. We have observed above that the glory of God in John, particularly when it is connected with the person and work of Jesus, has always revelational character. Jn 7.18b also needs to be understood in the same sense. Jesus seeks the δόξα of God in the sense that he reveals God among humans in his glory. If so, 7.18 implies that the mission of anyone who functions with human authority lacks revelatory nature and so ends up in self-seeking, but, in contrast, that the goal of Jesus' mission is to enable people to see the glory of God, that is, the very nature of God. Thus Loader maintains that the 'Glory' motif is associated with the revealer–envoy pattern developed by the sending-Christology in John.[7] This revealer–envoy pattern is reminiscent of the mission of the one who saw the glory of God in a Merkabah-like vision and who later on reveals his vision to his listeners, though in John *Jesus becomes both the revelation and the testimony*.

Important Aspects of the Son's Mission

The most significant work accomplished by sending the Son is the redemption of the world, which is the point in 3.16-17, where the verbs ἔδωκεν and ἀπέστειλεν are used in parallel. Beasley-Murray points out that the 'giving' of the Son includes both his incarnation and vicarious death for the world and hence that the entire mission of the Son for the redemption of the world is in view.[8] But John particularizes Jesus' suffering and death on the cross as the means by which Jesus accomplishes the work of the Father who sent him, as it is clear from his use of the verb τελειόω in important places (cf. 4.34; 5.36; 17.4; 19.28, 30). The redemptive work, thus accomplished, has three dominant motifs in itself: witnessing, judgment and eternal life.

Witnessing
The witnessing of Jesus to what he had seen and heard with the Father in heaven is an important dimension in God's redemptive plan. By presenting the idea of witnessing as a form of divine revelation, John asserts that Jesus bears witness about himself, but that even if he bears witness about himself, his witness is true (8.14; cf. 8.18). Meeks observes that the total testimony of Jesus in John is in fact about

---

7.   Loader, *Christology*, pp. 82-85; cf. pp. 77-82.
8.   Beasley-Murray, 'Logos-Son', p. 1858; *idem, Gospel of Life*, p. 21.

himself.[9] However, Jesus bears witness by uttering the words of God (3.11, 32, 34; cf. 8.26, 38a; 12.49; 14.24) and hence Jesus' διδαχή is not his own but of the one who sent him (7.16-17; 8.28b; 12.49; 14.24). Moreover, when Jesus speaks the words that the Father taught him, the Father Himself is with him (ὁ πέμψας με μετ᾽ ἐμοῦ ἐστιν—8.29) and gives witness about him (μαρτυρεῖ περὶ ἐμοῦ ὁ πέμψας με πατήρ—8.18b; 5.32). The witness concerning Jesus (περὶ ἐμοῦ) is the very fact that the Father has sent him (5.38). This means that it is hard to separate the witness borne by Jesus and that of the Father who sent him. When Jesus witnesses, it is the Father who is revealed and glorified.

There are two other significant witnesses who reveal Jesus through their ministry: ὁ παράκλητος (15.26; cf. 3.34) and the disciples (15.27).[10] The redemptive work of Jesus involves also his return to the Father (13.1, 3; 14.12, 28; 16.7, 28; 17.11, 13) in order to send the paraclete to be with his disciples (16.7; cf. 14.16-17, 26; 15.26), who, in turn, are sent into the world in the same way as the Son was sent (20.21-22; cf. 17.6). Thus, the sending of the Spirit and that of the disciples, being rooted in the sending of the Son, has the same revelatory effect, for 'the work of the disciples and the Spirit is revelatory only in the sense that it reveals the revelation of the Son'.[11]

T. Preiss recognizes the Spirit as the witness *par excellence*[12] and argues that although the word 'mystic' does not appear in John, there is what he calls 'juridical mysticism', that is, 'a sort of ontological unity of eternal reciprocal immanence as between the Father and the Son'—a unity that is juridical and almost military in character.[13] However, Preiss emphasizes in this context more the title 'Son of Man' as judge and witness than the title 'Son of God' which is directly connected with the Johannine sending-motif. The idea behind Preiss's *mystique juridique* is that the agent is a person identical with his principal (*Mek.* 12.3-4; *Qid.* 43a). But this halakhic principle, which belongs to a later

9.   Meeks, 'Man from Heaven', p. 56.
10.   There are other two witnesses for Jesus: τὰ ἔργα (5.36) and αἱ γραφαί (5.39). But even these ultimately derive from the Father who sent him.
11.   Loader, *Christology*, p. 92. For the missionary implication of the salvation-event of Jesus upon the Church, see M.R. Ruiz, *Der Missionsgedanke des Johannesevangeliums: Ein Beitrag zur johanneischen Soteriologie* (Würzburg: Echter Verlag, 1987).
12.   Preiss, *Life in Christ*, pp. 19, 22.
13.   Preiss, *Life in Christ*, pp. 25-27, esp. 25; see also above pp. 35-36.

date, can hardly illuminate the idea of Johannine sending. The *halakhah* does not identify the agent as a judge, but as the one who will *receive* judgment in a lawsuit on the property of his master (*b. Qam.* 70a), without having any connotation of 'judgment' as John has. Further, the unity that allegedly exists between the sender and his agent in the *halakhah* is not the same as the mutual indwelling of Father and Son. We will come back to the halakhic principle of agency later. Suffice it here to note that Preiss's juridical mysticisim does not do justice either to the Johannine theme of judgment (see further below) or to the reciprocal immanence of Father and Son.

Nevertheless, the mystagogical role of the Holy Spirit, who will lead (ὁδηγήσει) the disciples into all truth (16.13), points to the Merkabah mystical visions in which the angels escort the mystic in the latter's heavenly ascent, guide him to see the glory of God and reveal all cosmological and heavenly secrets. The angelic function of Jesus is now transferred by John to the Holy Spirit by whose witness a vision of God continues to be possible.[14] Windisch holds that the content of the Spirit's witness is apocalyptic.[15] However, in view of the Spirit's function of 'bringing home the glory of Christ to the world'[16] (16.14; 7.39) and thereby bringing a vision of God himself, we can suggest that the witness of the Spirit reflects also Merkabah mystical practice.

Judgment

It is striking that the act of bearing witness is closely tied up in John with that of judgment. In fact, both are spoken in parallel terms:

κἂν ἐγὼ μαρτυρῶ περὶ ἐμαυτοῦ, ἀληθής ἐστιν ἡ μαρτυρία μου (8.14a).
καὶ ἐὰν κρίνω δὲ ἐγώ, ἡ κρίσις ἡ ἐμὴ ἀληθινή ἐστιν (8.16a).

Similarly, the act of judging (5.27, 29-30) is connected by John with the μαρτυρία-motif in 5.31-47. The sending of the Son, though an act of God's love, evokes judgment, when the world does not believe in his witness (3.17-19; cf. 12.47-48).

14. Cf. 16.13-15, which describes that the Holy Spirit will reveal (ἀναγγελεῖ) the heavenly mysteries taught and revealed by Jesus himself and thus he will glorify Jesus. Brown, *John*, II, p. 1138, indicates that ἀναγγελεῖν is a verb used in apocalypses to describe the unveiling of the truth of a vision. Cf. below, p. 267.

15. H. Windisch, *The Spirit-Paraclete in the Fourth Gospel* (FBBS, 20; Philadelphia: Fortress Press, ET 1968), p. 12.

16. Barrett, *John*, p. 490. Beasley-Murray, *John*, p. 284, comments that in the glorifying function of the Spirit the revelation of God in Christ reaches its apex.

Nevertheless, the Son himself is not left without the responsibility to judge, for the Father has given all judgment to the Son (5.22, 28, 30; cf. the πάντα δέδωκεν ἐν τῇ χειρὶ αὐτοῦ of 3.35), precisely because he is the Son of Man (5.27), that is, the one who represents the restored and vindicated humanity by his suffering, death and resurrection.[17] The word spoken by Jesus will be the judge (12.48) and even this word is given to him by the Father (12.49-50). It is God, the Sender, who judges in and through Jesus by means of what he had spoken and 8.16 portrays judgment as the corporate act of the Father and the Son. Jesus judges as he hears the decision of his Father, who appointed him (5.30) and this judgment applies to judgment every day as well as on the last day (12.48).[18] In other words, the Son takes the place of the Father in executing judgment, implicitly on the throne of God.[19] Beasley-Murray, commenting on 8.17-18, states that in the act of judgment and testimony two complementary ideas, the unity of the Father and the Son and at the same time their distinctness, are present.[20] But the passages that he cites (5.30; 7.16-17) describe the Son as having the same will and authority as the Father rather than having his own.

Salvation or Eternal Life

The ultimate motive of God in sending his Son is to save rather than to condemn (κρίνειν) the world and thus to enable the world to have eternal life (3.16-17). The possibility of possessing eternal life lies for those who see (θεωρεῖν) the Son and believe in him both at present and in the eschatological day (6.40), whereas it is unbelief, rooted in the evil deeds of humans, which brings condemnation (3.18-20). The κρίσις of the Son divides humans into two: those who have done good and those who have done evil, and the former receive life, but the latter condemnation (5.27-29).[21] Hence Bultmann is correct in saying that the

17.	Cf. Barrett, *John*, p. 262, who remarks that Jesus does not judge simply because he is a human being in which case anyone would be at liberty to judge, but that he judges because he is humanity restored and vindicated by its union with God.

18.	See Beasley-Murray, 'Logos-Son', p. 1859.

19.	See above, pp. 243-45 for the idea of Jesus being seated on the judgment-seat in 19.13.

20.	Beasley-Murray, *John*, p. 129.

21.	Meeks's valuable study on the descent–ascent motif in John shows that this motif has a dualistic tendency, sharply dividing a small group of believers over against 'the world' that belongs to darkness and the devil (cf. ἐκ τῶν κάτω >< ἐκ

mission is the *eschatological event*,[22] though he did not observe the importance of the present tenses in 3.15-21. Jesus' authority to raise the dead and to give life derives from the Father who commissioned him (5.21-27) and therefore in and through Jesus God himself gives life and executes judgment.

Possible Background for Understanding John's Sending-Motif

We have analysed the key aspects embedded in the Johannine theme of 'sending' and now it is proper for us to examine the background against which it can be best understood.

The concept of sending occurs in the *Hermetica* on two occasions. At first, the visionary, Tat, is sent forth by Poimandres with the task of preaching the beauty of reverence (εὐσεβείας) and knowledge (γνῶσις) (*CH* 1.27-29).[23] This resembles partly the sending of the Merkabah mystics after their chariot-vision and also the commissioning of the Old Testament prophets. The second reference is in *CH* 4.4-6, which we have mentioned earlier.[24] Although the sending of the basin described in *CH* 4 resembles the sending of the Son in John, the purpose and the result of the sending radically differs in John from that described in the *Hermetica*. According to the *Hermetica*, people should leave their bodily pleasures and partake of the νοῦς that God has sent by dipping themselves in the basin and such people see the good by raising themselves even to what lies beyond heaven; after seeing the good, however, they regard the earthly life as only a calamity (*CH* 4.5). In contrast, John focuses on 'believing' in the Son of God who was sent by the Father in order to attain life here and now. Fowden observes that the idea of herald found in the *Hermetica* is an allusion to the language of the mystery religions, whereas Festugière connects the idea of basin with the Wisdom and gnostic traditions.[25] The reference to 'sending' in

τῶν ἄνω in 8.23)—Meeks, 'Man from Heaven', pp. 66-72.

22.   Bultmann, *John: A Commentary*, p. 154.

23.   Although neither πέμπειν nor ἀποστέλλειν has been used in this passage, the verb ἀνείθην gives the sense of commissioning.

24.   See above, pp. 66 and 184-85. For other parallels between Johannine sending-motif and the idea of sending in the *Hermetica*, see Odeberg, *Fourth Gospel*, pp. 117-20.

25.   See B.P. Copenhaver, *Hermetica: The Greek Corpus Hermeticum and the Latin Asclepius in a New English Translation with Notes and Introduction* (Cambridge: Cambridge University Press, 1992), p. 134.

the *Hermetica* only shows that the idea was familiar in Hellenistic circles.

Following Preiss, Borgen argues that at least six aspects of the Jewish halakhic principles of agent are reflected in John.[26] Although Borgen lists the points of similarities between the Johannine idea of sending and the halakhic principles of agency, he does not argue that the halakhic tradition could have influenced John. It is true that the halakhic rule, 'an agent can appoint an agent' (*Qid.* 41a; *Giṭ.* 29b), resembles the sending of the disciples by Jesus, the agent-Son, but the halakhah speaks of the divorce proceedings, which is not the point in John. The discussion of the rabbis on this question shows that when the husband dies they all cease to be agents (*Giṭ.* 29b). Moreover, our study shows that John's sending-motif exceeds the *shaliah* model in its emphasis on the permanent oneness of the Son with the Father both before and after creation.[27] Nevertheless, one of Borgen's conclusions that the Jewish background reflected in John should be characterized as the early stages of Merkabah mysticism, which exhibits a combination of *halakhah*, heavenly figures and the heavenly world,[28] leads us basically to the Merkabah mystical tradition as the possible source of inspiration for John to use his envoy model. But Borgen picks up only one aspect of Merkabah mysticism, the vision of God, important though it is, and compares it with Philo's ideas of Israel ('he who sees God'—*Conf. Ling.* 146 and *Leg. All.* 1.46) and of the 'second birth' of Moses at the Sinai-theophany (*Quaest. in Exod.* 2.46).[29] Other mystical aspects, which also occur in the Johannine concept of agent, as we will note below, remain unnoticed by Borgen and other scholars who have followed him.

The same *shaliah*-principle is applied by Meeks to the heavenly ascent of Moses who, as Meeks argues, was enthroned there as prophet-king and who was sent to his people both as revealer (prophet) and vice-regent (king).[30] He suggests that the description of Jesus as the

26.   Borgen, *Bread from Heaven*, pp. 158-64; *idem*, 'God's Agent', pp. 137-48.

27.   See Dunn, 'Let John Be John', pp. 329-30.

28.   Borgen, 'God's Agent', pp. 144-47.

29.   Borgen, 'God's Agent', pp. 144-45. According to Borgen, since Philo too was influenced by early Merkabah mysticism, his writings can throw light on Johannine ideas.

30.   Meeks, 'Moses as God and King', pp. 354-71. Cf. also above p. 38.

prophetic agent or envoy of God in John was modelled in part on the traditions of Moses' mission.[31] Meeks is certainly right in maintaining that kingship in John is being radically redefined,[32] but it is unlikely that it is redefined in terms of the mission of the prophet. Though Jesus' mission includes prophetic function in the sense that he received the words (ῥήματα) or teaching (διδαχή) from God and gave them to his hearers (cf. 3.34; 7.14-24; 8.28, 40; 12.49-50; 14.10; 17.8), in the final analysis it is his sonship that attains prominence in John's description of Jesus' mission.[33] As Meeks himself observes in another place, Jesus, the envoy of God, has not only delivered the name of God and his words to his disciples, as Moses did, but he has shown them God's *doxa*, enabling them to 'see' the Father.[34] Our study above shows that the ascent of Moses constitutes only one wing of the heavenly ascent type of mystical experience that was attributed to the patriarchs and prophets and that even the vision of Moses can only be explained against the background of Merkabah mysticism. Meeks's theory of Moses' mystical ascent to explain John's Christology points eventually then to the Merkabah mystical tradition.

Dodd argues that the description of the status and function of the Son of God as the one sent by the Father recalls the language of the Old Testament prophets (cf. Num. 24.13; Isa. 6.8; Jer. 1.5, 10; 9.24; Amos 3.7).[35] However, he is aware that the distinctively divine activities, ζωοποίησις and κρίσις, accomplished by the Son, his intimate unity or solidarity with the Father, which is known from his use of the divine name, ἐγώ εἰμι, and his pre-temporal existence implied in the Son's τὰ ἄνω to τὰ κάτω movement are those which distinguish the Son from the prophets.[36]

31. Meeks, *Prophet-King*, pp. 301-305.
32. Meeks, *Prophet-King*, p. 67.
33. See de Jonge, *Stranger from Heaven*, p. 57, who stresses that it is the title 'Son of God', his unique relationship with God and his obedience to his will attain significance in John as a whole and in chs. 5–7 in particular.
34. See W.A. Meeks, 'The Divine Agent and his Counterfeit in Philo and the Fourth Gospel', in E.S. Fiorenza (ed.), *Aspects of Religious Propaganda in Judaism and Early Christianity* (Notre Dame: University of Notre Dame Press, 1976), pp. 43-67 (58).
35. Dodd, *Interpretation*, pp. 254-55.
36. Dodd, *Interpretation*, pp. 93-96, 257-62. Dodd goes on to say that the name of God takes the form not merely of אֲנִי הוּא, ἐγώ εἰμι, but of וַאֲנִי הוּא, ἐγὼ καὶ ὁ πέμψας με. Cf. Bultmann, *John: A Commentary*, p. 250, who comments that

Ashton also argues that Jesus' relationship with God should be conceived on the analogy of the prophetic mission and the law of agency, for in the prophetic schema the king is greater than his emissary, while in the Jewish law of agency the emissary is the king's equal.[37] But Ashton does not produce enough evidence to prove his latter point. Like Borgen, Ashton too treats the halakhic principle, 'An agent is like the one who sent him (καθὼς...οὗτος)' as expressing the 'unity' or 'equality' between the agent and the sender.[38] But unfortunately this statement proves similarity only in will,[39] authority, and perhaps in rank, but not equality in life (ζωή) and glory (δόξα), as we have it in John. Ashton's argument is weakened by his contradictory views expressed on the same subject: while he accepts the law of agency as the background for understanding Jesus' equality with God in terms of divine status,[40] later on he says, 'The exceptional character of Jesus' relationship with God cannot be *explained* by the law of agency'.[41] Further, even if an agent *identifies himself* with the will and intention of him who sent him, this does not mean that both were naturally holding oneness in intention. A monarch sometimes may make his ambassador a plenipotentiary to fulfil his will,[42] but even here the scope and duration are limited, for an agent bears his master's authority only as far as the judicial function is concerned. Moreover, as we have noticed above, the juridical aspect of the halakhic agency does not identify the agent as a judge in the Johannine sense of bringing salvation and condemnation.

Bühner proposes that the quasi-juridical role of בן בית ('son of the house'), a term that was used in Jewish law in conjunction with the term בעל בית ('master of the house'), (*m. Ta'an.* 3.8; *m. Šeb.* 7.8.) can best explain Jesus' participation in the twin powers, power to give life and power to judge, which are the sole prerogatives of God (5.22, 27).[43] However, like the halakhic principle of שליח, the use of the בן בית

---

no Old Testament prophet was ever given divine status.

37. Ashton, *Understanding*, pp. 316-17.

38. Ashton, *Understanding*, p. 314.

39. Because an agent *identifies himself* with the will and intention of him who sent him (Borgen, *Bread from Heaven*, pp. 159-60).

40. Ashton, *Understanding*, p. 316.

41. Ashton, *Understanding*, p. 325; emphasis his.

42. Ashton, *Understanding*, p. 314; Borgen, *Bread from Heaven*, p. 160.

43. Bühner, *Der Gesandte*, pp. 195-98; Ashton, *Understanding*, pp. 322-23.

model also suffers inadequacy in interpreting Johannine sending-statements. We cannot do justice to the Johannine passages by interpreting
them in the light of later documents. Moreover, the total responsibility
bestowed on the בן בית as to administer the estate of the בעל הבית as a
legal heir does not explain, as Bühner thinks, the responsibility of
giving life, rendering judgment and even of raising the dead on the last
day (6.39; 5.25-29), which the Johannine Son exercises.

Bühner also thinks that the cultural-historical, religio-historical traditions, which include the idea of agency based on the prophetic-messen-
ger and the Moses traditions, and the apocalyptic traditions, have all
contributed to the development of the sending-concept in John. At the
level of cultural history, he highlights the universal custom of ancient
society in sending news, according to which a messenger goes through
three stages on his path: (1) he is sent out; (2) he implements; and (3)
he returns to the sender. Bühner finds that John's idea of sending fits
into these three stages.[44] At the religio-historical level, he argues for the
שליח-principle as underlying John's Christology. He conceives the
descent of a heavenly angel to function as prophetic שליחות as a possible background to the Son of Man Christology, which is also equal to
the Son Christology.[45] As Bühner's position centres around the analogy
of prophetic mission and the halakhic law of agency, the criticisms that
we have posed above regarding the insufficiency of these systems of
thought to enlighten the sending-concept in John are applicable also
against Bühner. Dunn points out that the notion of angelic messengers
is irrelevant to the Johannine Son of Man, who is not at all presented by
John as an angel.[46]

It is possible that John uses the sending-motif found both in the
synoptic tradition (cf. the parable of the wicked tenants in Mk 12.11
par.)[47] and in Pauline tradition (cf. 8.3; Gal. 4.4-5),[48] enriching it with

44.   Bühner, *Der Gesandte*, pp. 118-37, 423-25.
45.   Bühner, *Der Gesandte*, pp. 270-421, 430-32.
46.   Dunn, 'Let John Be John', p. 329; cf. also above, pp. 207-208. Ashton,
Understanding, pp. 325-26, maintains that Bühner's findings do not give due care
to the divine aspect of the agent Christology.
47.   The key ideas found in the parable—such as the sending of the son, his
death in the course of his mission, the anticipation of Jesus' resurrection, the sending of the son as king by a king, and the rendering of the twofold judgment:
destruction of the wicked and an offer of inheritance to the faithful—all have
parallel with the Johannine sending-motif—see esp. Schnackenburg, *St John*, II, pp.
78-79; Ashton, *Understanding*, pp. 319-29; F.J. Matera, *The Kingship of Jesus:*

the 'mutual indwelling' or 'oneness' formula. However, the following distinctive elements in Johannine sending-motif demand attention.

1. Jesus was sent into the world as the Son of God not merely to redeem humankind by his death, but more to make the unknowable and invisible God known and visible. In other words, if anything, it is the revelation of God that attains prominence in God's sending of his Son.

2. In the mission of the Son ultimately the Father is glorified, which means that the Son reveals the glory, that is, the very nature of God, to humans.

3. The Son utters the words received from God and bears witness to what he had seen and heard with the Father, which indicates the heavenly pre-existence of the Son with the Father before he was sent.

4. The sending of the Son evokes judgment, when the world does not believe in his witness and the Son himself renders judgment on behalf of the Father who sent him.

5. In the mission of the Son, the Father himself, who sent him, speaks, acts and bears witness, because both of them are one by means of their mutual indwelling.

It is precisely his pre-existence in heaven and oneness with the Father that make it possible for the Son to manifest God in his glory. This suggests that *John most likely interacts with the adherents of Merkabah mystical practice, by counter-arguing that the glory of God, which the mystics claim as having seen in their heavenly ascent, has been sent down to earth in his Son, Jesus.* In this sense, Jesus represents and manifests on earth God who appears in Merkabah mystical visions. The eternal life, which is available for those who believe in the Son, echoes the transformation of the Merkabah visionary to the heavenly life. The fact of judgment as integral to the Johannine sending-concept is parallel to the Merkabah mystical visions in which judgment is

Composition and Theology in Mark 15 (SBLDS, 66; Chico, CA: Scholars Press, 1982), pp. 74-91.

48.   E. Schweizer, 'υἱός, κ.τ.λ.', *TDNT*, VIII, pp. 363-92 (375), holds that the sending-formula, which occurs both in Paul and John, presupposes an already developed Christology of the pre-existent Lord in the sphere of Logos or Wisdom tradition. See also J.P. Miranda, *Die Sendung Jesu im vierten Evangelium: Religions- und theologiegeschichtliche Untersuchungen zu den Sendungsformeln* (SBS, 87; Stuttgart: Katholisches Bibelwerk, 1977), pp. 52-68. Dunn, *Christology*, pp. 44-45, argues that the parable of the wicked tenants probably gives a closer parallel to and explanation of Paul's sending-Christology in Rom. 8.3 than the sending of Wisdom.

rendered by a human who had been given authority by God to judge (cf. Dan. 7.9-14; 11QMelch; *T. Abr.* 11–13; *4 Ezra* 12–13; and *1 En.* 37–71).[49] John seems to take up these concepts and apply them to Jesus in his attempt to confront those who were engaged in mystical practice, by proclaiming that the heavenly life can be obtained here on earth simply by believing in the one sent by the Father (17.3) and that failure to do so has *already* caused God's condemnation (3.16-21).[50]

In short, the sending of Jesus to bear witness to what he had seen and heard with the Father and later on the sending of the disciples, who had seen the glory of God in his envoy-revealer, recall Merkabah mysticism in another dimension: the commissioning of the prophets and the patriarchs, who had seen God's glory on the Merkabah, to go to their people not only to narrate the vision, but also to warn them of the impending judgment of God.

Bühner maintains that the setting of the history of religion for Johannine Christology was formed in the framework of an interaction with the Judaism of apocalyptic-esoteric and rabbinic origin.[51] This Judaism, in our analysis, seems to be the one that took great interest in Merkabah mysticism, which itself is a part of the apocalyptic-esoteric tradition.

Conclusions

John describes Jesus as the emissary sent by God with a mission of revealing the hidden God to humans. He was sent as God's Son, who alone had seen the Father because of his intimate communion with him. The ultimate motive of the sending of the Son is to reveal God's glory among human beings. The envoy-revealer does this by redeeming the world by his death on the cross and offering his salvation to all who believe. The idea of revealing God in his glory is reminiscent of the central thought of Merkabah mysticism, but differs radically from any

---

49.   It is notable that the human figure who appears in the execution of God's judgment in these visions, except in 11QMelch, is called 'one like a son of man' or 'like unto a son of God' or 'a man', who is interpreted as 'God's Son', or 'the Son of Man' and that the same titles are applied to Jesus by John, especially in the judgment-motif.

50.   We have also learned that Jesus is sent into the world not only as the Son, but also as king, and that behind John's king-motif lies his polemic against Merkabah mysticism—see above, pp. 233-47.

51.   Bühner, *Der Gesandte*, pp. 332-35, 425.

kind of human commissioning in which it is possible to see the ruler only in isolation from his ambassador, but not in him.

The Johannine Jesus is sent to bear witness not only about the heavenly reality, as observed in the previous chapter, but also about himself, and in his witness about himself it is the Father who is revealed and glorified. The mission of the Son includes also the sending of the Holy Spirit and of his disciples, who will continue the task of witnessing and in whose witness the glory of Jesus will be revealed. Therefore the witness of the paraclete and the mutual indwelling of Father and Son do not seem to justify Preiss's view of 'juridical mysticism', but they echo Merkabah mysticism. However, unlike the Merkabah mystic, who is sent by God to bear witness to the heavenly vision, Jesus himself becomes the *manifestation* of God's glory on earth as well as the *testimony* to that glory.

The revelatory aspect of Jesus' mission includes an *execution* of judgment either in terms of salvation/life or of condemnation, depending upon the response one gives to his witness. This forensic nature of Jesus' revelation is not essentially the same as the halakhic agent who represents his master in legal proceedings to *receive* judgment. Instead, it reflects Merkabah visions, some of which portray a human figure as *rendering* judgment on behalf of God. Also, the Son's offer of eternal life is the echo of the heavenly life one obtains from God during one's mystical ascent to heaven.

Our study shows that various traditions concerning the sending of an agent had probably been known to John's readers, particularly to his Jewish readers. But they do not explain such key aspects in John's sending-motif as the heavenly origin of the Son, his permanent indwelling with the Father, his accomplishment of the Father's will by his death on the cross, his revelation of God's glory on earth, his mission to enable humans to 'see' God in him, and the act of *rendering* judgment on behalf of God.

It is clear that the idea of the sending of the Son, along with that of his vicarious death and of judgment, had been well established in the synoptic and Pauline traditions before John. John could have taken up these traditions, but was not hesitant to enrich it with his own doctrine of revelation based on the oneness of Father and Son. What prompted him to adapt the current idea of sending? The Merkabah mystical elements detected above suggest that the evangelist has used them with the aim of confronting those who had mystical interests with the message that God has manifested himself to humankind here on earth by sending his Son, whose revelation of the heavenly secrets is authentic because he reveals nothing but what he had seen and heard with the Father. However, for John, this message demands faith in the agent-Son of God so that one may attain eternal life.

Chapter 15

THE JOHANNINE IDEA OF INDWELLING

A number of scholars understand the Johannine expressions such as μένειν ἐν, εἶναι ἐν and γινώσκειν in the light of the Hellenistic mystical concept of the union of human soul with God.[1] We have also raised questions above as to whether John uses Philo's teaching on the divine indwelling or at least the ἐν θεῷ motif of the *Hermetica*.[2] Now it is appropriate for us to analyse the Johannine passages concerned to see what John has to say about indwelling. This, in turn, will enable us to grasp which tradition, if any, he follows and for what purpose he uses it.

μένειν ἐν *in John*

The verb μένειν ἐν is used in John mostly with a distinctive theological meaning to refer to the 'lasting immanence' between God and Christ or believers and Christ, emphasizing the sense of permanence.[3] God abides in Jesus (14.10b) and hence the expression μείνατε ἐν ἐμοί κἀγὼ ἐν ὑμῖν in 15.4 implies that in the mutual abiding of Jesus and his disciples they abide in God himself. John's choice of the imagery of the vine and its branches to describe the mutual unity (Jn 15) shows that the unity that John had in mind emphasizes first its communal aspect, though the individual abiding is not missing, and then the life shared by that community. It is the life that 'flows from the central stem, nourishes all the branches and issues in fruit'.[4] This notion is

1.   Notable among them are Underhill, Dodd, Mealand, Countryman and Sanford—see above pp. 23-25, 27-28, 31-33.
2.   See the conclusions in Chapters 2 and 3.
3.   See F. Hauck, 'μένω, μονή, κ.τ.λ.', *TDNT*, IV, pp. 574-81 (576); Brown, *John*, I, p. 510.
4.   Dodd, *Interpretation*, p. 196.

reinforced in 6.56: ὁ τρώγων μου τὴν σάρκα καὶ πίνων μου τὸ αἷμα ἐν ἐμοὶ μένει κἀγὼ ἐν αὐτῷ. It is by coming to the incarnate Son of God, which is the life-giving food, and by believing in him that one can absorb his life and be united with him permanently. This does not mean an 'absorption *into* the divine' or 'deification', as it is held in Hellenistic and Philo's mysticism and as Sanford has recently argued.[5] In contrast, it denotes the divine *life* absorbed *by* the believers.

Union with Jesus is God's Gift
In John's theme of 'abiding' a sense of 'givenness' can be envisaged. The reference to the Father's pruning (15.2) and the word ἤδη used in connection with the disciples' καθαρισμός (15.3) before John introduces the verb μείνατε in 15.4 suggest that union with Jesus is already granted by God as a gift to the disciples. What the disciples are exhorted to do is to hold on loyally and continually to that givenness.[6] Therefore the ἐν θεῷ motif, which makes union with God possible only after a striving on the part of νοῦς (*CH* 11.18-20), is not a reasonable parallel to John's thought of unity by indwelling. Even the statements, 'God is in νοῦς and νοῦς in the soul...and the soul is in matter' (*CH* 11.4b); and 'soul is in body, mind is in soul, and God is in mind' (*CH* 12.13b, though the text is so damaged that one can hardly derive a correct translation) are far from the idea of the mutual indwelling of God and human beings. The union of humans in God, as the *Hermetica* describe, does not seem to be direct and personal as we have it in John, for the relation of humans with God is due to the fact that the *kosmos* is ἐν τῷ θεῷ and the human beings are ἐν τῷ κόσμῳ (*CH* 8.5b; 9.9). Even the described union (συμπάθειαν) of humans with the second God (*CH* 8.5a) is no more than the human feeling that he is a part of the cosmos and organically connected with it.[7] Therefore the union with God, which Hellenistic mysticism advocates, has no conceptual or terminological parallel to John's life-sharing union of the disciples with Jesus and God.

Union with Jesus and the Heavenly Journey
Μονή in 14.23, as in 14.2, is the verbal noun derived from the verb

5. See above pp. 24-25.
6. Barrett, *John*, p. 474.
7. See W. Scott (ed.), *Hermetica*, I, p. 177 n. 10.

μένειν, denoting a permanent abiding place.[8] It bears the notion of life in 1 Macc. 7.38[9] and thus the dwelling of the Father and the Son with the one who loves Jesus can well imply a permanent sharing of their life with him. The eschatological promise of Jesus that he will come again to take the disciples to the μοναί in the Father's house (14.2) is partly realized with 'a paradoxical change of emphasis'[10] in the possibility of the coming of the Father and the Son to dwell with the believers here on earth. It is also notable that the act of God's dwelling with his people was expected to take place at the end-time (Ezek. 37.26-27; Zech. 2.14 MT; Rev. 21.3, 22-23), but that for John it is initially realized here and now in the ministry of Jesus.[11] The idea of mutual union is described in 14.2-3 and 14.23 with a different but complementary emphasis: whereas in 14.2-3 the Father becomes the spiritual sphere in which all believers dwell individually in union with Jesus, in 14.23 each believer individually becomes the spiritual sphere in which the Father dwells in union with Jesus.[12] According to McCaffrey, what is described in 14.2-3 is the journey of the disciples in union with the risen Jesus (παραλήμψομαι ὑμᾶς πρὸς ἐμαυτόν) and this in fact is dependent on the permanent union described in 14.23.[13] That is, the believer's union with Jesus is described by John in terms of a heavenly journey to the Father and this journey is initiated in the union of the Father and the Son in the believer here and now. However, this union is conditioned by the believer's love and obedience to Jesus (14.23a). While 14.2-3 portrays Jesus' ascent in union with the disciples, 14.23 portrays his descent in union with the Father prior to such an ascent. John's reinterpretation of the heavenly journey contains polemic against several mystical traditions, including Merkabah mysticism, to affirm that *the purpose of heavenly journeys, that is, union with God, is now available on earth in Jesus and that an eschatological heavenly ascent is possible for believers only in union with him.*

8.   See Hauck, 'μένω', pp. 579-81; Barrett, *John*, pp. 456, 466.
9.   The μὴ δῷς αὐτοῖς μονήν of 1 Macc. 7.38 LXX is translated in the NRSV as 'let them live no longer'.
10.   So Schnackenburg, *St John*, III, p. 81.
11.   Schnackenburg, *St John*, III, pp. 81-82, rightly holds that the eschatological promise to dwell with Jesus is not ultimately fulfilled here and now, but that it lies also in the future (cf. 12.26; 17.24).
12.   See McCaffrey, *The House with Many Rooms*, pp. 164-66, esp. p. 165.
13.   McCaffrey, *The House with Many Rooms*, p. 195.

Mutual Abiding Denotes 'Seeing'

Brodie shows that the language of mutual abiding in 15.4-10 is developed into the language of mutual seeing in 16.16-22.[14] This is possible by the continued presence of Jesus in the Christian by the paraclete/Spirit (16.12-15; cf. 14.15-17). By using the two verbs μένειν παρά and εἶναι ἐν in 14.17, John states that the Holy Spirit is the most effective means of divine indwelling within a believer. Brodie rightly comments that unless the Spirit first confronts and guides the disciples, one cannot see Jesus, that is, one cannot have 'an inner sense of the human face of God'.[15] He finds three progressive stages of mutual indwelling in 14.12-24: the initial involvement of the Spirit (14.15-17), the coming or seeing of Jesus (14.18-20) and finally the establishment of the divine abode within the disciple (14.23). In this deeper union the Spirit becomes fully active (16.7-15).[16] His role of leading on the way (ὁδηγήσει in 16.13) reminds us of an angel's function in Merkabah mystical visions.[17] Just as the guidance of angels is integral to Merkabah visions, the paraclete, as the indweller and guide, is integral to the disciples' perception of Jesus and in him God. It is notable that the indwelling of the Spirit is an impossible experience for the κόσμος, for it is incapable, because of its rebellious nature against God, of recognizing the Spirit and thus of accepting the divine revelation found in Jesus (14.17).[18] In contrast, the disciples are the spheres of the indwelling of the Spirit. Thus the idea of 'seeing' by union with Christ has in John an esoteric sense more than a dualistic sense and this again is reminiscent of Merkabah visions in which a selected few are able to see God and to have communion with him.

Fruit-Bearing Union

For John the act of 'mutual indwelling' (i.e. joining together with Jesus, the source of divine life) is not static, but a progressive act, which culminates in yielding fruit (15.4, 5, 8, 16). What does John mean by φέρειν καρπόν? Strachan suggests that the fruit is not merely

---

14. Brodie, *John*, p. 494.
15. Brodie, *John*, p. 494.
16. Brodie, *John*, p. 495.
17. See also above, p. 253.
18. For the Johannine understanding of κόσμος, see Beasley-Murray, *John*, p. 257; Bultmann, *John: A Commentary*, p. 616; Barrett, *John*, pp. 161-62; Brown, *John*, I, pp. 508-10.

excellencies of character, but a will and capacity for service, including missionary work.[19] Schnackenburg, Brown and Beasley-Murray interpret φέρειν καρπόν as denoting all forms of Christian life lived in close communion with Christ.[20] Perhaps the clue for understanding this key concept lies in the expressions: 'Apart from me you can do nothing' (15.5) and 'By this my Father is glorified' (15.8a).

The energizing source for fruit-bearing is Jesus himself, for 'χωρὶς ἐμοῦ οὐ δύνασθε ποιεῖν οὐδέν' (15.5). That is, in fruit-bearing it is the very character of Jesus that is revealed to and experienced by humankind. By perceiving Christ's character manifested in the lives of those who live in union with him as well as with one another, people can recognize them as those who follow Jesus (15.8).[21] Christ's life becomes visible in the Church in its exercise of love for one's fellow-being (i.e. union with one another) and of obedience to the words of Jesus (15.7, 9, 10). John speaks of love and obedience as one single component in his theology of mutual indwelling (cf. 14.23) and they are presented as the highest mark of Christian life (13.35; 15.12-17). Moreover, in the disciples' experience of indwelling in Jesus and of his words in them a blending of wills seems to take place, for if they ask whatever they will, it shall be done to them (15.7).[22] Thus John's idea of indwelling reflects neither the pantheistic belief of absorption *into* the divine nor an ecstatic state caused by divine inspiration, but rather it speaks of a community, which absorbs divine life *from* Christ and which, as a result, can intimately relate with God.[23]

The ultimate goal of indwelling, as John portrays it, is to reveal the glory of the Father, for in the fruit-bearing of the believers the world will recognize them as Jesus' followers and glorify the Father (15.8).[24]

19.   Strachan, *Fourth Gospel*, pp. 289-90; so too Hoskyns, *Fourth Gospel*, p. 476; Lindars, *John*, pp. 489, 492.

20.   Schnackenburg, *St John*, III. p. 100; Brown, *John*, II, pp. 662-63; Beasley-Murray, *John*, p. 273. Brown treats 'bearing much fruit' and 'proving to be my disciples' synonymous.

21.   Whether we read γένησθε or γένησεσθε, ἐμοί or μου in 15.8 the meaning does not change much.

22.   Cf. Brodie, *John*, p. 481.

23.   Dodd, *Interpretation*, p. 197. McPolin, 'Johannine Mysticism', p. 27, says that John does not separate morality from mysticism.

24.   The ἵνα-clause denotes the content of the term ἐν τούτῳ. The aorist passive ἐδοξάσθη needs to be understood as gnomic aorist, denoting an act that is valid for all time, though Blass and Debrunner, *Greek Grammar*, §333 (1) treats it

That is, in the daily life of the believers, humankind is able to see God's glory and honour him. We have observed above that John uses the verb δοξάζω to indicate primarily the revelation of God's glory in Jesus,[25] which echoes the heart of Merkabah mysticism. Now the same glory is pictured by John as visible in the life of the believers living in union with Christ. The self-manifestation of God's glory, which was commonly held in the mystical circles of John's time, is given a new interpretation. For John the divine glory is to be seen in the historical life of Jesus and continues to be seen in the life of the Church. The Church could mediate this vision not because of its organizational structure, but because of the indwelling presence of Jesus, the manifestation of God's glory within it. If people could perceive the love and obedience of Jesus being reflected in the life of the Church and if Jesus had given to his own his glory, which he had always shared with God (cf. 17.1, 4-5, 10, 22-23), the corollary is that people could see God's glory in the Church and honour him.[26] This confirms our earlier conclusion that, for John, mystical vision is possible now on earth rather than by means of an ascent to heaven. Moreover, John's emphasis on the responsibility of the believers to manifest God's glory in their daily life recalls the belief of Yohanan's school that a true perception of God includes both mysticism and the daily life lived in love and honour to one's neighbour.[27]

The Joy of Being in Union with Jesus
The act of fruit-bearing, that is, of revealing the glory of the Father by means of exercising love and obedience, is directly related to Christ's joy experienced by the community. This is expressed in 15.11: ταῦτα λελάληκα ὑμῖν ἵνα ἡ χαρὰ ἡ ἐμὴ ἐν ὑμῖν ᾖ καὶ ἡ χαρὰ ὑμῶν πληρωθῇ, a verse that forms the centre in the chiastic structure of 15.7-17.[28] The phrase ταῦτα λελάληκα refers back not only to the injunction

---

as futuristic aorist. In support of the sense 'is glorified', see C.F.D. Moule, *An Idiom Book of New Testament Greek* (Cambridge: Cambridge University Press, 2nd edn, repr. 1988), p. 146; Barrett, *John*, pp. 474-75.

25. See above, pp. 227-30.

26. Cf. R. Kysar's comment: 'The incarnation of God's presence moves from Jesus of Nazareth (1:14) to the community of faith'—cited by Brodie, *John*, p. 481.

27. Cf. above, p. 156-58.

28. See Brown, *John*, II, p. 667; C.H. Talbert, *Reading John: A Literary and*

to keep Jesus' commandments and abide in his love (15.10), but to the whole discourse on the vine.[29] The term 'my joy' indicates the joy caused by Jesus and hence it is the result of the disciples' union with him. It is the result of experiencing God's love that is in Jesus (15.9, 10), of being loyal to Jesus' ῥήματά (15.7), and of reflecting the glory of God to the world (15.4-8). In brief, χαρά in 15.11 'expresses a blossoming which flows from God's realm'.[30] John seems to have in mind the current Merkabah mystical practice in which the mystic rejoices finally at the vision of God on the throne, but seems to correct it by saying that the joy that flows from God is not purely of ecstasy, but an outward expression of the inward relationship of love and obedience.

It also has an eschatological dimension. The expression ἵνα ἡ χαρὰ ἡ ἐμὴ ἐν ὑμῖν ᾖ καὶ ἡ χαρὰ ὑμῶν πληρωθῇ echoes the ἵνα ἔχωσιν τὴν χαρὰν τὴν ἐμὴν πεπληρωμένην ἐν ἑαυτοῖς of 17.13, which speaks of the eschatological joy fulfilled in the life of the Church, particularly after the resurrection (cf. 14.28; 16.16-24, which refer to the joy of the disciples in Christ's lasting presence after his resurrection).[31] Therefore the joy of the disciples is the eschatological joy initiated by Jesus on earth. As the mutual indwelling makes the eschatological joy real in the present experience of Christ's disciples, so also it makes the eschatological judgment a present reality. The removal by the Father of any branch that bears no fruit (15.2; cf. Lk. 13.6-9) and the ingathering of those branches to be thrown into the fire and burned (15.6) echo the synoptic passages on judgment (cf. Mt. 3.10b par., 40, 42, 50; Mt. 7.19). John, then, indicates the urgency of living in union with Christ, failure of which will bring even now eschatological judgment— destruction to those who are not united with Christ and thus bear fruit, and joy to those who live in constant union with him and hence bear fruit.[32] This again is reminiscent of the eschatological judgment and salvation which was part of Merkabah visions in the first century. John

---

Theological Commentary on the Fourth Gospel and on the Johannine Epistles (London: SPCK, 1992), p. 213.

29.   See Schnackenburg, *St John*, III, p. 103.

30.   Brodie, *John*, p. 483. Cf. also his connection of 15.11 with 13.31.

31.   See Bultmann, *John: A Commentary*, pp. 541-42.

32.   In the Old Testament (Ps. 80; Isa. 5.1-7; Jer. 2.21; Ezek. 15; Hos. 10.1-2) the description of Israel as the vine or vineyard carries the notion of judgment. Cf. Beasley-Murray, *Gospel of Life*, pp. 104-105; Haenchen, *John*, II, p. 131, sees in 15.2 the Father's judgment.

seems to confront the Merkabah tradition by pointing out where lies the eschatological joy or judgment.

The Theme of Union in the Light of Merkabah Mysticism
The Johannine concept of μένειν ἐν, then, shows traces of influence more of Merkabah mysticism than of Hellenistic mysticism. Does Philo's mysticism offer closer parallel to the Johannine theme of union? Philo's ἐν θεῷ does not speak of the mutual abiding of God and humans. Mealand quotes *Somn.* 1.63 (1.64 also should be included) to argue that Philo speaks of humans dwelling in God or of God dwelling in them.[33] But this passage actually describes God as the τόπος or χώρα that contains τὰ ὅλα (i.e. all that exists), echoing pantheism and without exhibiting any moral implications. The idea that the cosmos is ἐν θεῷ and God in the cosmos can hardly be reconciled with the fact of the existence of evil in the world,[34] an idea that John maintains throughout his Gospel. Philo does use the word μένειν (see particularly *Ebr.* 212; *Leg. All.* 3.100; *Somn.* 2.221; *Fug.* 13), but not in connection with mutual indwelling. The Philonic idea that 'mystical' union with God can be attained by 'mystic marriage' or by union with Sophia[35] resembles the Johannine idea that union with God is now possible by having union with Jesus. However, for Philo the human soul needs to be tortured by God before Virtue/Sophia comes into it. This is not the picture one gets in John. Union with Jesus, for John, is a gift given by God to the believers. This idea comes closer to Wisdom tradition, as we see below, than to the Hellenistic-Jewish mystical tradition. Therefore Philo's writings are inadequate to illuminate John's doctrine of union.

The theology of union cannot be confined to the Hellenistic milieu or to Philo's mysticism alone. Abelson has shown that Jewish mysticism in the sense of 'inward experience of God' or 'union with reality' is as old as some of the oldest parts of the Old Testament and that such mystical elements are found in the New Testament too.[36] He finds the idea of divine presence filling the people in Isa. 40.22; Prov. 20.27; Job 32.8; Eccl. 12.7; Psalm 139 and the idea of Yahweh dwelling among his people in Exod. 25.8; Ezek. 37.27; cf. Jub. 1.17; Rev. 3.20; 21.3.[37]

---

33. Mealand, 'Mystical Union', pp. 27-28.
34. Abelson, *Immanence*, pp. 59, 67.
35. See above, pp. 74-75.
36. See Abelson, *Jewish Mysticism*, pp. 1-15.
37. See Abelson, *Immanence*, pp. 12-45.

The reciprocal relationship between God and his people can be envisaged in Lev. 26.12; 2 Sam. 7.14; and Song 6.3. Moreover, the dwelling of Jesus in his disciples and thus of God in them echoes also the Wisdom tradition, as M. Scott has demonstrated. Scott finds the use of μένειν in 15.1-17 as forming a closer parallel to Wis. 7.27, which refers to Wisdom abiding (μένουσα) in herself, renewing all things and entering into (μεταβαίνουσα) holy souls to make them friends of God.[38] Besides this, the statement that wisdom will not enter (εἰσελεύσεται) a deceitful soul or dwell in (κατοικήσει ἐν) a body enslaved to sin (Wis. 1.4) resembles John's view that the world can neither receive the indwelling Spirit (14.17) nor abide in Jesus (cf. 15.1-17 with 15.18-27). The statements that nothing defiled can enter into her (μεμιαμμένον εἰς αὐτὴν) and that God loves the one who lives with wisdom (τὸν σοφίᾳ συνοικοῦντα) (Wis. 7.25, 28) come closer to the abiding of the disciples in Jesus. It is not improbable that John has used the indwelling concepts found in the Old Testament and Wisdom literature. The element of mutuality is probably the mark of his creativity nurtured by the Christian and apocalyptic traditions (cf. Col. 3.3; Rev. 3.20; 21.3).[39] However, the notion of 'mutual indwelling' between God and his self-manifesting glory is implied in Merkabah visions.[40] Therefore we do not overstate the case if we suggest that by using the indwelling-motif, which points to an experience of obtaining divine life in Jesus and manifesting God's glory, the heavenly journey of the believers in Jesus, and to the eschatological joy and judgment available even now, John is combating those who took interest in Merkabah mysticism. For him it is not by moral purity or by regular meditation on the Torah or by undertaking a heavenly journey, but by receiving the gift of union with God in Christ and continuing in that union, that one can commune with God.

38.   M. Scott, *Sophia and the Johannine Jesus* (JSNTSup, 71; Sheffield: JSOT Press, 1992), pp. 156-58. For Scott, wisdom abiding in herself is an implicit reference to her abiding in God.

39.   Paul uses ἐν θεῷ in Rom. 2.17; 5.11; Eph. 3.9 and 1 Thess. 2.2 without implying union with God or the idea of Χριστὸς ἐν θεῷ. However, he considers the believers as being in the Spirit and the Spirit being in them (Rom. 8.9; cf. 1 Cor. 3.16); and the believers as indwelling in Christ (Rom. 8.10; 1 Cor. 15.22; 2 Cor. 5.17; Gal. 2.20) and the universe being in Christ (Col. 1.16-20).

40.   See below, pp. 274-76.

The Idea of γινώσκειν in John

Dodd maintains that the reciprocal immanence between God and humans is closely associated with the Johannine idea of knowing.[41] The concept of knowledge is often associated with Hellenistic mysticism[42] and Jewish mysticism.[43] Therefore a study of 'knowing' will throw further light both on Johannine indwelling and Johannine mysticism.

The Possibility for Humans to Know God
According to Dodd, in the Old Testament, in Hellenistic mysticism, and in John alike human knowledge of God is dependent on God's knowledge of humans and John's idea of knowing is based on the Hebrew concept of יִדַּע, which claims that God, having a deeper insight into the hearts of his people, intimately relates with them by choosing them, delivering them from their enemies, and leading them to himself.[44] By using the two verbs γινώσκειν and εἰδέναι almost synonymously, John describes God's knowledge of humans uniquely in terms of Jesus knowing his own, for both God and Jesus are inseparably one (10.30) and both exist in one another (14.10; 17.21, 23). Therefore it is impossible to know God without knowing Jesus (8.19 [εἰδέναι] and 8.28 [γινώσκειν]).

Knowing as 'Seeing'
The human knowledge of God described by John has two levels of meaning, similar to the Johannine 'seeing': the initial apprehension (implied by the aorist subjunctive γνῶτε, for example, in 10.38) and a continuous appreciation and understanding (implied by the present subjunctive γινώσκητε in 10.38). In 1.48 Jesus answers in terms of 'seeing' (εἶδόν) for Nathanael's inquiry as to how Jesus knows (γινώσκεις) him. A similar shift from γινώσκειν to ὁρᾶν is found in 14.9 and in

41. Dodd, *Interpretation*, pp. 169, 187; cf. Brodie, *John*, p. 512; McPolin, 'Johannine Mysticism', pp. 31-32.

42. See above, p. 65. According to E. Norden, the conception of knowledge is a common possession of Oriental-Hellenistic mysticism (cited by Barrett, *John*, pp. 375-76).

43. See Scholem, *Jewish Gnosticism* (1960), pp. 1-10, who attempts to trace out 'gnostic' elements in Jewish mysticism. Cf. Alexander, 'Gnosticism', pp. 1-18 for the relation between later Gnosticism and Merkabah mysticism.

44. Dodd, *Interpretation*, pp. 160-62.

14.7 'knowing' and 'seeing' are inseparably linked together. Jesus' coming from God articulates and authenticates both his knowledge and vision of the Father (cf. 6.46; 7.28). The knowledge of God is mediated to human beings by a vision of Jesus himself:

ὁ ἑωρακως ἐμὲ ἑώρακεν τὸν πατέρα (14.9).
ὁ θεωρῶν ἐμὲ θεωρεῖ τὸν πέμψαντά με (12.45).

Those who perceive the glory of God in the life of Jesus have attained the knowledge of Jesus, which is the real 'vision of God'. Similarly, in 14.19-20 θεωρεῖν and γινώσκειν appear interrelated. In similar vein, one can argue from 17.3, which speaks of knowing both God and Jesus Christ as eternal life in connection with the glorification of the Son and the Father (17.1, 4, 5), that knowing is an experience of beholding the glory of God in Jesus and of having a share in it (17.22, 24).[45] Thus, it is clear that γινώσκειν and θεωρεῖν or ὁρᾶν in John complement each other. Dodd argues that knowing God as a vision in John is close, on one hand, to the direct vision claimed by Hellenistic mystics and, on the other hand, to the vision mediated by Philo's λόγος as well as by the νοῦς of the *Hermetica*.[46] But for John, as Dodd himself rightly perceives, the mediating principle of the vision is not in abstraction, but embodied in a living person, to which no exact parallel can be found.[47] However, the overall picture of Johannine seeing as well as the idea of knowing God as an experience of beholding the δόξα of God, point to Merkabah mysticism as the most probable source of inspiration for the evangelist. Other aspects of Johannine knowing, which we discuss below, support our view.

Knowing as Mutual Indwelling
The knowledge of God and Jesus Christ is rooted in Jesus' knowledge of his own and the mutual knowledge of God and Jesus:

καὶ γινώσκω τὰ ἐμὰ καὶ γινώσκουσί με τὰ ἐμά, καθὼς γινώσκει με ὁ πατὴρ κἀγὼ γινώσκω τὸν πατέρα (10.14-15).

That is, knowing God is based on the unity that exists between Father and Son and this unity is the pattern and ground for the reciprocal unity

45.   Cf. Bultmann, *John: A Commentary*, pp. 494-95, who comments that 17.3 shows wherein the δόξα of God and of the Son consists, i.e. in the fact that God is revealed through his Son.
46.   Dodd, *Interpretation*, pp. 167-68.
47.   Dodd, *Interpretation*, p. 168.

between Christ and his followers, and between his followers and God. Knowing God and this threefold union is inseparable and in fact only by knowing this existing union can one really know God and Jesus, as 10.38 shows: ἵνα γνῶτε καὶ γινώσκητε ὅτι ἐν ἐμοὶ ὁ πατὴρ κἀγὼ ἐν τῷ πατρί[48] (cf. 10.30; 14.20; 17.21). What is the nature of this union? Is it functional unity as 10.25, 32, 37-38 (cf. 5.17, 19; 8.28-29; 9.4) seem to suggest? Does it denote a merging of personalities? Appold has rightly denied the *unio mystica* view of 'merging identities', but asserts that Jesus' inseparable oneness with the Father is unique and revelational, which *qualifies* the factors of mutual knowledge, glory, love, witness, work and the sending-motif.[49] Strictly speaking, the unity between Father and Son denotes the sharing of one life (ζωή), which is eternal or absolute (cf. 5.26; 6.57)[50] and it is this divine life that is expressed by Jesus in his love, glory, obedience to the Father's will and ministry.

Just as this ζωή enables the Son to perform God's works in obedience to his commands, the ζωή of the disciples, derived from the Son, enables them to perform the works of Jesus in obedience to his words (14.12, 21, 23-24). The love of the Father to the disciples is assured by virtue of the fact that they love Jesus and obey his commandments and is expressed in his coming with Jesus to anyone who loves Jesus and in their making their home with that person (μονὴν παρ᾽ αὐτῷ ποιησόμεθα) (14.21, 23). It is by this kind of mutual indwelling that God manifests himself to humans, for the reference to the threefold union in 14.23 is set in response to Judas's question as to why Jesus will manifest (ἐμφανίζειν) himself to the disciples, and not to the world (14.22). Schneider has aptly stated, 'To "see Jesus" is essentially to experience him as indwelling'.[51] God's revelation in terms of indwelling is clearly

---

48.   Dodd, *Interpretation*, p. 169, comments on this verse that to apprehend truly the nature of God is to apprehend him in the unity of Father and Son. Cf. Appold, *Oneness Motif*, pp. 280-83.

49.   Appold, *Oneness Motif*, pp. 18-34, 45-47. However, his discussion centres mainly on εἷς, while it is the neuter ἕν that is used to describe the union between Father and Son.

50.   See Dodd, *Interpretation*, pp. 194-95. Dodd observes (p. 155) that the formula οἶδά σε, Ἑρμῆ, καὶ σὺ ἐμέ, which appears in a magical papyrus, is very likely taken from the liturgy of a Hermetic cult. The expression ἀλλὰ πάνυ γνωρίζει καὶ θέλει γνωρίζεσθαι in *CH* 10.15 indicates God's *willingness* to acknowledge humans, but not the 'mutual knowing' as we have it in John.

51.   Cited by Brodie, *John*, pp. 429, 494.

esoteric, for it is confined only to those who love Jesus and follow his words and not to the κόσμος, which, by its nature, neither loves him nor obeys him (cf. the κόσμος neither sees nor knows the paraclete—14.17). The esoteric nature of indwelling as the intensive form of 'seeing' the Father and the Son echoes Merkabah mysticism in which the privilege of seeing God and of having communion with him and the heavenly beings is confined only to a selected few, who would obey the Torah, although such language as μένειν ἐν, εἶναι ἐν and γινώσκειν is not used in this tradition.

As it is the union of love and obedience, John's mutual knowing denotes 'a thoroughly personal relationship in which the integrity of the persons is preserved', which Brodie calls 'mystical'.[52] It is precisely this mutual and personal relationship, accompanied by the idea of revelation, that distinguishes John's theme of knowing from Hellenistic mysticism in which the relationship between God and mystic is a circular process, causing the mystic to finally claim equality with God for himself.[53] Although Bultmann notes this difference, he argues that the description of mutual γινώσκειν between the Revealer and his own (10.14) is taken from the terminology of mysticism or Hellenistic Gnosticism.[54] But surely John's 'mutual indwelling' has no conceptual parallel with Hellenistic mysticism, but it fits well into Merkabah mysticism. For in John knowing includes beholding God's glory in Jesus and having a share in it. The appearance of God's glory in Merkabah mystical visions is nothing but the *Offenbarungsgestalt* of God and thus God and his glory are one and it is the same as stating that they indwell one another.[55] It is the same glory that is to be seen in Jesus, according to John.

Knowing is Eternal Life

Knowing includes not only 'beholding the glory of God in Jesus', but it itself is ἡ αἰώνιος ζωή, as 17.3 shows. Eternal life, for John, *consists* in knowing the only true God and the one he has sent. The ἵνα-clause in

52. See Brodie, *John*, p. 370, who cites Kysar.

53. So Bultmann, *John: A Commentary*, p. 382.

54. Bultmann, *John: A Commentary*, pp. 380-81. However, Bultmann does not show any literary evidence for the existence of the idea of 'mutual' knowledge in any of the mystical traditions at the time of John.

55. See above, pp. 249-51, 274, for the nature of the union between Father and Son as sharing of the same glory, will and, above all, life.

17.3 indicates the *content* of eternal life and not the purpose, as Schnackenburg construes.[56] According to Bultmann, since γινώσκειν denotes a relationship in which the partners are by nature bound together, it is possible to speak of the knowledge of God and of his messenger as eternal life.[57] Haenchen views γινώσκειν as 'the beginning of man's life dedication and his union with God (and Jesus)'.[58] The fact that John does not use in 17.3 the noun γνῶσις in parallel to ἡ αἰώνιος ζωή shows that eternal life for John is not a static phenomenon, but active participation in the very life of God. This life, denoted by חיי עולם, was expected to be possessed only in the age to come (cf. Dan. 12.2), but for John one can participate in the divine life even now by entering into a deeper communion with God through Jesus Christ.[59]

Dodd argues that the idea that to know the Lord is to have eternal life comes closer to the τοῦτο μόνον σωτήριον ἀνθρώπῳ ἐστίν, ἡ γνῶσις τοῦ θεοῦ of *CH* 10.15.[60] However, this does not imply that John was influenced by Hellenistic mysticism. First, in *CH* 10.15 the knowledge of God is the ascent to Olympus (αὕτη εἰς τὸν Ὄλυμπον ἀνάβασις) and even this ascent does not guarantee a permanent salvation, for the soul, by being dragged down to the body's grossness, becomes evil again. This is not implied even remotely in 17.3. Secondly, the knowledge of God in the *Hermetica* (*CH* 1.3) is attainable by anyone by learning the things that are (τὰ ὄντα) and their nature (φύσις). In contrast, John maintains a distinction between the world (or 'the Jews'), which cannot know God because of its unbelief in the incarnate Logos (1.10; 7.28-29; 8.14, 19, 55; 9.29; 14.17; 15.21; 16.3; 17.25; cf. 1 Jn 3.1), and the disciples who, by faith, could receive the mystery of knowing Jesus and thus God himself (cf. 3.19; 6.69).[61] It is true that Tat

---

56.   Schnackenburg, *St John*, III, p. 172. Blass and Debrunner, *Greek Grammar*, §338, which he cites in support of his view, does not include 17.3. In fact 17.3 is constructed in the pattern of 3.19: αὕτη δέ ἐστιν ἡ κρίσις ὅτι..., where the content of the κρίσις is in view.

57.   Bultmann, *John: A Commentary*, pp. 381, 495.

58.   Haenchen, *John*, II, p. 151.

59.   Care should be taken not to confuse participation in the divine life with participation in the divinity itself. Bultmann's statement, 'It is a knowing in which God discloses himself to man, and in so doing transforms him into a divine being' (Bultmann, *John: A Commentary*, p. 381) presents this confusion.

60.   Dodd, *Interpretation*, p. 163.

61.   Cf. Mussner, *Historical Jesus*, p. 27.

learns τὰ ὄντα in a vision of Poimandres (*CH* 1.3), but this, unlike the Johannine idea of 'seeing', remains a philosophical speculation without any link with human history. The Johannine knowledge of Jesus is not bound to the time of the historical Jesus alone, but is carried beyond the limits of the original historical situation, as the perfect πεπιστεύκαμεν and ἐγνώκαμεν in 6.69 show.[62] In other words, John speaks of the knowledge of God in an esoteric tone. The notion of participation in divine life, along with the implied esotericism, echoes first-century Palestinian mysticism, in which the knowledge of God and transformation into divine life simultaneously occur to a privileged few, who ascend to heaven. But John proclaims the availability of the divine life here on earth in Jesus Christ.

Knowing in Relation to Worship and Witness
Johannine γινώσκειν can adequately be expressed by the Church in two complementary ways: by offering worship and bearing witness.

The idea of worship in connection with 'knowing' occurs in 4.22: ὑμεῖς προσκυνεῖτε ὃ οὐκ οἴδατε· ἡμεῖς προσκυνοῦμεν ὃ οἴδαμεν... The neuter ὃ expresses the person of God[63] and thus the one whom the Church knows (ὃ οἴδαμεν) is precisely the object of worship. Dodd defines Christian worship as the acknowledgment of God's glory that was revealed in the Word incarnate and points out that God is known in Jesus Christ rather than by 'mystical union' with God or by means of a 'nature-mysticism' (i.e. an attempt to attain mystical union with the Absolute through created things).[64] Though Dodd sees this idea in the prologue, his point is well attested by 4.22-25. By treating the eschatological worship as worship ἐν πνεύματι καὶ ἀληθείᾳ,[65] John stresses that such a worship can be offered to God here and now (4.23-24).[66] By living in union with Jesus and his disciples (cf. 14.19-20), the Spirit of God enables the believers to rise above the earthly level, the level of flesh, in order to offer true worship to God. Such a worship gives a new

---

62. Mussner, *Historical Jesus*, p. 31.
63. Beasley-Murray, *John*, p. 62, citing Schlatter.
64. Dodd, 'Christian Worship', pp. 9-22, esp. pp. 13-18.
65. Bultmann, *John: A Commentary*, p. 190. The term πνεῦμα refers to God's Spirit, not to man's spirit, as Odeberg holds (Odeberg, *Fourth Gospel*, p. 170). Against Odeberg, see Brown, *John*, I, p. 180; Bultmann, *John: A Commentary*, p. 190 n. 6.
66. See Bruce, *John*, p. 110.

significance to the temple worship, for in 4.23-24, 'Jesus is speaking of the eschatological replacement of temporal institutions like the temple, resuming the theme of ii 13-22'.[67] The new temple is Christ, in and through whom comes salvation and a real perception of God (cf. 2.19-22),[68] for the expression ἀναγγελεῖ ἡμῖν ἅπαντα in 4.25 indicates the coming of the Messiah as the source of the knowledge of God, of his salvation and of the manner of worship; and in 4.26 the revelation of Jesus as the Christ has an overtone of divinity.[69] Thus we find three important features intertwined in John's portrayal of worship: the mediatory role of Christ, the new temple, in bringing divine knowledge; the inspiration of the divine Spirit to know and worship God; and the initiated eschatological worship at present.

These features, along with the notion of revelation, indicates the Merkabah mystical vision, described in the Sabbath Songs, as a more acceptable parallel to the Johannine notion of knowing and worshipping God. We have seen that, by practising 'community mysticism', the Qumranites acquired a deeper knowledge of God and communion with him by the mediation of the angels, who, as the most holy spirits, represented the presence of God in worship.[70] John seems to take up this picture of worship and combines it with his own formula of 'mutual knowing' to say that the knowledge of God as well as true worship are possible in Jesus Christ and the Holy Spirit. John uses the concept of mutual knowing, because he replaces the angels with Jesus, who is one with God and hence in whom the real mystical experience is viable.

The experience of knowing God or the heavenly reality leads one to bear witness to that reality and this is clear in 3.11: ὃ οἴδαμεν λαλοῦμεν καὶ ὃ ἑωράκαμεν μαρτυροῦμεν (cf. 12.49-50). In 4.42; 15.26-27 the connection between 'knowing' and 'witnessing' is implied. Similarly, 'seeing', 'witnessing', 'knowing' and 'believing' occur together complementing each other in 19.35 (cf. 21.24). Painter outlines the idea of 'knowledge expressed in witness', but he has not given sufficient atten-

---

67. Brown, *John*, I, p. 180; cf. Bultmann, *John: A Commentary*, pp. 189-90; Schnackenburg, *St John*, I, pp. 438-39. For the replacement-motif in John, see above pp. 194, 201 n. 70.

68. Cf. Wohlgemut, 'Where Does God Dwell?', pp. 87-93.

69. See Hanson, *Prophetic Gospel*, p. 257.

70. See above, pp. 95-98.

tion to the verses that directly connect 'knowing' and 'witnessing'.[71] Here also Merkabah mysticism provides a more reasonable background.[72] There is a parallel in *CH* 1.26b, 27-29, 30-32, which describes the witnessing of the one who got γνῶσις (i.e. an entering into God), but we have little evidence to prove that the *Hermetica* were the motivating factor for John's conception of 'knowing'. In view of the other factors that show influence of Merkabah mysticism, the combination of γινώσκειν and μαρτυρεῖν also can attest the influence of the same tradition.

To sum up, it emerges to our view that the Johannine concept of 'knowing' in the sense of 'seeing' God and his glory in their 'mutual' oneness, of 'participating' in the divine life, and of expressing the knowledge acquired by communal worship and witnessing, bears the stamp of Merkabah mysticism more than of Hellenistic mysticism.

Conclusions

We have analysed two major concepts embedded in the Johannine indwelling-motif: μένειν ἐν and γινώσκειν and found that both of them show evidence of the influence of Merkabah mysticism.

The experience of indwelling is based on the already-existing oneness between God and Jesus, which is uniquely life-sharing and revelational, and Jesus' abiding in the disciples. One can have union with God only by being united in Jesus. This tripartite union is portrayed by John by the imagery of vine and branches. The indwelling of Jesus in the disciples is essentially an experience of 'seeing' Jesus and in him God. In John this indwelling is not one-sided but mutual and this mutuality is described in terms of a heavenly journey undertaken by Jesus and in him the believers, which is partly realized here and now in the indwelling of Father and Son within the believers. The Holy Spirit in John functions as the *mystagogue* who will effectively reveal Jesus' glory by dwelling in the disciples. John emphasizes the transformation of the disciples' lives into the divine life that flows from Jesus. Thus he has accommodated not the idea of 'absorption *into* God', but that of 'absorption of life *from* God' through Jesus, which basically differen-

71.   J. Painter, *John: Witness and Theologian* (London: SPCK, 1975), pp. 90-91.

72.   For 'witnessing' involved in Merkabah visions see above, pp. 84, 111, 127-28, 164, 169, and Conclusion (for Part II), p. 180.

tiates Johannine mysticism from Hellenistic and Philonic mysticism. This life enables them to manifest the divine glory to the inquisitive world by practising love and obedience and to have fullness of joy. John does not ignore the impending divine judgment against those who fail to live in union with Christ. All these features are found in Merkabah mysticism. Undoubtedly John is using the Merkabah mystical concepts that were familiar to the people of his time, but radically alters them to stress the personal and historical nature of union with God which, for him, is attainable only in Jesus rather than by contemplation. For John, as it was for Yohanan, true mysticism is marked not by seclusion, but by active participation in the affairs of human beings with love and obedience to Jesus' words.

John presents almost the same mystical thoughts as we have shown above by means of the knowing-concept. His description of 'knowing' as 'seeing' God and his glory in their mutual oneness, as 'participation' in the divine life, and as an intimate experience with God that is expressed in communal worship and effective witnessing, throws new light on the Merkabah mysticism then current and calls the authorial audience of John's Gospel (i.e. those who had been engaged in mystical experiences based on the throne-chariot of Ezekiel) to come to Christian faith.

Chapter 16

THE LIGHT-MOTIF IN JOHN

We have noticed that φῶς appears as a common phenomenon both in the Jewish and in the Hellenistic mystical traditions in their descriptions of the possibility of seeing God.[1] John also uses the term φῶς primarily to describe Jesus and the effect of his mission (see 1.4, 5, 7-9; 3.19-21; 8.12; 9.5; 11.9, 10; 12.35, 36, 46). An inquiry into the Johannine concept of light will enable us to understand whether or not John, by using the term φῶς, shows any conceptual affinity with the mystical trends of his day and if he does, to what extent.

φῶς as God's Self-Manifestation

John treats the ζωή inherent in the Logos, both in the pre-incarnate and incarnate state, as light (1.4-9) and its revelatory role is clearly perceived in the so-called 'revelatory declaration': ἐγώ εἰμι τὸ φῶς τοῦ κόσμου (8.12; 9.5).[2] Moloney thinks that, as the whole of 8.12-20 is concerned with Jesus' revelation of the Father, there is every possibility that 'light' is used here in the sense of revealing the Father.[3] In the Old Testament the phrase ἐγώ εἰμι is used to reveal God in his divine prerogative and his relationship with his chosen ones (cf. Gen. 28.13, 15; Exod. 3.14; Isa. 43.10-11; 45.5, 6, 18, etc.).[4] We have also observed above that ἐγώ εἰμι constitutes a part of the divine name and that in John it is displayed in various dimensions. One such dimension here is revealed as the light of the world, since for a Jew God is Light (Ps. 27.1). Thus, by using ἐγώ εἰμι along with τὸ φῶς for Jesus, John

1.   See above, pp. 66-67, 70, 81.
2.   See Beasley-Murray, *John*, p. 127.
3.   Moloney, *Son of Man*, p. 125; cf. Bultmann, *John: A Commentary*, pp. 342-43.
4.   See Schnackenburg, *St John*, II, pp. 79-89.

claims that Jesus, having a unique relationship with the Father, is the revelation of the one and only God. The attached ἦλθον-saying with the light-motif in 8.12-14 indicates the heavenly origin of Jesus from the beginning of time and his closeness of continuity with the Father.[5] Therefore one can argue with Moloney that the light is drawn from the Father.[6]

That in the light manifested in Jesus people see and encounter God himself is clear from John's description that the deeds performed by those who come to the light are the works done ἐν θεῷ, that is, in the sphere of God or in fellowship with him (3.21).[7] What is explicit in 1 Jn 1.5 (ὁ θεὸς φῶς ἐστιν) is implicit in 3.21. By coming to the light, people express their commitment to Jesus[8] or listen to 'the Revealer's voice in faith and obedience'[9] and by doing this, they become υἱοὶ φωτὸς (12.35, 36). Brodie aptly comments that the light, as someone to be followed (cf. 18.12b), does not denote an isolated Jesus, but a Jesus in union with the Father and that the light comes from the Logos who is in intimate relationship with God (1.1).[10] The Johannine theme of light, then, exhibits the two sides of the same coin: on the one hand, it reveals the divine life or the very characteristics of God; and, on the other hand, it reflects the same life imparted to those who believe in Jesus (3.18).[11]

The revelatory nature of φῶς in John can also be envisaged by its parallelism with John's δόξα-theme. Deissmann and Schneider have argued that the most concrete meaning of δόξα that emerges from the LXX and the New Testament is 'light' or 'radiance'.[12] Although Kittel

5. See Dunn, 'Let John Be John', pp. 328-29; Bühner, *Der Gesandte*, pp. 148-75, suggests that it is the ἦλθον-saying (8.14; 12.47; 18.37) that supports the 'message' stated in 8.12; 12.44-46; 18.36.

6. See Moloney, *Son of Man*, p. 129; cf. J.P. Weisengoff, 'Light and its Relation to Life in St John', *CBQ* 8 (1946), pp. 448-51 (451).

7. See Westcott, *St John*, p. 57; Lindars, *John*, p. 161.

8. ἀκολουθεῖν here means 'commitment' to Jesus (see Moloney, *Son of Man*, p. 128 n. 28).

9. See Schnackenburg, *St John*, II, p. 191.

10. Brodie, *John*, p. 324. Jesus as light leads to the one true God, the Father— Haenchen, *John*, II, p. 26.

11. See Odeberg, *Fourth Gospel*, pp. 290-92, who cites Lindblom in this connection.

12. See Kittel, 'δόξα', p. 235.

dismisses this meaning as belonging to the pre-Judaeo-Christian world,[13] it is not out of place in John. For example, Dodd, who demonstrates a parallelism between δόξα and φῶς from the LXX (Isa. 60.1-3; 58.8), finds a reference to the eternal light in God's act of revealing his glory through the Logos incarnate.[14] The pre-existent Logos was coming into the world as φῶς (1.4-5, 9) and what was revealed in him was the δόξα of the Father (1.14), and therefore there is no doubt that the δόξα of 1.14 exhibits the character of φῶς in the sense that both contain the thought of revelation.[15] John, then, identifies the light with the divine glory that was manifested in Jesus.

God's self-manifestation in the form of light is also known by the close connection John makes between φῶς and the idea of 'seeing' and/or 'believing'. The claim that Jesus is the light of the world (φῶς εἰμι τοῦ κόσμου—9.5) as long as he is in the world is immediately followed by the 'seeing' of the blind man in terms both of physical vision (βλέπω in 9.7) and of a deeper insight (ἑώρακα in 9.35-39).[16] A clear reference to seeing the light occurs in 11.9, 10. Though it is a parable, the notion of seeing the sunlight (τὸ φῶς τοῦ κόσμου τούτου) in 11.9 is used to indicate an experience of having Jesus, the true light, within oneself (τὸ φῶς οὐκ ἔστιν ἐν αὐτῷ—11.10). Because Jesus is one with the Father, he could see clearly what the will of God is (cf. 4.34; 9.4-5) and therefore he, as the one who walks in the daylight, does not stumble even in the phase of death (11.8). But the disciples, who were challenged to travel towards death, could not face the challenge and therefore stumbled, because they lacked 'the inner light which is given by Jesus who is himself the light'.[17] Viewed thus, the ἐν αὐτῷ of 11.10 does not suggest a 'mystical meaning' that one has the light of God within oneself just like the Logos is believed to be indwelling within the human soul.[18] Nowhere in his Gospel does John seem to contribute

13.   Kittel, 'δόξα', pp. 235-36.
14.   Dodd, *Interpretation*, pp. 206-207; I. Abrahams, *The Glory of God: Three Lectures* (Oxford: Oxford University Press, 1925), pp. 52-61, argues that John had the idea of light (or *Shekinah*) in mind in 1.14.
15.   See Thüsing, *Die Erhöhung*, pp. 246-47.
16.   See above, pp. 217-18 for the relation between 'seeing' and 'believing'. In 12.44-46 πιστεύειν εἰς and θεωρεῖν occur in identical sense with a reference to the coming of the light into the world (cf. 9.36-38).
17.   Brodie, *John*, p. 391; cf. Beasley-Murray, *John*, p. 188.
18.   See Sanford, *Mystical Christianity*, pp. 23-24, 223. Cf. the stoic principle

to this idea. 'To have the light in oneself' implies one's close relationship with a deeper level of commitment to Jesus and thus the preposition ἐν should mean 'with', denoting 'accompaniment'.[19]

Possible Background to the Johannine Light-Motif

That God's light can be perceived in Jesus, the Logos-Son, raises the question: what then is the religio-historical background to this concept? We investigate this below.

Poimandres reveals himself as the primal light who existed in the beginning of the cosmos (*CH* 1.4) and from whom came forth the holy word, which is also known as the voice of the light and the Son of God (*CH* 1.5, 6, 9-12). Barrett sees this as close to John's thought.[20] However, in *Poimandres* it is the νοῦς, rather than ὁ θεός or ὁ λόγος, that is the light (*CH* 1.12b, 13). Poimandres's statement, 'τὸ φῶς ἐκεῖνο... ἐγώ νοῦς', seems to be no more than what Bultmann calls 'the identification formula'[21] without any implication of revealing the Absolute Being. Poimandres describes νοῦς, rather than the λόγος, as ζωή καὶ φῶς (*CH* 1.9, 12, 21). The description of ζωή and φῶς as the final destination of the visionary (*CH* 1.26b) may seem to have conceptual affinity with τὸ φῶς τῆς ζωῆς of 8.12b. However, in John this expression, having τῆς ζωῆς as the genitive of source, means 'light, such as the ζωή gives', for in 1.4 the divine life inherent in the Logos is described as the φῶς.[22] Here John is in close parallel with Philo, whose thoughts we discuss below.

For Philo λόγος, as God's fullness (ὁ πληρέστατος... αὐτοῦ), is φῶς, but the illuminating nature of the Johannine light in the sense that it 'dispels the darkness of sin and unbelief'[23] (cf. 3.19-21; 8.24, 34-36) has no parallel in Philo. Similarly, the parallel between John's φῶς ἀληθινόν and Philo's φωτὸς ἀρχέτυπον (cf. *Somn.* 1.75), suggested by

that people have naturally been possessed with σπερματικοὶ λόγοι, parts of the λόγος, the rational principle.

19. Bernard, *St John*, II, p. 378, comments that ἐν αὐτῷ emphasizes the idea of spiritual enlightenment.

20. Barrett, *John*, p. 336.

21. Bultmann, *John: A Commentary*, p. 226 n. 3 of p. 225.

22. Bultmann, *John: A Commentary*, p. 342 n. 5.

23. See Bruce, *John*, p. 36; Schnackenburg, *St John*, II, p. 191.

Dodd,[24] overlooks the fact that John's φῶς ἀληθινόν is not an abstract entity of which all empirical lights are mere copies, but the truth of the light lies in its act of reaching out to humans to illuminate their lives. Philo, who quotes Ps. 27.1 ('the Lord is my illumination and my Saviour') in *Somn.* 1.75, does not refer to the illuminating and the saving power of the light, but only describes God as the archetype of every other light.[25]

Nevertheless, Philo speaks of the illumination of the soul (τήν ψυχὴν ἀφώτιστον) by the divine word (*Somn.* 1.117-18; cf. *Fug.* 139, where he uses the verb φωτίζει). When he mentions the possibility of seeing God who is light, Philo says that this light is perceptible to mind (παραπεμφθεὶς τῶν νοητῶν) and to the eye of the understanding (τὸ τῆς διανοίας ὄμμα) (*Op. Mund.* 71) and that God, being light, can be discerned (θεωρεῖν) and envisaged (φαντάζειν) through himself (light) alone (*Praem. Poen.* 45–46). Similarly, Poimandres too refers to the mystic's gazing at the light, but more in the sense of seeing in one's mind than with the physical eyes (cf. θεωρεῶ ἐν τῷ νοΐ μου τὸ φως in *CH* 1.7 and εἶδες ἐν τῷ νῷ τὸ ἀρχέτυπον εἶδος in *CH* 1.8a). Sanford has these traditions in mind when he understands the Johannine light as a source of 'enlightened consciousness'.[26] Undoubtedly John shares the Philonic and Hellenistic views of the possibility of seeing the light, but for him 'seeing' contains two gradations: physical sight and a deeper insight. Moreover, as we have observed, 'to have the light in oneself' for John is concerned with one's *relationship* with and *faith commit-ment* to the Logos incarnate. Dodd argues that the 'light mysticism' current in Hellenistic circles has been adapted by John to convey the message that the archetypal light was manifested in the person, Jesus Christ.[27] Although this is plausible, we should note that the idea of light illuminating the νοῦς or ψυχή is very vague both in Philo and *Poimandres*, whereas John, without using such abstract terms as νοῦς and ψυχή, expresses the idea of illumination in terms of transformation of human lives from the darkness of unbelief and sin to a life that will

24. Dodd, *Interpretation*, p. 203.

25. Barrett, *John*, p. 336, comments that the Lord, as the Light, illumines is missed by Philo in *Somn.* 1.75.

26. According to Sanford (*Mystical Christianity*, pp. 100-106; esp. 101, 180-81), the light of which John speaks is 'a quality of the ego as such' and it 'comes from a deeper reality' and lights the ego to give forth light.

27. Dodd, *Interpretation*, pp. 204, 210.

exhibit divine characteristics and deeds (cf. 1.9; 3.19-21; 8.12; 12.35-36, 45-46). Viewed thus, the light-motif of John fits better into first-century Merkabah mysticism, which describes the possibility of seeing God as light and of the resultant transformation of the visionary unto divine glory.

Parallels to John's light-motif have been deduced from Qumran literature which presents light and darkness as representing two opposite ways of life (1QS 3.20-21; cf. 1QS 4.11-14; 1QM 1.1-17; 13.12).[28] Also, the phrase 'light of life' or 'eternal light' occurs in 1QS 3.7; 1QH 12.15; 1QM 13.5; 17.6 in the eschatological sense, and the expression 'sons of light' is widely used (cf. 1QS 1.9; 2.16; 3.13, 24-25; 1QM *passim*). However, these texts do not express the revelatory nature of God through light and even the idea of 'illumination' by light is associated with 'the eternal place' of the end time (1QH 12.15, 29). Therefore, a more plausible parallel with Qumran texts lies in the Merkabah vision of the Sabbath Songs, which describe the presence of God not only in terms of כבוד but also in terms of אור that is surrounded by אש.[29]

Odeberg argues that the self-predication, 'I am the light of the world', reflects the characteristics of the Jewish mystical presentations of Metatron (*3 En.* 3–15) and of the first man, Adam (*y. Šab.* 5b).[30] However, these documents that are later than John can hardly be used for understanding John's light-motif. Conzelmann's argument that the description of the deity or the Revealer as the light of the world derives from the world of Hellenistic syncretism rather than the Old Testament or the Greek tradition[31] is unconvincing because of his treatment of both ζωή and λόγος as two different concepts in the Prologue, which actually affirms: in the Logos was life (1.4a).

It is conspicuous, then, that John's presentation of φῶς as the revelation of God in Jesus and as divine glory recall more the 'dazzling light' of Merkabah visions than the 'light-stream' of Philo or the 'life and light' of *Poimandres*. The Merkabah mystical background is

28.   See J.H. Charlesworth, 'A Critical Comparison of the Dualism in 1QS 3:13–4:26 and the "Dualism" Contained in the Gospel of John', in J.H. Charlesworth (ed.), *John and the Dead Sea Scrolls* (New York: Crossroad, 1991), pp. 76-106.

29.   See above, pp. 91, 94.

30.   Odeberg, *Fourth Gospel*, pp. 286-87.

31.   H. Conzelmann, 'φῶς, κ.τ.λ.', *TDNT*, IX, pp. 323-36, 343-55 (351).

further confirmed by the ideas of salvation and judgment embedded in John's light-motif, as demonstrated below.

The Salvific Effect of the Johannine φῶς

By connecting τοῦ κόσμου with τὸ φῶς, in conformity with the Christian tradition,[32] John emphasizes the soteriological function of the light in 8.12, because the very purpose of the Son's coming into the world is to save the world. That is, the mission undertaken by the light to bring salvation was basically anchored in the filial relationship of the Logos with the Father.[33] The soteriological function of the light can clearly be envisaged in the background of the Feast of Tabernacles. The statement ἐγώ εἰμι τὸ φῶς τοῦ κόσμου in 8.12 is set within an occasion of the celebration of the Feast of Tabernacles (cf. 7.2, 10-14, 28). How was this feast celebrated? According to later rabbinic testimony, every night during the feast people used to rejoice by dancing and singing in the court of women which had been illuminated by four golden lamps, and men known for their good works danced before them with torches in their hands (*m. Suk.* 5.14).[34] The celebration was the means of commemorating the presence of Yahweh in the pillar of fire and of cloud, which saved the Israelites from their enemies and led them in the wilderness (Exod. 13.21-22; 14.19-25; 40.38). Since light and Yahweh's salvation are linked together (Pss. 27.1; 44.3; Hab. 3.3-4), light in Hebrew thought is Yahweh in his saving activity.[35] Beasley-Murray shows that the same idea is found also in Ezekiel's chariot-vision (Ezek. 1.4, 13, 26-28).[36] The Jews expected not only the pillar of fire and cloud to return in the endtime (Isa. 4.5; Bar. 5.8-9; *Song R.* 1.8), but also Yahweh himself to be the light in his eschatological coming (Isa. 60.19-22; Zech. 14.5b-7).

Therefore a statement such as ἐγώ εἰμι τὸ φῶς τοῦ κόσμου at the Feast of Tabernacles shows that, for John, Jesus is the bearer of the

---

32.   See Mt. 5.14, where the expression τὸ φῶς τοῦ κόσμου indicates the disciples; cf. Acts 13.47; Eph. 5.8; Phil. 2.15; Col. 1.12-13; 1 Pet. 2.9.

33.   Cf. Brodie, *John*, p. 324. I replace his phrase 'the inner parental relationship' with 'filial relationship'.

34.   See Barrett, *John*, p. 335; Beasley-Murray, *John*, p. 127; Talbert, *Reading John*, pp. 152-53.

35.   See Conzelmann, 'φῶς', p. 320.

36.   Beasley-Murray, *John*, p. 128.

light of Yahweh, which appeared in several theophanies including Ezekiel's chariot-vision, in order to lead unto salvation not only the Israelites but all people both now and at the end-time. Thus the Jesus of John fulfils the Old Testament as well as the rabbinic concept of light by replacing it with his own person and ministry. It is precisely because Jesus claimed for himself the position of Yahweh by using both the ἐγώ εἰμι-formula and τὸ φῶς and thus made the eschatological hope of salvation a universal privilege, that the pharisees were provoked and debated with him (8.13-20).

Within the sphere of salvation lies the Johannine motif of judgment. The coming of the light into the world prompts judgment (κρίσις) in the sense that it exposes the evil deeds of those who live in darkness because of their unbelief and thus condemns (κρίνειν) them, but that it provides salvation (σώζειν) to those who believe in the Son (3.16-21; 12.47, 48; cf. also 1.4, 9-12 and the κρίσις/σχίσμα theme developed in chs. 6–12). In other words, the light, which has the same effect as that of the sending of the Son, 'sets a true standard for judging reality'.[37]

Dodd argues that the effect of the light in the world is judgment and that this has no real parallel in Hellenistic mysticism.[38] But the idea of salvation and judgment occur together in Merkabah tradition, according to which the manifestation of God, as a human-like figure, was surrounded by light and offered divine salvation and eschatological judgment.[39] This implies that Merkabah mysticism was developing in parallel with similar tradition found in the Feast of Tabernacles and that John was familiar with them both.

Conclusions

The term φῶς, which constitutes one element in Merkabah mystical visions, is used by John not only to indicate God's revelation in Jesus, but also as a source of divine life imparted to those who believe in him, the light of the world. We have noticed that the revelatory nature of

37. Brodie, *John*, p. 324.
38. Dodd, *Interpretation*, p. 212. However, he argues that John has entirely transformed the Hellenistic conceptions.
39. Cf. 11QMelch; *1 En.* 39, 41, 45, 46, 48, 58, 61, 62, 71; *4 Ezra* 11–13. The visions described in the *Similitudes* refer to light coupled with salvation for the elect ones and destruction to their enemies (cf. *1 En.* 39.7; 41.2, 9; 48.4, 7-10; 58.3-4, 6; cf. 61.6-12 with 62–63; cf. 71.2, 5 with 71.15-17).

light is referred to both in Philo and the *Hermetica*, but that John's presentation of the essence of the Logos as light has closer resemblence to Philo. The idea of illumination also is common both in Philo and John. However, whereas for John the light illuminates the whole person in general, the ethical side in particular, for Philo light is the illuminating agency of one's νοῦς. Although the ideas of 'light and life' occur both in John and *Poimandres*, the mythological notions embodied in the hermetic 'light and life' are missing in John. For him the light, as τὸ φῶς τῆς ζωῆς, imparts life to those who follow it.

In spite of the terminological similarities between John and *Poimandres*, on the one hand, and between John and Philo on the other, John's conception of φῶς as identical with δόξα, its function of revealing God in a human figure, Jesus, its transforming effect over the lives of those who see and follow him, and its task of bringing God's salvation and judgment all point to Merkabah mysticism as the most probable source of background. In conformity with other themes, here too John shows evidence of polemic against those who had been associated with mystical practices, proclaims that the 'mystical' light is revealed in Jesus, and, by so doing, persuades his readers to believe in and be enlightened by that light.

Chapter 17

THE JOHANNINE LOGOS

Having found that the Johannine motifs of δόξα, φῶς, ὄνομα and ζωή are better understood in the light of first-century Jewish mysticism, we now proceed to analyse the Logos-concept, with which these motifs are inseparably linked. We have noticed that λόγος plays a vital role in Philo's mysticism, according to which God, who is otherwise unknowable, can be seen supremely through his Logos which exists nearest to him.[1] It is worth investigating, then: does the Johannine Logos resemble in any way the Logos in Philo's 'mystical' teaching? Or does it exhibit 'mystical' character in any other way? As 'the absolute, specific, unrelated ὁ λόγος is never found outside the prologue',[2] we will focus on the Johannine prologue.

The Revelatory Nature of the Logos

Brown maintains that the title 'Word' in John indicates a revelation, not so much a divine idea, but a divine communication.[3] The revelatory nature of the Johannine Logos can be examined in its three dimensions.

The Logos in its Pre-existent State
For John the Logos was in existence even before the beginning of time (ἐν ἀρχῇ in 1.1a) and the sphere of its existence was God himself, as καὶ ὁ λόγος ἦν πρὸς τὸν θεόν (1.1b) shows. The preposition πρός here does not carry the sense of 'motion towards' God or of 'accompaniment with' God, but the idea of closeness to God and communion in divine life. For, as Schnackenburg shows, πρὸς τὸν θεόν in Koine

---

1.   See *Mut. Nom.* 7-10; *Conf. Ling.* 97; cf. Goodenough, *By Light, Light*, pp. 27-28; Dunn, *Christology*, pp. 223-28.
2.   G. Kittel, 'λόγος, κ.τ.λ.', *TDNT*, IV, pp. 91-136 (128).
3.   Brown, *John*, I, p. 24.

Greek is the equivalent of παρὰ τῷ θεῷ (cf. Mt. 26.18; Mk 6.3; 9.19; 14.49; Lk. 22.56; etc.) and παρά + dative is used in 17.5 to refer to the pre-existent glory, which the Father had given to Jesus (17.24).[4] Thus, the eternal Logos is the one who existed in union with God before anything was created, reflecting his very glory. This is in line with the Christology developed in John as a whole and in the prologue in particular, for we have seen above that John insists that Jesus, the Logos incarnate, is one with the Father by 'reciprocal indwelling'.[5] The same idea of intimacy is brought out by the phrase εἰς τὸν κόλπον τοῦ πατρός in 1.18 (cf. 1 Jn 1.2).

The sense of such a close union between God and the Logos is missing in Philo and even in Wisdom tradition. Though in Philo the Logos is placed nearest to the Existent with no intervening distance, the term ὁ ἐγγυτάτω used by Philo, along with the other titles, 'the image of God', 'the chiefest of all beings' and 'the charioteer' who himself is directed by God (*Fug.* 101), do not make it probable that Philo meant communion between God and the Logos. As a parallel to John's ὁ λόγος ἦν πρὸς τὸν θεόν, Dodd suggests *Deus Imm.* 31, which says that God purposed to have the νοητὸς κόσμος (= Logos) in his own keeping (παρ' ἑαυτῷ).[6] However, we cannot simply identify Philo's intelligible world with the Logos, for the intelligible world is something that was formed by the Logos (i.e. rational principle) in association with the incorporeal ideas (*Vit. Mos.* 2.127-28; cf. *Op. Mund.* 16). Moreover, *Deus Imm.* 31 conceives χρόνου θεός ('maker of time' = δημιουργός), not ὁ θεός, as the one who has the intelligible world in his own keeping.

The union that exists between God and the Logos does not, however, make the Logos ὁ θεός, although the word θεός occurs in the predicate position in the statement: καὶ θεὸς ἦν ὁ λόγος (1.1c), for this will contradict what John says in 1.1b, 2 and in 14.28. The sentence in 1.1c cannot be translated as 'the Word was divine', for the Logos is not described as θεῖος. The word θεός is not a genus here, but signifies 'the nature proper to God and the Logos in common'.[7] The Logos is θεός,

4.	Schnackenburg, *St John*, I, p. 234. But there is no idea of 'proceeding from' God, as Schnackenburg thinks. Similarly, M. Scott's suggestion of the meaning 'in the company of' does not take into consideration John's Christology as a whole (M. Scott, *Sophia*, pp. 96-97).

5.	See above, pp. 237-38, 249-50, 274-76.

6.	Dodd, *Interpretation*, pp. 71-72, 280.

7.	Schnackenburg, *St John*, I, p. 234.

because he exists in 'the closest union of being and life' with ὁ θεός. As Bruce puts it, 'The Word shared the nature and being of God, or...was an extension of the personality of God'.[8]

John designates the Logos as θεός also because he is the Son of God (or μονογενής), who reveals the Father and his glory to humankind (1.14c, 18). Dunn sees in this sense a conflation of Logos Christology with John's own Son of God Christology.[9] In other words, the Logos is God precisely because he is the self-revelation of God and, as the Son of God, he bears and reveals the same glory as that of God (1.14c).[10] Thus, John highlights the revelatory nature of the Logos by placing θεός in an emphatic position in such a bold statement as καὶ θεός ἦν ὁ λόγος. It is only in the sense of making God knowable to people that Jesus, the Logos incarnate and exalted, is confessed as ὁ θεός μου (20.28; cf. *Leg. All.* 3.207). The Logos is θεός, whose deeds and words are the deeds and words of ὁ θεός[11] because of their 'mutual indwelling'. Thus John safeguards monotheism even while he describes the Logos as a personal being. However, we should note that the emphasis is primarily on God's relation to humans rather than on God himself.[12]

Philo also describes λόγος as θεός, but with a cautioning note, 'improperly so called' and with a firm statement: ὁ μὲν ἀληθείᾳ θεὸς εἷς ἐστιν (*Somn.* 1.229-30). The context of *Somn.* 1.227-30 suggests that Philo conceives λόγος as the place (τόπος) of God's self-manifestation. Dunn holds that the Logos for Philo stands for that limited apprehension of the one God which the mystic may attain to.[13] The

8.   Bruce, *John*, p. 31; cf. the NEB rendering: 'And what God was, the Word was.'

9.   Dunn, *Christology*, p. 244; cf. his debate on this point with M. Wiles in 'Some Thoughts on Maurice Wiles's "Reflections"', *Theology* 85 (1982), pp. 96-98 (92-98); M. Wiles and J.D.G. Dunn, 'Christology: The Debate Continues', *Theology* 85 (1982), pp. 324-32.

10.   M. Dahood argues, on the basis of the Ebla place-name 'Temple of the Word', that the Word was already divinized by the Canaanites in north-western Syria c. 2500 BCE and that when John described Jesus as the Word, he might have been indebted to the Canaanite religion rather than to Greek philosophy—see M. Dahood, 'Ebla, Genesis and John', *ChristCent* 98 (1981), pp. 418-21. Though valuable his observation is, Dahood fails to understand Logos in the religio-historical context of John.

11.   Barrett, *John*, p. 156.

12.   So suggests Brown (see Brown, *John*, I, p. 24).

13.   Dunn, *Christology*, p. 241.

same idea of God's self-manifestation through the Logos is alluded to in 1.1, but it can properly be grasped only in the light of John's oneness motif, which is not the case in Philo. All we can say is that John's christological idea that the unknowable God became knowable in the Logos must have been well understood particularly in the Hellenistic-Jewish circles.

John describes the Logos also as the one who was involved in creation in his pre-existent state. For him, the creation *in toto* came into being through the Logos (πάντα δι' αὐτοῦ ἐγένετο in 1.3). The negative repetition in 1.3b emphatically states that all realms of creation owe their existence to the Logos.[14] However, 1.3 does not imply that the Logos is an intermediary between God and his creation, nor that he is the demiurge, who, in later gnostic thought, was responsible for the material world that is evil, but it implies that the creative activity of the Logos is the creative activity of God through him.[15] Painter argues that God is designated as the Logos in his creative role and thus that John understands God 'as the God who speaks in his works, as the God who reveals himself in all that he does'.[16] In this sense, 1.3 clearly reflects Genesis 1, where God creates everything by his utterance (cf. Pss. 33.6; 147.15; Isa. 55.11). In fact, the first λόγος uttered by God was 'Let there be light' (Gen. 1.3) and the light was the first manifestation of life in the world (cf. Ps. 36.9). As the Father has life in himself so also the Son, who pre-existed as the Logos, has life in himself (5.26; 6.57) and precisely this life is the light for all humans (1.4-5). We have noticed above that the Johannine φῶς reveals God to humans with an impact of salvation and judgment and that this can better be understood against

14.   Cf. Schnackenburg, *St John*, I, p. 238. Taking ὃ γέγονεν with v. 3, as Nestle-Aland and UBS do, gives better sense. It also justifies the evangelist's theology and style of writing (cf. 13.35; 15.8; 16.26, where John starts the sentence with ἐν followed by a demonstrative pronoun; cf. 5.26, 39; 6.53, which gives the sense that the Son has life in himself). See further Metzger, *Textual Commentary*, pp. 195-96. Even Schnelle, who argues that in text-critical terms the reading that takes ὃ γέγονεν with v. 4 should be favoured, concludes that in terms of content, the reading that takes ὃ γέγονεν with v. 3 should be preferred—U. Schnelle, *Antidocetic Christology in the Gospel of John: An Investigation of the Place of the Fourth Gospel in the Johannine School* (Minneapolis: Fortress Press, ET 1992), p. 216.

15.   So T.E. Pollard, as cited by Beasley-Murray, *John*, p. 11.

16.   J. Painter, 'Christology and the History of the Johannine Community in the Prologue of the Fourth Gospel', *NTS* 30 (1984), pp. 460-74 (471).

the background of Merkabah mysticism. Is this true here with the Logos-concept also? Since both λόγος and φῶς occur here in connection with the creation of the world, it is possible that at least an early form of *Ma'aseh Bereshit* underlies it. Our study below will shed more light on this.

The Logos as Light in the World

John presents λόγος as the true light that was coming into the world (1.9). That is, God reveals himself through the Logos not only in creation, but particularly in the world (κόσμος) which he created, for the life in the Logos is light to human beings, who otherwise would live in the darkness of evil, being estranged from their Creator. In other words, the revelation wrought by the Logos has salvific effect in the sense that its light of life purges away the evil (cf. ἡ σκοτία αὐτοῦ οὐ κατέλαβεν in 1.5b; cf. the word of Jesus as a cleansing agent in 15.3) and gives life to every human being who will receive it (1.9-12a).[17]

However, the coming of the Logos as light into the world seems to denote his pre-incarnate coming, as 1.4-5, 9-12 suggests. By reading ὃ γέγονεν with 1.4 (i.e. 'What has appeared in him was life'), Miller argues that John refers to incarnation even in v. 4.[18] However, we can hardly arrive at any firm conclusion on the basis of a phrase that still poses difficult textual problems. Schnackenburg thinks that 1.5 is concerned with the historical coming of the Logos into the world and the time of the evangelist.[19] Against this position, Schnelle has convincingly argued that 1.5 speaks of a fruitless working of the λόγος ἄσαρκος in history just as wisdom, though non-incarnated, was believed to shine within history (cf. Wis. 7.29-30), but to have found no dwelling on earth (*1 En.* 42.1-2; Sir. 24.2-22).[20] Also, 1.10-12b echoes the idea of wisdom as hidden from humans or rejected by them, but revealed to Israel in the Torah (Sir. 24; Bar. 3.9-4.4; *1 En.* 42).[21] It is quite probable that 1.4-5, 9-12 refers to the pre-incarnate coming of the Logos into history through Torah and to the human failure to identify it and accept

17. E.L. Miller, *Salvation-History in the Prologue of John: The Significance of John 1:3/4* (Leiden: E.J. Brill, 1989), argues that the Logos-hymn, particularly 1.1-5, is a salvation-historical representation of the Logos's saving activity.
18. Miller, *Salvation-History*, pp. 90-109.
19. Schnackenburg, *St John*, I, p. 245.
20. Schnelle, *Antidocetic Christology*, p. 217.
21. See Dunn, *Christology*, p. 242; M. Scott, *Sophia*, pp. 101-104.

it. Thus, for John, the Logos revealed himself not only in creation, but also in the Scripture (cf. 5.39, 46-47), although the idea of revelation through Scripture is not so explicit in John as it is in Philo. There is no doubt that for John the Logos is φῶς both in his pre-incarnate and incarnate states. However, the illumination of the Logos can ultimately be understood only on the basis of the incarnation and the revelation in Christ.[22]

The revelation of God through the Logos as light both at the time of creation and in human history recalls the two integral aspects of Jewish mysticism: *Ma'aseh Merkabah* and *Ma'aseh Bereshit*. Dunn points out that the linking of the Logos with life and light is similar to what is found in Wisdom and Philo.[23] Our study also shows that John's presentation of the essence of the Logos as light and its illuminating character has closer resemblance with Philo than with the *Hermetica*.[24] Such similarities between Philo and John can well be attributed to the common use of the Genesis story and to the common Graeco-Jewish environment.[25] Further, as Dunn suggests, Philo is using the sort of cosmological speculation that must have been present at least in some sophisticated circles of his day.[26] Painter also recognizes that cosmological speculation was a popular form for the proclamation of a message (e.g. the *Poimandres*; 1QS 3.13–4.26; Heb. 1; Col. 1).[27] The proposed cosmological speculation can well be identified with the mystical tradition of *Ma'aseh Bereshit*, or at least its earlier form, which served as a vehicle for both writers to present the theology of God's communication to the world. However, it is hard to derive any conclusion before we analyse the Johannine idea of incarnation.

The Revelation of the Logos in Flesh
After mentioning the divine revelation by the Logos in creation and in the Torah, the evangelist states in 'the harshest available terms' (Barrett, *John*, pp. 164-65) the climax of that revelation: in and through the Logos God came to live and to be seen on earth (1.14).

The affirmation, καὶ ὁ λόγος σὰρξ ἐγένετο, which stresses the

22.   See Schnelle, *Antidocetic Christology*, p. 217.
23.   Dunn, *Christology*, p. 242.
24.   See above, pp. 70, 76, 285-86.
25.   See Wilson, 'Philo and the Fourth Gospel', pp. 47-49.
26.   Dunn, *Christology*, p. 229.
27.   Painter, 'Christology and the History', p. 472.

transition of the Logos from his pre-existence to become a real human
being in human history, lacks any true parallel in pre-Christian thought,
particularly in Philo and in the *Hermetica*. In Philo, the Logos never
descends from the intelligible world into the sensible world, but man
must move into the intelligible world to encounter the Logos.[28] Philo's
description of Moses as the law-giving Word (*Migr. Abr.* 23-24; cf.
Rer. Div. Her. 205-206) may be argued as closer parallel to John's portrayal of the Logos incarnate, but Dunn points out that such a description is partly allegorical and partly that Moses is the wise man, the man
of reason *par excellence*.[29] Dunn goes on to say, 'To speak of Moses as
the "incarnation of the Logos" is to use the word "incarnation" in a
broader and looser way than is appropriate to John 1.14'.[30] Philo's
statement, 'Sooner could God change (μεταβαλεῖν) into a man than a
man into God' (*Leg. Gai.* 118) may seem to come closer to John's
incarnation theology, but in Philo it is only a hypothetical statement to
stress the impossibility for humans to attain deification. Now no longer
is the Torah the means to know God as he is in himself, as Philo's
'mystical' way suggests (*Migr. Abr.* 130, 174), but the Logos which
became a person through whom one can reach God (14.6).[31] If Philonic
mysticism does not provide adequate background to John's understanding of divine revelation through the λόγος, does any other tradition
shed enough light on this?

The key lies in the fact that the Logos incarnate is the expression of
God's pre-existent glory which is now perceivable in the only Son of
the Father. We undertook a detailed study of the δόξα-theme in Chapter
13, where we have learned that the revelation of Jesus' glory can be
best understood against the background of Merkabah mysticism. If so,
it is likely that the glory revealed in human-like form in Merkabah
mystical visions is, for John, the glory of the pre-existent Logos-Son. If
our observation that the Johannine δόξα can be identified with the
divine ὄνομα and φῶς is correct, then it implies that the pre-existent
Logos was the embodiment of divine glory, name and light, all of

28.   See Sandmel, *Philo of Alexandria*, p. 95. Cf. above, p. 72.
29.   Dunn, *Christology*, p. 243.
30.   Dunn, *Christology*, p. 243.
31.   Dodd, *Interpretation*, p. 69, observes that, though Philo personifies the
Logos, he is not really thinking of a personal guide and companion. Cf. Bernard, *St
John*, I, p. cxl.

which form several aspects of the same revelation of God in Merkabah mysticism.

Scripture affirms that the Throne of Glory had been set on high from the beginning (Jer. 17.12 MT; cf. Pss. 45.6; 92.2 LXX) and a later Jewish text also reiterates this (*Pes.* 54a).[32] Since the Logos was also in existence ἐν ἀρχῇ, there is a possibility that the Logos had been closely associated with the Throne of Glory. This is confirmed by Wis. 18.15: 'Your all-powerful word leaped from heaven, from the royal throne...' This makes it probable that the Logos had been occupying the royal throne of God in heaven before it became a human being, as John portrays. In that case the link between the Logos and Merkabah mysticism, which Scholem calls 'Throne mysticism', becomes stronger than we have so far seen. The corollary is that the Word that was occupying the royal throne in heaven became man, Jesus Christ, and that just like he was revealing the kingly glory in the heavenly throne, he manifested his glory on earth on the throne of the cross.

However, in no mystical visions that we have examined so far, is there an obvious reference to the Logos as a person. If John had Merkabah mysticism in mind in his Logos-doctrine, why then did he choose the term λόγος to describe God's self-manifestation? It is notable that in most of the Merkabah visions the one seated on the throne *speaks* or his will is communicated to the mystic either through the angels or through a man-like figure. Probably John found this term, more than terms such as δόξα, θρόνος, φῶς, etc., as denoting the most effective way of communication with and revelation to human beings. Moreover, Dunn has argued that late-first-century Judaism felt that monotheistic faith was being endangered by the growing interest in some of the Jewish and Christian circles on the apocalyptic and mystical visions of the heavenly throne, angels and the man-like figure in Daniel 7.[33] Our previous study also attests this factor. John, in this situation, found the term λόγος, which better expresses the 'sameness and continuity' between the Logos-Son and the Father,[34] as appropriate to express the unity of God, even while conveying the news that God has indeed revealed himself to humans in a more *personal* way. Since for John the same word was uttered by God in creation, his Logos Christology remarkably interweaves the two trends of Jewish mystic-

---

32. See Kittel, 'λόγος', p. 135; Schnackenburg, *St John*, I, p. 495.

33. Dunn, *Christology*, pp. xxviii-xxxii.

34. See Dunn, 'Let John Be John', p. 335 and n. 92.

ism: *Ma'aseh Merkabah* and *Ma'aseh Bereshit*. John's use of current mystical traditions again betrays his concern for those who had a mystical disposition to proclaim to them that *the beauty of God's glory and the secret that lies behind all creation are to be seen in Jesus, the Logos-Son.*

Conclusions

Like Philo, John presents the Logos as the supreme revelation of God. Although both the writers recognize the Logos as θεός, the manifestation of ὁ θεός, for Philo it is improperly so called, whereas for John it is θεός because of its eternal existence in closest communion with ὁ θεός. Philo's treatment of the Logos remains only at the philosophical level, whereas John brings it to the historical and practical level by saying that the Logos became flesh, in which one can encounter God. Philo treats the Law as the divine Word that guides people to the knowledge of God, but for John the Word, which had been temporarily revealed in the Torah, became a human who alone is now the way to God. Although both in Philo and in John the Logos is the prime source of creation, in John the emphasis is more on God who *speaks* and reveals himself in all that he does. Due to these conceptual differences, it is less probable that John was influenced by Philo's mystical reflection on the Logos than that both had used the contemporary cosmological speculation based on Genesis 1.

At the same time the revelatory aspect of the Logos, which is inseparably linked in John with the motifs of life, light and glory, inevitably leads us to consider Merkabah mysticism as a possible background to his Logos-concept. For John describes the Logos as the one who was existing with God sharing his glory and light, but who now has become flesh to reveal the same glory and light to humankind. The Logos is none but the Son of God, whose life was the light that transforms human lives. John's stress on the pre-existence of the Logos as the Son, who was equal to God, can best be explained by reference to the Merkabah mystical visions of the late first century in which the pre-existence of the Son of Man/the Messiah/the Son became a focal point. However, in order to preserve monotheism, John seems to use Logos-Christology and fuses it with the Son-Christology. We have also noticed that the pre-existent Logos had occupied the pre-existent Throne of Glory, embodying δόξα, φῶς and ὄνομα within itself. This suggests that

John replaces the Jewish throne-mysticism with the vision of divine glory available in the Logos incarnate on the cross. In short, John, in his peculiar way, has intertwined the two aspects of Jewish mysticism, *Ma'aseh Merkabah* and *Ma'aseh Bereshit*, by using the Logos-concept. By so doing, he seeks to confront and persuade the mystics of his time to come to faith in Jesus, the Logos-Son, who is the revelation of God's glory on earth and who embodies the reality behind God's creation.

Chapter 18

THE ESOTERIC ELEMENTS IN JOHN

We have observed above that 'esotericism', that is, mysterious experience or teaching grasped only by the initiated, but not by the 'outsiders', was an integral part of Merkabah mysticism as early as the first
century BCE.[1] If John contains Merkabah mystical elements, as our
study has proved beyond doubt, more plausibly it may also contain
esoteric elements. We have already detected in some passages John's
esoteric mind. In this chapter we will consider the literary forms by
which the esoteric character of the Gospel is expressed.

John's Literary Devices

Some Johannine scholars have repeatedly pointed out that John uses a
special literary device characterized principally by 'misunderstanding',
'irony', 'symbolism' and 'signs' to communicate the mystery of his
Gospel to the readers.[2] Brodie observes that through its many forms of
contradiction—including shocks, style changes, obscurities, riddles and
breaks—John invites the readers to move beyond superficiality and to
grasp the deeper level of meaning of some of his words and concepts.[3]
Thus by means of 'silent' communication, the evangelist conveys a

---

1. See above pp. 56-57, 99-101; cf. p. 106.
2. See particularly G.W. MacRae, 'Theology and Irony in the Fourth
Gospel', in M.W.G. Stibbe (ed.), *The Gospel of John as Literature: An Anthology
of Twentieth-Century Perspectives* (Leiden: E.J. Brill, 1993), pp. 103-13; D.A.
Carson, 'Understanding Misunderstandings in the Fourth Gospel', *TynBul* 33
(1982), pp. 59-91; Duke, *Irony*; G.R. O'Day, *Revelation in the Fourth Gospel*
(Philadelphia: Fortress Press, 1986); and R.A. Culpepper, *Anatomy of the Fourth
Gospel: A Study in Literary Design* (Philadelphia: Fortress Press, repr. 1989), pp.
151-202.
3. Brodie, *John*, p. 19.

great deal without actually saying it.[4] Sometimes he has allowed
incongruities in meaning in such a way that the readers could grasp the
inner significance of certain events or expressions while the character in
the scene knows only their outward meaning. For example, by record-
ing the astonishment and ignorance of the steward of the wedding-feast,
John silently turns the attention of his readers to Jesus, the one
who reveals his glory (2.9-11). Occasionally, he communicates the
truth about Jesus by making Jesus' enemies speak it out unaware (see
Caiaphas's 'prophecy' about Jesus' vicarious death in 11.50-51 and
Pilate's testimony about Jesus' kingship in 18.39; 19.5, 14, 19-22).
Sometimes the author records people's questions but leaves them unanswered, recognizing the readers' pre-knowledge. Pilate's question,
'What is truth?' (18.38) is left unanswered so that the readers may
grasp that Jesus is the truth (14.6). Thus John uses such literary techniques so that he may lead his audience closely to Jesus and enable
them to see his kingly glory for themselves. Is this true with other
major devices that John uses? A brief analysis will bring us closer to
the answer.

Irony in John

Irony is basically a 'two-storey' phenomenon in which the higher level
of meaning is 'contradictory, incongruous, or incompatible' with the
apparent lower-level meaning.[5] Culpepper cites as examples the dualistic references in John: τὰ ἐπίγεια and τὰ ἐπουράνια of 3.12; Jesus'
origin as from ἄνω in contrast to his opponents as from κάτω (8.23) or
from the earth (3.31).[6] However, the Johannine irony, instead of con-
tributing to dualism, points beyond the clues and glimpses to 'a reality
incapable of being spelled out'.[7] For, as O'Day shows, when irony is
understood as 'a mode of revelatory language', that is, as the means to
make the reader 'really see' the truth, it does not create incongruities,
but intensifies meaning and comprehension; and John's irony belongs
to the revelatory mode which shows 'how' God is revealed in Jesus.[8]

---

4.   Culpepper, *Anatomy*, p. 151.
5.   So H. Chevalier, as cited by Culpepper, *Anatomy*, pp. 166-67. Cf. Duke,
Irony, p. 15.
6.   Culpepper, *Anatomy*, p. 167; cf. Duke, *Irony*, p. 142.
7.   Duke, *Irony*, p. 155.
8.   O'Day, *Revelation*, pp. 31, 43-46. E.M. Good, *Irony in the Old Testament*
(Sheffield: Almond Press, 1991), pp. 24-26, 32-33, argues that the basis of irony in

The presentation of τὰ ἐπιγεία, for example, is to lead the ignorant pharisee to the perception of a higher realm, τὰ ἐπουράνια, and eventually to identify who Jesus really is (3.12-21).

Jesus' dialogue with the Samaritan woman, the disciples and the Samaritans in John 4 shows, by displaying more distinctively the literary technique of irony, how the partners of the dialogue were finally led to the knowledge of Jesus. The revelation of who Jesus is, which is to be offered to the Samaritan woman, is anticipated in 4.10: 'If you knew the gift of God, and who it is that is saying to you, "Give me a drink", you would have asked him, and he would have given you living water.' As O'Day puts it, 'The woman will not be able to interpret living water correctly until she can recognize the identity of the person with whom she speaks.'[9] The readers can identify a shift from the earthly ὕδωρ to the heavenly concept of τὸ ὕδωρ τὸ ζῶν, which, for John, denotes the gift of the Holy Spirit to be granted by Jesus himself (cf. 7.37-39). Prior to receiving this gift, however, the woman should identify him not simply as 'a thirsty Jew', but more as the 'Messiah' and as the one sent by God to reveal God (4.26, 34). It is worth calling this ironical treatment 'ironic vision', for it is in irony that John expresses the meaning of Christ for the world.[10] The ironic theological vision of John is also expressed through symbols, as we see below.

Symbols
According to Culpepper, a symbol as 'a connecting link between two different spheres' expresses something more or something less than its superficial meaning. In other words, it serves as 'a meeting point between the finite and the infinite'.[11] John uses the earthly things such as water, bread, light, vine, etc., as symbols that point to the heavenly reality. By linking them with ἐγώ εἰμι, he elucidates the revelatory nature of Jesus. We have seen above how the 'water' is used by John to enable the readers to know the mystery of Jesus. Similarly, the water in which the blind man washed points to Jesus as God's ἀπόστολος (Siloam = ἀπεσταλμένος—9.7).[12] The symbols, bread and light, point

---

a vision of truth is aimed at amendment of the incongruous rather than its annihilation.

9. O'Day, *Revelation*, p. 60.
10. MacRae, 'Theology and Irony', p. 109.
11. Culpepper, *Anatomy*, pp. 182-83.
12. Dodd, *Interpretation*, p. 140.

to Jesus himself as the one who comes from heaven into the world to transform human lives (6.35, 51; 1.4, 9; 8.12; 9.5).

For John, Jesus reveals God and the heavenly reality to humans and hence Jesus himself is 'the unique and totally adequate symbol of God'.[13] Furthermore, the symbolic languages of John call the readers not just to understand Jesus as God's revelation, but particularly to participate in that revelation by believing in him. The ὕδωρ ζῶν is to be drunk (4.10, 14), the ἄρτος τῆς ζωῆς is to be eaten (6.51), the φῶς needs to be followed (8.12) and the ἄμπελος necessitates the 'abiding in' (15.1-7). Schneiders rightly stresses the two dimensions of the Johannine symbol: revelatory and mediatory, that is, the symbol is the sensible expression of the transcendent and also of participation in that which is revealed.[14] She goes on to say that both these dimensions took place in history, in the life-history of Jesus, and that Jesus is the sensible expression of the glory of God (1.14; 2.11; cf. 10.30; 14.9, 10) as well as the locus of the disciples' participation in that glory.[15] Therefore, the Johannine symbol is altogether 'an historical event'[16] in which the secret of eternal reality is revealed.

Signs
The idea of the revelation of the hidden glory of God can also be learned from John's use of σημεῖον. Nicol argues that the σημεῖον of Jesus, being more than a mere miracle, has a deeper meaning, even while the original meaning, 'miracle', is not rejected.[17] Just like the Old Testament אוֹת, the σημεῖον also refers to 'a symbolical anticipation or showing forth of a greater reality'.[18] In 6.2, 14, 26 the word is connected with the act of 'seeing' and therefore, according to Nicol, σημεῖον implies a deeper vision.[19] What do the Johannine signs stand for? What does the Johannine Jesus want the crowd to see? Brown's

13. S.M. Schneiders, 'History and Symbolism in the Fourth Gospel', in M. de Jonge (ed.), *L'évangile de Jean: Sources, rédaction, théologie* (Leuven: Leuven University Press, 1977), pp. 371-76 (373).
14. Schneiders, 'History and Symbolism', p. 372.
15. Schneiders, 'History and Symbolism', pp. 372-73.
16. See Dodd, *Interpretation*, p. 140.
17. Nicol, *Sêmeia*, pp. 113-16.
18. See Barrett, *John*, p. 76; cf. Brown, *John* I, pp. 529-30; for Dodd (*Interpretation*, p. 90) the σημεῖον symbolizes eternal realities.
19. Nicol, *Sêmeia*, p. 114.

study of signs[20] is helpful in answering these questions. From this study we can list at least two elements that differentiate Johannine signs from the Synoptic miracles.

1. There is little emphasis in John on the material results of the miracle, but more emphasis on the spiritual symbolism. For example, the raising of Lazarus back to his physical life is the sign of the gift of eternal life granted by Jesus (11.24-26); Jesus' healing of the blind man is followed by his restoration of spiritual sight, but, at the same time, a deepening of the spiritual blindness of the pharisees (9.35-41).[21] Temporally also, the signs anticipate the spiritual life and sight that will be granted after Jesus is glorified and the Spirit is given.[22]

2. John presents the miracles as a work of revelation which is closely connected with salvation. That is, signs are not just to be marvelled at, but to reveal Jesus and his oneness with the Father. The healing of the official's son enabled him and his household to believe in Jesus (4.53) and at the end of the feeding miracle, Peter could acknowledge Jesus as the Holy One of God (6.69). So also Jesus' identity is emphasized in 9.38, 11.25-27 and 20.30-31. The ἔργα, which Jesus does, manifest his oneness with the Father (10.38; cf. 5.36).[23] Jesus' signs also reveal his glory to those who believe (2.11; 11.40; 12.37, 41; cf. Num. 14.22). John probably uses the Isaianic prophecy that a sign is a part of the proclamation of God's glory to the Gentiles (Isa. 66.19).[24]

The significance of the signs in John shows that John intended his readers to understand more than what can be seen at the surface level. He uses them as 'symbolic revelation' of Jesus as the Messiah, the Son of God, and his glory. However, only those who believed in him were able to grasp the reality behind the signs, but others could see Jesus as no more than a wonder-worker who came from God.

Misunderstanding
Misunderstanding or failure to understand is another important device, which John uses to give his readers a deeper perception of Jesus' words

20. See Brown, *John*, I, pp. 525-32.
21. Brown, *John*, I, p. 529.
22. Brown, *John*, I, p. 530.
23. Brown, *John*, I, pp. 526-29, treats σημεῖα and ἔργα as having the same connotation.
24. Barrett, *John*, p. 76, maintains that a σημεῖον in the Old Testament draws the attention of the Gentiles to the glory of God.

and themes. Culpepper finds three important elements incorporated in Johannine misunderstanding:[25] (1) often misunderstandings arise from an ambiguous statement, metaphor or double-entendre in Jesus' conversations; (2) his dialogue partners, being incapable to grasp the intended meaning, respond with a question, derision, challenge, request or mystification; and (3) at times Jesus explains, sometimes the narrator comments and on other occasions the readers are given the choice to resolve the misunderstanding.

The term ἄνωθεν in 3.3 was by and large misunderstood or partly understood by Nicodemus. But his questions led him and the readers not only to know the heavenly origin of new birth, but also to identify Jesus as the Son of Man who descended to earth from heaven and as the Son of God who was sent by the Father, by believing in whom one can attain eternal life (3.9-21).[26] Similarly, the failure to understand the term ὑψωθῆναι by the Jews (8.27-28) and by the crowd (12.34) as denoting the exaltation of the Son of Man in terms of his crucifixion led the crowd to question: who is this Son of Man? The author leaves this question unanswered so that the readers can discern the identity of the Son of Man as ἐγώ εἰμι from the earlier reference (8.28), though this will be revealed only when Jesus is glorified in his death.[27]

Similarly, the people as well as many of his disciples could not understand the origin and identity of Jesus as 'bread from heaven', but understood the whole discourse on the flesh and blood of the Son of Man in earthly terms (6.30-60). The misunderstanding of Jesus' statement about the raising up of Lazarus by Martha led her to grasp the inner meaning that Jesus, the Son of God, is the hope of resurrection and life (11.23-27). Ironically, misunderstanding becomes a means of furthering the reader's understanding.[28] Culpepper rightly recognizes that the theme that appears most frequently in the misunderstandings is Jesus' death, resurrection and glorification—all as one event (cf. 2.19-

25.   Culpepper, *Anatomy*, pp. 152, 160.
26.   See de Jonge, 'Nicodemus and Jesus', p. 351.
27.   See Meeks, 'Man from Heaven', pp. 63-64. Carson, 'Understanding Misunderstandings', p. 66, shows that misunderstanding is the characteristic of the unbelieving Jews, whereas non-understanding is the characterisitc of the disciples. He also notes that sometimes Jesus clears away the non-understanding of the disciples and on other occasions they are allowed to understand only after the salvific event of Jesus' death and resurrection.
28.   So Duke, *Irony*, p. 146.

21; 6.51-53; 7.33-36; 8.21-22; 12.32-34; 13.36-38; 14.4-6; 16.16-19).[29] However, the Johannine misunderstandings do not seem to rule out the literal or earthly meanings, as Culpepper thinks,[30] but they guide the readers to perceive the inner and heavenly sphere of meanings through the literal aspect.

Nevertheless, only those who believe in Jesus are able to perceive the hidden reality and for others, that is, the unbelievers and the enemies of Jesus, it remains hidden (2.20-21; 3.11-12; 4.1-15; 6.41-42, 52, 60-65; 7.3-5, 12-13, 20; 8.21-59; etc.), because they are not of God (ἐκ τοῦ θεοῦ οὐκ—8.47) and they discern his words and deeds by appearance (7.24) and according to the flesh (8.15). Although Jesus had said nothing ἐν κρυπτῷ, but ἐν παρρησίᾳ to the κόσμος (18.20), for unbelievers his deeds are still performed ἐν κρυπτῷ, and hence the demand to manifest himself ἐν παρρησίᾳ (7.4); but for believers the words of Jesus were ἐν παρρησίᾳ, no more ἐν παροιμίᾳ (16.29).[31] Just like esoteric doctrines, Johannine misunderstandings, then, enforce a 'marked distinction between "insiders" and "outsiders", between those who understand Jesus and those who do not'.[32]

The Mystery behind These Literary Techniques
Our survey of the four of John's literary devices justifies Duke's observation that all literary devices point in the same direction, the direction that is *beyond*. 'It is mystery, height, depth—hidden significance in need of crucial illumination.'[33] What is precisely the mystery that John has placed behind his narrative techniques? It is not merely the person Jesus, who is the Christ, the Son of God, but, more specifically, his glory, which is the same as that of the Father. This is particularly brought out by Culpepper who states, 'John points to the mystery made present in Jesus, but what is seen in him is glory (1.14), the glory of the Father...'[34] This is presented in an 'esoteric' sense,

29. Culpepper, *Anatomy*, p. 163; however, 11.23-27 is not included in his list.
30. Culpepper, *Anatomy*, p. 165.
31. Barrett, *John*, p. 528, comments that it is unbelief that makes Jesus' words cryptic; cf. Duke, *Irony*, p. 149.
32. Culpepper, *Anatomy*, p. 164; cf. Duke, *Irony*, p. 146.
33. Duke, *Irony*, pp. 146-47. Culpepper's study (*Anatomy*, pp. 151, 165, 180-81) proves beyond doubt that all literary devices are interrelated to one another.
34. Culpepper, *Anatomy*, p. 200. Cf. also Schneiders, 'History and Symbolism', p. 373.

because John, by using those techniques, speaks of the divine secrets (Jesus' identity and his glory), revealed to the initiated (i.e. the believers), but hidden for others. This makes it clear that John, just like the Qumranites, treated the δόξα of God as esoteric.[35] Since 'esotericism' is an element inherent in Jewish mysticism, it is natural that he used the esoteric mode of communication when he had Merkabah mysticism in mind. Duke's point that irony implies that 'beyond the clues and glimpses is a reality incapable of being spelled out'[36] is essentially the same as the central aspect of Jewish mysticism. The author of the Fourth Gospel, reflecting the Jewish esoteric and mystical tradition, seems to say silently that the eternal reality, which is behind all contemplation and for which the mystics are longing, has been revealed in Jesus, the Son of God.

The Community Background

An important aspect of the secrecy-motif, particularly of irony, in John is its presupposition of a community with which the author and his readers alike had been associated. The readers can hardly get a glimpse of the hidden meaning communicated by the author unless they had already been 'informed by the "language-world" of the community for which the text was intended'.[37] The idea that behind the composition of the Fourth Gospel lies a community has been upheld by several scholars.[38] Whether this community consisted of only John and his close associates, or it included Christians from other traditions as well,[39] we are not certain. Culpepper's analysis of the schools, which were roughly contemporary of John, shows that they all contained traces of

35. See above, pp. 222-23, for the esoteric notion found in the glory-motif of John.

36. Duke, *Irony*, p. 155; what Duke claims for irony is applicable to all literary devices that we have examined.

37. J. Camery-Hoggatt, *Irony in Mark's Gospel: Text and Subtext* (SNTSMS, 72; Cambridge: Cambridge University Press, 1992), pp. 13-14; cf. W. Booth, *A Rhetoric of Irony* (Chicago: University of Chicago Press, repr. 1975), p. 28; Duke, *Irony*, p. 151.

38. Duke, *Irony*, p. 194 n. 28, cites R.E. Brown, O. Cullmann, R.A. Culpepper, J.L. Martyn and R. Kysar.

39. See T.L. Brodie, *The Quest for the Origin of John's Gospel: A Source-Oriented Approach* (New York: Oxford University Press, 1993), pp. 144-55; esp. pp. 150-51.

esotericism, if not 'mysticism', in their mode of communication.[40] Therefore the highly esoteric nature of the Gospel presupposes a community in which teaching, learning, studying the Scriptures and writing were regular activities.[41] Our study earlier has shown that it is not improbable that the 'Johannine' community was a 'mystical' community, which used to see God's glory in Christ especially at the time of worship.[42] It is also possible that John, as a priest, himself had undergone mystical trance and visionary experiences. If so, as far as the 'Johannine' community is concerned, 'mysticism' and 'esotericism' complement each other. The presence of esoteric elements in John, then, attests the mystical tendency not only of the community but also of the Gospel.

The indirect mode of communication becomes more sensible only in a context of conflict or persecution of that community by a hostile society.[43] The thesis that John was written in a context of conflict between the 'Johannine' community and the synagogue in the late first century has gained ground in Johannine studies.[44] Whether Martyn's proposal of 'two-level drama' does justice to the ἀποσυνάγωγος passages (9.22; 12.42; 16.2) or not,[45] these passages imply that the Christian community of John's time was in constant threat of excommunication and death. In such a situation it is natural for John to seek to strengthen the Christians in their faith by communicating his message about Jesus in an esoteric mode. This justifies Wilkens's view that John is an 'esoteric' Gospel.[46]

Conclusions

An important feature of Merkabah mysticism is 'esotericism'. Our study shows that John adopts the esoteric method of communication so

40. See Culpepper, *Johannine School*, p. 262.
41. Culpepper, *Johannine School*, pp. 261-89, esp. pp. 234-35, 264-79, 287-89.
42. See above, pp. 230-31.
43. MacRae, 'Theology and Irony', p. 108, observes that Johannine irony, like any dramatic irony, is born out of a conflict situation and that the conflict can be historical or theological or metaphysical.
44. See above p. 44.
45. Carson's argument against Martyn's position is not convincing (see Carson, 'Understanding Misunderstandings', pp. 81-88).
46. As mentioned by de Jonge, 'Nicodemus and Jesus', p. 355.

that the readers, the members of his community in particular, can grasp the secret meaning that lies behind some of the words and themes in his Gospel. This esoteric feature becomes more obvious in Johannine irony, symbolism, misunderstanding and, not the least, signs, which lead the readers not only to perceive the mystery behind the clues—the mystery being the identity of Jesus and the glory he reveals—but also to participate in that vision by faith. For this mystery can be appreciated only by those who believe in Jesus as the Son of God. John's use of esotericism is also confirmed by the historical root of John's Gospel, for the whole idea of esotericism presupposes a community that lived in the phase of conflict and/or persecution. A situation of conflict between 'the Jews' and Christians is implied in John.

Thus the esoteric way of passing on divine secrets gives one more piece of evidence for the presence of 'mysticism' in John, for 'mysticism' in general, and Merkabah mysticism in particular, is concerned with the revelation of God and the secrets of heaven. By using Merkabah mystical ideas along with their esoteric character, John effectively argues that the eternal reality for which the mystics are longing is manifested in Jesus and that those who believe in him will be able to see the glory of God. We have also noticed that the theme that most frequently appears in misunderstandings (and even in signs) is Jesus' death, resurrection and glorification. This means that, as we have observed in previous chapters, the revelation of God's character is very much bound with Jesus' death on the cross. Thus John seems to attempt to strengthen the Christians on one hand, and to persuade the mystics of his time to come to faith on the other, by proclaiming the Gospel that communion with God is possible in Jesus, the Son of Man and Son of God, who, for this purpose, reveals God in his kingly glory supremely on the cross.

Chapter 19

CONCLUSION

We have examined seven key motifs in the Gospel of John—ascent,
glory, king, sending, indwelling, light, and the Logos—and found that
the conceptual and phraseological parallels with Hellenistic mysticism
and Philo's 'mystical' teachings are very slender. But they show strong
influence of the Merkabah mysticism that was familiar in the late first
century. The esotericism that underlies some of the themes and literary
techniques of John confirms this all the more.

Hellenistic Mysticism
We have seen that Hellenistic mysticism is mainly concerned with
acquiring the knowledge of God by means of a 'mystic' vision of God
and by union with him. The goal of 'mystical' experience, in Hellenistic tradition, seems to be deification of the mystic in his ascent to God
by partaking in the νοῦς that God sent to earth. John too is mainly
concerned with 'seeing' God and having union with him, but, for him,
it is possible by means of the life and work of a historical person, Jesus,
the Son of God, who was sent by the Father to the world. The idea of
the mystic's deification is foreign to John. Instead, he emphasizes a
personal and loving relationship between God and those who believe in
Jesus. Unlike in Hellenistic mysticism, in John rebirth is possible not ἐν
θεῷ but ἐκ θεοῦ, that is, by believing in the Son of Man who descended from heaven. Hellenistic ideas such as sending and witnessing
do fit into John's thought, but the total picture of those concepts in John
point to the Merkabah mystical background that was prevalent at the
time of John.

Philo's Mysticism
Like Hellenistic mysticism, Philo's 'mystical' thought also is based on
two important aspects: to see God, τὸ ὄν, and to have union with him.

Both Philo and John agree in presenting the Logos as God's self-manifestation and as the agent of creation. But the close link that exists
between the Johannine Logos and the concepts of δόξα, ζωή, φῶς and a
broader picture of divine revelation in human form points to Merkabah
mysticism as the best possible source of inspiration for John. It is
probable that God's access to humans in the Logos *ensarki* and the
tripartite union that exists between God, Jesus and his followers are
unique to John. The idea of creation underlying Philo's Logos and the
Johannine Logos probably shows the existence of a cosmological
speculation based on Genesis 1, which may well be identified with the
earlier form of one branch of Jewish mysticism, *Ma'aseh Bereshit*.

From our analysis we list below the major elements of Jewish mysticism in John, based on Ezekiel 1 and Genesis 1, and this will show
how John's message can be best understood against that mystical background.

An Ascent to Heaven

The Merkabah mystical experience of an ascent to heaven is described
as a heavenly journey of Jesus' disciples with him to go to the Father's
οἰκία at the end-time. However, this experience is the outcome of the
prior descent–ascent of Jesus. That is, the Son of Man, who, as Son,
pre-existed in heaven in closest communion with the Father, descended
into the world as the Logos incarnate in order to express God from
within human flesh. His incarnate life, works, and, in climax, death on
the cross manifested God's glory to humans. In fact, his life and works
manifested God's glory by ultimately pointing to the cross. Thus, for
John, the mystical experience of 'seeing' God's glory, promised by
Jesus to all his disciples, is possible here on earth even now and hence
it is unnecessary to undertake a heavenly ascent. However, only those
who believe in Jesus could perceive this glory and for others Jesus was
merely a wonder-worker or even a threat to Jewish monotheism (cf.
5.18; 10.30; 19.7). His ascent to the Father, after his resurrection, was
to prepare a place for his followers in his Father's chambers, to come
again to them and to bring them to the Father's house, where they will
permanently behold his glory. This experience of heavenly journey and
heavenly dwelling is already realized in the indwelling of the Father
and the Son with believers. The only preparation to enter the heavenly
realm is a life transformed by the Spirit rather than ascetic types of
practices, as performed in Merkabah mystical circles.

Throne-Chariot

The Merkabah mystical understanding of 'seeing God on the throne-chariot' is reinterpreted by John by using the noun δόξα and its verb δοξάζω, which the word 'throne-chariot' symbolizes. According to him, Jesus, the Logos-Son, who is eternally one with the Father and hence who alone bears the very nature or the δόξα of God, reveals God's glory to humans. As in Merkabah mysticism, in John also the manifested glory is the kingly glory of God, for Jesus is portrayed as a king who, as ὁ ἄνθρωπος, reveals God's kingship to the world not in a splendid manner, but in utter humiliation and death on the cross. The majestic throne of mystical visions is replaced by John with the cross of Christ, whence he supremely revealed God's kingly glory. This means that only by death could he triumph over evil and offer salvation to humans. Ironically, then, Jesus' death becomes his exaltation and the effective means of communicating God's love and saving power. We can hardly mark John's mysticism as Christ-mysticism, as A. Schweitzer has argued for Pauline mysticism. For, in John, Christ is not simply the place in which God reveals his glory, as Philo's Logos is, but he himself is the glory of God and by seeing him one can have communion with God. In this sense Jesus, as the Son of Man, represents the human-like figure on the throne. But the place in which God supremely manifests his glory is the cross of the King of the Jews just like Ezekiel's chariot-throne is the seat on which God revealed his glory.

We have seen that almost all earthly events of Jesus, which manifest God's glory, are narrated by John in the context of Jesus' death and resurrection so that his readers can perceive the shadow of the cross in all those events until they could see the δόξα of God clearly at the crucifixion. Traditionally, Jewish mysticism has been identified as throne-mysticism (for example, Scholem, Gruenwald and Segal have argued so), for the crux of the mystical experience lies in the descent of the mystic on the chariot-throne where he sees God's glory and has communion with him. If John had Merkabah mysticism in mind in his Gospel, it is only natural that he gives so much emphasis to the place of God's glory, the cross, as he gives to the bearer and revealer of God's glory. John also was aware of the tradition that claimed that the Logos was occupying a heavenly throne whence he was revealing the kingly glory and whence he leaped. Since John presents Jesus as the Logos incarnate, he was not hesitant to portray cross as the throne on which

Jesus manifested his glory here on earth. This attests our thesis that John replaces the Jewish throne-mysticism with cross-mysticism underlining Jesus' hour of suffering and death as the supreme hour of his mission to reveal God's glory to human beings and that for him Christ-on-the-cross is the one who fulfils the aspirations and the longings of the Merkabah mystics. We have also observed the oft-repeated theme of replacement that appears in John's Gospel as the whole and in the early chapters in particular.

Streams of Fire/Light

The appearance of brightness round about the human-like figure in Merkabah visions is echoed in John's light-motif. Our analysis shows that John's description of Jesus as the light of the world cannot be fully matched with the light-mysticism of Philo or that of the *Hermetica*. Light in John, just as in Merkabah mysticism, has two main functions: revelatory and enlightening. That is, the light in Jesus reveals God's glory and transforms the lives of those who believe in the light and follow it so that they might be called υἱοὶ φωτός. It is not that one has light within oneself, but it is a matter of faith commitment to Jesus and the resultant ethical conduct.

Retinue of Angels

Although there is no particular angelology in John, he gives a picture of angelic accompaniment. He makes a quick reference to the ascending and descending angels by citing Gen. 28.12 in conjunction with Ezek. 1.1. The enthroned king on the cross is surrounded by hostile forces, 'the Jews', rather than by angelic beings, for God's glory with redemptive significance can meaningfully be revealed to humans only in such a humility. Further, the angelic function of leading the mystics to the Throne of Glory is transferred by John to Jesus, who, as the stairway, will lead his followers to the Father, and to the paraclete, who will reveal Jesus' glory by leading the disciples into all truth. The angelic mediation of God's vision, which is prominent in the Sabbath Songs, is ascribed by John to Jesus.

The Man-Like Figure/The Son of Man

We have also observed that, in Merkabah visions, God's glory was revealed temporarily in a human-like form and that the angelomorphic Son of Man represents God's glory in apocalyptic visions. Moreover, in the late first century the figure, Son of Man, was regarded in Merkabah visions as God's vicegerent or even as the Son of God and the Messiah. John seems to take up this idea and apply it to Jesus, the Son of Man. For John, Jesus is none but the manifestation of the same glory that appeared in mystical and prophetic visions (cf. 1.51; 12.41). The Son of Man, who is the communication between heaven and earth, is referred to in John as the one who will be exalted on the cross which is also the time of his glorification. He is the man, but is at the same time also the king, who displays his kingly glory by being enthroned on the cross. Therefore the glory is seen not in a *human-like* figure, as it is in Merkabah visions, but in a man himself who lived in history and who was lifted up on the cross. Here again it emerges to our view that the Jewish throne-mysticism is replaced by cross-mysticism just like the Son of Man replaces the human-like figure of Merkabah mystical visions.

Salvation and Judgment
We have observed that judgment, which offers salvation/eternal life for God's people and destruction for 'outsiders', is a recurring theme in Merkabah mysticism. John has accommodated this theme throughout his Gospel, stressing the necessity of leading a life that will glorify God. This echoes not only the judgment-motif embedded in Merkabah visions, but also the integral unity between ethics and mysticism stressed by Yohanan. The most obvious reference for the influence of Merkabah mysticism in John's judgment-motif is his description of God's bestowal of authority on his Son to execute judgment, because (ὅτι) he is υἱὸς ἀνθρώπου (5.27), for in Merkabah visions the Son of Man or a man appears as rendering judgment on behalf of God.

Transformation of the Mystic
The result of 'gazing on the king on the throne' is the participation of the visionary in God-given glory and his joy with heavenly beings. It is not an 'absorption into the divine', but a reception of divine glory by him. We have seen that this idea occupies an important place in John. The light that is in Jesus transforms the lives of those who follow him. God's glory revealed in Jesus, is granted to the disciples to enable them to love one another and obey Jesus' words. According to John, the believers thus have the responsibility to manifest God's glory in their daily life inasmuch as Jesus reveals his Father's glory. The fullness of

joy of those who bear fruits of love and obedience is reminiscent of the joy of the Merkabah mystic with the angels. Therefore Johannine mysticism is not concerned with 'merging' of identities, but with the relationship of love and obedience to Jesus, both individually and as a community. If Christ's glory could be revealed more meaningfully only in his suffering and death on the cross, then it follows that the community of believers also can effectively show forth the character of God in their suffering even to the point of death.

Divine Commissioning

The idea that the mystic is sent by God to bear witness to his vision is not absent in John. This is expressed in two phases: the sending of the Son into the world to reveal God's glory and to bear witness to the heavenly realities that he had seen and heard with the Father; and the sending of the disciples, equipped by the Holy Spirit, to reveal the same glory by bearing witness to Jesus. Here also John makes a remarkable change in the traditional Merkabah visions. For him, Jesus is not merely the witness, but he himself is the revelation. This envoy-revealer manifests God's glory on earth by redeeming the world by his death on the cross and by offering his salvation to all who believe.

The Name of God

John's identification of δόξα with the ὄνομα of God reflects primarily the mystical tradition of *Ma'aseh Bereshit*, though Merkabah mysticism too is not out of place. John's affinity with the mystical tradition centred on Genesis 1 is explicit in his presentation of the Logos as the revealer of God's glory in creation as much as in incarnation. The divine name, 'I AM/I WILL BE THERE', is also portrayed in various dimensions in ἐγώ εἰμι statements. John was not hesitant to use Merkabah mysticism in association with the cosmological speculation, which probably later came to be known as *Ma'aseh Bereshit*, enriching it with the theology of 'mutual indwelling'.

The Communal Mysticism

The 'mystical' experience of the Qumranites in terms of realizing a sense of union with the priestly angels in the heavenly temple is recalled in John mainly in two motifs: first, in John's description of 'seeing' God's glory as a community experience (1.14), perhaps in a context of worship; secondly, in his portrayal of the eschatological worship that can be offered at present by the inspiration of the Spirit and in union with Christ, the new temple, in whom a real perception of God is possible (4.19-25). Since, for John, Jesus is the one who represents and constitutes God's glory, it is Jesus, rather than the angels in heaven, who becomes the mediator of communal mysticism.

The Esoteric Character of John

We have learned that Jewish mysticism belongs to the esoteric tradition which emphasizes the ultimate reality behind the world of appearance and the secret teachings that are revealed exclusively for the initiates and not for the vulgar. The same tradition is reflected in John precisely in his use of the literary devices such as irony, symbols, signs and misunderstanding—all of which point beyond the clues and glimpses to the ultimate reality who is Jesus Christ, particularly his glory as revealed on the cross of Christ.

Our study suggests that John has used two strands of Jewish mysticism: principally the mystical experience centred on Ezekiel 1; Isaiah 6; and Daniel 7, and occasionally the mystical practice based on Genesis 1, by making necessary alterations to suit his christological purpose. If the mystical tradition centred on Moses was in his mind, probably it was so only as a secondary source. Why then did he use the current mystical traditions? Does it show that John himself was a mystic? The idea of seeing God's glory in Jesus during worship and the communal aspect of mysticism portrayed in John make it possible that John and his group might have had mystical visions of Christ. John's polemic purpose in using Merkabah materials is quite obvious in his statement, 'No one has ascended into heaven but he who descended from heaven, the Son of Man' (3.13). However, his constant emphasis on 'seeing' and 'believing' shows that he had a proclamative motive to persuade people to believe in Jesus in whom alone one can see God in his kingly glory (cf. 12.41). This leads us to the conclusion that the Gospel of John is a 'mystical' document, written, at least as one of its purposes, to address with the Gospel those who were preoccupied with Merkabah mystical practice and with cosmological speculations. The esoteric character of the Gospel, however, makes it probable that John himself, hailing from a priestly family, had Merkabah mystical background and that naturally he adopted the esoteric tendency to proclaim the message of Christ to his fellow-Christians as well in order to strengthen them in Christian faith in the wake of persecution.

BIBLIOGRAPHY

Abbott, E.A., *Johannine Vocabulary* (London: A. & C. Black, 1905).
—*Johannine Grammar* (London: A. & C. Black, 1906).
Abelson, J., *The Immanence of God in Rabbinical Literature* (London: Macmillan, 1912).
—*Jewish Mysticism* (London: G. Bell and Sons, 1913).
Abrahams, I., *The Glory of God: Three Lectures* (Oxford: Oxford University Press, 1925).
Aland, K., M. Black *et al.* (eds.), *Nestle–Aland Novum Testamentum Graece* (26th edn) as reprinted in *Greek–English New Testament* (Stuttgart: Deutsche Bibelgesellschaft, 6th edn, 1992).
Aland, B., J. Aland and K. Karavidopoulos *et al.* (eds.), *Nestle–Aland Novum Testamentum Graece* (Stuttgart: Deutsche Bibelgesellschaft, 27th rev. edn, 1993).
—*The Greek New Testament* (Stuttgart: Deutsche Bibelgesellschaft, 4th rev. edn, 1994).
Aland, K. (ed.), *Synopsis Quattuor Evangeliorum: Locis parallelis evangeliorum apocryphorum et patrum adhibitis* (Stuttgart: Deutsche Bibelgesellschaft, 12th edn, 1982).
Albright, W.F., 'Recent Discoveries in Palestine and the Gospel of John', in W.D. Davies and D. Daube (eds.), *The Background of the New Testament and its Eschatology: Studies in Honour of C.H. Dodd* (Cambridge: Cambridge University Press, 1956), pp. 153-71.
Alexander, P.S., 'Comparing Merkabah Mysticism and Gnosticism: An Essay in Method', *JJS* 35 (1984), pp. 1-18.
—'3 (Hebrew Apocalypse of) Enoch', *OTP*, I, pp. 223-315.
—'The Family of Caesar and the Family of God: The Image of the Emperor in the Heikhalot Literature', in L.C.A. Alexander (ed.), *Images of Empire* (Sheffield: JSOT Press, 1991), pp. 276-97.
—'The Historical Setting of the Hebrew Book of Enoch', *JJS* 28 (1977), pp. 156-80.
—(ed. and trans.), *Textual Sources for the Study of Judaism* (Manchester: Manchester University Press, 1984).
Andersen, F.I., '2 (Slavonic Apocalypse of) Enoch', *OTP*, I, pp. 91-213.
Appasamy, A.J., 'The Mysticism of Hindu Bhakti Literature, Considered Especially with Reference to the Mysticism of the Fourth Gospel' (DPhil Thesis, University of Oxford, 1922).
Appold, M.L., *The Oneness Motif in the Fourth Gospel: Motif Analysis and Exegetical Probe into the Theology of John* (WUNT, 2.1; Tübingen: J.C.B. Mohr [Paul Siebeck], 1976).
Argyle, A.W., 'Philo and the Fourth Gospel', *ExpTim* 63 (1951–52), pp. 385-86.
Ashton, J., *Understanding the Fourth Gospel* (Oxford: Clarendon Press, 1991).
—*Studying John: Approaches to the Fourth Gospel* (Oxford: Clarendon Press, 1994).
Aune, D.E., 'Christian Prophecy and the Messianic Status of Jesus', in J.H. Charlesworth (ed.), *The Messiah: Developments in Earliest Judaism and Christianity* (Minneapolis: Fortress Press, 1992), pp. 404-22.

Augustine, St, *Homilies on the Gospel According to St John and his First Epistle* (2 vols.; trans. H. Browne; Oxford: John Henry Parker, 1848–49).

Balthasar, H.U. von, *The Glory of the Lord: A Theological Aesthetics*. I. *Seeing the Form* (Edinburgh: T. & T. Clark, 1982).

Balz, H.R., *Methodische Probleme der neutestamentlichen Christologie* (WMANT, 25; Neukirchen–Vluyn: Neukirchener Verlag, 1967).

Barker, M., *The Great Angel: A Study of Israel's Second God* (London: SPCK, 1992).

Barrett, C.K., 'Christocentric or Theocentric? Observations on the Theological Method of the Fourth Gospel', in *idem*, *Essays on John* (London: SPCK, 1982), pp. 1-18.

—*A Commentary on the Second Epistle to the Corinthians* (HNTC; New York: Harper & Row, 1973).

—' "The Father is Greater than I" John 14.28: Subordinationist Christology in the New Testament', in *idem*, *Essays on John*, pp. 19-36.

—'The Flesh of the Son of Man', in *idem*, *Essays on John*, pp. 37-49.

—*The Gospel According to St John* (London: SPCK, 1955).

—*The Gospel According to St John* (Philadelphia: Westminster Press, 2nd edn, 1978).

—*The Gospel of John and Judaism* (London: SPCK, 1975).

—(ed.), *The New Testament Background: Selected Documents* (London: SPCK, rev. edn, repr. 1993).

—'The Old Testament in the Fourth Gospel', *JTS* 48 (1947), pp. 155-69.

Barton, J.M.T., 'The Ascension of Isaiah', in H.F.D. Sparks (ed.), *The Apocryphal Old Testament* (Oxford: Clarendon Press, 1984), pp. 775-812.

Bauer, W., *Das Johannes-Evangelium* (HNT, 6; Tübingen: J.C.B. Mohr [Paul Siebeck], 3rd edn, 1933).

Bauer, W., W.F. Arndt, and F.W. Gingrich, *A Greek–English Lexicon of the New Testament and Other Early Christian Literature* (Chicago: University of Chicago Press, rev. 2nd edn, 1979).

Beasley-Murray, G.R., *Gospel of Life: Theology in the Fourth Gospel* (Peabody, MA: Hendrickson, 1991).

—*John* (WBC, 36; Dallas: Word Books, 1987).

—'John 3:3,5: Baptism, Spirit and the Kingdom', *ExpTim* 97 (1986), pp. 167-70.

—'The Mission of the Logos-Son', in F. van Segbroeck *et al.* (eds.), *The Four Gospels 1992* (3 vols.; Festschrift F. Neirynck; Leuven: Leuven University Press, 1992), III, pp. 1855-68.

Bernard, J.H., *A Critical and Exegetical Commentary on the Gospel According to St John* (ICC; 2 vols.; Edinburgh: T. & T. Clark, repr. 1948–49).

Bietenhard, H., *Die himmlische Welt im Urchristentum und Spätjudentum* (WUNT, 2; Tübingen: J.C.B. Mohr [Paul Siebeck], 1951).

—'ὄνομα', *TDNT*, V, pp. 242-83.

Biram, A., 'Ma'aseh Bereshit; Ma'aseh Merkabah', *JewEnc*, VIII, pp. 235-36.

Black, D.A., 'The Text of John 3:13', *GTJ* 6 (1985), pp. 49-66.

Black, M. (ed.), *Apocalypsis Henochi Graece: Fragmenta Pseudepigraphorum Quae Supersunt Graeca* (Leiden: E.J. Brill, 1970).

—*An Aramaic Approach to the Gospels and Acts* (Oxford: Clarendon Press, 2nd edn, 1954).

—*The Book of Enoch or 1 Enoch* (Leiden: E.J. Brill, 1985).

—'The Eschatology of the Similitudes of Enoch', *JTS* 3 (1952), pp. 1-10.

—'The Throne-Theophany Prophetic Commission and the "Son of Man": A Study in

Tradition History', in R. Hamerton-Kelly and R. Scroggs (eds.), *Jews, Greeks and Christians: Religious Cultures in Late Antiquity* (Festschrift W.D. Davies; Leiden: E.J. Brill, 1976), pp. 57-73.

Blass, F., A. Debrunner and R.W. Funk, *A Greek Grammar of the New Testament and Other Early Christian Literature* (Chicago: University of Chicago Press, 1961).

Bliss, A.J., *A Dictionary of Foreign Words and Phrases* (London: Routledge & Kegan Paul, repr. 1972).

Booth, W., *A Rhetoric of Irony* (Chicago: University of Chicago Press, repr. 1975).

Borgen, P., *Bread from Heaven: An Exegetical Study of the Concept of Manna in the Gospel of John and the Writings of Philo* (NovTSup, 10; Leiden: E.J. Brill, 1965).

—'God's Agent in the Fourth Gospel', in J. Neusner (ed.), *Religions in Antiquity: Essays in Memory of E.R. Goodenough* (NumSup, 14; Leiden: E.J. Brill, 1968), pp. 137-48 (reprinted in Borgen, *Philo, John and Paul: New Perspectives on Judaism and Early Christianity* [BJS, 131; Atlanta: Scholars Press, 1987], pp. 171-84).

—'Observations on the Targumic Character of the Prologue of John', in *idem, Logos Was the True Light and Other Essays on the Gospel of John* (Trondheim: TAPIR Publishers, 1983), pp. 13-20.

—'Some Jewish Exegetical Traditions as Background for Son of Man Sayings in John's Gospel (Jn 3,13-14) and Context', in M. de Jonge (ed.), *L'évangile de Jean: Sources, rédaction, theólogie* (Leuven: Leuven University Press, 1977), pp. 243-58 (reprinted as 'The Son of Man Saying in John 3:13-14', in Borgen, *Logos Was the True Light and Other Essays on the Gospel of John*, pp. 133-48; and also in *idem, Philo, John and Paul*, pp. 103-20).

—'The Unity of the Discourse in John 6', in *idem, Logos Was the True Light and Other Essays on the Gospel of John*, pp. 21-29.

Bornkamm, G., 'Die eucharistische Rede im Johannes-Evangelium', *ZNW* 47 (1956), pp. 161-69.

—'μυστήριον, μυέω', *TDNT*, IV, pp. 802-28.

Borsch, F.H., *The Son of Man in Myth and History* (London: SCM Press, 1967).

Bousset, W., *Die Himmelreise der Seele* (Darmstadt: Wissenschaftliche Buchgesellschaft, 1971).

Bowker, J.W., '"Merkabah" Visions and the Visions of Paul', *JSS* 16 (1971), pp. 157-73.

Bowman, J., 'The Background of the Term "Son of Man"', *ExpTim* 59 (1947–48), pp. 283-88.

Box, G.H., *The Apocalypse of Abraham* (London: SPCK, 1918).

—*The Ezra-Apocalypse* (London: Pitman, 1912).

—*The Testament of Abraham* (London: SPCK, 1927).

Boyd, R.H.S., *An Introduction to Indian Christian Theology* (Delhi: ISPCK, repr. 1989), pp. 110-43.

Bratcher, R.G., 'What does "Glory" mean in Relation to Jesus? Translating *doxa* and *doxazo* in John', *BT* 42 (1991), pp. 401-408.

Brodie, T.L., *The Gospel According to John* (New York: Oxford University Press, 1993).

—*The Quest for the Origin of John's Gospel: A Source-Oriented Approach* (New York: Oxford University Press, 1993).

Brooke, G.J., *Exegesis at Qumran* (Sheffield: JSOT Press, 1985).

Brown, R.E., *The Community of the Beloved Disciple* (New York: Paulist Press, 1979).

—*The Gospel According to John* (AB, 29, 29A; 2 vols.; New York: Doubleday, 1966, 1970).

—*The Semitic Background of the Term 'Mystery' in the New Testament* (FBBS, 21; Philadelphia: Fortress Press, 1968).

Brownlee, W.H., *Ezekiel 1–19* (WBC, 28; Waco, TX: Word Books, 1986).

—'Whence the Gospel According to John?', in J.H. Charlesworth (ed.), *John and the Dead Sea Scrolls* (New York: Crossroad, 1991), pp. 166-94.

Bruce, F.F., *The Gospel of John* (Grand Rapids: Eerdmans, 1992).

—'The Oldest Greek Version of Daniel', *OTS* 20 (1977), pp. 25-26.

Brückner, K., 'A Word Study of *Doxazo* in the Gospel of John', *NOT* 2 (1988), pp. 41-46.

Bühner, Jan-A., *Der Gesandte und sein Weg im 4. Evangelium: Die kultur- und religions- geschichtlichen Grundlagen der johanneischen Sendungschristologie sowie ihre traditionsgeschichtliche Entwicklung* (WUNT, 2.2; Tübingen: J.C.B. Mohr [Paul Siebeck], 1977).

Bultmann, R., 'Die Bedeutung der neuerschlossenen mandäischen und manichäischen Quellen für das Verständnis des Johannesevangeliums', *ZNW* 24 (1925), pp. 104- 109.

— 'γινώσκω, κ.τ.λ.', *TDNT*, I, pp. 689-719.

—*The Gospel of John: A Commentary* (Philadelphia: Westminster Press, ET 1971).

—*Theology of the New Testament* (2 vols.; London: SCM Press, ET 1955).

Burkett, D., *The Son of the Man in the Gospel of John* (JSNTSup, 56; Sheffield: JSOT Press, 1991).

Burney, C.F., *The Aramaic Origin of the Fourth Gospel* (Oxford: Clarendon Press, 1922).

Cadman, W.H., *The Open Heaven: The Revelation of God in the Johannine Sayings of Jesus* (Oxford: Basil Blackwell, 1969).

Caird, G.B., 'The Glory of God in the Fourth Gospel: An Exercise in Biblical Semantics', *NTS* 15 (1968–69), pp. 265-77.

Camery-Hoggatt, J., *Irony in Mark's Gospel: Text and Subtext* (SNTSMS, 72; Cambridge: Cambridge University Press, 1992).

Caragounis, C.C., *The Son of Man: Vision and Interpretation* (Tübingen: J.C.B. Mohr [Paul Siebeck], 1986).

Carrell, P.R., 'Jesus and the Angels: The Influence of Angelology on the Christology of the Apocalypse of John' (PhD Thesis, University of Durham, 1993).

Carrol, K.L., 'The Fourth Gospel and the Exclusion of Christians from the Synagogues', *BJRL* 40 (1957–58), pp. 19-32.

Carson, D.A., *The Gospel According to John* (Leicester: IVP; Grand Rapids: Eerdmans, 1991).

—'Understanding Misunderstandings in the Fourth Gospel', *TynBul* 33 (1982), pp. 59-91.

Casey, M., *Son of Man: The Interpretation and Influence of Daniel 7* (London: SPCK, 1979).

—'The Use of the Term "Son of Man" in the Similitudes of Enoch', *JSJ* 7 (1976), pp. 11- 29.

Charan Singh, M., *St John the Great Mystic* (Punjab: Radha Soami Satsang Beas, 3rd edn, 1974).

Charles, R.H., *The Apocrypha and Pseudepigrapha of the Old Testament* (2 vols.; Oxford: Oxford University Press, 1913).

—*The Ascension of Isaiah* (London: SPCK, 1917).

—*The Book of Enoch or 1 Enoch* (Oxford: Clarendon Press, 1st edn, 1893 and 2nd edn, 1912).

—*The Book of the Secrets of Enoch* (Oxford: Clarendon Press, 1896).

—*A Critical and Exegetical Commentary on the Book of Daniel* (Oxford: Clarendon Press, 1929).

—*A Critical and Exegetical Commentary on the Revelation of St John* (2 vols.; ICC; Edinburgh: T. & T. Clark, 1920).

Charlesworth, J.H., 'A Critical Comparison of the Dualism in 1QS 3:13–4:26 and the "Dualism" Contained in the Gospel of John', in Charlesworth (ed.), *John and the Dead Sea Scrolls*), pp. 76-106.

—(ed.), *The Old Testament Pseudepigrapha* (2 vols.; New York: Doubleday, 1983–1985).

—*The Pseudepigrapha and Modern Research with a Supplement* (Chico, CA: Scholars Press, 1981).

Chernus, I., *Mysticism in Rabbinic Judaism: Studies in the History of Midrash* (SJ, 11; Berlin: W. de Gruyter, 1982).

—'Visions of God in Merkabah Mysticism', *JSJ* 13 (1982), pp. 123-46.

Chilton, B.D., *The Glory of Israel: The Theology and Provenience of the Isaiah Targum* (JSOTSup, 23; Sheffield: JSOT Press, 1983).

—*The Isaiah Targum: Introduction, Translation, Apparatus and Notes* (Edinburgh: T. & T. Clark, 1987).

—'John XII. 34 and Targum Isaiah LII. 13', *NovT* 22 (1980), pp. 176-78.

—'Regnum Dei Deus Est', in *idem*, *Targumic Approaches to the Gospels: Essays in the Mutual Definition of Judaism and Christianity* (New York: Lanham, 1986), pp. 99-107.

Cohen, M.S., *The Shi'ur Qomah: Liturgy and Theurgy in Pre-Kabbalistic Jewish Mysticism* (New York: Lanham, 1983).

Collins, A.Y., 'The "Son of Man" Tradition and the Book of Revelation', in Charlesworth (ed.), *The Messiah*, pp. 536-68.

Collins, J.J., 'The Son of Man and the Saints of the Most High in the Book of Daniel', *JBL* 93 (1974), pp. 50-66.

—'The Son of Man in First Century Judaism', *NTS* 38 (1992), pp. 448-66.

Colpe, C., 'ὁ υἱὸς τοῦ ἀνθρώπου', *TDNT*, VIII, pp. 420-29, 464-70.

Colson, F.H., G.H. Whitaker *et al.* (trans.), *Philo* (12 vols.; LCL; Cambridge, MA: Harvard University Press, repr. 1979–93).

Colwell, E.C., 'A Definite Rule for the Use of the Article in the Greek New Testament', *JBL* 52 (1933), pp. 12-21.

Conzelmann, H., 'φως, κ.τ.λ.', *TDNT*, IX, pp. 323-36, 343-55.

Cook, W.R., 'The "Glory" Motif in the Johannine Corpus', *JETS* 27 (1984), pp. 291-97.

Copenhaver, B.P., *Hermetica: The Greek Corpus Hermeticum and the Latin Asclepius in a New English Translation, with Notes and Introduction* (Cambridge: Cambridge University Press, 1992).

Countryman, L.W., *The Mystical Way in the Fourth Gospel* (Philadelphia: Fortress Press, 1987).

Coutts, J., 'The Messianic Secret in St John's Gospel', *SE* 3 (ed. F.L. Cross; TU 88; Berlin: Akademie Verlag, 1964), pp. 45-57.

Cullmann, O., *Early Christian Worship* (London: SCM Press, 1953).

Culpepper, R.A., *Anatomy of the Fourth Gospel: A Study in Literary Design* (Philadelphia: Fortress Press, repr. 1989).

—*The Johannine School: An Evaluation of the Johannine-School Hypothesis Based on an Investigation of the Nature of Ancient Schools* (SBLDS, 26; Missoula, MT: Scholars Press, 1975).

Dahl, N.A., 'The Johannine Church and History', in W. Klassen and G.F. Snyder (eds.), *Current Issues in New Testament Interpretation: Essays in Honour of O.A. Piper* (New York: Harper & Row, 1962), pp. 124-42.

Dahn, K., 'See (ὁράω)', *NIDNTT*, III, pp. 511-18.

Dahood, M., 'Ebla, Genesis and John', *ChristCent* 98 (1981), pp. 418-21.

Dan, J., 'Mysticism in Jewish History, Religion and Literature', in J. Dan and F. Talmage (eds.), *Studies in Jewish Mysticism* (Cambridge, MA: Association for Jewish Studies, 1982), pp. 1-14.

—'The Religious Experience of the Merkavah', in A. Green (ed.), *Jewish Spirituality*. I. *From the Bible through the Middle Ages* (London: Routledge & Kegan Paul, 1986), pp. 289-307.

—'The Revelation of the Secret of the World: The Beginning of Jewish Mysticism in Late Antiquity' (Brown University Program in Judaic Studies Occasional Paper No. 2; Rhode Island: Brown University, 1992).

Danby, H., *The Mishnah* (Oxford: Clarendon Press, 1933).

Davidson, A.B., *Hebrew Syntax* (Edinburgh: T. & T. Clark, 3rd edn, repr. 1954).

Dean-Otting, M., *Heavenly Journeys: A Study of the Motif in Hellenistic Jewish Literature* (JU, 8; Frankfurt: Peter Lang, 1984).

Derrett, J.D.M., 'Christ, King and Witness (John 18,37)', *BeO* 31 (1989), pp. 189-98.

—'The Parable of the Wicked Vinedressers', in *idem*, *Law in the New Testament* (London: Darton, Longman & Todd, 1970), pp. 286-312.

Dodd, C.H., *The Bible and the Greeks* (London: Hodder & Stoughton, 2nd edn, 1954).

—*Historical Tradition in the Fourth Gospel* (Cambridge: Cambridge University Press, repr. 1965).

—*The Interpretation of the Fourth Gospel* (Cambridge, Cambridge University Press, repr. 1958).

—'The Prologue to the Fourth Gospel and Christian Worship', in F.L. Cross (ed.), *Studies in the Fourth Gospel* (London: A.R. Mowbray, 1957), pp. 9-22.

Duke, P.D., *Irony in the Fourth Gospel* (Atlanta: John Knox Press, 1985).

Dunn, J.D.G., 'Christology as an Aspect of Theology', in A.J. Malherbe and W.A. Meeks (eds.), *The Future of Christology: Essays in Honour of L.E. Keck* (Minneapolis: Fortress Press, 1993), pp. 202-12.

—*Christology in the Making: An Inquiry into the Origins of the Doctrine of the Incarnation* (London: SCM Press, 2nd edn, 1989).

—'The Colossian Philosophy: A Confident Jewish Apologia', *Bib* 76 (1995), pp. 153-81.

—*Jesus and the Spirit: A Study of the Religious and Charismatic Experience of Jesus and the First Christians as Reflected in the New Testament* (Philadelphia: Westminster Press, 1975).

—'John VI: A Eucharistic Discourse?', *NTS* 17 (1970–71), pp. 328-38.

—'Let John Be John: A Gospel for its Time', in P. Stuhlmacher (ed.), *Das Evangelium und die Evangelien: Vorträge vom Tübinger Symposium 1982* (WUNT, 28; Tübingen: J.C.B. Mohr [Paul Siebeck], 1983), pp. 309-39 (reprinted in P. Stuhlmacher [ed.], *The Gospel and the Gospels* [Grand Rapids: Eerdmans, 1991], pp. 293-322).

—*The Partings of the Ways: Between Christianity and Judaism and their Significance for the Character of Christianity* (London: SCM Press; Philadelphia: Trinity Press International, 1991).

—*Romans 9–16* (WBC, 38B; Dallas: Word Books, 1988).

—'Some Thoughts on Maurice Wiles's "Reflections" ', *Theology* 85 (1982), pp. 92-98.

—'The Washing of the Disciples' Feet in John 13.1-20', *ZNW* 61 (1970), pp. 246-52.

Dupont-Sommer, A., *The Essene Writings from Qumran* (Oxford: Basil Blackwell, 1961).

Eichrodt, W., *Ezekiel: A Commentary* (London: SCM Press, 1970).

Eisenman, R., and M. Wise, *The Dead Sea Scrolls Uncovered* (Shaftesbury, Dorset: Element, 1992).

Eissfeldt, O., 'אָדוֹן ,אֲדֹנָי' in *TDOT*, I, pp. 59-72.

Elior, R., *Hekhalot Zutarti* (Jerusalem: Magnes Press, 1982).

—'Merkabah Mysticism: A Critical Review', *Numen* 37 (1990), pp. 233-49.

—'Mysticism, Magic, and Angelology: The Perception of Angels in Hekhalot Literature', *JSQ* 1 (1993–94), pp. 3-53.

Ellis, E.E., *The World of St John* (London: Lutterworth; New York: Abingdon Press, 1965).

Epstein, I. (ed.), *The Babylonian Talmud* (London: Soncino, 1935–52).

Evans, C.A., *Noncanonical Writings and New Testament Interpretation* (Peabody, MA: Hendrickson, 1992).

—*To See and Not Perceive: Isaiah 6.9-10 in Early Jewish and Christian Interpretation* (JSOTSup, 64; Sheffield: JSOT Press, 1989).

—*Word and Glory: On the Exegetical and Theological Background of John's Prologue* (JSNTSup, 89; Sheffield: JSOT Press, 1993).

Faivre, A., 'Hermetism', *ER*, VI (1987), pp. 293-94.

Farrer, A., *The Revelation of St John the Divine* (Oxford: Clarendon Press, 1964).

Flusser, D., 'Scholem's Recent Book on Merkabah Literature', *JJS* 11 (1960), pp. 59-68.

Fossum, J., 'Jewish-Christian Christology and Jewish Mysticism', *VC* 37 (1983), pp. 260-87.

—*The Name of God and the Angel of the Lord: Samaritan and Jewish Concepts of Intermediation and the Origin of Gnosticism* (WUNT, 36; Tübingen: J.C.B. Mohr [Paul Siebeck], 1985).

Freedman, H., and M. Simon (eds.), *Midrash Rabbah* (London: Soncino, 1951).

Fry, E., 'Translating "Glory" in the New Testament', *BT* 27 (1976), pp. 422-27.

Fuchs, H.F., *Ezekiel 1–24* (Die Neue Echter Bibel; Würzburg: Echter Verlag, 1984).

Fulco, W.J., *Maranatha: Reflections on the Mystical Theology of John the Evangelist* (New York: Paulist Press, 1973).

Furnish, V.P., *II Corinthians* (AB, 33; New York: Doubleday, 1984).

Gärtner, B., *The Temple and the Community in Qumran and the New Testament: A Comparative Study in the Temple Symbolism of the Qumran Texts and the New Testament* (SNTSMS, 1; Cambridge: Cambridge University Press, 1965).

—'The Pauline and Johannine Idea of "To Know God" against the Hellenistic Background: The Greek Philosophical Principle "Like by Like" in Paul and John', *NTS* 14 (1967–68), pp. 209-31.

Gaster, T., *The Scriptures of the Dead Sea Sect* (London: Secker & Warburg, 1957).

Geyser, A.S., 'Israel in the Fourth Gospel', *Neot* 20 (1986), pp. 13-20.

Gitay, Y., *Isaiah and his Audience: The Structure and Meaning of Isaiah 1–12* (Assen: Van Gorcum, 1991).

Glasson, T.F., *Moses in the Fourth Gospel* (SBT, 40; London: SCM Press, 1963).

Goldberg, A., 'Der Vortrag des Ma'asse Merkawa: Eine Vermutung zur frühen Merkawamystik', *Judaica* 29 (1973), pp. 9-12.

Good, E.M., *Irony in the Old Testament* (Sheffield: Almond Press, 1991).

Goodenough, E.R., *By Light, Light: The Mystical Gospel of Hellenistic Judaism* (New Haven: Yale University Press, 1935).

Goulder, M., 'Nicodemus', *SJT* 44 (1991), pp. 153-68.

Gove, P.B. (ed.), *Webster's Third New International Dictionary of the English Language* (London: G. Bell & Sons, 1961).

Greenberg, M., *Ezekiel 1–20* (AB, 22; New York: Doubleday, 1983).

Grese, W.C., '"Unless One is Born Again": The Use of a Heavenly Journey in John 3', *JBL* 107 (1988), pp. 677-93.

Gruenwald, I., *Apocalyptic and Merkavah Mysticism* (Leiden: E.J. Brill, 1980).

—'Further Jewish Physiognomic and Chiromantic Fragments', *Tarbiz* 40 (1970), pp. 301-19 ('English Summaries', p. v).

—'The Jewish Esoteric Literature in the Time of the Mishnah and Talmud', *Immanuel* 4 (1974), pp. 37-46.

—'Jewish Merkavah Mysticism and Gnosticism', in Dan and Talmage (eds.), *Studies in Jewish Mysticism*, pp. 41-55.

—'Knowledge and Vision: Towards a Clarification of Two "Gnostic" Concepts in the Light of their Alleged Origins', *IOS* 3 (1973), pp. 63-107.

—'New Passages from Hekhalot Literature', *Tarbiz* 38 (1968), pp. 354-72 ('English Summaries', pp. iii-iv).

Gundry, R.H., 'In my Father's House are many μοναί', *ZNW* 58 (1967), pp. 68-72.

Haag, H., 'אָדָם בֶּן', in *TDOT*, II, pp. 159-65.

Haenchen, E., *John* (Hermeneia; 2 vols.; Philadelphia: Fortress Press, ET 1984).

— 'Der Vater der mich gesandt hat', *NTS* 9 (1962–63), pp. 208-16.

Hagner, D.A., 'The Vision of God in Philo and John: A Comparative Study', *JETS* 14 (1971), pp. 81-93.

Hahn, F., 'Sehen und Glauben im Johannesevangelium', in H. Baltensweiler and Bo Reicke (eds.), *Neue Testament und Geschichte: Historisches Geschehen und Deutung im Neuen Testament* (Festschrift O. Cullmann; Tübingen: J.C.B. Mohr [Paul Siebeck], 1972), pp. 125-41.

Halperin, D.J., 'The Exegetical Character of Ezek. x. 9-17', *VT* 26 (1976), pp. 129-41.

—*The Faces of the Chariot: Early Jewish Responses to Ezekiel's Vision* (Tübingen: J.C.B. Mohr [Paul Siebeck], 1988).

—*The Merkabah in Rabbinic Literature* (New Haven: American Oriental Society, 1980).

—'Origen, Ezekiel's Merkabah, and the Ascension of Moses', *CH* 50 (1981), pp. 261-75.

Hanson, A.T., *The Image of the Invisible God* (London: SCM Press, 1982).

—*The Prophetic Gospel: A Study of John and the Old Testament* (Edinburgh: T. & T. Clark, 1991).

Harrington, D.J., 'Pseudo-Philo', *OTP*, II, pp. 297-377.

Harris, J.R., 'Traces of Targumism in the New Testament', *ExpTim* 32 (1920–21), pp. 373-76.

Hartman, L.F., and A.A. Di Lella, *The Book of Daniel* (AB, 23; New York: Doubleday, 1977).

Hauck, F., 'μένω, μονή, κ.τ.λ.', *TDNT*, IV, pp. 574-81.

Hayward, C.T.R., 'The Holy Name of the God of Moses and the Prologue of St John's Gospel', *NTS* 25 (1979), pp. 16-32.

Heil, J.P., 'Jesus as the Unique High Priest in the Gospel of John', *CBQ* 57 (1995), pp. 729-45.

Hengel, M., *The 'Hellenization' of Judaea in the First Century after Christ* (London: SCM Press; Philadelphia: Trinity Press International, 1989).

—'The Interpretation of the Wine Miracle at Cana: John 2:1-11', in L.D. Hurst and N.T. Wright (eds.), *The Glory of Christ in the New Testament: Studies in Christology* (Festschrift G.B. Caird; Oxford: Clarendon Press, 1987), pp. 85-112.

—*The Johannine Question* (London: SCM Press; Philadelphia: Trinity Press International, 1989).

—*Judaism and Hellenism* (Minneapolis: Fortress Press, 2nd edn, 1991).

—'The Old Testament in the Fourth Gospel', *HBT* 12 (1990), pp. 19-41.

—'Reich Christi, Reich Gottes und Weltreich im Johannesevangelium', in M. Hengel and A.M. Schwerner (eds.), *Königsherrschaft Gottes und himmlischer Kult im Judentum, Urchristentum und in der hellenischen Welt* (Tübingen: J.C.B. Mohr [Paul Siebeck], 1991), pp. 163-84.

Heschel, A.J., 'The Mystical Element in Judaism', in L. Finkelstein (ed.), *The Jews: Their History, Culture and Religion*, II (London: Peter Owen, 1960), pp. 932-53.

Higgins, A.J.B., *Jesus and the Son of Man* (London: Lutterworth, 1964).

Hill, D., ' "My Kingdom is not of this World" (John 18:36): Conflict and Christian Existence in the World According to the Fourth Gospel', *IBS* 9 (1987), pp. 54-62.

—'The Request of Zebedee's Sons and the Johannine δόξα-Theme', *NTS* 13 (1966–67), pp. 281-85.

Hines, H.W., 'The Prophet as Mystic', *AJSL* 40 (1923–24), pp. 37-71.

Hollander, H.W., and M. de Jonge, *The Testaments of the Twelve Patriarchs* (Leiden: E.J. Brill, 1985).

Hooker, M.D., *The Son of Man in Mark: A Study of the Background of the Son of Man and its Use in St Mark's Gospel* (London: SPCK, 1967).

Horgan, M.P., *Pesharim: Qumran Interpretations of Biblical Books* (Washington: Catholic Biblical Association, 1979).

Horst, P.W. van der, 'The Birkat ha-minim in Recent Research', *ExpTim* 105 (1993–94), pp. 363-68.

—'Moses' Throne Vision in Ezekiel the Dramatist', *JJS* 34 (1983), pp. 21-29.

Horton, F.L., *The Melchizedek Tradition: A Critical Examination of the Sources to the Fifth Century AD and in the Epistle to the Hebrews* (SNTSMS, 30; Cambridge: Cambridge University Press, 1976).

Hoskyns, E.C., *The Fourth Gospel* (ed. F.N. Davey; London: Faber & Faber, 2nd rev. edn, repr. 1961).

Howard, W.F., *The Fourth Gospel in Recent Criticism and Interpretation* (London: Epworth Press, 1931).

—*The Fourth Gospel in Recent Criticism and Interpretation* (London: Epworth Press, 4th rev. edn, repr. 1961).

Hügel, B.F. von, 'John, Gospel of St', *Encyclopaedia Britannica*, XV (Cambridge: Cambridge University Press, 11th edn, 1911), pp. 452-58.

Hurtado, L.W., *One God, One Lord: Early Christian Devotion and Ancient Jewish Monotheism* (London: SCM Press, 1988).

Inge, W.R., *Christian Mysticism: The Bampton Lectures 1899* (London: Methuen, 1899).

—*Personal Idealism and Mysticism* (London: Longmans Green, 1907).

Isaac, E., '1 (Ethiopic Apocalypse of) Enoch', *OTP*, I, pp. 5-89.

Jacobs, L., *Jewish Mystical Testimonies* (New York: Schocken Books, 1976).

James, M.R., *The Biblical Antiquities of Philo* (London: SPCK, 1917; repr. New York: Ktav, 1971).

—*The Testament of Abraham* (Cambridge: Cambridge University Press, 1892).

Jastrow, M., *A Dictionary of Targumim, the Talmud Babli and Yerushalmi, and the Midrashic Literature* (2 vols.; New York: Choreb, 1926).

Jeremias, J., *Jerusalem in the Time of Jesus: An Investigation into Economic and Social Conditions during the New Testament Period* (repr.; Philadelphia: Fortress Press, repr. 1975).

John, M.P., 'Johannine Mysticism', *IJT* 5 (1956), pp. 15-21.

Johnston, G., 'Ecce Homo! Irony in the Christology of the Fourth Evangelist', in Hurst and Wright (eds.), *The Glory of Christ in the New Testament*, pp. 125-38.

—*The Spirit-Paraclete in the Gospel of John* (SNTSMS, 12; Cambridge: Cambridge University Press, 1970).

Jones, R.M., 'Mysticism', *ERE*, IX, pp. 83-84, 89-90.

Jonge, M. de, 'Christology and Theology in the Fourth Gospel', in F. van Segbroeck *et al.* (eds.), *The Four Gospels 1992*, III (Festschrift F. Neirynck; Leuven: Leuven University Press, 1992), pp. 1835-53.

—'Jesus as Prophet and King in the Fourth Gospel', in *idem*, *Jesus: Stranger from Heaven* (Missoula, MT: Scholars Press, 1977), pp. 49-76.

—'Nicodemus and Jesus: Some Observations on Misunderstanding and Understanding in the Fourth Gospel', *BJRL* 53 (1970-71), pp. 337-59.

Kaiser, O., *Isaiah 1–12: A Commentary* (London: SCM Press, 1972).

Käsemann, E., *The Testament of Jesus: A Study of the Gospel of John in the Light of Chapter 17* (London: SCM Press, ET 1968).

Katz, S.T., 'Issues in the Separation of Judaism and Christianity after 70 C.E.: A Reconsideration', *JBL* 103 (1984), pp. 43-76.

Kautzsch, E. (ed.), *Gesenius' Hebrew Grammar* (Oxford: Clarendon Press, 2nd edn, 1910).

Kee, H.C., 'Testaments of the Twelve Patriarchs', *OTP*, I, pp. 775-81, 788-95.

Kilpatrick, G.D., 'The Religious Background of the Fourth Gospel', in Cross (ed.), *Studies in the Fourth Gospel*, pp. 36-44.

Kinman, B., 'Jesus' "Triumphal Entry" in the Light of Pilate's', *NTS* 40 (1994), pp. 412-48.

Kinniburgh, E., 'The Johannine "Son of Man" ', *SE*, TU, IV (1968), pp. 64-71.

Kittel, G., 'δόξα', *TDNT*, II, pp. 232-55.

—'λόγος, κ.τ.λ.', *TDNT*, IV, pp. 91-136.

Klein, E., *A Comprehensive Etymological Dictionary of the English Language* (repr.; Amsterdam: Elsevier, 1971).

Kleinknecht, H., 'λόγος', κ.τ.λ.', *TDNT*, IV, pp. 77-91.

Klinzing, G., *Die Umdeutung des Kultus in der Qumrangemeinde und im Neuen Testament* (Göttingen: Vandenhoeck & Ruprecht, 1971).

Knibb, M.A., 'Martyrdom and Ascension of Isaiah', *OTP*, II, pp. 143-76.

Koester, C., 'Hearing, Seeing, and Believing in the Gospel of John', *Bib* 70 (1989), pp. 327-48.

Köhler, K., 'Merkabah', *JewEnc*, VIII, pp. 498-500.

Kysar, R., 'The Fourth Gospel: A Report on Recent Research', *ANRW*, II, 25.3, pp. 2389-480.

Lampe, G.W.H. (ed.), *A Patristic Greek Lexicon* (Oxford: Clarendon Press, 1961).

Larsen, I., 'The Use of Hina in the New Testament, with Special Reference to the Gospel of John', *NOT* 2 (1988), pp. 28-34.

Leaney, A.R.C., 'The Johannine Paraclete and the Qumran Scrolls', in Charlesworth (ed.), *John and the Dead Sea Scrolls*, pp. 38-61.

Lenski, R.C.H., *The Interpretation of St. Paul's First and Second Epistles to the Corinthians* (Minneapolis: Augsburg, 1963).

Levey, S.H., *The Targum of Ezekiel* (ArBib, 13; Edinburgh: T. & T. Clark, 1987).

Levi, P., *The Holy Gospel of John: A New Translation* (Worthing, W. Sussex: Churchman Publishing, 1985).

Liddell, H.G., and R. Scott, *A Greek–English Lexicon* (repr.; Oxford: Clarendon Press, 9th edn, 1966).

Lightfoot, R.H., *St John's Gospel: A Commentary* (ed. C.F. Evans; Oxford: Clarendon Press, 1956).

Lindars, B., *The Gospel of John* (NCBC; London: Oliphants, 1977).

—'John and the Synoptic Gospels: A Test Case', *NTS* 27 (1981), pp. 287-94.

—'The Son of Man in the Johannine Christology', in B. Lindars and S.S. Smalley (eds.), *Christ and Spirit in the New Testament: Essays in Honour of C.F.D. Moule* (Cambridge: Cambridge University Press, 1973), pp. 43-60.

—'The Son of Man in the Theology of John', in *idem*, *Jesus Son of Man: A Fresh Examination of the Son of Man Sayings in the Gospels in the Light of Recent Research* (London: SPCK, 1983), pp. 147-53, 218-21 (reprinted in *idem*, *Essays on John* [ed. C.M. Tuckett; Leuven: Leuven University Press, 1992], pp. 153-66).

Loader, W., *The Christology of the Fourth Gospel: Structures and Issues* (BEvT, 23; Frankfurt: Peter Lang, rev. edn, 1992).

Louth, A., *The Origins of the Christian Mystical Tradition: From Plato to Denys* (Oxford: Clarendon Press, 1981).

Lust, J., 'Daniel 7,13 and the Septuagint', *ETL* 54 (1978), pp. 63-69.

Macleod, C.W., 'Allegory and Mysticism in Origen and Gregory of Nyssa', *JTS* 22 (1971), pp. 362-79.

MacKenzie, R.A.F., *Sirach* (OT Message, 19; Wilmington, DE: Michael Glazier, 1983).

MacRae, G.W., 'Theology and Irony in the Fourth Gospel', in M.W.G. Stibbe (ed.), *The Gospel of John as Literature: An Anthology of Twentieth-Century Perspectives* (Leiden: E.J. Brill, 1993), pp. 103-13.

Maddox, R., 'The Function of the Son of Man in the Gospel of John', in R.J. Banks (ed.), *Reconciliation and Hope: New Testament Essays on Atonement and Eschatology* (Festschrift L.L. Morris; Exeter: Paternoster Press, 1974), pp. 186-204.

Maggioni, B., 'La Mistica di Giovanni Evangelista', in E. Ancilli and M. Paparozzi (eds.), *La Mistica: Fenemenologia e Riflessione Teologia* (2 vols.; Rome: Citta Nuova, 1984), I, pp. 223-50.

Mahé, J.-P., 'Hermes Trismegistos', *ER*, VI (1987), pp. 287-93.

Maier, J., *Vom Kultus zur Gnosis: Studien zur Vor- und Fruhgeschichte der judischen Gnosis: Bundeslade, Gottesthron und Merkabah* (Salzburg: Otto Müller Verlag, 1964).

Mansoor, M., *The Thanksgiving Hymns* (Leiden: E.J. Brill, 1961).

Marcus, J., 'Entering into the Kingly Power of God', *JBL* 107 (1988), pp. 663-75.

Marcus, R. (trans.), *Philo: Questions and Answers on Genesis* (LCL, 1; Cambridge, MA: Harvard University Press, repr. 1993).

Marsh, J., *The Gospel of St John* (repr.; London: Penguin, 1988).

Martin, R., *2 Corinthians* (WBC, 40; Waco, TX: Word Books, 1986).

Martínez, F.G., *The Dead Sea Scrolls Translated: The Qumran Texts in English* (Leiden: E.J. Brill, ET 1994).

—*The Dead Sea Scrolls Translated: The Qumran Texts in English* (Leiden: E.J. Brill; Grand Rapids: Eerdmans, 2nd edn, ET 1996).

—*Qumran and Apocalyptic: Studies on the Aramaic Texts from Qumran* (Leiden: E.J. Brill, 1992).

Martyn, J.L., 'Glimpses into the History of the Johannine Community', in de Jonge (ed.), *L'évangile de Jean: Sources, rédaction, theólogie*, pp. 149-75.

—*History and Theology in the Fourth Gospel* (Nashville: Abingdon Press, 2nd edn, 1979).

Mary, S., *Pauline and Johannine Mysticism* (London: Darton, Longman & Todd, 1964).

Matera, F.J., *The Kingship of Jesus: Composition and Theology in Mark 15* (SBLDS, 66; Chico, CA: Scholars Press, 1982).

McCaffrey, J., *The House with Many Rooms: The Temple Theme of Jn. 14:2-3* (AnBib, 114; Rome: Pontificio Istituto Biblico, 1988).

McKelvey, R.J., *The New Temple: The Church in the New Testament* (Oxford: Oxford University Press, 1969).

McPolin, J., 'Johannine Mysticism', *Way* 1 (1978), pp. 25-35.

Mealand, D.L., 'The Language of Mystical Union in Johannine Writings', *DownRev* 95 (1977), pp. 19-34.

Meeks, W.A., '"Am I a Jew?": Johannine Christianity and Judaism', in J. Neusner (ed.), *Christianity, Judaism and Other Greco-Roman Cults: Studies for M. Smith* (SJLA, 12; Leiden: E.J. Brill, 1975), I, pp. 163-86.

—'The Divine Agent and his Counterfeit in Philo and the Fourth Gospel', in E.S. Fiorenza (ed.), *Aspects of Religious Propaganda in Judaism and Early Christianity* (Notre Dame: University of Notre Dame Press, 1976), pp. 43-67.

—'The Man from Heaven in Johannine Sectarianism', *JBL* 91 (1972), pp. 44-72.

—'Moses as God and King', in Neusner (ed.), *Religions in Antiquity*, pp. 354-71.

—*The Prophet-King: Moses Traditions and the Johannine Christology* (NovTSup, 14; Leiden: E.J. Brill, 1967).

Mettinger, T.N.D., *The Dethronement of Sabaoth: Studies in the Shem and Kabod Theologies* (ConBOT, 18; Lund: C.W.K. Gleerup, 1982).

Metzger, B.M., 'The Fourth Book of Ezra', *OTP*, I, pp. 517-59.

—*A Textual Commentary on the Greek New Testament* (Stuttgart: United Bible Societies, corrected edn, 1975).

Michaelis, W., 'Joh. 1,51, Gen. 28,12 und das Menschensohn-Problem', *TLZ* 8 (1960), cols. 561-78.

—'ὁράω, κ.τ.λ.', *TDNT*, V, pp. 319-66.

Milik, J.T. (ed.), *The Books of Enoch: Aramaic Fragments of Qumran Cave 4* (Oxford: Clarendon Press, 1976).

Miller, E.L., 'The Johannine Origins of the Johannine Logos', *JBL* 112 (1993), pp. 445-57.

—*Salvation-History in the Prologue of John: The Significance of John 1:3/4* (Leiden: E.J. Brill, 1989).

Milne, B., *The Message of John: Here is Your King!* (BSTS; Leicester: IVP, 1993).

Miranda, J.P., *Die Sendung Jesu im vierten Evangelium: Religions- und theologie-geschichtliche Untersuchungen zu den Sendungsformeln* (SBS, 87; Stuttgart: Katholisches Bibelwerk, 1977).

Mlakuzhyil, G., *The Christocentric Structure of the Fourth Gospel* (AnBib, 117; Rome: Pontificio Istituto Biblico, 1987).

Moloney, F.J., *The Johannine Son of Man* (Biblioteca di scienze Religiose, 14; Rome: Las, 2nd edn, 1978).

Montgomery, J.A., *A Critical and Exegetical Commentary on the Book of Daniel* (ICC; Edinburgh: T. & T. Clark, 1927).

Morgan, M.A. (trans.), *Sepher Ha-Razim: The Book of the Mysteries* (Chico, CA: Scholars Press, 1983).

Morray-Jones, C.R.A., 'Merkabah Mysticism and Talmudic Tradition: A Study of the Traditions Concerning Hammerkabah and Ma'aseh Merkabah in Tannaitic and Amoraic Sources' (PhD Thesis, Cambridge University, 1988).

—'Paradise Revisited (2 Cor 12:1-12): The Jewish Mystical Background of Paul's Apostolate. Part 1: The Jewish Sources', *HTR* 86 (1993), pp. 177-217.

—'Paradise Revisited (2 Cor 12:1-12): The Jewish Mystical Background of Paul's Apostolate. Part 2: Paul's Heavenly Ascent and its Significance', *HTR* 86 (1993), pp. 265-92.

—'Transformational Mysticism in the Apocalyptic-Merkabah Tradition', *JJS* 43 (1992), pp. 1-31.

Moule, C.F.D., *An Idiom Book of New Testament Greek* (Cambridge: Cambridge University Press, 2nd edn, repr. 1988).

—'The Individualism of the Fourth Gospel', *NovT* 5 (1962), pp. 171-90.

—'A Note on "Under the Fig Tree" in John 1.48,50', *JTS* 5 (1954), pp. 210-11.

Mowvley, H., 'John $1^{14\text{-}18}$ in the Light of Exodus $3^{37}\text{-}34^{35}$', *ExpTim* 95 (1984), pp. 135-37.

Müller, K.W., 'König und Vater: Streiflichter zur metaphorischen Rede über Gott in der Umwelt des Neuen Testaments', in Hengel and Schwerner (eds.), *Königsherrschaft Gottes*, pp. 21-43.

Mussner, F., *The Historical Jesus in the Gospel of St John* (Freiburg: Herder; London: Burns & Oates, 1967).

Myers, J.M., *I and II Esdras* (AB; New York: Doubleday, 1974).

Neusner, J., *Development of a Legend: Studies on the Traditions Concerning Yohanan ben Zakkai* (Leiden: E.J. Brill, 1970).

—'The Development of the Merkavah Tradition', *JSJ* 2 (1971), pp. 149-60.

—*Early Rabbinic Judaism: Historical Studies in Religion, Literature and Art* (Leiden: E.J. Brill, 1975).

—*A Life of Yohanan ben Zakkai: Ca. 1–80 C.E.* (Leiden: E.J. Brill, 2nd rev. edn, 1970).

—'The Traditions Concerning Johanan ben Zakkai: Reconsiderations', *JJS* 24 (1973), pp. 65-73.

Newbigin, L., *The Light has Come: An Exposition of the Fourth Gospel* (Edinburgh: Handsel Press, repr. 1987).

Newsom, C., 'Merkabah Exegesis in the Qumran Sabbath Shirot', *JJS* 38 (1987), pp. 11-30.

—*Songs of the Sabbath Sacrifice: A Critical Edition* (HSS, 27; Atlanta: Scholars Press, 1985).

Neyrey, J.H., 'The Jacob Allusions in John 1:51', *CBQ* 44 (1982), pp. 586-605.

Nicholson, G.C., *Death as Departure: The Johannine Descent–Ascent Schema* (SBLDS, 63; Chico: Scholars Press, 1983).

Nickelsburg, G.W.E., *Jewish Literature between the Bible and the Mishnah* (London: SCM Press, 1981).

Nicol, W., *The Sēmeia in the Fourth Gospel* (NovTSup, 32; Leiden: E.J. Brill, 1972).

Noll, S.F., 'Angelology in the Qumran Texts' (PhD Thesis, University of Manchester, 1979).

O'Day, G.R., *Revelation in the Fourth Gospel* (Philadelphia: Fortress Press, 1986).

Odeberg, H., *3 Enoch or the Hebrew Book of Enoch* (New York: Ktav, repr. 1973).

—*The Fourth Gospel: Interpreted in its Relation to Contemporaneous Religious Currents in Palestine and the Hellenistic-Oriental World* (Uppsala: Almqvist & Wiksell, 1929; repr.; Chicago: Argonaut Publishers, 1968).

O'Neill, J.C.O., 'The Kingdom of God', *NovT* 35 (1993), pp. 130-41.

Painter, J., 'Christ and the Church in John 1,45-51', in de Jonge (ed.), *L'Évangile de Jean*, pp. 359-62.

—'Christology and the History of the Johannine Community in the Prologue of the Fourth Gospel', *NTS* 30 (1984), pp. 460-74.

—'The Enigmatic Johannine Son of Man', in van Segbroeck, *et al.* (eds.), *The Four Gospels 1992*, III, pp. 1869-87.

—*John: Witness and Theologian* (London: SPCK, 1975).

Pamment, M., 'The Son of Man in the Fourth Gospel', *JTS* 36 (1985), pp. 56-66.

—'The Meaning of *doxa* in the Fourth Gospel', *ZNW* 74 (1983), pp. 12-16.

Panackel, C., ΙΔΟΥ Ο ΑΝΘΡΩΠΟΣ *(Jn 19, 5b): An Exegetico-Theological Study of the Text in the Light of the Use of the Term* ΑΝΘΡΩΠΟΣ *Designating Jesus in the Fourth Gospel* (Rome: Pontificia Università Gregoriana, 1988).

Pantuck, A., 'Paul and the Dead Sea Scrolls: Ascent and Angelification in First-Century Judaism' (Unpublished paper, 1988).

Phillips, G.L., 'Faith and Vision in the Fourth Gospel', in Cross (ed.), *Studies in the Fourth Gospel*, pp. 83-96.

Plummer, A., *A Critical and Exegetical Commentary on the Second Epistle of St Paul to the Corinthians* (ICC; Edinburgh: T. & T. Clark, repr. 1925).

Porteous, N.W., *Daniel: A Commentary* (London: SCM Press, 1965).

Preiss, T., *Life In Christ* (London: SCM Press, 1954).

Preuss, H.D., 'דְּמוּת/דְּמָה', *ThWAT*, II, cols. 266-74.

Pring, J.T., *The Oxford Dictionary of Modern Greek: Greek–English and English–Greek* (Oxford: Clarendon Press, 1982).

Pryor, J.W., 'The Johannine Son of Man and the Descent–Ascent Motif', *JETS* 34 (1991), pp. 341-51.

Quispel, G., 'Ezekiel 1:26 in Jewish Mysticism and Gnosis', *VC* 34 (1980), pp. 1-13.

—'Nathanael und der Menschensohn (Joh 1.51)', *ZNW* 47 (1956), pp. 281-83.

Rad, G. von, *Genesis: A Commentary* (ET; London: SCM Press, 1961).

—*Old Testament Theology*. II. *The Theology of Israel's Prophetic Traditions* (ET; London: SCM Press, 1965).

Reim, G., 'Targum und Johannesevangelium', *BZ* 27 (1983), pp. 1-13.

Rengstorf, K.H., 'ἀποστέλλω (πέμπω)', *TDNT*, I, pp. 398-447.

Rensberger, D., 'The Politics of John: The Trial of Jesus in the Fourth Gospel', *JBL* 103 (1984), pp. 395-411.

Rhea, R., *The Johannine Son of Man* (ATANT, 76; Zürich: Theologischer Verlag, 1990).

Richardson, Charles, *A New Dictionary of the English Language: Volume the Second* (London: William Pickering, 1844).

Riedl, J., 'Wenn ihr den Menschensohn erhöht habt, werdet ihr erkennen (Joh 8, 28)', in
    R. Pesch and R. Schnackenburg (eds.), *Jesus und der Menschensohn* (Festschrift
    A. Vögtle; Freiburg: Herder, 1975), pp. 355-70.
Rissi, M., 'John 1:1-18 (The Eternal Word)', *Int* 31 (1977), pp. 394-401.
Robertson, A.T., *A Grammar of the Greek New Testament in the Light of Historical
    Research* (London: Hodder & Stoughton, 1914).
Robertson, P.E., 'Glory in the Fourth Gospel', *TheolEduc* 38 (1988), pp. 121-31.
Robertson, R.G., 'Ezekiel the Tragedian', *OTP*, II, pp. 803-19.
Robinson, J., 'Dunn on John', *Theology* 85 (1982), pp. 332-38.
Robinson, J.A.T., 'The Destination and Purpose of St John's Gospel', *NTS* 6 (1959-60),
    pp. 117-31.
Rowland, C.C., 'Apocalyptic, the Poor, and the Gospel of Matthew', *JTS* NS 45 (1994), pp.
    504-18.
—'The Influence of the First Chapter of Ezekiel on Jewish and Early Christian Literature'
    (PhD Thesis, Cambridge University, 1974).
—'John 1.51, Jewish Apocalyptic and Targumic Tradition', *NTS* 30 (1984), pp. 498-507.
—*The Open Heaven: A Study of Apocalyptic in Judaism and Early Christianity* (London:
    SPCK, 1982).
—'The Vision of the Risen Christ in Rev. i.13ff.: The Debt of an Early Christology to an
    Aspect of Jewish Angelology', *JTS* 31 (1980), pp. 1-11.
—'The Visions of God in Apocalyptic Literature', *JSJ* 10 (1979), pp. 137-54.
Rubinkiewicz, R., 'Apocalypse of Abraham', *OTP*, I, pp. 681-705.
Ruckstuhl, E., 'Abstieg und Erhöhung des johanneischen Menschensohns', in Pesch and
    Schnackenburg (eds.), *Jesus und der Menschensohn*, pp. 314-41.
Ruiz, M.R., *Der Missionsgedanke des Johannesevangeliums: Ein Beitrag zur
    johanneischen Soteriologie* (Würzburg: Echter Verlag, 1987).
Russell, E., 'Possible Influence of the Mysteries on the Form and Interrelation of the
    Johannine Writings', *JBL* 51 (1932), pp. 336-51.
Sanders, E.P., *Judaism: Practice and Belief 63 BCE–66 CE* (London: SCM Press;
    Philadelphia: Trinity Press International, 1992).
—'Testament of Abraham', *OTP*, I, pp. 871-902.
Sanders, J.N., and B.A. Mastin, *A Commentary on the Gospel According to St John*
    (London: A. & C. Black, 1968).
Sandmel, S., *Philo of Alexandria: An Introduction* (Oxford: Oxford University Press,
    1979).
Sanford, J.A., *Mystical Christianity: A Psychological Commentary on the Gospel of John*
    (New York: Crossroad, 1993).
Schäfer, P., 'The Aim and Purpose of Early Jewish Mysticism', in *idem, Hekhalot–Studien*
    (Tübingen: J.C.B. Mohr [Paul Siebeck], 1988), pp. 277-95.
—'Engel und Menschen in der Hekhalot-Literatur', in *idem, Hekhalot–Studien*, pp. 250-76.
—(ed.), *Geniza-Fragmenta zur Hekhalot-Literatur* (TSAJ, 6; Tübingen: J.C.B. Mohr [Paul
    Siebeck], 1986).
—*Konkordenz zur Hekhalot-Literatur* (2 vols.; Tübingen: J.C.B. Mohr [Paul Siebeck],
    1988).
—'New Testament and Hekhalot Literature: The Journey into Heaven in Paul and in
    Merkabah Mysticism', *JJS* 35 (1984), pp. 19-35.
—(ed.), *Synopse zur Hekhalot-Literatur* (TSAJ, 2; Tübingen: J.C.B. Mohr [Paul Siebeck],
    1991).

—'Tradition and Redaction in Hekhalot Literature', in *idem, Hekhalot–Studien*, pp. 8-16.

—*Der verborgene und offenbare Gott* (Tübingen: J.C.B. Mohr [Paul Siebeck], 1991).

Schiffman, L.H., 'Merkavah Speculation at Qumran: The 4Q Serekh Shirot 'Olat ha-Shabbat', in J. Reinharz and D. Swetschinski (eds.), *Mystics, Philosophers, and Politicians: Essays in Jewish Intellectual History in Honor of A. Altmann* (Durham, NC: Duke University Press, 1982), pp. 15-47.

Schmidt, N., 'The Son of Man in the Book of Daniel', *JBL* 19 (1900), pp. 22-28.

—'The Two-Recensions of Slavonic Enoch', *JAOS* 41 (1921), pp. 307-12.

Schmitz, E.D., 'γινώσκω', *NIDNTT*, II, pp. 392-406.

Schnackenburg, R., *The Gospel According to St John* (3 vols.; New York: Crossroad, ET 1968).

Schneiders, S.M., 'History and Symbolism in the Fourth Gospel', in de Jonge (ed.), *L'évangile de Jean*, pp. 371-76.

Schnelle, U., *Antidocetic Christology in the Gospel of John: An Investigation of the Place of the Fourth Gospel in the Johannine School* (Minneapolis: Fortress Press, ET 1992).

Scholem, G.G., *Jewish Gnosticism, Merkabah Mysticism, and Talmudic Tradition* (New York: Jewish Theological Seminary of America, 1960; 2nd edn, 1965).

—'Kabbalah', *EncJud*, X, cols. 489-654.

—*Major Trends in Jewish Mysticism* (London: Thames & Hudson, 3rd rev. edn, 1955).

Schulz, S., *Das Evangelium nach Johannes* (Göttingen: Vandenhoeck & Ruprecht, 1978).

Schürer, E., *The History of the Jewish People in the Age of Jesus Christ (175 B.C.–A.D. 135)*, III.1 (Edinburgh: T. & T. Clark, rev. edn, 1986).

Schweizer, E., 'υἱός, κ.τ.λ.', *TDNT*, VIII, pp. 363-92.

Schweitzer, A., *The Mysticism of Paul the Apostle* (London: A. & C. Black, ET 1931).

Scott, J.M., 'The Triumph of God in 2 Cor 2:14: Additional Evidence of Merkabah Mysticism in Paul', *NTS* 42 (1996), pp. 260-81.

Scott, M., *Sophia and the Johannine Jesus* (JSNTSup, 71; Sheffield: JSOT Press, 1992).

Scott, R.B.Y., *Proverbs–Ecclesiastes* (AB, 18; New York: Doubleday, 1965).

Scott, W. (ed.), *Hermetica* (2 vols.; Oxford: Clarendon Press, 1924, 1925).

Segal, A.F., 'Heavenly Ascent in Hellenistic Judaism, Early Christianity and their Environment', *ANRW*, II, 23.2 (1980), pp. 1352-89.

—*Paul the Convert: The Apostolate and Apostasy of Saul the Pharisee* (New Haven: Yale University Press, 1990).

—*Rebecca's Children: Judaism and Christianity in the Roman World* (Cambridge, MA: Harvard University Press, 1986).

—*Two Powers in Heaven: Early Rabbinic Reports about Christianity and Gnosticism* (Leiden: E.J. Brill, 1977).

Segovia, F.F., *The Farewell of the Word: The Johannine Call to Abide* (Minneapolis: Fortress Press, 1991).

—'John 13:1-20: The Footwashing in the Johannine Tradition', *ZNW* 73 (1982), pp. 31-51.

Sidebottom, E.M., 'The Ascent and Descent of the Son of Man in the Gospel of John', *ATR* 39 (1957), pp. 115-22.

—*The Christ of the Fourth Gospel in the Light of First-Century Thought* (London: SPCK, 1961).

Simon, U.E., 'Eternal Life in the Fourth Gospel', in Cross (ed.), *Studies in the Fourth Gospel*, pp. 97-109.

Skehan, P.W., and A.A. Di Lella, *The Wisdom of Ben Sira* (AB; New York: Doubleday, 1987).

Smalley, S.S., 'The Johannine Son of Man Sayings', *NTS* 15 (1968–69), pp. 278-301.

Smith, J.Z., 'Prayer of Joseph', *OTP*, II, pp. 699-714.

—'The Prayer of Joseph', in Neusner (ed.), *Religions in Antiquity*, pp. 253-94.

Smith, M., 'Observations on Hekhalot Rabbati', in A. Altmann (ed.), *Biblical and Other Studies* (Cambridge, MA: Harvard University Press, 1963), pp. 142-60.

—'Palestinian Judaism in the First Century', in Moshe Davis (ed.), *Israel: Its Role in Civilization* (New York: Harper & Brothers, repr. 1956), pp. 67-81.

Sparks, H.F.D. (ed.), *The Apocryphal Old Testament* (Oxford: Clarendon Press, 1984).

Spittler, R.P., 'The Limits of Ecstasy: An Exegesis of 2 Corinthians 12:1-10', in G.F. Hawthorne (ed.), *Current Issues in Biblical and Patristic Interpretation: Studies in Honour of M.C. Tenney* (Grand Rapids: Eerdmans, 1975), pp. 259-66.

Stone, M.E., 'The Messiah in 4 Ezra', in Neusner (ed.), *Religions in Antiquity*, pp. 303-10.

—'Paradise in 4 Ezra iv:8 and vii:36, viii:52', *JJS* 17 (1966), pp. 85-88.

Strachan, R.H., *The Fourth Gospel: Its Significance and Environment* (London: SCM Press, rev. 3rd edn, repr. 1946).

Strugnell, J., *The Angelic Liturgy at Qumran: 4Q Serek Shirot 'Olat Ha-shabat'* (VTSup, 7; Leiden: E.J. Brill, 1959), pp. 318-45.

Suggit, J., 'John 19[5]: "Behold the Man" ', *ExpTim* 94 (1983), pp. 333-34.

Tabor, J.D., *Things Unutterable: Paul's Ascent to Paradise in its Greco-Roman, Judaic, and Early Christian Contexts* (New York: Lanham, 1986).

Talbert, C.H., 'The Myth of a Descending-Ascending Redeemer in Mediterranean Antiquity', *NTS* 22 (1976), pp. 418-40.

—*Reading John: A Literary and Theological Commentary on the Fourth Gospel and on the Johannine Epistles* (London: SPCK, 1992).

Theobald, M., *Die Fleischwerdung des Logos: Studien zum Verhältnis des Johannesprologs zum Corpus des Evangeliums und zu 1 Joh* (NTAbh, 20; Münster: Aschendorff, 1988).

Thompson, M.M., *The Humanity of Jesus in the Fourth Gospel* (Philadelphia: Fortress Press, 1988).

Thüsing, W., *Die Erhöhung und Verherrlichung Jesu im Johannes-evangelium* (NTAbh, 21; Münster: Aschendorff, 2nd edn, 1970).

Toy, C.H., *A Critical and Exegetical Commentary on the Book of Proverbs* (ICC; Edinburgh: T. & T. Clark, 1899).

Trumbower, J.A., *Born from Above: The Anthropology of the Gospel of John* (Tübingen: J.C.B. Mohr [Paul Siebeck], 1992).

Underhill, E., *The Mystic Way* (London: J.M. Dent, repr. 1914).

Untergassmair, F.G., *Im Namen Jesu: Der Namensbegriff im Johannesevangelium* (Stuttgart: Katholisches Bibelwerk, 2nd edn, 1977).

Urbach, E.E., 'Ha-Masorot 'al Torat ha-Sod bi-Tequfat ha-Tannaim', in A. Altmann (ed.), *Studies in Mysticism and Religion: Presented to G.G. Scholem on his Seventieth Birthday* (Jerusalem: Magnes Press, 1967), pp. 2-11.

Vaillant, A. (ed.), *Le livre des Secrets d' Henoch: Texte slave et traduction française* (Paris: Textes Publies par l' Institute d' Etudes Slaves, IV, 1952).

Vermes, G., *The Dead Sea Scrolls in English* (Sheffield: JSOT Press, 3rd edn, 1987).

—*The Dead Sea Scrolls in English* (Sheffield: Sheffield Academic Press, 4th edn, 1995).

—*Discovery in the Judaean Desert* (New York: Desclée Company, 1956).

Wadsworth, M., 'The Death of Moses and the Riddle of the End of Time in Pseudo-Philo', *JJS* 28 (1977), pp. 12-19.
—'A New Pseudo-Philo', *JJS* 29 (1978), pp. 186-91.
Watts, J.D.W., *Isaiah 1–33* (WBC, 24; Waco, TX: Word Books, 1985).
Wedderburn, A.J.M., *Baptism and Resurrection: Studies in Pauline Theology against its Graeco-Roman Background* (Tübingen: J.C.B. Mohr [Paul Siebeck], 1987).
Weisengoff, J.P., 'Light and its Relation to Life in St John', *CBQ* 8 (1946), pp. 448-51.
Weiss, H-F., *Untersuchungen zur Kosmologie des hellenistischen und palästinischen Judentums* (TU, 97; Berlin: Akademie-Verlag, 1966).
Wengst, K., *Bedrängte Gemeinde und verherrlichter Christus: Der historische Ort des Johannesevangeliums als Schlüssel seiner Interpretation* (Biblisch-theologische Studien, 5; Neukirchen–Vluyn: Neukirchener Verlag, 1981).
Westcott, B.F., *The Gospel According to St John* (London: John Murray, 1882).
Westermann, C., *Genesis 12–36: A Commentary* (Minneapolis: Augsburg, ET 1985).
Whitacre, R.A., *Johannine Polemic: The Role of Tradition and Theology* (SBLDS, 67; Chico, CA: Scholars Press, 1982).
Wildberger, H., *Isaiah 1–12: A Commentary* (Minneapolis: Fortress Press, ET 1991).
Wiles, M., 'Reflections on James Dunn's *Christology in the Making*', *Theology* 85 (1982), pp. 92-96.
Wiles, M., and J.D.G. Dunn, 'Christology: The Debate Continues', *Theology* 85 (1982), pp. 324-32.
Wilson, R. McL., 'Philo and the Fourth Gospel', *ExpTim* 65 (1953–54), pp. 47-49.
Windisch, H., 'Angelophanien um den Menschensohn auf Erden', *ZNW* 30 (1931), pp. 231-35.
—'Joh 1$_{51}$ und die Auferstehung Jesu', *ZNW* 31 (1932), pp. 199-204.
—*The Spirit-Paraclete in the Fourth Gospel* (FBBS, 20; Philadelphia: Fortress Press, 1968).
Winston, D., 'Philo and the Contemplative Life', in Green (ed.), *Jewish Spirituality*, I, pp. 198-231.
Wohlgemut, J.R., 'Where Does God Dwell? A Commentary on John 2:13-22', *Direction* 22 (1993), pp. 87-93.
Wolfson, H.A., *Philo: Foundations of Religious Philosophy in Judaism, Christianity, and Islam* (2 vols.; Cambridge, MA: Harvard University Press, 1948).
Woude, A. van der, 'Melchisedek als himmlische Erlösergestalt in den neugefundenen eschatologischen Midraschim aus Qumran Höhe XI', *OTS* 14 (1965), pp. 354-73.
Yadin, Y., 'The Excavations at Masada: A Scroll of the Songs of the Sabbath Sacrifice (1039–200; Pl. 20B)', *IEJ* 15 (1965), pp. 105-108.
York, A.D., 'The Dating of the Targumic Literature', *JSJ* 5 (1974), pp. 49-62.
Young, E.J., *The Book of Isaiah* (3 vols.; Grand Rapids: Eerdmans, 1965).
Young, F.W., 'A Study of the Relation of Isaiah to the Fourth Gospel', *ZNW* 46 (1955), pp. 215-40.
Zimmerli, W., *Ezechiel*, I (BKAT, 13.1; Neukirchen–Vluyn: Neukirchener Verlag, 1969).
—*Ezekiel* (2 vols.; Philadelphia: Fortress Press, ET 1979, 1983).

INDEXES

INDEX OF REFERENCES

OLD TESTAMENT

Genesis		6.2-3	39, 233	40.34-35	90, 163,
1	41, 294,	12.7	271		222
	299, 312,	13.21-22	288	40.34	223
	317	14.19-25	288	40.38	288
1.3	294	16.7	90, 163		
1.14	192	16.10	223	Leviticus	
1.18	192	19.9	168	26.12	74, 272
12–36	191	19.16	146		
14.9	192	19.18	125, 168	Numbers	
14.10	192	19.21	166, 223	14.9	73
14.16	191	20.18-19	223	14.22	305
22.6	73	20.18	223	21.8-9	206
28	189, 191,	23.20-21	172	21.8	204, 205
	211	23.20	140	21.9	204, 205
28.12-17	191	23.21	136	24.13	257
28.12-13	119	24.10-11	148		
28.12	36, 189-	24.10	224	24.17	242
	91, 193,	24.15-18	168		
	211, 314	24.16-18	163	Deuteronomy	
28.12b	188	24.16-17	90	4.12	223
28.13	191, 192,	24.16	222, 223	4.15	223
	282	24.16a	224	4.24	171
28.15	282	24.17	223	5.24	223
32.30	166	28.4	142	18.15-19	236
49.9	130, 147	29.43	163	18.15	239
		33.18-23	223	29.29	88
Exodus		33.18-19	222, 233	30.4	198
1.14-18	223	33.20-23	223	33.2	171
2.39-40	71	33.20	163, 166		
2.45	224	33.23	224	Judges	
3.2	171	34.5-7	222	5.4-5	168
3.13-14	39, 233	34.5-6	233	6.22-23	166
3.14	282	39.29	142	13.22	166

NEW TESTAMENT

OTHER EARLY JEWISH AND CHRISTIAN LITERATURE

Weisengoff, J.P. 283
Weiss, H.-F. 50, 89
Wellhausen, J. 129
Westcott, B.F. 20, 207, 222, 224, 283
Westermann, C. 191
Whitaker, G.H. 47
Wholgemut, J.R. 279
Wildberger, H. 106, 166-68
Wiles, M. 293
Wilson, R. McL. 47, 296

Windisch, H. 253
Wise, M. 89, 100
Wohlgemut, J.R. 201
Wolfson, H.A. 73

Yannai, R. 189
Young, E.J. 166
Young, F.W. 226

Zimmerli, W. 94, 160, 161, 163, 164

JOURNAL FOR THE STUDY OF THE NEW TESTAMENT
SUPPLEMENT SERIES